# INNER CONFLICT AND DEFENSE

BY

Daniel R. Miller
*University of Michigan*

Guy E. Swanson
*University of Michigan*

IN COLLABORATION WITH

Wesley Allinsmith
*Harvard University*

Elton B. McNeil
*University of Michigan*

AND

Beverly B. Allinsmith
*Concord, Massachusetts*

Justin Aronfreed
*University of Pennsylvania*

Betty J. Beardslee
*Connecticut State Hospital*

Leonard M. Lansky
*Fels Research Institute, Ohio*

# INNER CONFLICT AND DEFENSE



A HOLT-DRYDEN BOOK

HENRY HOLT AND COMPANY, NEW YORK

Library of Congress Catalogue Card Number: 58-6334

25715-0110

Printed in the United States of America

# PREFACE

The plans for this book gradually became crystallized in the years between 1949 and 1953, when we conducted a seminar at the University of Michigan. The seminar was attended by a group of psychologists and sociologists who were interested in the different ways people resolve inner conflict. It was the goal of the group to formulate testable hypotheses concerning the origins of these individual differences. To that end, we re-examined the meanings of the basic concepts often invoked in analyses of conflict and then decided on our methods of classification and measurement. Most helpful in planning our research were certain theoretical advances that have been made in psychoanalysis, psychology, and sociology.

The psychoanalytic concepts that were of greatest service to us were the mechanisms of defense. We devoted much of our time to defining and classifying the different mechanisms, and to speculating about their origins and possible effects on the resolution of conflict. Academic theory of learning contributed the concepts of generalization and habit family, which were very helpful in classifying defense mechanisms and moral standards. Our readings in academic psychology also cultivated our interest in expressive movement and in the perceptual and conceptual styles that might affect the resolution of conflict. And it was the findings of recent epidemiological research on personality disorders that ultimately prompted us to phrase our hypotheses in terms of the social and familial origins of psychological reactions.

At the conclusion of two seminars, we had developed systems

for classifying the concepts in which we were interested. We had also phrased a number of questions which lent themselves to empirical testing and seemed crucial to theories of personality and socialization. It was then time to get some answers. To test parts of the theory, some participants in the seminars conducted a group of investigations from 1951 to 1955. The studies were reported in doctoral dissertations that were supervised by the two senior authors, and provided the empirical contents of this book.

Our research associates on the project, Wesley Allinsmith and Elton B. McNeil, were of inestimable help in planning some of the investigations and in collecting data. In addition to the senior authors and Allinsmith and McNeil, the project staff included Beverly B. Allinsmith, Justin Aronfreed, Betty J. Beardslee, J. Edwin Keller, Leonard M. Lansky, and David A. Rhodes, all of whom contributed to theory and methods and helped to obtain the data. Doctors Wesley Allinsmith and Beverly Allinsmith, and Doctors Aronfreed, Beardslee, Lansky, and McNeil had primary responsibility for planning and executing certain of our studies. After each person completed his dissertation he re-analyzed some of his data and prepared one or more chapters for this book.

As will become evident, each of the studies required the simultaneous exploration of a number of problems. It was often necessary for us to clarify the difference between two concepts, such as defense mechanism and expressive style. Since we constructed our own instruments, we also had to find out about their properties. And, of course, the primary purpose of each study was to test a number of hypotheses about the social origins and the child-rearing practices that predispose children to favor particular methods of resolving conflict. Naturally, our viewpoints kept changing as we obtained the results of our most recent investigations, and we modified our concepts and methods accordingly. The reports of our research represent, then, a proliferating and continuously evolving picture of conflict and of methods for studying it.

The preparation of the present book was undertaken by the senior authors, who wrote a number of chapters on the theory of the project, re-analysed some of the data, and edited and coordinated the writing of all the chapters. In this task, we received significant and patient aid from all the individuals who were responsible for the empirical studies and from Wesley Allinsmith, Elton

B. McNeil, and Leonard M. Lansky, who provided editorial suggestions. As our manuscript took shape, we received many helpful suggestions from colleagues who either read a part or all of the book: John W. Atkinson, Raymond Bauer, Jack Block, Urie Bronfenbrenner, Henry Brosin, Freda Fromm-Reichmann, Nathan Glazer, Ernest R. Hilgard, Alex Inkeles, Morris Janowitz, Donald G. Marquis, Helen Peak, Albert J. Reiss, Gertrude Selznick, and Edward L. Walker.

The work of such a project could not have been accomplished without the assistance of many other people. We are deeply indebted to the Boards of Education of the cities of Detroit, Highland Park, and Dearborn, Michigan, for their unstinting help and support. Wherever necessary, they made their records available to our staff, provided us with clerical help, explained the purpose of our project to parents, and gave us generous amounts of class time to see the subjects. We are also grateful to the mothers of our subjects for providing us with essential information. In the daily work of the project we could always depend on the help of Robert Fagot, Julie Gray, and Heinz Hohler in statistical analysis; of Harry Dillingham, A. Freda Milstein, Elaine Platsky, and George Witt in the collection of data: and of June Crockett, Dona Lansky, and Mary Jo Winer in administrative and clerical tasks. We are obligated to the directors of the military training programs of the University of Michigan for allowing us to test their students during class time, and to Mr. S. S. Dunn of the Australian Council for Educational Research for permission to use the Franck Test.

Although an initial sample of subjects was obtained without financial assistance, it would have been impossible to continue the many activities of the project without the financial support of the United States Public Health Service (U.S.P.H.S. Project M-564). We owe a special debt to the Center for Advanced Study in the Behavioral Sciences, which granted the authors considerable time to work on the manuscript and also provided the intellectual stimulation of a group of scholars who contributed greatly to the present structure of this book.

To gain additional information about some of our results, we decided to conduct an independent investigation of the methods used to rear children by a representative sample of mothers in the metropolitan area. This research, which has been published elsewhere,* produced a number of concepts about social position that enriched our understanding of conflict. For financial support of the study of Detroit mothers we are indebted to the Horace H. Rackham Fund of the University of Michigan and to the Ford Foundation, which subsidizes the Detroit Area Study, an on-going research facility of the University of Michigan. We are grateful to Ronald Freedman, the director of the D.A.S., for his invaluable counsel, and to the many graduate students who helped in our work.

D.R.M.
G.E.S.

Ann Arbor, Michigan
October, 1959

* D. R. Miller and G. E. Swanson, *The changing American parent* (New York: Wiley, 1958).

# CONTENTS

Preface v

PART ONE
The Problem

1. Reactions to Conflict and Their Origins: An Overview 3

PART TWO
Expectations

2. Social Positions and Reactions to Conflict 43
3. Child-rearing Practices and Reactions to Conflict 69

PART THREE
Populations Studied

4. Selecting Subjects 99

PART FOUR
Results

5. Moral Standards: I. Needs and Moral Standards 119
6. Moral Standards: II. The Learning of Moral Standards 141

7. Moral Standards: III. Moral Behavior and Sex Identity 177
8. Mechanisms of Defense: I. The Mechanisms of Defense 194
9. Mechanisms of Defense: II. Denial of Failure 213
10. Mechanisms of Defense: III. Repression of Failure 231
11. Mechanisms of Defense: IV. Aggression and the Second Family of Defenses 256
12. Mechanisms of Defense: V. Sex Identity and Defenses Against Aggression 272
13. Expressive Styles: I. Substitution and Expressive Style 289
14. Expressive Styles: II. Directness with which Anger Is Expressed 315
15. Expressive Styles: III. Two Styles of Expression: Motoric and Conceptual 337

PART FIVE
Postscript

16. A Final Review 359
Appendixes 407
Index 445

## PART ONE

# THE PROBLEM

# 1

# REACTIONS TO CONFLICT AND THEIR ORIGINS:

## An Overview

Each of us experiences inner conflict many times a day. Man often strives to battle the desire of the moment because of guilt or fear, or because of his sense of responsibility to himself and to others. It is usually difficult for him to relinquish the immediate gratification, but it may be equally difficult to ignore the ultimate consequences of the action. The inevitable choice among unwelcome alternatives is even more onerous. He is reluctant to make a decision because at least one of his impulses must be frustrated. And once he acts, he may not have another opportunity to make the same decision. The choice can become particularly troublesome when it is an important one, and the pulls of contradictory desires are approximately equal.

Because conflict is ubiquitous and decisions can be so important, each man develops his own characteristic methods of defining the alternatives and of choosing among them. Even casual observations readily reveal considerable variations in individual reactions to incompatible impulses. Such variations emerge when both trivial and momentous choices must be made. For example, it is instructive to observe different people's behavior when they must choose between seeing a motion picture, which they want very much to do, and completing some urgent work. One person will go to the motion picture and feel guilty about neglecting his job. Another will go and blame his superior for assigning too much work. A third will remain in his office and feel inadequate because he has not kept up with his assignments. A fourth will give up the movie, do his work, feel grateful for his superior's dedication to the activities of the organization, and then go home and become irrationally angry at his wife. There are many other possibilities.

Characteristic responses to conflict usually become organized in a pattern which also affects many other aspects of behavior. The understanding of man's personality, therefore, requires the examination of different reactions to inner conflict and an explanation of how they develop. These were the goals of the research that will be reported in this book. In this chapter we will describe the problems we phrased in our attempts to implement these goals.

Our research was the product of a somewhat unusual integration of psychoanalytic and sociological principles. Originally, we developed many of our hypotheses after considering Faris and Dunham's (6) * now classic study of the distribution of psychoses in Chicago. Of primary importance to our research was their finding that schizophrenics tend to come from the poorest districts of the city, while manic-depressives come from the sections occupied by white-collar workers. This difference in socio-economic origins of psychoses has since been corroborated by investigations in other cities and is also reported to exist for certain neuroses. As yet, the data are fragmentary, but they seem sufficiently trustworthy to establish the fact that patients from the working class are inclined to develop symptoms different from those of patients from the middle class.

In interpreting these data, we assumed that symptoms of personality disorders represent particular solutions of inner conflict. Schizophrenics solve their problems by retreating from reality; depressives by attacking themselves. If our assumption is correct, Faris and Dunham's results suggest that the experiences unique to a particular class create characteristic reactions to conflict. As a result, when members of the middle and working classes become psychotic, they develop different symptoms.

As indicators of particular means of resolving conflict, symp-

* Parenthetical numbers refer to the lists of references, which will be found at the end of each chapter.

toms may throw as much light on the reactions of normals as they do on abnormals. The techniques employed by mental patients to resolve their problems cannot have developed overnight, or even shortly before the time of crisis. Before a person can resolve a conflict in a particular way, he must first have learned many social rules and many different ways of expressing his needs. Such skills are very complicated and can develop only over a long period of time. This development usually begins during the first years of life. Hence, the differences in symptoms may have their counterparts in reactions of normal members of various social classes.

We carried our thinking one step further. Differences in techniques for resolving conflict must reflect the contrasting experiences of people in different social classes. How can such experiences be identified? Since some of the major conflicts that affect character structure begin in the bosom of the family during the first years of life, we decided to concentrate on the study of child-rearing practices. It seemed reasonable that certain parental methods that differ in terms of social class might reinforce particular reactions to conflict.

## Indices of Our Subjects' Backgrounds

In line with our thinking, we used normal subjects in most of the studies reported on herein. Our work focused on those aspects of the subjects' experiences that led them to favor particular reactions to conflict. We investigated two general sources of our subjects' experiences. One was *social class;* the second was the *method of child rearing* used by their parents. We now review these two sources of experience to show how they may be related to each other and to the resolution of conflict.

### Social class

Investigators typically assign an individual to a social class in terms of such indices as income, prestige, education, or power. Usually, these are interrelated. Education provides a means of increasing income; the higher the education or income, the greater the power. With more power, education, or income, we often find greater prestige. Power refers to the degree to which a man's decisions can affect the lives of others. The decisions of a judge, for example, can affect more people than can those of a truck driver.

Members of the middle class usually earn incomes which permit them to accumulate some savings after the essentials are purchased. Quite often they attain a relatively advanced level of education, so that they may acquire marketable skills in using ideas. Members of the American working class grow up in a very different world. Many do not earn enough to permit any savings. A few may even have to worry about lack of food. Since they make a living by manipulating objects rather than symbols, blue-collar workers do not have to undertake a protracted formal education to prepare themselves for their jobs. Because of their limited schooling, they lack some of the skills necessary for advancement into white-collar jobs.

Membership in a social class signifies much more than a particular amount of income, or education, or prestige, or power. As a result of his lifelong experience as a member of his class, each person acquires certain characteristic traits. A man of the middle class, for example, can manipulate symbols with ease, speak grammatically, and display the social amenities. His styles of walking, speaking, and gesturing are unique. Because he can be optimistic about economic advancement, he respects the abilities and qualities that are usually required to accomplish this end. He places great store in advanced education, and is often impressed by self-sacrifice, hard work, and ethical conduct.

### CHILD REARING

In part, it is by its profound imprint on child-rearing practices that social status affects reactions to conflict. However, methods of rearing children are influenced by many factors in addition to social class. These factors include social categories, such as race and ethnicity, and parental characteristics, such as values and degrees of anxiety. The traits of the children, such as physical deformities and levels of intelligence, may affect the parents' methods. It was necessary, therefore, to devise an instrument for obtaining information about parental practices.

Some of the practices that we investigated were being used

by mothers at the time they were interviewed by members of our staff. These methods included type of discipline, extent to which requests for obedience were explained, and frequency and type of reward. We also obtained information about the harshness of weaning and toilet training, two practices that the women had used when their sons were young children. Finally, the unconscious and conscious masculinity of the subjects provided us with indirect indices of earlier parental methods.

To convey the flavor of our thinking, we now list three of our predictions about child-rearing practices and reactions to conflict. We expected that, with class controlled, harshness of weaning would be directly related to guilt about death wishes. We also anticipated that a tendency on the part of the parents to rely on a particular kind of discipline would be associated with the directness with which aggression was expressed. If the discipline was predominantly corporal, we predicted that the children would express themselves directly. Finally, it seemed probable that consciously feminine subjects would be more likely to favor the defense mechanisms of denial than would consciously masculine subjects.

So intimately are social status and the methods of training children connected that we did not think it advisable to investigate the relation to conflict of either topic without taking the other into account. To illustrate some of the possible connections that we anticipated, we cite some representative hypotheses which were confirmed by our results.

The different aspects of middle-class life—the parents' income, their prestige, their values, the people to whom they have access—inevitably influence methods of rearing children. Since the parents believe in responsibility and self-control, we predicted that they would have initiated even such early practices as weaning sooner than would parents in the working class. Because people in the middle class are accustomed to solving many problems conceptually, we anticipated that they would discipline their children by appealing to their guilt in terms of such abstractions as honesty and consideration of others. We thought that wives of blue-collar workers would be more inclined to enforce discipline by physical means.

We did not anticipate that the same child-rearing practice

would sometimes have different meanings within the two social classes. The results made it very clear, however, that we would have overlooked some important associations if we had not considered the simultaneous effect on conflict of both status and practice. Arbitrariness of parental requests, for example, was not, by itself, significantly related to such defense mechanisms as turning on the self or reversal. When variation in social class was introduced, the relationship between parental requests and the defenses became significant.

Our illustrations highlight two points about the significance of social class. First, social class defines the conditions under which parents come to favor certain patterns of child-rearing. These patterns then exert a basic influence on the children's reactions to conflict. Second, social class provides a context for interpreting the meaning of various parental techniques. Without such information, it is often impossible to predict the relationship between a technique and an inclination toward a specific method of resolving conflict. These two implications of social class will emerge frequently when we report our results.

## The Components of Conflict

Given the bewildering variety and complexity of reactions to conflict, how were we to classify them? We were not interested in conflict in general, but in specific reactions. Until we identified the different varieties and their components, we could not trace their origins to social position and child-rearing. At the present stage of our knowledge, the theoretical framework which best describes the nature of inner conflict and its resolution is the one originally developed by Freud to explain, first, the symptoms of conversion hysteria and obsessive-compulsive neurosis, and, later, the meaning of such phenomena as dreams, art forms, and slips of the tongue. In essence, the theory explains all these forms of behavior as unconsciously selected substitutes or indirect expressions of needs whose direct expressions are in conflict with other needs or with moral norms.

This interpretation helped us to phrase our problem more specifically. We defined our task as the prediction of substitute expressions. To convey the implications of this definition, we must first describe the kind of conflict on which we concentrated and then examine some of the facets of conflict that affect the selection of different kinds of substitutes.

## Substitution and Stabilized Conflicts

We were particularly interested in a kind of conflict involving forces approximately equal in strength. To illustrate some of the characteristics of such a conflict we now describe it in the light of one of its occasional results: it can be very difficult to resolve because the relative strengths of the antagonistic needs alternate somewhat like a seesaw. First, one need becomes stronger; then, as it is about to be gratified, the impending frustration of the opposing need suddenly makes it more dominant. This vacillation in strength is illustrated by the confusions of an adolescent girl who has just been kissed by her boy friend. She wants to engage in further sexual play, but is deterred by a number of forces. One is her conscience, another is her fear of pregnancy, a third is the fear that she may get the reputation of being an "easy mark." Thus, as she is about to act on her sexual need, she loses courage. She steels herself to retreat. But her anticipation of withdrawing makes her boy friend seem more attractive and diminishes her fears. These alternations in the relative dominance of needs do not occur in response to a specific external event. The struggle is largely internal.

What kinds of conflict become stabilized because of these alternations in dominance? Two conditions are necessary before such stability can occur: The needs must be closely matched in strength, and at least one of the needs must impel the person to retreat (15).

We begin with the first condition. Because antagonistic sets of pressures are created by complex groups of needs, they are seldom precisely equal. The person is first impelled in one direction, but then reverses his behavior and is impelled in the opposite direction. If the needs are very unequal in strength, there is little reason for indecision. The young lady mentioned above would have no problem if her escort were much less attractive. Or she might experience only temporary conflict if her fear of a blemished reputation was much stronger than her sexual need. Since one need would clearly outweigh the other, there would be no alternation in their dominance. As she decided to withdraw, she would still become increasingly concerned with the boy's strength or his good looks, but the increase in her sexual desire would not be sufficient to overcome her fear. The necessity of making a choice would then terminate as she said "good night" to her escort and left him at her doorstep. Of course, she would still have to find some outlet for the sexual need.

A conflict may also become stabilized when neither of the alternatives is sufficiently attractive. This is the problem of a boy who almost decides to go to a baseball game one day because he hates the drudgery of attending school. He changes his mind when he thinks of the truant officer's visit to his home, the confrontation by his mother, and the unpleasant interview with the principal. He has almost resigned himself to a boring day at school when he remembers the interminable classes, the repetitive exercises, and his poor grades. So the conflict becomes stabilized. Because of the oscillation in needs, he finds it extremely difficult to make a decision.

The type of conflict which is the most frequent source of pathological behavior involves the tendency to both approach and avoid the same object. Because a penalty is attached to a pleasure, the impulses toward approach and avoidance often oscillate. If the young lady engages in sexual relations, she worries about her reputation or about becoming pregnant. If a boy expresses his irritation at his sister, he becomes concerned about losing his parents' love. Realistic solutions of such conflicts are often impossible. How can an unmarried person solve the conflict between his moral standards and his sexual cravings? How can a man who is extremely religious ever satisfy his wish to behave ethically if he must compete with men who are using unethical practices? How can the ambitious worker adopt the speech, dress, and manners of the middle class and yet avoid being rejected by his working-class friends?

There are many, many needs and a myriad of possible substitutes. To simplify our empirical analyses of such complex phenomena, we decided to concentrate on two particular types of conflict. We chose conflicts between aggression and moral needs, and between ambition and fear of failure. We were guided in these choices by the universality and significance of these problems. Every society must educate its young in the rules about appropriate and inappropriate outlets of aggression, and many societies instill standards of achievement which exceed the potentialities of some members. The skills required to achieve adequate control of aggression and to avoid failure are many, and the educational process is long and difficult. To resolve the ensuing conflicts, everyone must develop a number of techniques. A person's aggressive needs and anxieties about failure are aroused by so many of the frustrations inherent in his social relations that the frequency of his conflicts, and his characteristic means of resolving them, provide keystones to his basic relationships with his fellow men.

When we tried to analyze the origins of different substitutes, we found that we had to take three components of conflict into account. First, it was necessary for us to know the nature of the relevant *standards,* the violation of which initiated the conflict. Standards proscribe some substitutes and define others as acceptable. Second, we had to identify the *mechanisms of defense:* the techniques of self-deception which, according to our definition, determine a preference for certain groups of substitutes over others. Finally, it was important to consider differences in *expressive style.* This term refers to a man's habitual manner of doing things, such as the tenseness of his muscular movements when he walks and the concreteness or abstractness of his ideas. Styles describe not *what* a man does, but *how* he does it. A particular expressive style tends to restrict the range of possible substitutes to those the person is accustomed to performing with some comfort. We shall now consider each of the components of conflict in turn and discuss its possible relationship to the selection of substitutes.

## Internalized Standards and Conflict

Conflicts about aggression are usually initiated because aggression violates moral standards. These are internalized rules, which are commonly accepted as implementing the goals of a social group and by which people regulate their lives.

THE LEARNING OF SOCIAL RULES

As a child participates in the activities of his family, his neighborhood, his religion, or his social class, he gradually acquires the information and skills that the group has devised to satisfy its common needs. This knowledge has been tested by the mutual efforts of many people over long periods of time. Hence it is usually superior to anything he could develop on his own. Because of the many rewards that he gains from participating in the group, the typical child undertakes his apprenticeship with enthusiasm.

But this process requires many inhibitions. All impulses cannot be gratified immediately. Cooperative enterprise cannot prosper if people sacrifice common goals to immediate personal impulses. The code of every group requires that its members either postpone or completely inhibit the gratification of some impulses.

The list of regulations in any society is very long. It takes the child many years to understand the codes that are intended to regulate his behavior, and to develop the capacity to inhibit many of his desires. As a member of society, he must control his anger, his ambition, and other needs which, if unregulated, might threaten the existence of the group.

When he is a little older, he finds that there are complicated variations of the rules. For example, he learns only gradually to tell the difference between permissible and forbidden targets of anger. If he destroys people on the battlefield, he may become a hero. If he commits the same act in his home town, he may be executed. If he gossips about politicians or high-pressure salesmen, most people will agree with him, but he cannot, without unpleasant consequences, criticize the friends whose goals he shares —unless they in turn have violated the code by some act such as spreading malicious gossip about him. As a member of various subgroups within the society, he must learn to live by special sets of regulations: to attend school regularly or jeopardize his occupational future, to play games only with boys or have others cast aspersions on his masculinity.

INTERNALIZATION AND GUILT

When the child first learns these rules, he does not necessarily use them as a basis for evaluating his behavior. It requires years of his parents' pressures before he begins to judge himself by their standards. Only then can the rules be said to have been internalized. When tempted to engage in immoral acts, he refrains even when no one can observe him. If he does transgress, even secretly, he reproaches himself. In part, a person's maturity is judged by the degree to which he has internalized and learned to live by certain rules. The mature adult can inhibit certain pleasurable acts and express himself by means of constructive alternatives which are neither harmful to himself nor to other people.

The acquisition of the information and skills that facilitate the expression of needs in a socially approved manner is a very complicated process, one which is so difficult that many people stumble before they reach the end of the long path. The 750,000 mental patients in American hospitals, the millions more who are seen in clinics and in private practice, many of the inmates of prisons and wards for alcoholics—all bear vivid testimony to the uneven success with which members of our society can live in accordance with the social rules.

While internalization is a social necessity, it creates certain problems. Some of the needs that are subject to moral regulation are anchored in human biology. Sexual needs provide a good example. They may recur frequently, even periodically, they cannot be abolished by social dicta, and they do not evaporate when an attempt is made to inhibit them. Other needs, such as the desire for status, are learned as responses to certain social situations. This latter type of need is found in all societies. And because needs to establish sexual contacts or to acquire higher status must be regulated in order to avoid social disruption, inner conflict seems inevitable.

## Dimensions of Moral Standards and Substitution

The outlawing of recurrent needs with organic components, or of needs which are the inevitable products of social experience, is not the only, or even the most frequent, cause of conflict. The growing child must learn that many social behaviors are appropriate in one context, but not in another. A man who drinks heavily may be accepted by his friends, but not if they learn that he is depriving his family of food. Helping a friend is generally approved, but, with few exceptions, it is condemned if he has deliberately committed an antisocial act. It takes the child many years to learn the differences between situations to which the rules apply and those to which they do not apply. These discriminations are often very hard to make. The youngster is often puzzled by the contradictions in the standards of different groups, and the shifts in peoples' expectations as he matures.

We have tried to convey the significance of internalized social standards for the initiation of conflict. Equally important for the research to be reported are the limitations that these standards impose on the resolution of conflict. For example, a standard that defines as sinful many of the alternative expressions of an aggressive need requires the adoption of less direct substitutes than a standard that defines as sinful only a few alternative expressions. In other words, members of a religious sect whose doctrines forbid most recognizable expressions of aggression feel constrained to use less direct outlets than members of a socially rebellious Bohemian group do.

To predict the substitutes, it is necessary to know not only the range of forbidden actions but also their specific contents. Only if a man has learned to become guilty about a particular impulse does he experience conflict. If his social standard proscribes the blaming of anyone but oneself, he feels impelled to employ the defense of self-attack rather than indiscriminate scapegoating.

Depending on his previous experiences, each person develops a somewhat unique pattern of social needs. In our research we focused on individual differences in the *extensity* of moral standards. The term refers to the range of acts defined as immoral. We inferred extensity from *severity of guilt* after a standard was violated. We also studied *resistance to temptation,* and *externalization,* or projection of moral disapproval. We related individual differences in these expressions of morality to social status and to direct and indirect indices of the child-rearing methods to which the subjects had been exposed.

## Anxiety and the Mechanisms of Defense

When needs and moral standards are approximately equal in strength, the conflict does not always, or even usually, become stabilized for any period of time. While the equilibrium lasts, it builds up an increasing amount of anxiety. Finally, the experience becomes so unpleasant that it stimulates attempts to resolve the conflict. Among the techniques that fulfill that aim are the defense mechanisms.

To describe the function of defense mechanisms, the second component of conflict that we investigated, we must begin with the topic of anxiety. We summarize the problems of a nine-year-old boy to illustrate its significance for conflict and defense.

Bill, a "spoiled" child, was referred to a clinic because he was doing poor work in school. Since Bill was a very bright boy, his teacher ascribed the problem to some sort of emotional block. She reported that he was easily distracted; he seemed to be daydreaming so much of the time that he could not learn his lessons. In addition, he insisted on teasing some of the girls. He did not defend himself when they complained to the teacher, but remained silent and depressed.

Bill's mother could not think of any reason why her son should be disturbed. She said that he had recently lost his appetite and occasionally had spells of crying. The mother had just given birth to a daughter, but did not think this had anything to do with Bill's emotional state.

Bill acted more like an adult than a boy during his interview at the clinic. His speech was precise, his vocabulary impressive, and his general behavior overcontrolled and evasive. He obviously was not going to trust a strange adult. Rather than press the boy to confide his troubles, the clinician tried to get at them indirectly by allowing him to draw anything he wished, to make up dramatic situations with dolls, and to tell interesting stories about some pictures.

The first drawing, a multi-colored swastika, was depicted in loving detail. Later discussions revealed that Bill knew the meaning of the symbol, and realized the horror with which his Jewish parents would react to it. A second drawing portrayed the family: The father, mother, and six-month-old sister were in a close group, but Bill placed himself at some distance from the rest. His stories and dramatic situations revealed his problems very clearly. There were affectionate references to babies, but also tales in which they stole the love of their parents from their elder siblings. The examiner learned that the advent of Bill's sister had had a marked effect on his relationship with his parents. Following her birth, he had lost his privileged position. The parents, thinking that he was mature enough to take care of himself, neglected all but his physical necessities for the next few months. It is not difficult to imagine the effect of this change on the previously indulged boy.

Later Bill admitted that in many of his daydreams he killed his sister and recaptured his favored position. One conflict thus involved his homicidal and loving impulses toward his sister. A second involved simultaneous love and hatred for the fickle parents. A story about people preferring girls to boys was the clue to a final difficulty. Although Bill desperately wanted to remain a boy, he also had daydreams about being a girl. In his stories he revealed the unconscious impression that this was the only way he could recapture the attention that was reserved for his sister. At times he even had fleeting fantasies of an operation which converted him into a girl.

At this point we would like to focus on the methods by which Bill resolved his conflicts. He could not gain exclusive rights to his parents' love, but he could get their attention—and hurt them—by failing in school. He could not harm his sister, but he could substitute the teasing of other girls for such activity. He could not become a girl, but he could have daydreams of operations on his genitals. It is notable that none of the three solutions ameliorated his real problems. Failing in school did not increase parental affection, teasing strange girls did not hurt Bill's sister, and fantasies about operations did not transform him into a girl. Nor, for that matter, would becoming a girl have helped him to replace the baby in the parents' affection. If Bill could have been rational, he would have been able to see the shortcomings in his methods. But when anything pertaining to his symptoms came up, he found it very difficult to think clearly. He was torn by many conflicting impulses and could not make any choices between them. He became so tense that it was difficult for him to sleep at night. Even when he could rest, he often felt exhausted. He was also extremely anxious. To understand how his emotional state affected his view of his problems and created a need for his nonrational solutions, we parenthetically direct our attention to the nature of anxiety.

## Anxiety

We have noted that incompatible impulses to approach and to avoid the same object often result in protracted indecision. Because of the swings in the relative strengths of the impulses, neither can be directly gratified. Thus the conflict persists. It mounts in intensity as the individual delays his attempts at solutions.

When a conflict becomes stabilized, any decision is costly. If the problem continues for some time, the person soon experiences a very unpleasant emotional state. Often he does not know its meaning. His anxiety may take many forms. He may be restless; his behavior may become inflexible; he may become preoccupied with his physical state—his sweating hands, his startle responses, his frequent urination, his rapid breathing, and his insomnia. If the conflicting needs are very strong, his symptoms may finally become so overwhelming that he cannot continue his customary activities.

Anxiety is not clearly understood. The experience is even difficult to describe. Subjectively, it seems akin to fear, but need not be as overwhelming. Its causes are only vaguely understood, and it seems to persist without reason. Scholars are agreed that it develops from fear, that it may turn into panic, and that it is often indistinguishable from the two. Most commonly, when the person clearly perceives the source of danger he is said to experience fear; when he is not sure about the nature of the danger, he is anxious.

Depending on its intensity, anxiety can be helpful or handicapping. This is easily illustrated by the behavior of a child. At first he resists various maternal attempts to wash him, or to stop him from running into the street. When he deliberately disobeys, even a patient mother who does not retaliate physically or punish him by withdrawing some privilege cannot help being cool to him for a time. Since he fears the loss of her love, he may become very disturbed by the exclusion from her favor. The next time he wants to avoid washing, he anticipates the coldness or the spanking. These may not yet be sufficient to deter him immediately. If he resists washing, he is punished. If he conforms, he is praised or, possibly, given some special privilege. After much repetition he finally learns to judge the situation and to control his actions accordingly. He has associated his reluctance to wash with the subsequent emergency of being unloved, and consistent praise has helped him to conform.

The anxiety that the boy experiences when he anticipates that he will be deserted, while similar to the feeling associated with the real event, is much less intense. It is therefore less disruptive. Anxiety thus becomes a useful signal (8). When the average person is tempted to engage in an act that may earn the scorn of others or create excessive guilt, his anxiety is usually low enough in intensity to stimulate a temporary state of inhibition. As a result, he is free to consider the problem, to examine various alternative solutions, and to take appropriate action.

People vary in the degree of anxiety that they can tolerate before deliberate behavior yields to panic. Some show a poor tolerance for difficulties which others can take in their stride. There may be congenital as well as environmental reasons for such differences. Certain clinicians are inclined to stress innate differences in the physiological thresholds of organs which participate in emotional expression. Such clinicians consider a low threshold a congenital predisposition to neuroses (11).

A more obvious cause of a low threshold is an inadequate mastery of the skills required for self-control. These include the abilities to anticipate future opportunities for satisfaction, to trust others, and to tolerate mild discomforts. If an adult lacks such abilities, even small emergencies may elicit intense anxiety. It is then impossible for him to make an active, realistic attempt to solve his problems. He must resort to more automatic, less deliberate, nonrational techniques.

Once anxiety becomes too painful, its origins are easily distorted. Because the signs of anxiety are so diffuse, it is easy to deceive oneself about their meanings and causes. Uneasiness about one's guilt, the disruptive effect of emotion, the vagueness of the signs of anxiety—these forces work together to distort the understanding of one's conflicts.

When anxiety is not excessive, many personal problems can be solved rationally. Most men can make a rational choice between the momentary unpleasantness of visiting the dentist and the intolerable prospect of pain or of loss of teeth. But supposing a man had an experience in childhood which led him to expect unbearable pain when his teeth were drilled. He might have become convinced that all dentists go out of their way to hurt their patients, or he might have developed a lasting hatred of his mother who insisted on the treatment. Even as an adult he may find the prospect of visiting the dentist so overwhelming that he cannot be objective about these obviously untenable childish impressions.

### THE MECHANISMS OF DEFENSE

When a man cannot face a conflict, or is too overwhelmed by anxiety to resolve it by rational means, he must resort to other methods. Then the defense mechanisms come into play. By using a particular mechanism, he blinds himself to the nature of his real wishes, usually by substituting more permissible versions. Defenses operate as automatically as breathing. They are applied without awareness that a choice is being made, or even that a conflict exists. Regardless of the defense, it reduces the anxiety produced by impending or actual awareness of the true needs. This point may be illustrated by Bill's conflicts and his methods of resolving them.

Obviously, his difficulties were created by the sudden loss of his parents' support. The loss made him hate his sister, whose sudden appearance on the scene created the emergency. He hated his parents, too, but he also wanted their love. To resolve his problem rationally, he would have had to accomplish two things: to recapture his parents' attention, and to express his hostility in a manner that did not forfeit their affection. Bill might have achieved these ends by controlling his anger for a few months until his parents were less preoccupied with the physical care of the baby. Then they might have been genuinely appreciative of his consideration and lavished the love on him that he craved so desperately. He might have called his needs to their attention in a tactful enough manner to modify their complete dedication to the baby. He might have expressed his aggression in outside activities, such as rough sports. Such rational problem-solving would have had obvious advantages over Bill's distorted solutions. Unfortunately Bill could use none of these rational solutions. He was too passive to tolerate the sudden curtailment of support or to take the initiative with his peers. And he was probably too young to educate his parents.

So Bill took another path in solving his problems. Instead of a rational approach, he used defensive distortions. He *repressed* his anger and became unaware of it. Still having the unwelcome need to hurt his sister, he *displaced* or transferred his unwelcome need to hurt his sister: He teased other girls. He also expressed his anger at his parents by indirect rather than direct action. He failed in school, knowing that his father, who was an ambitious professional man, would be very disturbed. The failure also reflected the defense of *turning* aggression *against the self.* By means of these defenses, Bill (1) became unaware of his incompatible reactions to the members of his family, and (2) thus reduced his anxiety. Instead of attacking his parents, and thus forfeiting more of their love, he (3) turned his anger on himself, and instead of hurting his sister, he (4) vented his aggression on some safe scapegoats.

Bill could have diverted his anger in still other ways. Instead of attacking himself with it, he might have *projected* it: He might have viewed as exceptional anger a temporary irritation of his mother's. He would not then have had to acknowledge his own hostility. He might also have *reversed* his impulse so that he was inordinately affectionate and anxious to help her in some way.

Usually, defenses occur in combination. If Bill had fantasies of hurting his parents, he might have "accidentally" cut his hand while whittling. This would have served the double purpose of *undoing,* or symbolically canceling, the hostile impulse, and of diverting the attack from its original object. He might also have reversed his impulse by assisting his mother with the housework.

Some of the most interesting defenses are those which obliterate awareness of a painful sight or reinterpret it in accordance with wishful fantasy. *Denial in fantasy* is such a mechanism. It helps to distort observable facts. To illustrate it, Anna Freud (7) describes the behavior of a small girl who could not reconcile herself to the sexual difference between herself and her brothers.

Instead of finding consolation in approved feminine activities for what she regarded as a crucial malformation, the patient pretended to herself that she had a penis. She lifted her skirts and exhibited herself, meanwhile daydreaming that she was displaying masculine genitals. This invidious concern with genital differences is not restricted to girls. Bill might have denied his burdensome masculinity by assuming the feminine position while urinating and picturing himself as being a girl.

*Repression,* a related defense, helps to obliterate events which are closely associated with forbidden needs (9). The resultant unawareness reduces anxiety about impulses which, if expressed, would lead to unpleasant consequences, such as guilt. Following repression, there is no memory of the forbidden impulse. Yet it survives in a distorted form whose meaning, while thinly veiled to the trained observer, is nevertheless not available to the person in conflict. Bill, for example, would have been astonished to learn that his sentiments for his parents involved anything but love.

Sometimes the self-deception resulting from repression is so transparent to others that the person's lack of insight seems surprising. A man who was very troubled by his unconscious hostility spent many hours each evening saying his prayers. If, at any point, he deviated from the correct procedure, he had to begin over again. This prolonged the process painfully, but he could not go to sleep unless he followed the exact ritual. Exploration of the symptom revealed that the patient was very preoccupied with the fear that his father, who was in reasonably good health, might die. The son felt that only if he said his prayers in just the right way, would he be able to save his father. Such obsessive concern with death is often the superficial mask of a coveted wish. An excessive preoccupation with an improbable death may seem very close to the original need, at least from the viewpoint of the observer, but its meaning can be disguised when the concern is shifted to the slavish performance of ritual that is intended to help the hated person.

### Substitution and families of defenses

Every defense depends for its effectiveness upon the substitution of a socially acceptable alternative for the original form of the need. Sometimes the original is revealed by an unintentional error. Freud (10) cites the case of the printer who made a "mistake" in setting type for a story about a member of the royal family. This nobleman had been involved in many escapades. Instead of "crown prince," the article referred to the "clown prince." When the printer set type for the retraction, he made the same mistake. Erickson (4) provides another illustration of this type of error. During hypnosis, a subject was told that the experimenter was an irritatingly dull person. When the two were talking later, and the subject had presumably repressed the events of the hypnotic session, he felt a draft and said he shut the "bore."

Everyone probably avails himself of all the defenses that are common in his society. People are likely to differ, however, in their orders of preference. Given the same conflict, one person immediately begins to look for a scapegoat; another concentrates on the good qualities of those who are causing his difficulties. How are such individual differences learned? In analyzing them we first divided the defenses we studied into two *families*. Mechanisms in the first family, such as denial, have in common the obliteration of objective events and the substitution for them of more tolerable fantasies. Such defenses depend on responses that are available shortly after birth, and are applicable to most kinds of conflict. Because their use results in gross distortions, it creates social difficulties.

Defenses in the second family, such as reversal, have in common a displacement within one or more dimensions of a need. Such mechanisms may involve displacements of *objects,* or *acts,* or *affects,* or *agents*. Unlike members of the first family, those in the second require very complex skills. Each of the defenses is applicable only to a certain kind of conflict, and results in minimal distortion of the actual events. Usually, the distortion is of a type which avoids social difficulty.

In our research we thought in terms of the two families when we made predictions. We assumed that the second family has obvious social advantages over the first but requires more complex skills. Hence, it seemed to us that the first is favored when the situation is very difficult or conditions for learning the complex skills are not favorable. In various studies we investigated both families and such individual members as turning against the self and denial. We related predilections for them to social positions and to child-training practices favored by the subjects' parents.

## Expressive Style

Each defense mechanism limits the total range of solutions to a group of substitutes having a common characteristic. The knowledge that a person is using a particular defense eliminates many possible substitutes, but leaves a broad range of alternatives from among which his selection must be predicted. Displacement, for example, involves a change of object. If this is a man's only defense, it is certain that he is not changing his affect or act. But how is the final object to be explained when there are still so many possibilities? When a man displaces, does he tend to favor certain objects over others? An angry boy may shift the attack from his father to an uncle, an aunt, an unrelated older man or woman, a boy or girl, himself, a dog or cat, or an inanimate object, such as a piece of furniture or the family automobile.

The problem of explaining specific substitutes applies to a number of mechanisms. Rather than shifting to another object, a man may project his aggression and incorrectly attribute it to someone else. To whom? A father, mother, sister, stranger, animal, or railroad train can all serve to terminate the conflict. It is helpful to know that all the substitutes must have the capacity of fulfilling his forbidden desire, but there still remains a wide range of possible resolutions. How can the kinds that he selects be determined?

To shed some light on this problem we decided to investigate *expressive style.* By this term we refer to certain individual differences in the manner of perceiving and responding to one's environment. In everyday conversation they are typically depicted by adjectives like "rigid," "neat," "passive," and "diffident." Such styles of behavior are not contingent on the presence of incompatible impulses. They are usually enduring characteristics, and seem relatively independent of temporary conditions. Expressive styles are, however, very pertinent to the resolution of conflict. To demonstrate the connection, we shall review three kinds of expressive style that we investigated in our research.

Let us consider first the *directness of aggression.* Two boys are troubled by conflicting impulses toward their fathers. One may typically displace his aggression to objects that are similar to the original: He relieves his anger by provoking his brother into a fight. The other boy usually substitutes remote objects: He relieves his anger by kicking the furniture.

The directness with which anger is expressed also applies to the substitution of acts. The angry boy who can be direct may play a trick on his father, or try to humiliate him by revealing one of his indiscretions to a neighbor. The boy with the indirect style is more likely to help his father.

In the resolution of conflict, defense and directness of expression are independent: Directness can refer to the substitution of objects, acts, affects, or agents. The more direct the style, the more similar the substitute is to the blocked impulse. The less direct the style, the less similar is the substitute.

The other two styles—the *conceptual* and *motoric orientations*—describe the relative extent to which a person employs his muscles and his mind in resolving his problems. Some people can think through a problem only if they can work on it with their hands. Unless they can manipulate objects physically, they cannot perform adequately. Other people feel more comfortable if they can get a picture of the task and then solve it in their heads. They may be handicapped in attacking problems which require a motoric orientation. An inclination to favor either a motoric or a conceptual orientation probably affects the nature of substituted acts. When disturbed or confused about aggressive impulses, motoric subjects are likely to substitute physical rather than conceptual acts. Such people probably prefer playing football to debating. Conceptual subjects are inclined to make the opposite kinds of choices.

We also investigated three other expressive styles. *Passivity* is the extent to which a person attempts to gratify a need by appealing to others to do something to or for him. The other two styles were *emotional dilation-constriction* and *degree of control.* The former refers to the directness with which feelings are expressed; the latter refers to size of discrepancy between internalized standards and actions.

On the assumption that expressive styles are relatively enduring aspects of people's personalities, we anticipated that individual stylistic differences among our subjects would affect their methods of resolving conflicts. In our research we related differences in expressive style to social position and to various patterns of parental child-rearing practices.

## The Thinking Behind Our Predictions

The antecedent variables in our studies included social class and such parental methods as type of discipline, the extent to which requests were explained, the type and frequency of reward, and the harshness of weaning and toilet training. Different aspects of conflict were traced to these variables in the various investigations. In studies of morality we measured severity of guilt, resistance to temptation, and defenses against guilt. When we turned to conflict resolution we studied both families of defense, the specific mechanisms of denial, turning against the self, and repression, and realistic problem solving. Expressive styles which we explored included directness of aggression, motoric and conceptual orientation, passivity, emotional dilation-constriction, and control of behavior.

Now, how does one arrive at a basis for postulating relations among such variables? Our general purpose was to explain the origins of different reactions to conflict. To this end, we tried, as far as possible, to test the kinds of claims which appear most often in articles on personality. Unfortunately, there are many gaps in the theory. It is also possible to formulate many contradictory hypotheses. One may postulate, for example, that late weaning is not traumatic because the child is finally ready to stop sucking, or that late weaning is traumatic because the child is so accustomed to oral gratification that he cannot relinquish it.

While some of the literature provided fruitful ideas, we needed more specific theoretical guidance in formulating hypotheses. We consider two kinds of principles. The first and more general kind of principle was usually derived from the literature on learning and perception. The second, which was more specific, pertained to variables themselves. We shall now illustrate each of these types.

GENERAL PRINCIPLES

Fundamental to all our predictions was the assumption that moral standards, defenses, and expressive styles are learned. Some of the reactions may be acquired deliberately; some may be acquired unintentionally or even without awareness. Our hypotheses pertained to the conditions under which reactions were learned.

We tried to predict what a boy would learn when his mother acted in a particular way, and also how well he would learn it. Since we investigated a variety of reactions, we had to invoke a number of different explanatory processes. One group pertained to the lessons learned when parents offer positive incentives. The second group pertained to the lessons learned from negative incentives.

Three principles guided us in predicting the content of learned materials. We anticipated that much of the content would be taught verbally, that it would be obtained from important adults, and that the boys would be most inclined to adopt the adults' methods of exerting power. We now consider each of these in turn.

In analyzing the boys' choices of motoric and conceptual jobs, we inquired into the mothers' preferences. We did this on the assumption that preferences would differ in terms of social class, and that they would be communicated verbally to the offspring.

In other studies we postulated a second source of reactions. We assumed that sons would pattern their own behavior after that of their parents. This principle seemed particularly relevant to expressive style, since it is so visible. We predicted, for example, that if the mothers were inclined to use abstract appeals, such as symbolic rewards, the sons would probably develop a conceptual style.

It seemed to us that in identifying with their mothers, children would internalize the characteristics most pertinent to the women's manipulations of power. If they usually reinforced their requests with their hands, we thought that the boys would be fighters; if the mothers did not beat their sons but appealed to their guilt, we anticipated that they would not be fighters.

The remaining issues all pertained to the effects of negative reinforcement. We anticipated that painful methods would create strong avoidance tendencies, that lack of understanding would make it difficult for children to act in many situations, and that the timing of requests would affect the learning of certain skills. Let us consider each of these assumptions.

Pain can be so intense or so widespread as to create generalized avoidance of reality. In line with this principle, we assumed that the combination of harsh physical punishment and lack of reward would lead to frequent denial.

Pain and confusion may both occur if parents enforce requests without explaining their purposes. It is easier to learn a complex skill if reasons for it have been explained than if it has been arbitrarily required. We looked, therefore, for an association between explained requests for obedience and resistance to temptation.

Earliness of requests may be interpreted in two ways. Very early ones can have the same effect as lack of explanation if they are made before the child can understand the reasons for them or what he is to do. Premature demands may then disrupt learning or lead to avoidance. It was the postulated connection between very early requests and avoidance which led us to test the association between the timing of toilet training and frequency of denial. On the assumption that very early requests interfere with learning, we anticipated that the time when they occurred would fixate a child at that stage of development. We thought he would favor the skills of that period because it would be difficult for him to learn the more mature skills of subsequent periods. Timing was, therefore, a primary consideration when we predicted the reactions to conflict of subjects who were unconsciously feminine. In line with certain clinical observations, we first postulated that these boys had not acquired the masculine traits of later stages because of the difficulties caused by particular parental requests during earlier stages of development. We also predicted that our subjects would favor the defenses and expressive styles reinforced most strongly during the same stages of development.

Early, but not premature, requests which the child can obey need not be disruptive. In fact, earliness of weaning or toilet training, for example, may even be used to establish high standards of behavior. It did not seem surprising, therefore, to find that harshness of weaning was significantly associated with severity of guilt about the violation of a moral standard.

### Predictions involving social class

In addition to the general principles just discussed, we also took the nature of specific variables into account when we tried to define our expectations. Just how we thought about individual variables is explained in chapters containing our results. At this point we will illustrate some of the issues in terms of our thinking about social class.

The concept of social status is a very complicated one. The assignment of a man to a particular social class may signify a number of facts. It may signify such things as his relative power in the community, the area of the city in which he lives, the nature of his job, the amount of property he owns, the extent of his education, or the social status of people to whom he has access. His socio-economic status also provides a key to such varied characteristics as his values, dress, style of speech, the size of his family, and the number of organizations to which he belongs. It is not necessary to add the many more possible examples to highlight the main problem posed by social class in our research. Only with difficulty could we predict associations between the many-faceted concept of social class and other variables. From a general picture of life in the middle and working classes, we were able to make some predictions with confidence in the probable results. To gain advancement in the economic order, people in the middle class must have self-control. Thus we anticipated that they would get more practice in the defenses needed for self-control than would people in the working class. The defenses we investigated were reversal and turning against the self. Because white-collar occupations require the manipulation of symbols, we predicted that children in the middle class would favor conceptual skills more than would children in the working class.

We also made other predictions, which, while they seemed plausible, differed from the results in ways that revealed some of the fuzziness in our conception of social class. Some of us anticipated, for example, that boys from the working class would express their aggression more directly than boys in the middle class.

Boys in the two classes did not differ significantly on the total distribution of directness; they did in the frequency of the most direct forms of aggression. We had overgeneralized from accounts of frequent fighting in the working class. It was this kind of inexactitude which led members of our project to disagree or to be uncertain about some of our predictions. While we investigated the connections between social class and such variables as severity of guilt and fear of failure, we did not always anticipate significant associations. We shall have more to say about the prediction of behavior from socio-economic status in our reports of results and in the final chapter.



## Significance of Conflict

We now come to a topic which ordinarily would have been introduced earlier. We delayed our discussion until we could describe our basic concepts. Why study conflict at all? We had four primary reasons. One has already been introduced: It is the dependence of particular patterns of internalized social standards, defenses, and expressive styles on the experiences most typical of particular social positions in American society. We will delay further treatment of this topic until later chapters. Another reason for our interest in conflict, particularly of the unresolved type, is its frequency and importance in the everyday life of most normal people. A third source of interest is the information which knowledge of a man's typical reactions to conflict provides about his behavior in conflict-free situations. Finally, reactions to conflict help us to understand the symptoms of certain personality disorders. We will consider each of the last three reasons in turn.

### Frequency of unresolved conflicts

Among the most common inner conflicts are those that are hard to resolve in any reasonable manner. Everyone has had to face the frustrations of wanting to hurt someone he likes, feeling guilty because of a sexual attraction to someone beyond his reach, aching to achieve certain unattainable goals, or feeling unworthy because of his wishes to exploit others. The mature person tries to adjust to the realities of the situation. If he can accept the inevitability of some antisocial wishes, he need not feel very guilty when they occur. To avoid conflict, he learns to control himself and to seek socially acceptable outlets for his needs.

Objective assessment of the facts sometimes produces little but humiliation. This is particularly true because of the rapid social change in American society. The forbidden practice in one decade sometimes becomes the approved one in the next. Standards of child rearing provide a good example. The many shifts in fashion are vividly illustrated in Wolfenstein's (22) analysis of the recommendations of the United States Children's Bureau. In the second decade of this century parental demonstrations of affection were definitely frowned upon. In the fourth, loving was strongly advocated. More recently, the publications have stressed the setting of limits. Because of the frequent shifts, many mothers have become confused and insecure about the correctness of their methods, and about the extent to which they should limit their children's aggression, sexuality, or ambition.

Even if rapid change were less serious a problem, aggressive and sexual needs would probably be involved in many conflicts. Few socially approved forms of gratification are available for these needs. In what ways can the mistreated child express his hostility to his parents without being condemned or attacked? How can the dull child achieve self-respect when his parents want him to prepare for a professional school? At best, some conflicts afford only partially adequate resolutions, so that many people keep searching continuously for acceptable substitutes.

A quest for the vicarious expression of unacceptable needs may account for the universal interest in the artistic depiction of conflict. For example, some of our classic dramas picture men divided against themselves. Some of the popularity of *Oedipus* or *King Lear* must reflect the fact that the primary characters are struggling with conflicts which have plagued all peoples throughout time.

Often the theme of conflict has earned for the artist or philosopher a popular appeal that he might not have had otherwise. Because of St. Augustine's struggles with "lust of the flesh, lust of the eyes, and pride" (20), he is far better known to the layman than is Aquinas, who was his superior as a formal philosopher.

Similarly, Hogarth and Dostoevsky provide unique interest in their portrayals of self-torment and depravity.

The vicarious expression of needs involved in conflict is as frequently a goal in the applied arts as it is in the fine arts. In the sale of soap and beer, a tried-and-true appeal is a semi-clothed model in a seductive pose suggesting passionate fulfillment. Some of the most popular detective stories seem to sell because of their bone-crushing, face-smashing sadism. Many housewives seek to escape from their drab existence by vicariously living the exciting lives of the heroines of soap operas. There seems little doubt that the commercial potency of such appeals must derive from the synthetic fulfillment of needs which have few other legitimate expressions.

### CONFLICT AND CHARACTER

Conflict is important not only because of its great frequency, but also because methods of resolving it are used so often and in so many situations that they tend to spread to many reactions which originally had nothing to do with competing needs. Writers often display an intuitive grasp of this principle in portraying their characters. They seem keenly aware of the fact that defensive maneuvers emerge during life's crises, so that information about a man's reactions at such times often reveals more about his probable responses in many different kinds of situations than a much more detailed description of his behavior during less tense periods. Crisis is required for tragedy, and tragedy is the tool of the writer who wishes to portray the character of a man. Lancelot is caught between his love for Guinevere and his devotion to King Arthur; Lady Macbeth is torn between ambition and guilt. Don Jose can have Carmen only if he betrays his country, and Faust must choose between eternal damnation and his thirst for knowledge. Popular stereotypes of famous heroes often depend upon their characteristic reactions to conflict. Hamlet is known by his constant introspection, Peer Gynt by his escape from his problems through wanderlust, and the young George Washington by his honesty.

Psychologists have also noted the close connections between characteristic methods of resolving conflict and many other kinds of behavior. A man who keeps his emotions in order as a means of controlling his aggression is also likely to be concerned with having his desk in order, meeting appointments at the exact time, and keeping a detailed budget. Or, if he is inclined to attribute to others the anger that he cannot tolerate in himself, his suspiciousness may lead him to be unduly secretive about his personal affairs, very sensitive to the motives of others, and preoccupied with methods of avoiding trouble. He is not usually an enthusiastic or outgoing person. There are hundreds of clinical cases which illustrate the connections between reactions to conflict and such varied forms of behavior as the jokes a person tells, his dreams and fantasies, the patterns of his doodles, his vocational interests, his styles of physical expression, or his reactions to threat of failure. In view of the congruence among these types of behavior, Reich (17) suggests that techniques of resolving conflict form the nucleus of a "character structure."

### Conflicts and pathological symptoms

Reactions to conflict are also of interest because they throw light on the symptoms of certain personality disorders. A conflict can be resolved in a number of ways. If a man can be deliberate, he prefers a socially acceptable resolution. If, for example, he is angry at a friend who has unintentionally inconvenienced him, he considers it more realistic to discuss the matter and to work out a mutually satisfactory solution than to attack the friend. An attack may be gratifying, but it may also create unpleasant complications.

When a problem cannot be solved directly, some mature solution, such as concentrated activity in a sport or hobby, can occasionally be found. Some conflicts are so intense, however, that they cannot be resolved by means of very indirect expressions. Others afford no mature substitutes. In either case a man may be forced to seek solutions which were adequate in earlier years—solutions which, while they provide relief, also create social difficulty. They may result in puzzling pains for which the sufferer seeks attention, they may produce a pleasure in sarcastic humor that exposes the frailties of others, or they may maximize a tendency to appeal for help in performing tasks that one can readily do on his own. Unrealistic substitutes that create certain problems in one's relations with other people are called symptoms. The following case history of a hysterical conversion illustrates the relief, as well as the difficulties, which occur when that symptom results from a particular solution of a conflict.

An apprentice at a punch press had been the object of his foreman's public taunts for some time. They began when the apprentice removed the automatic safety device which pulled his arm out of the way as the press descended, because he found it too unpleasant to have his arm jerked thousands of times a day. From the foreman's point of view, the devices were installed because there had been many serious accidents in the plant. He was very worried about the accidents, and he decided to make an issue of the apprentice's act. So the foreman started a barrage of sarcastic comments about the false bravery and lack of intelligence of the apprentice. Since the latter needed the job, he did not retaliate. At times he would even convince himself that the foreman's intent was justified. At other times he was so furious that he feared he might lose control and strangle the foreman.

While the apprentice was operating the press one day, he was taunted continuously. He became increasingly inaccurate in his work, and his fingers would have been crushed had it not been for the guard. That afternoon, his right arm became paralyzed. A physician found that there was nothing physically wrong with the nerve tracts involved in the functioning of the arm, and diagnosed the symptom as conversion hysteria. Patients who suffer from this disorder, because they cannot resolve a particular conflict in a mature manner, banish it from awareness and express it symbolically in a physical disturbance.

After spending some time with the patient, a psychotherapist discovered the covert meanings of the symptom. Because the arm was immobile, it could not be used to attack the tormentor. In addition, the paralysis prevented the apprentice from performing his job. This removed him from an intolerable situation.

The apprentice resolved the conflict between his hatred of the foreman and his fears and guilts by repressing the hatred. Had he been more fortunate he could have overcome his difficulty with more mature kinds of defense, which would have enabled him to express his feelings in acceptable ways. Had he been more unfortunate he would have resorted to more pathological defenses, each of which would have exacted its own penalty. He could have turned his hatred on himself and become sufficiently depressed to require psychiatric treatment. Or he could have used the defense of projection. He then would have attributed his own anger to the foreman, thus exaggerating his hostility. This would have relieved the apprentice's guilt about his own hatred. If he began to elaborate his ideas of being persecuted so that he interpreted the actions of others as systematic plots, he would have been diagnosed as paranoid. Finally, he might have gradually retreated from reality into a fantasy world that was closer to his wishes, and gradually stopped responding to people. He then would have been labeled as schizophrenic.

These are a few of many possible examples of the meanings of symptoms of personality disorders when viewed as indirect expressions of desired but unavailable acts—substitutes which are determined in part by the patient's particular combinations of defense mechanisms. When we come to understand the conditions that produce conflict, and the variety of methods used to terminate it, we will have made considerable progress in explaining the origins of personality disorders.

## A Note on the Statistical Methods and Tables

Chapters containing the reports of investigations usually include only the minimal information required to convey the significance of certain relations. In most tables we have summarized a group of results by identifying the variables, indicating the trends, and reporting significances. To highlight the primary results of each study, we have shifted other statistical details to an appendix. Unless otherwise stated, the frequencies of cells for each relation cited in a summary table are contained in Appendix D, which is divided according to the chapters in which the results are reported.

The significance of each relation has been evaluated in terms of the probability that the obtained chi square or tau, depending on the statistic, could have arisen by chance. If the probability is .05 or less, we consider it significant. If a probability is less than .20, its exact figure is cited. If it is more than .20, it is given to the closest tenth: .30, .40, and so on.

When the direction of the association is not apparent from the figures, it is reported in the table. It is indicated by a description of the box, or boxes, with the largest frequencies. Thus, in presenting the association between social class and reward, we indicate the trend with the statement that the combination of working class and occasional reward was most frequent. Once this fact is known, the relative frequencies in the other three boxes can be inferred. In the statistician's language, a table with two rows and two columns has only one degree of freedom. If the working-class mothers give occasional rewards, they cannot give rewards frequently. And if the association is significant, the fact that the working-class mothers favor occasional rewards means that the middle-class mothers must give rewards frequently.

To test the significance of relations involving one degree of freedom, we calculated the chi square with a correction for continuity when the marginal sums did not exceed twenty (14). The Fisher Exact Test (12) was used for smaller samples. For tables with more than one degree of freedom, we obtained an approximation of chi square from the maximum likelihood ratio, or lambda, described by Mood (16). When there is more than one degree of freedom, this approximation provides a more sensitive test than the usual Pearson formula. Chi square is minus two times the log to the base *e* of lambda.

In some instances we anticipated not only that two variables would be related, but also that the relation would be monotonic. In other words, the prediction meant that increasing values of one variable would be associated with increasing, or decreasing, values of the other. This principle is illustrated by the relation, explained in Chapter 15, between social class and a conceptual orientation in paintings. We anticipated that the largest proportion of boys from the middle class would be most conceptual, that a smaller proportion would be intermediate, and that the smallest proportion would be least conceptual. Furthermore, we anticipated that the largest proportion of boys from the working class would be least conceptual, that fewer boys would be intermediate, and that the smallest proportion would be most conceptual. To calculate the significance of such relations, with the progressive changes in proportions taken into account, we used Smith's (18) modification of Kendall's tau, or rank correlation. It is a tau with ties:

Every case in the same class is treated as though it were tied with every other case. When we report the results of such calculations, we also include the progressive changes in proportions as part of the table.

The ordinary chi square test is not uniquely sensitive to such monotonic relationships. The chi square would remain the same if the column with most conceptual cases were interchanged with the column containing the intermediate cases, so that there was no longer a monotonic trend in proportions. For tables involving two or more rows, and three or more columns, Kendall's statistic is approximately normal in distribution. Hence, it permits the use of one-tailed tests. For tables with one degree of freedom, chi square obtained by Pearson's method is $N$ times the square of the tau obtained by Kendall's rank correlation index. The two methods are equivalent for a large $N$. We made the arbitrary decision of using the ordinary chi square technique.

## Plan of the Book

Our research represented an attempt to extend psychoanalytic principles, not by means of the clinical methods originally used to develop them, but by the controlled empirical techniques of the social scientist. This decision posed some difficult problems. In terms of the therapeutic purposes for which psychoanalytic concepts were devised, they have been very useful. The theoretical seedlings that Freud planted have matured into hardy and adaptable organisms. There is little question that they constitute the most influential theory of personality. But any system, particularly one with such wide scope, can always be improved. At one time or another Freud discussed motivation, learning, poetry, war, thinking, defense mechanisms, religion, psychiatric symptoms, the family, and humor, to name a few of his topics. While his success was phenomenal, he was realistic enough to regard many of his principles as first approximations and to stress many of the lacunae in his theory. The flexibility of his system is indicated by its continuing change, not only during his lifetime but also since his death. Recent innovations, for example, include explorations of the early years of childhood, the processes of socialization in different societies, and the nature of voluntary conscious reactions. Obviously, we could not agree with the position of some psychoanalysts who seem to find it difficult to accept any change in current concepts. We also rejected the position of some social scientists who point a finger of scorn at the methodological inadequacy of some psychoanalytic principles without taking cognizance of the clinical tradition and the relative youth of the movement.

The clinical literature contains many observations which helped us to clarify our hypotheses. However, our problems were relatively new. While the clinical literature is rich with suggestions, few of the concepts and principles have been carefully defined or systematically organized. The possible relationships between social position and reactions to conflict have been mentioned but not explored. A number of psychologists have made valuable progress in identifying and classifying the various methods of child rearing (1, 2, 19, 21), but thus far they have not agreed on standard definitions. Such key concepts as needs, moral standards, and defense still remain to be carefully defined. It is generally agreed that moral standards create the basis for certain kinds of conflict and delimit the methods of resolving them. There is no clear picture, however, of the dimensions of moral needs, nor has any attempt been made to trace their interrelationships. Of all topics, defense mechanisms have been explored the least. They are viewed roughly as techniques for distorting perceptions of unacceptable impulses, but psychoanalysts do not agree among themselves in their descriptions of certain defenses. Psychologists have tested some extremely fruitful hypotheses relating defense to perception (3–5). Still to be made are initial attempts to examine the similarities and differences in the characteristics of various defenses, or the backgrounds that predispose an individual to avail himself of one defense rather than another.

Because of such considerations, we have devoted considerable space in the next few chapters to definitions of concepts and to descriptions of methods used to obtain information about the subjects' backgrounds. In fact, such topics are the primary concern of the initial part of the book.

The next two chapters contain descriptions of our categories of social status and of child-rearing practices. A fourth chapter on the recruitment and selection of subjects concludes this introductory section.

The middle section of the book is devoted to reports of empirical studies. It contains three parts, each of which concerns an aspect of conflict. First, we describe studies of internalized social standards, then of defense mechanisms, and, finally, of expressive styles. Each aspect of conflict is introduced by a theoretical chapter on such problems as definition, classification, and the derivation of hypotheses. Because an attempt has been made to be broadly systematic, these introductory chapters include more concepts and hypotheses than we have had time to test.

It is not until we reach the concluding section of the book that we consider a topic which is ordinarily introduced much earlier in reports of empirical work. The topic is the nature of techniques for measuring moral standards, defenses, and expressive styles. We consider such issues as the reasons for selecting the method of story completion, evidence for its validity, and technical and ethical problems involved in devising methods of arousal. While some of these issues are discussed in the chapters containing the reports of findings, we left the review of our methods to the end because we wanted to describe the exploratory work which preceded the development of the techniques we used, and the extent to which the results of the studies changed our conceptions of adequate methods. It would not have been feasible to present a developmental account of our methods before summarizing the individual studies. The concluding chapter also contains an evaluation of our findings and a discussion of their significance for further research.

## References

1. Baldwin, A. L., Kalhorn, Joan, & Breese, Fay H. The appraisal of parent behavior. *Psychol. Bull.*, 1949, *63*, 1–85.
2. Champney, H. The variables of parent behavior. *J. abnorm. soc. Psychol.*, 1941, *36*, 525–42.
3. Cowen, E. L., & Beier, E. G. The influence of "threat-expectancy" on perception. *J. Pers.*, 1950–51, *19*, 85–94.

4. Erickson, M. H. Experimental demonstrations of the psychopathology of everyday life. *Psychoanal. Quart.*, 1939, *8*, 338–53.
5. Eriksen, C. W. The case for perceptual defense. *Psychol. Rev.*, 1954, *61*, 175–82.
6. Faris, R. E. L., & Dunham, H. W. *Mental disorders in urban areas.* Chicago: Univ. of Chicago Press, 1939.
7. Freud, Anna. *The ego and the mechanisms of defence.* London: Hogarth, 1937.
8. Freud, S. *Inhibitions, symptoms, and anxiety.* London: Hogarth, 1936.
9. ——— Repression. *Collected Papers,* Vol. IV. London: Hogarth, 1949.
10. ——— *The basic writings of Sigmund Freud.* New York: Modern Library, 1938.
11. Greenacre, Phyllis. The predisposition to anxiety. In Tomkins, S. (Ed.), *Contemporary psychopathology.* Cambridge: Harvard Univ. Press, 1947.
12. Latscha, R. Tests of significance in a 2X2 contingency table: Extension of Finney's table. *Biometrika,* 1953, *40,* 74–75.
13. Lazarus, R. S., Eriksen, C. W., & Fonda, C. P. Personality dynamics and auditory perceptual recognition. *J. Pers.,* 1950–51, *19,* 471–82.
14. McNemar, *Q. Psychological statistics.* New York: Wiley, 1955.
15. Miller, N. Experimental studies of conflict. In Hunt, J. McV. (Ed.), *Personality and the behavior disorders.* New York: Ronald, 1944.
16. Mood, A. McF. *Introduction to the theory of statistics.* New York: McGraw-Hill, 1950.
17. Reich, W. *Character analysis.* New York: Orgone Inst. Press, 1949.
18. Smith, J. E. K., On the analysis of contingency tables with ordered classifications. Unpublished manuscript.
19. Sears, R. R., Maccoby, Eleanor, & Levin, M. *Patterns of child rearing.* New York: Row, Petersen, 1958.
20. *St. Augustine's Confessions,* Wm. Watts (trans.), Cambridge: Harvard Univ. Press, 1950.
21. Whiting, J. W. M., & Child, I. L. *Child training and personality: a cross-cultural study.* New Haven: Yale Univ. Press, 1953.
22. Wolfenstein, Martha. The emergence of fun morality. *J. soc. Issues,* 1951, *7,* 15–25.

# PART TWO

# EXPECTATIONS

# 2

# SOCIAL POSITIONS AND REACTIONS TO CONFLICT

Differences in internalized standards, mechanisms of defense, and expressive styles may be traced to differences in previous learning experiences. A child who withdraws as a means of ending a conflict, for example, has probably been reared differently from another who faces the same conflict without retreating. If we knew the relevant features of each person's background, we would be able to predict his reactions. But how does one select background variables for experimental study? We have taken a social psychological approach. To explain different kinds of substitution, we started with some of the social conditions that create particular types of learning experiences. From these, we derived child-rearing practices and then the various reactions to conflict.

In this chapter we will examine different class positions in American society and speculate on the consequences of being in one class rather than another both for child rearing and for types of experience with conflict. We arrive at our hypotheses by placing in juxtaposition two types of evidence: that socio-economic groups in American society differ in their methods of training children (11, 12); and that socio-economic groups also differ in their proportions of patients with various disorders. To connect these facts, we will first explore the kinds of experience that are most characteristic of each social position. Then we will speculate on the possible influences that the child-rearing practices used in a particular class may have on methods of resolving conflict.

## Culture and Pathology

The greatest differences in reactions to conflict can probably be obtained from cross-cultural comparisons. So varied are child-rearing methods in different societies that the range of practices probably cannot be approximated by studies in any one culture, no matter how many groups it contains. While the resolution of conflict has not been studied directly by many anthropologists, the reports on pathological states in different societies provide a sizable body of indirect evidence. Of course, it is hazardous to interpret such reports. Adequate descriptive information is meager, methods of classifying disorders have not been sufficiently standardized, and most anthropologists have had little or no training in diagnosing symptoms even in their own societies.

### Cross-cultural studies of personality disorders

Despite the fallibility of ethnological data, it is impossible to escape the impression that there are great differences in the frequencies of certain pathologies in various societies. The mental disorder of depression provides a good example. In Hawaii it occurs more often among the Filipinos, Japanese, and Koreans, than among the Chinese and Portuguese (2). Among the Hutterites, a religious group with communities on the Northwestern border of the United States, manic-depressives are more than four times as frequent as schizophrenics, a ratio opposite to that of the rest of the American population (15). The incidence of manic-depressive psychosis is exceptionally low among the Formosan Chinese (25). Among African Negroes, too, depression is extremely rare (31).

Suicide in our society is sometimes a turning against the self of a homicidal wish. This mechanism of self-punishment may help to explain the high suicide rate among the Japanese (2) and some Polynesian peoples (19). Possibly an infrequent use of the mechanism in certain African Negro groups accounts for the fact that the rates of suicide are "almost unbelievably low by Western standards" (4).

It is much harder to interpret reports on the incidence of the schizophrenias, a group of disorders which can take many forms and is often difficult to diagnose. One trend in the reports does merit consideration. No field worker has reported a high rate of schizophrenia in a stable primitive society which is isolated from white influences (14). Wherever schizophrenia is recorded, the society is in the process of change. This suggests that the incidence of the disorder is connected in some way with the structure and functioning of the society.

The neuroses have been the object of few cross-cultural studies. While the frequency of hysteria seems to be diminishing in Western countries, its rates are high among Hindus (35) and Chinese (25). Data on obsessive-compulsive neurosis are scarce, but there are indications that it is much more common in Western European countries than among the Africans (8) or Chinese (25).

Apart from the indirect evidence provided by the differential occurrence of personality disorders, the observations of numerous field workers indicate that the more "normal" members of different societies also have distinct preferences for various defenses. The natives of Ifaluk (30) are a peaceable group who, in the opinion of the ethnologist, project their needs onto ghosts. This distortion may enable these people to remain at peace with each other. According to Benedict (5), most Dobuans have paranoid traits. While they favor the defense of projection, their objects are not supernatural figures but their peers. The result is continuous hostility.

PATHOLOGY AND SOCIAL CLASS IN AMERICAN SOCIETY

While it would have been tempting to conduct a broad cross-cultural study, we planned to test most of our hypotheses by studying two sub-cultures within American society, those of the middle and working class. There were some obvious advantages in working within our own society. Fewer problems were involved in interpreting the subjects' languages and methods of communication, in understanding their social institutions, and in devising tests with comparable meaning for different populations. There was also a burgeoning literature at our disposal, indicating the differential occurrence of certain disorders in the two social classes.

In their study of the distribution of psychoses, Faris and Dunham (18) analyzed rates of first admissions to state and private hospitals in the Chicago area. These rates were tabulated in terms of urban zones. In Chicago, as in most American cities, there is a central business district. Beside it is a zone occupied by the poor people who live near the factories. This is intermixed with a district of rooming houses. Then we find an apartment house section; next, multiple and single-family dwellings; and, finally, there are the suburbs. Each zone has its special characteristics. Some zones, usually those closest to the center of the city, are the foci of certain social difficulties. Crime rates are high, school services are often inadequate, and the proportion of broken homes is high. In other areas, mostly those toward the outskirts of town, these social problems are much less frequent.

Faris and Dunham found distinct differences in the proportions of patients from the various zones of the city. The central district produced the largest rate. Next were the adjacent hobo and rooming house neighborhoods. The smallest incidence occurred in the outlying residential areas which were economically the most prosperous. These findings—that the lower the socio-economic status, the greater is the incidence of psychosis—have been confirmed by studies in Providence (28), New York (32), St. Louis (29), and New Haven (23).

Since we ourselves were concerned with the social origins of defenses, we felt that the most interesting finding of Faris and Dunham was their discovery that the geographic distribution of all mental disorders did not follow the same general pattern. While the schizophrenias were most numerous in the central part of the city, the rates for different types of schizophrenia varied within this area. Catatonic schizophrenics lived most often in the poverty ridden slums containing heavy populations of foreign born and Negroes. Patients suffering from paranoid schizophrenia tended to come from the hobo and rooming house districts. There were also many hebephrenic schizophrenics who resided in the same areas. By contrast, manic-depressives appeared more frequently in the areas with high rentals.

Faris and Dunham favored the interpretation that the conditions under which patients mature—conditions connected with areas of residence—contribute to the disturbances. Other social scientists insisted that psychotics grow up in various parts of the city and that, as they become sick and find it harder to get along with others, they lose jobs and friends and drift to the lower rental districts. There is evidence that some schizophrenics do go down in the occupational scale prior to hospitalization (10), but whether or not this change causes them to cluster in certain districts is the issue involved in the dispute about Faris and Dunham's data.

Studies of this issue are inconclusive, but tend not to support the postulated decline in social status as a result of the psychoses. If it were correct, the average social status of schizophrenic patients would be lower than that of their parents. It was not possible for Faris to locate the parents of most patients, but he did the next best thing (17). He used the average rentals in districts in which the patients resided during childhood as the closest approximation of their parents' socio-economic status. He found no significant differences between parents and children on this criterion. With the exception of one pathological group, the average rentals paid years before by the parents showed the same associations with the frequencies of the different disorders as the social positions of the patients in adulthood. This finding makes tenuous the notion that the low socio-economic status of psychotics results from their deteriorated social skills.

According to Faris, depressives are the one major group of psychotics whose areas of residence in adulthood differ in economic status from those of their parents. Instead of coming from all the different parts of the city, manic-depressives usually grow up in high rent districts. As children, they typically live in apartment houses and hotels, dwellings occupied by middle- and high-income groups, especially by those who tend to be migrants from other parts of the city and from other cities (20). Possibly rapid social change, in addition to status in the middle class, is required in order for the psychosis to occur.

Other investigators who have studied the backgrounds of patients suffering from personality disorders report results in essential agreement with those of Faris. During the childhood of schizophrenics their parents' incomes are significantly lower than those of the parents of manic-depressives (24, 27, 36). If we assume that the number of years the patient remains in school reflects his parents' economic position, then the fact that schizophrenics have less schooling than manic-depressives (10) indicates that the schizophrenics must come from poorer families. This assumption, however, is questionable.[1] We can account for the curtailed education of the schizophrenic in terms of his retreat from the reality rather than in terms of his family's income.

## Deductions from the Differential Incidence of Disorders

The researches we have just summarized interested us mostly because they suggested differences in methods of resolving conflict among people from various social backgrounds. We assumed that the distributions of pathologies, if interpreted correctly, could tell us much about the moral standards, defensive preferences, and expressive styles of normals as well as of abnormals.

### Defenses

The internalization of standards and learning of defenses starts in childhood, and the effect of both must be apparent long before an illness is recognized. To the extent that most members of a given society have previously been subjected to a common set of influences, they may be expected to develop similar sets of moral needs and a similar repertory of defenses. If there is a high incidence of depressive disorders among the Hutterites, Koreans, and middle-class Americans, both the normal and abnormal members of these societies must have many experiences which reinforce the defense against anger by turning it on oneself. Their experiences must be different from those of the African Negroes and the Chinese who seem to have fewer depressives. Similarly, the high proportion of obsessives among middle-class

[1] While we are on the topic of questionable assumptions, we want to stress that the epidemiological data reported in the literature do not bear on the validity of our results, and were of great value to us primarily because of the richness of their theoretical implications. Actually, the reported distributions of psychoses may be distorted. Hospitals vary in their policies of accepting different kinds of patients and in their acceptability to different kinds of patients, in diagnostic criteria, and in the adequacy of records. The differences in methods of finding cases used by different investigators also complicates the interpretation of data. In view of the many possible sources of error, we are impressed by the relative agreement in most of the reported trends, and we are not surprised by some of the disagreements in obtained proportions.

Americans signifies that both the normal and abnormal members of this group must mature under conditions which teach them to favor the defenses of undoing, isolation, and reversal. The low incidence of obsessives among the African Negroes, Chinese, and working-class Americans indicates that members of these groups, both normal and abnormal, must learn to avail themselves of defenses other than undoing, isolation, and reversal. In making these derivations, we are following Freud's assumption that the defenses are learned.[2]

If all members of a society learn similar methods of reacting to conflict, then how do the patients differ from the normals? One reason for a difference may be the excessive use by patients of certain common defenses. Another may be the patients' favoring of defenses to which normal adults resort only in times of greatest stress.

Turning against the self is a good example of the former. Everyone, at one time or another, has felt remorse and guilt about hostile wishes or acts. Who has not thought himself unworthy and been unhappy when he has failed in an important undertaking? Such reactions are extremely common. But our society labels as pathological the tendency to blame oneself to such a degree that the whole world seems black and the only way out is self-destruction. We are purposely oversimplifying our account of depression to stress our point. In his self-attack, the depressive differs from other men less in his methods than in the frequency and intensity with which he applies them.

The abandonment of the common defenses in favor of those that are much less obvious in the everyday behavior of normals produces some of the bizarre symptoms of psychotics: the visions, the accusatory voices, the ideas of being influenced by cosmic rays, the persecutory misinterpretations. The defenses which give rise to such symptoms are not without influence on the behavior of normal adults. Visions are not restricted to psychotics. They may occur when we are drugged, asleep, and, under special conditions, such as driving at night, when we are visually unstimulated

[2] "No individual makes use of all the possible mechanisms of defense. [As a result of his particular early experiences] each person merely selects certain of them. . . . [They become] regular modes of reaction . . . which are repeated throughout life whenever the situation occurs similar to that which originally invoked them" (21, p. 340).

(6). As for false beliefs, under great stress normal men often require little evidence to become unduly suspicious of the motives of others. And psychotic convictions of being magically manipulated are not unrelated to such superstitious practices as throwing salt over one's shoulder or knocking on wood.

Defenses which lead to visions or hallucinations are available to anyone. Beginning in early childhood, we all get some gratification from them. Given the appropriate conditions, they may gain ascendance over the more subtle defenses, which, as we shall see, are probably learned later on. In societies with high incidences of schizophrenia both the normal adults and the mentally ill must develop more of a preference for the more primitive defenses than do members of societies in which schizophrenia is infrequent.

### Moral standards

We may deduce characteristics of moral standards from the incidence of obsessional neuroses and depressions. Such symptoms are substituted for the direct expression of aggression because they are more compatible with moral standards. When we feel we have sinned because we want to hurt someone, we can reduce the pressure or our consciences by attacking ourselves and becoming depressed, or we can become obsessed with a "meaningless" topic which we cannot get out of our minds. The high proportion of obsessives and depressives in middle-class American society signifies that people in this group internalize moral standards that require frequent self-attack.

While the causes of depression may differ with the society, this symptom also seems to have some common meaning. Hutterites judge their self-worth in terms of moral standards which would be deemed extraordinarily stringent in other societies. Obviously, the contents [3] to which standards apply—the specific reasons for turning on the self—vary considerably from one society to another. In developing principles of conflict that apply cross-culturally, we have to abstract the functional characteristics from

[3] To avoid a possible misunderstanding of our position, it may be necessary at this point to stress, parenthetically, that our deductions apply to the functional aspects of moral standards and defenses and not to their contents. By functional, we refer to such properties of the standards as the range of forbidden elements. By contents we mean the specific values themselves, such as fealty to one's family or the avoidance of physical attack.

the content. For example, even though the acts that define the relationships between parents and their offspring are quite different in Japanese and American societies, few people would doubt that the Japanese have the higher standards of family loyalty. In the past if the well-born son of a distinguished Japanese family fell in love with a girl of lower status, the possible shame to his family sometimes caused him such "loss of face" that he committed suicide. The extreme loyalty that was expected in Japan also created great difficulties for the wife. She came to live with her husband and his parents, and judged her own worth in terms of her ability to meet her mother-in-law's standards. But since few women could have satisfied some of the critical mothers-in-law, there was much friction. Often the wife blamed herself. If her guilt became intolerable, she sometimes diverted her aggression from the source of her troubles to herself. The result was a psychogenic illness.[4]

## Structure of American Society

Although cross-cultural information helped us to formulate some of our questions, it was the research on the structure of our own society which determined more of our hypotheses. Specifically, it contributed the basic independent variable of social status. From this variable, we predicted parental child-rearing practices and the children's moral needs, defenses, and expressive styles. We analyzed experiences inherent in a particular socioeconomic status because we anticipated that they would explain the origins of different reactions to conflict. To convey the reasoning behind our hypotheses, we shall now compare the backgrounds of children whose families occupy different social positions in American society.

Each society consists of component parts, all of which carry out collective attempts to solve the common problems of the society. Certain groups produce and distribute economic goods. Others perform such functions as caring for the aged or educating children. In selecting independent social variables from which we might predict differences in moral standards, defenses, and ex-

[4] We are indebted to Richard Beardsley for this example.

pressive styles, we tried to find some important characteristics of the society that would help us to understand how it is organized to solve its problems. There are, of course, certain relationships among the members of a society which affect the structures of many of the component groups, and ultimately the reactions of the individuals to conflict. For reasons cited in greater detail elsewhere (26), and to which we devote the remainder of this chapter, we decided to concentrate on two aspects of the organization of a society—*stratification* and *integration*.

Stratification refers to levels of social status. Two of the more fundamental sets of strata in our society are caste and social class. Caste refers to differences based on social boundaries, often hereditary, such as those that divide whites and Negroes in American society. Members of a caste have no legitimate avenues of upward mobility. Class refers to differences in economic power and influence. In our investigations we controlled caste by selecting only white subjects, and compared members of different classes.

Integration represents the degree to which people depend on each other and the nature of their dependence. Since Miller and Swanson (26) found that both social stratification and integration relate significantly to child-rearing practices, we anticipated that these social positions might also predict moral standards, expressive styles, and defenses. As our next task, we shall define social strata and types of integration, and describe some hypotheses about their probable relationships to the origins and resolutions of conflicts.

## Stratification: Social Class

We defined a position within the American system of stratification in terms of education and occupation. We chose these indices because they help to classify an individual's power within the system. Power refers to the ability to influence markedly the behavior and future of others and oneself. In American society the owner of a large department store can usually make decisions which have potent effects on the lives of more people than can the decisions made by any of his salesmen. Such differences in power are determined in great part by the contrasting positions these two types of men take in the processes of production and distribution of goods and services.

Differences in power vary, not only in amount but also in legitimacy and stability. Compared to the power of a businessman, that of a racketeer, let us say, is less legitimate and may be less stable. In our studies social classes were taken to represent categories of people in economic positions having roughly the same amount and stability of legitimate power. This power is usually associated with a particular income, level of education, type of occupation, social access to people of a particular stratum, and often residence in the same neighborhood. These and other correlated criteria have often served as indices of social status. Consistent with these indices are the styles of life that are developed at different class levels and which influence techniques for resolving conflict.

### American social classes

In everyday conversation people refer to three classes. There is an upper class, a middle or white-collar class, and a working or blue-collar class. Students of stratification have used the same three categories (9, 33).[5]

In order to tell whether a subject came from a family in the middle or working class, we had to decide on criteria. As an aid in developing our requirements, we first made an inventory of the characteristics of American social classes noted by various sociologists (13, 22, 33).

Compared to the economic position of blue-collar workers, that of white-collar workers entails skill in manipulating symbols

[5] In our remarks on stratification we shall devote most attention to the middle and working classes because they provided the sources of our samples. It would have been very difficult to recruit enough upper-class children. Many leave their home communities for private schools in other parts of the country, and we did not have the funds to reach them. In addition, we lacked prior information about their parents' child-rearing practices. The omission of children from the upper class was not damaging to our research, since we did not contemplate a descriptive study of all social strata. We were primarily interested in locating groups of children who clearly differed in the types of early experience that might be related to conflict. We could be fairly confident of the differences between the two lower groups, but we could not be certain of the differences between either of them and those in the upper category.

or ideas, payment in the form of salary, fee, commission, sometimes profits, an income sometimes high enough to permit some saving after the essentials are purchased, and, often, a bargaining relation to the employer on an individual rather than a group basis. Americans in the working class use manual skills, receive their incomes in the form of wages, and may or may not earn enough to be able to save part of their incomes.[6]

Students of American society have located important subdivisions within the middle and working classes, the strata of concern in this book. Upper middle-class people, for example, earn larger and more stable incomes than do men in the lower middle class, who perform tasks requiring a lower level of skill or less authority.[7] It is specialized skill which distinguishes the physician from the nurse, the certified public accountant from the bookkeeper, and the office manager from the file clerk. Specialized skill also determines the differences in status between the businessmen who establish the policies of large enterprises, the smaller entrepreneurs, such as operators of cleaning establishments, who perform more manual and fewer symbolic tasks, and the administrators who carry out policy in their supervision of simple functions. Since higher skill usually requires special training or broader knowledge, upper middles are more likely than lower middles to have some education beyond high school.

People in the upper working class are also distinguished from members of the lower working class in terms of greater skill or

[6] Members of the upper class usually make policy decisions for others, receive some payment in the form of interest or dividends, and earn enough money to be able to invest a sizable percentage of it.

[7] There are some obvious exceptions to our assumption that the members of the middle class have more, or more stable, power in our society than do the members of the working class. In northern industrial cities, such as Detroit, many skilled and semi-skilled laborers have average incomes higher than those whom the United States Census labels as "clerks and kindred workers." This exception may herald a realignment of power. If there is a realignment, it still may not change our assumptions about the reactions to conflict of people in the two social classes. An increase in income is not immediately accompanied by a comparable change in style of life. The family may need two or three generations to train its members effectively in skills and interests appropriate to the higher economic position. Conversely, once children in the middle class have developed the moral standards, the defenses, and the expressive styles characteristic of white-collar workers, they have an asset that is not available to most children of the working class.

responsibility. These create the differences in pay between such skilled and semi-skilled jobs as carpenter and die maker, and such unskilled jobs as ditch digger and sweeper. The latter require no special training. Among working-class Americans, the upper half differs from the lower in years of schooling. Many skilled workers have completed high school and two or three years of special courses. The semi-skilled may complete high school; they often take some additional training for their jobs. Unskilled laborers often have completed only the minimal education required by law and do not acquire any special training for their jobs.

## Life Style of the Middle Class

Both the middle and working classes have developed a coherent culture, functionally adapted to the economic positions of their members. This culture, by its effect on child rearing, contributes to individual psychology. In our research we were primarily interested in one direction of influence, that of the culture on the individual. Our account of the differences between classes was further simplified because we stressed those which seemed likely to cast light on the resolution of conflict. In other words, we were interested in a heuristic description rather than one that faithfully depicted all the differences between the classes.

We have assumed that methods of resolving conflict are a product of the experiences characteristic of each social class. If we explore these experiences in greater detail, we are in a better position to specify those aspects that are most closely related to moral standards, defenses, and expressive styles.

### Values

The American white-collar worker can usually look forward to some possibility of improving his economic position. Often the pursuit of this goal requires considerable effort and sacrifice, and he must postpone gratification of many needs in the hope that they will later be fulfilled. He must develop a reputation as an honest, responsible, and hard-working member of the community. Just as he accumulates savings to invest in a business, he often acquires social graces and contributes to charity as an investment in conspicuous respectability. Usually, he feels that the results justify the sacrifice.

The intellectual abilities necessary to maintain status in the middle class are no more easily acquired than the necessary personal traits and social skills. Abstract thinking is mastered only after many years of regular practice. To invest the required amount of time, the learner must have the necessary funds. He must also feel that proficiency is important in getting approval from people who are important to him, such as his family and friends, his teacher, or some future employer.

The focus of the middle class on individual advancement, self-denial, and competent performance helps to explain many of their dominant values. Highly esteemed are formal education, rationality, a reputation for controlled and respectable behavior, hard work, responsibility, and saving. Together, these values define the goals of an internally consistent way of life. Characteristic methods for resolving conflict are a part of that way of life.

Those values of the middle class that seem most relevant to a study of conflict include an acceptance of responsibility for one's own conduct, mastery of self by rational means as a prelude to mastering the world, and a feeling that control and sacrifice are worth the effort because they are for one's own good. The white-collar worker with these values is inclined to distort certain needs because their direct expression may threaten his position in the community. Before the member of the middle class can change his world, he must first change himself.

### Social status and conflict

From these values, we inferred a number of principles about moral standards, defenses, and expressive styles. The tests of some of these principles are reported in the chapters on results. We anticipated that the major conflicts of the middle-class citizen arise when he is tempted to engage in acts that may damage his social status. These are codified in the form of specific, and apparently extensive, moral prohibitions. If a man's socially unacceptable needs are very strong, he is likely to avoid guilt by defensive distortions that are compatible with his internalized standards. He cannot run away, or have trances. Such behavior would threaten his economic endeavors. He can shift blame from others to himself and he can play down the bad qualities in others. In addition, he can learn to express his sexual and aggressive needs in complex and symbolic forms. In short, we anticipated that he would favor defenses in the second family rather than the first, and that he would express his aggression indirectly and conceptually.

Our predictions about reactions to conflict were partially supported by the kinds of personality disorder which are common in the middle class. We inferred from the frequency of depressions and compulsions that the white-collar worker has severe standards about aggression, is likely to brood rather than act, and is inclined to favor the defenses that produce these symptoms: turning against the self, isolation, undoing, and reversal. Turning of aggression against the self shifts the target of the forbidden need. A man can then feel guilty about his impulse and avoid the violation of his moral standards. Isolation of the affect enables him to consider the action tendency rationally without fear of losing control. Reversal of an intended act bars it from awareness and replaces it by another that is compatible with his standards and social goals.

## Life Style of the Working Class

While many manual workers have moved into the middle class, their prospect of mobility is usually not promising. The barriers that these men must hurdle are created as much by their way of life as by their economic position. They lack the social skills and contacts, the values, and the personal characteristics needed for reasonably rapid advancement into the middle class. Even with free public education, the objective fact is that most manual laborers do not succeed in jumping the class barriers.

### Values

Limitations in economic power and in the possibility for advancement create distinctive values and behaviors. These, in turn, often limit the mobility even further. Because success and even security are so uncertain, the working-class citizen is usually oriented more to the present than to the future. He may consider formal education desirable, but not as vital as getting a job and keeping it. While he may pay lip service to the virtues of self-control and responsibility, they are often less evident in his behavior than in that of the white-collar worker.

The manual laborer is not inclined to regard each act as an investment in the future; he is more concerned with the pleasures of the moment. He sets great store by his family and personal comforts. His concern with friendship is motivated by more than a quest for social expression. It is critical for him that he fit into the informal groups of friends and fellow workers who are his point of contact with the union, and on whose solidarity rests much of his opportunity to improve his economic status. Very important to him are his principal economic assets, physical strength and manual skills. Should he become physically impaired, he would be handicapped in bargaining for a job.

### Social status and conflict

These values, like those of the middle class, have a number of implications for moral standards, defenses, and expressive styles. The working-class boy takes pride in physical prowess. He perfects his fighting skill as a weapon for maintaining his position among his peers. In certain cases he avoids scholarly pursuits because this would lower his standing with his friends. Some of the standards that he internalizes and uses as yardstick for self-evaluation are contradictory to the norms of middle-class boys and may even violate the law. The working-class child may get into trouble by being a good member of his own group—with the middle-class teachers for his poor work, with the middle-class truant officer for staying away from school, with the middle-class storekeepers for his escapades, with the middle-class judge for violations of the law, and so forth. Even if he does not get into trouble, the boy is handicapped in a number of ways. The teacher is sometimes unsympathetic because of her pupil's poor manners and indifferent dress, and is impatient with his lack of ambition and inadequate verbal facility.

The son of the blue-collar worker may live in a section of town in which schools and recreational facilities are barely adequate or substandard. If his mother works, he remains unsupervised by a responsible adult for much of the day. Consequently, he may be hurt or exploited by strangers from whom the middle-class boy is protected.

The fact that the working-class person is a member of his own group probably does not prevent him from internalizing some of the middle-class morality of the larger society of which he is also a member. This must create some unique moral problems for him when the standards of the two groups are contradictory. Because of this complication, he may find it difficult to satisfy his incompatible standards. In some instances, he may feel guilty regardless of his reaction to conflict.

The many people in the working class who are exposed to hardship throughout most of their lives may not be able to change their real world, but they can gain solace from their daydreams. If they cannot obtain certain cherished objects or goals, they may deny their needs and withdraw. Such techniques, while they impede the adjustment to reality, may offer the only means of protecting self-esteem. Excessive hardships may also establish a predilection for projection, a mechanism which allows a member of the working class to blame others for his difficulties. These speculations are supported by the high proportions of paranoid schizophrenics and hysterics in the working class. Patients suffering from such symptoms tend to resolve conflicts by blotting the difficult reality out of awareness in favor of a substitute world of fantasy.

In addition to fantasy, the kinds of substituted acts favored by the working class usually involve physical expression. The high incidence of hysteria and catatonic schizophrenia, both disturbances in the functions of the large voluntary muscles, suggests that the working class citizen learns to express many of his needs on a physical level.

Since the working-class citizen often holds the world, rather than himself, responsible for his misfortunes, he can be more direct in his substitute expressions of aggression than can members of the middle class. If he is angry, for example, and displaces the object, he is inclined to hurt someone similar to the original object. And he is most likely to use some form of direct attack, rather than an act which signifies a reversal of his anger. In summary, we expected him to have internalized many of the standards common to all members of the society, to favor the defense of denial, and to express his needs directly and by physical means.

## Assigning Subjects to Class Positions

In the foregoing we have attempted to illustrate some of the possible connections between membership in a social class and reactions to conflict. We shall now describe the specific means by which we assigned each subject to a particular social class.

Many indices have been proposed for identifying social class (1, 3, 7). Some theorists picture a social class as a position in a system of economic power. Consequently, they use such indices of economic power as income and occupation. Other theorists consider social participation the primary sign of social position. To classify an individual, they locate the groups who accept him on intimate terms. Since certain skills provide an avenue to economic security, education is sometimes used as an index of social status. Social class has likewise been defined in terms of the group with which an individual identifies. To determine the group the subject is asked for his own estimate of his class position. Political power and prestige have also been proposed as signs of social status, but often the criteria have not been specified.

Fortunately, all current indices of social class are highly interrelated. All we needed to do, then, was to choose the smallest number of criteria that would give us a reliable measure of social class. We decided on these criteria when we selected our first sample of subjects, who were boys in seventh, eighth, and ninth grades of schools in the Detroit area. As a basis for choosing the boys, we obtained information from school records and from interviews with the mothers. Included in each interview, in addition to the questions on child training, were questions concerning the husband's education, occupation, and income, which we thought relevant to the family's social position. It was our hope to develop an objective technique for placing families in the class system.

We finally assigned our children to social class positions by means of an index, developed at Yale University,[8] which combines father's occupation and education. The following technical description of our methods can be omitted by readers whose interest in such matters is satisfied by the naming of our two criteria.

[8] Described in personal correspondence from A. Hollingshead.

METHOD OF CLASSIFICATION

As a first step in placing families in class positions, one member of our group [9] examined the data gained from the interviews on husbands' occupations, on sources of family income, on parental ages, on educational and religious affiliations, and on occupations of the children's grandfathers. From these data, and his knowledge of the descriptive studies of social class, the rater subjectively assigned each family to a class position. When he was in doubt about the correctness of his classification of a family, he had two other raters [10] make independent judgments. The agreement of all three raters was required to determine the final class placements.

While we were involved in rating our subjects, we learned that Hollingshead and Myers had developed a class-typing procedure on the basis of a 5 per cent sample of the population of New Haven, Connecticut in 1951. Like ourselves, these investigators had conducted interviews and had independently made subjective ratings of the social class positions of their respondents. The agreement between the raters' independent judgments was extremely high. Hollingshead and Myers then correlated their subjective ratings with a variety of potential objective indices of economic position, such as income, occupation, and education. Using the technique of multiple correlation, they found that the best objective predictors of their subjective ratings were occupation, education, and area of residence. The multiple correlation coefficient was .94.

While we had data on occupation and education, we had no information about areas of residence in Detroit comparable to the material available for New Haven. Fortunately, Hollingshead and Myers had also found a very high multiple correlation, .92, between social class ratings and two of the three best predictors, occupation and education. We obtained exactly the same coefficient between occupation, education, and our subjective ratings when we used the multiple regression weights from the study in New Haven.

The categories of occupation developed at Yale and used in

[9] G. E. Swanson.

[10] M. Janowitz and G. E. Lenski.

our study were: (1) higher executive, professional, or proprietor, (2) lesser executive, professional, or proprietor, (3) small independent businessman, (4) clerical worker, (5) skilled worker, (6) semi-skilled worker, and (7) unskilled worker. The educational categories were: (1) graduate work or professional school, (2) college graduate, (3) 1 to 3 years of college, (4) high school graduate, (5) 10 to 11 years of school, (6) 7 to 9 years of school, and (7) less than 7 years of school. The respective multiple regression weights for occupation and education were .36 and .22 in both studies.

We may illustrate the application of these weights by the case of a father with a clerical job and a college degree. The job has a rank of four in the occupational categories, and a rank of two in the educational categories. Thus, his family would obtain a score of (4) (.36) + (2) (.22) or 1.88.

We divided our group of subjects into four social-class levels by inspecting the correlation table composed of subjective ratings and the objective ratings obtained by the Yale technique. In defining the levels we took advantage of the natural breaking points in the data which separated occupational and educational groups usually ascribed to each of the classes in current descriptive studies.[11]

## Integration

### Entrepreneurial and bureaucratic organization

We have just cited the relationships between social class and reactions to conflict which we anticipated when we first planned our research. In a later study Miller and Swanson (26) found that these relationships reflect a tradition which is changing rapidly. The ways of life that we have attributed to the middle and working class, and the concomitant reactions to conflict, originated during a period when most enterprises, whether business, industry or

[11] Usually men in the middle class have white-collar jobs and men in the working class have manual jobs, but the method of classification created some exceptions. If a laborer had an unusual amount of education, for example, he could earn a score which placed him in the middle class.

farm, large or small, were organized in simple patterns. These were *entrepreneurial* organizations. They usually had a few managers and many unskilled workers. There was a surplus of labor, and, among small retailers, intense competition. Each man was considered capable of protecting his own welfare. He was on his own, and the community was not responsible for his social security.

In recent years the number of small businesses with entrepreneurial organization has been declining. They are being replaced by large corporations with national and international markets. Such corporations are molded on a very different pattern from the entrepreneurial. The *bureaucratic* pattern is characterized by the integration of functions carried out by many specialists. Because white-collar workers are most likely to have a specialization, their jobs are reflecting the influence of bureaucratization earlier than those of blue-collar workers.

A number of social changes are promoting the growth of bureaucratic organizations. There has been a considerable increase in the sizes of organizations, owing largely to the continuous improvement of the machinery of production, the installations of assembly lines, and the creation of the corporate structure. The three class levels of the entrepreneurial society—upper, middle, and working—also exist in the bureaucratic, but their styles of life and their reactions to conflict are changing. At least, this assumption underlies some of the associations we tested in the studies.

### Class differences in bureaucratic organizations

No sharp line separates the entrepreneurial from the bureaucratic organization. Most companies with simple organization have some specialization. But this is far exceeded by the differentiation of function in the bureaucracies. The differentiation in turn requires special training and special coordination. Consider a member of the bureaucratic middle class. Usually, he is part of a group. The group has to integrate its products with the work of the rest of the organization. Since he produces only part of a unit, his contribution, even if its quality is excellent, is often not conspicuous. If he takes too much time to improve quality, he may slow down the production of the entire organization. But if he does an adequate or even an indifferent job, he may get along quite well. Dependability on the job is the primary requisite for security. Because the functions are specialized, the employer makes a considerable investment in training procedures. Consequently, he may be loathe to shift an employee very quickly, since this would mean an additional training cost.

Yet there is a good deal of mobility in some bureaucratized industries. Promotion often depends less on quality or pace of work than on the worker's seniority or his sensitivity to concerns of top management and to forces which affect the group's coordination. Because corporations have grown so large, it is becoming increasingly meaningless for a man in the middle class to save money in order to start his own business. Education is still important, and rationality and self-control are still highly valued, but they are dedicated to different goals—less to self-sacrifice or to the improvement of quality and more to the resolution of interpersonal pressures within the organization.

Like the white-collar worker, the laborer in a bureaucratic organization has been gaining increasing job security. In fact, he has had a proportionately greater increase in income. Because his education is limited, his possibilities of advancement are correspondingly curtailed. He is inclined to substitute a concern with the consumption of goods for pleasurable purposes for high valuations of productive skill and mobility.

Members of bureaucratic organizations are an emerging group, and we were not at all clear about their reactions to conflict. We could say more about what they were not than about what they were: We guessed how the defenses and expressive styles of bureaucrats might differ from those of people in the better understood entrepreneurial organizations. We imagined that some of the traditional internalized controls would loosen for all bureaucrats. While their concern with the group's performance may sensitize them to the moral standards of their peers, we pictured their conformity as being motivated less by guilt than by sensitivity to social pressure. It seemed to us that to the extent that bureaucrats do not internalize traditional standards, they need not be guilty when they privately behave in a manner that the society condemns. As a result of this diminished internalization, we thought that middle-class bureaucrats would seldom resort to defenses like turning on the self and reversal, which facilitate self-advancement in entrepreneurial organizations. Because the jobs of working class bureaucrats are becoming increasingly simple and routine, thus making the daily existence less meaningful, we thought these men would resort increasingly to denial and to the cultivation of leisure activities. As opposed to the marked differences between middle and working classes, which we predicted for the two classes in entrepreneurial organizations, we expected a diminution of contrasts in the reactions to conflict of the two social strata in bureaucratic organizations.

## Identifying Membership in Entrepreneurial and Bureaucratic Organizations

Miller and Swanson (26) classified a family as entrepreneurial if it met any one of five criteria. The first two required that one or both parents of a subject be born on a farm, or born outside the United States. Those born on farms are migrants from small entrepreneurial organizations, and it takes at least a generation before their economic positions in the city affects their child-rearing practices. Most of the foreign born in Detroit come from rural backgrounds. Furthermore, almost all come from countries with little bureaucratic organization as compared to the United States.

If wife or husband were not born on a farm or in a foreign country, the family could still be included in the entrepreneurial group if the husband met any one of three criteria: if he was self-employed; if he gained at least half of his income in the form of profits, fees, or commissions; or if he worked in an organization having only two levels of supervision.[12] We felt that the self-employed and those whose incomes depended in great part on the fortunes of their businesses were most likely to be taking the risks typical of an entrepreneurial style of life.

When we planned the present studies, we had not yet defined the distinctions between entrepreneurs and bureaucrats. Therefore, we did not collect all the information necessary to classify mothers

[12] By two levels, we mean a job in which a man has either a superior or a subordinate. This often occurs in a retail store. If the superior reports to another man above him, then there are three levels of supervision.

within these categories. However, we did have information concerning self-employment and the birth of either parent on a farm. Since we excluded the foreign born from our samples, we did not have to worry about that criterion of entrepreneurial status. From descriptions of the husbands' occupations, particularly the responses to questions about the people whom they supervised and who supervised them, we were able to gauge the number of levels of supervision in almost all cases. But we had no information that would help us to estimate whether a father had gained at least half of his income in the form of profits, fees, or commissions. This omission was not very serious. In a later study of a representative sample of families in the Detroit general area, the groups for whom we could account—farm born, foreign born, self-employed, and members of two-level organizations—constituted the vast majority of entrepreneurial subjects.

## Summary

In this chapter, we have described the thinking behind the kinds of connections we anticipated between social position and reactions to conflict. Very influential in the derivations of some of our hypotheses have been the distributions of psychoses in two social classes. These data suggest that the experiences most characteristic of the social positions create contrasting methods of resolving conflict. Membership in a particular social class, or in an entrepreneurial rather than a bureaucratic organization, requires a large number of adjustments which are organized as a style of life. Given a particular pattern of experiences, certain types of moral standards, defense mechanisms, and expressive styles tend to develop. In the middle class these reactions to conflict are likely to include very extensive standards, defenses like turning against the self and reversal, and indirect expression of aggression. In the working class the reactions are likely to include less extensive standards, defenses like denial and withdrawal, and direct expression of aggression.

Following our discussions of social status and type of integration, we cited our criteria for classifying subjects. To determine social class, we used scores based on the fathers' education and occupation. We classified as entrepreneurial those boys whose fathers were born on a farm or in a foreign country, were self-employed, or worked in organizations with two levels of supervision. All other subjects were classified as bureaucratic.

## References


1. Barber, B. *Social stratification.* New York: Harcourt, Brace, 1957.
2. Beaglehole, E. Culture and psychosis in New Zealand. *J. Polynes. Soc.,* 1939, *48,* 144–55.
3. Bendix, R., & Lipset, S. M. *Class, status, and power.* Glencoe, Ill.: The Free Press, 1953.
4. Benedict, P. K., & Jacks, I. Mental illness in primitive societies. *Psychiatry,* 1954, *17,* 377–90.
5. Benedict, Ruth. *Patterns of culture.* New York: Houghton, Mifflin, 1934.
6. Bexton, W. H., Heron, W., & Scott, T. H. Effects of decreased variation in the sensory environment. *Canad. J. Psychol.,* 1954, *8,* 70–76.
7. Broom, L., & Selznick, P. *Sociology.* New York: Row, Peterson, 1958.
8. Carothers, J. C. A study of mental derangement in Africans etc. *Psychiatry,* 1948, *11,* 47–86.
9. Centers, R. *The psychology of social classes.* Princeton: Princeton Univ. Press, 1949.
10. Clark, R. E. Psychoses, income, and occupational prestige. *Amer. J. Sociol.,* 1949, *54,* 7, 434–40.
11. Davis, A. Child training and social class. In Barker, R. G., Kounin, I. S., & Wright, H. F. (Eds.), *Child behavior and development.* New York: McGraw-Hill, 1943.
12. ——— Social class and color differences in child rearing. *Amer. Sociol. Rev.,* 1946, *11,* 698–710.
13. ———, Gardner, B. B., & Gardner, Mary R. *Deep South.* Chicago: Univ. of Chicago Press, 1941.
14. Demerath, N. J. Schizophrenia among primitives. In Rose, A. M. (Ed.), *Mental health and mental disorder.* New York: Norton, 1955.
15. Eaton, J. W., & Weil, R. J. *Culture and mental disorders.* Glencoe, Ill.: The Free Press, 1955.
16. Ericson, Martha C. Social status and child rearing practices. In

Newcomb, T. M., & Hartley, E. L. (Eds.), *Readings in social psychology*. New York: Holt, 1947.

17. Faris, R. E. L. Demography of urban psychotics with special reference to schizophrenia. *Amer. Sociol. Rev.*, 1938, *3*, 203–209.
18. ———, & Dunham, H. W. *Mental disorders in urban areas*. Chicago: Univ. of Chicago Press, 1939.
19. Firth, R. *Elements of social organization*. London: Watts, 1951.
20. Freedman, R. *Recent migration to Chicago*. Chicago: Univ. of Chicago Press, 1950.
21. Freud, S. Analysis terminable and interminable. *Collected Papers*, Vol. V. London: Hogarth, 1953.
22. Hollingshead, A. B. Selected characteristics of classes in a middle western community. *Amer. Sociol. Rev.*, 1947, *12*, 385–95.
23. ———, & Redlich, F. C. *Social class and mental illness*. New York: Wiley, 1958.
24. Landis, C., & Page, J. *Modern society and mental disease*. New York: Farrar & Rinehart, 1938.
25. Lin, T. Y. A study of the incidence of mental disorders in Chinese and other cultures. *Psychiatry*, 1953, *16*, 313–37.
26. Miller, D. R., & Swanson, G. E. *The changing American parent*. New York: Wiley, 1958.
27. Pollack, H. M., Malzberg, B., & Fuller, R. C. *Hereditary and environmental factors in the causation of manic depressive psychoses and dementia praecox*. Utica, New York: State Hospitals Press, 1939.
28. Queen, S. A. The ecological study of mental disorders. *Amer. Sociol. Rev.*, 1940, *5*, 201–209.
29. Schroeder, C. W. Mental disorders in cities. *Amer. J. Sociol.*, 1942, *48*, 40–47.
30. Spiro, M. E. Ghosts, Ifaluk, and teleological functionalism. *Amer. Anthrop.*, 1952, *54*, 497–503.
31. Tooth, G. *Studies in mental illness in the Gold Coast*. London: Colonial Research Publication, 1950, No. 6.
32. Tietze, C., Lemkau, P., & Cooper, M. Manic depressive psychoses and socio-economic status. *Amer. J. Sociol.*, 1941, *47*, 167–75.
33. Warner, W. L., & Lunt, P. S. *The social life of a modern community*. New Haven: Yale Univ. Press, 1941.
34. ———, Meeker, Marcia, & Eells, K. *Social class in America*. Chicago: Science Research Associates, 1949.
35. Williams, A. H. A psychiatric study of Indian soldiers in the Arakan. *Brit. J. Med. Psychol.*, 1950, *23*, 130–80.
36. Wilson, D. C. Families of manic depressives. *Dis. Nerv. Sys.*, 1951, *12*, 362–69.

# 3

# CHILD-REARING PRACTICES AND REACTIONS TO CONFLICT

We can explain reactions to conflict in a number of ways. We can trace the reactions to particular positions in society, as we have just done. But even if we find that a particular social position is related to the tendency to favor a particular defense mechanism, we are left with some important unanswered questions. Just how does membership in the middle class, let us say, cause a person to favor the defense of reversing his aggression? Is it through the values which his parents and friends espouse? Is it through the unverbalized pressures which are part of many social interactions? Is it through his parents' child-rearing practices?

While we acknowledged the importance for conflict of all three forces, we chose to concentrate on the latter. One reason was the evidence that many behaviors which are learned very early persist throughout life. Another was the existence of many institutions which are concerned with the imparting of certain skills to children.

To survive, a society must develop in a large number of its members the capacities to carry out collective tasks. If an individual is to participate in this collective endeavor, he must learn to express his needs in ways that are appropriate to the social structure. Different traits are required, for example, depending on whether the social structure is bureaucratic or assertive-individidualistic (13). To educate the child, each society employs a special group of organizations which impart the expectations of others, provide him with models, reward and coerce him, and supervise his practice of skills. Both children and adults are thus under constant pressure to avoid behavior not in a socially approved range. If the organizations are effective, the socially required personality configurations are generally achieved, and are transmitted from parents to children.

Some of the greatest efforts of each society are devoted to the education of the young in the socially acceptable expression of needs. An American child who expresses his aggression by creative initiative in play wins the approval of his peers and parents, but if he engages in destructive acts, he may be snubbed by his friends or spanked by his mother.

We will now describe the child-rearing practices that we investigated and our methods of measuring them, and consider their possible influences on the resolution of conflict. The practices include: type of parental discipline, nature of requests for obedience, type and frequency of reward, manner of weaning, coerciveness of toilet training, and types of experiences with parents, which we infer from differences in sex identity. We begin by showing how child-rearing practices may be influenced by the father's economic position: The father makes his own characteristic adjustment to his job, an adjustment he often transfers to his relationships with his wife and children.

## Social Position and Child Rearing

In our work we hoped to select child-rearing practices which would highlight the characteristic styles of resolving conflict in each social class. However, the choice of practices posed some difficult questions, for these practices are part of a long and complicated sequence of experiences, and there is no way of determining which part of the sequence is contributing most to the adult's characteristics. For example, when later behavior is significantly related to some objective and deliberate action of parents, such as weaning the child at a certain age, it is often difficult to determine whether it is the timing of the act or some more subtle, possibly unconscious, communication between mother and child which has influenced that behavior. It is even possible that the action and the subtle communication are products of a more basic source. Despite these problems in interpreting data, most social scientists are generally agreed that the ways in which men and women treat their children mold many aspects of their adult personalities.

Within the American family the father's economic position provides a key to many of the values and behavior patterns that he and his wife try to teach their children. An economic position is the focus of many social forces to which the father adjusts by adopting a particular style of life. His children reveal the effects of his position when they occupy jobs as adults, and as early as their first years of life as well. How are such customary styles of behavior transmitted from one generation to the next? How does the father who takes great pride in his physical skill teach his son to develop a comparable pride? How does the mother who would make any sacrifice to improve her son's social status convey her sense of urgency? How does she convey her values about physical attack, or reward her son for reversing his anger? To date, such problems have not been systematically investigated. However, we arrived at some tentative answers that guided us in phrasing our hypotheses.

Each man becomes accustomed to carrying out the duties of his job in his own characteristic ways: He customarily expresses himself with his hands or with ideas; he creates as nearly perfect a product as possible, or he modifies his standards in accordance with the pressures of various administrators; he saves for the future, or he lives for the present. He carries out these and many other related practices automatically and unwittingly at home as well. If he solves his problems on the job conceptually, he may regulate his son's behavior in the same manner. If he aims at perfect quality on his job, he may similarly be a perfectionist in the household work that he shares with his son. If he concerns himself with the cost of job operations, he may plan a personal budget with his wife and insist that she adhere to it when making purchases for the family. If he is socially mobile, he may unintentionally convey his respect for members of the upper class in conversations with his child.

Social position may also affect certain deliberate parental

techniques. On the basis of his experiences the adult gradually develops a picture of the nature of society and a formula for successful living within it. If the father is, let us say, the middle-class member of an entrepreneurial organization, he may decide that to get ahead one must engage in such activities as saving money, improving one's education, and acting respectably. In short, he develops an ideology. If he is fortunate, his wife has a compatible ideology because she has had a similar background. She may come from a family like his, or she may have identified with people who are like him. The parents' ideology guides them in rearing their children. To give their young son a "good start," for instance, they may establish high standards of performance and reward him generously if he fulfills them. They may also send him to particular schools in the hope that he will learn the social skills requisite for economic advancement.

The pressures inherent in the father's position are not the only determinants of child rearing. The practices that go with a particular position in society are often affected by the expectations of friends and neighbors. Families in similar social positions tend to occupy the same neighborhoods. Any mother who deviates markedly from the child-rearing practices of her neighbors is often subjected to social pressure. We recall the case of a psychologist who insisted that the toilet training of his daughter be delayed far beyond the age at which other mothers in the neighborhood began their training. When attempts by the other mothers to persuade his wife to mend her ways proved fruitless, they instructed their children to ostracize the "dirty girl." Had the family not moved from the neighborhood, they probably would have been forced to conform.

There are still other pressures on parents to employ child-rearing practices appropriate to their social positions. Some mothers feel that they must keep up with the latest literature on child psychology and participate in the local Parent Teachers' Association. Their relationship with their children may be strongly influenced by these activities. Since both activities also provide contacts with friends, the failure to engage in either may damage a mother's social relationships.

## Type of Discipline

Many of the major conflicts of childhood presumably originate in parental demands for obedience and the methods by which they are enforced. Most parents seem convinced that certain techniques are superior to others, and that disciplinary methods have lasting effects on children's behavior.

Why does the request for obedience or the type of discipline exerted affect a child's reactions to conflict? One reason is the amount of time he spends with his parents. In his early childhood they are the most significant people in his world. A baby spends more time with his mother than with any other single adult. Thus if others behave differently than she does, he usually has little chance to know about it. It is she who defines and enforces standards. Because her approval is so important to him, her rewards have special potency in prompting him to repeat certain acts; her punishments are equally potent in prompting him to avoid other acts. In the learning of new skills it is only natural that he pattern his own reactions after hers. The patterning also often represents a deliberate attempt to gain her approval. She will be proud of him if he greets friends in the polite manner that she uses. The patterning may be unconscious. The child may take over some of his mother's characteristic reactions without being aware of it. The process by means of which such internalization occurs has been called identification.[1]

### Identification and the Modification of Behavior

We can illustrate identification by the case of a small boy who wanted to hurt his young sister because he felt that she had stolen his parents' love. When he tried to hurt her, his mother intervened, sternly reprimanding him and consoling his sister. The fear of losing his mother's love deterred him for a while, but his

[1] There is considerable disagreement among students of personality concerning the mechanisms involved in identification. We shall not review the different viewpoints here; this has already been done very thoroughly by others (14, 17). While the concept is poorly understood, it will help us to describe, if not to explain, some of the most crucial aspects of socialization.

anger was so great that before long he became aggressive once more. Again he met with disapproval, and this time he was punished by being put to bed. Shortly afterward, when his anger at his sibling was still slightly stronger than his fear and guilt, he was seen slapping his own face, as though with his mother's hand, and saying to himself, "Bad Richie." Then he hit his sister. Apparently, his control was not yet adequate enough to inhibit his aggressive attack. Some days later, however, he displayed solicitude toward his sister and a control of his needs that were identical with his mother's behavior. He had resolved his conflict by identifying with her.

Initially, a person in conflict requires the presence of a model, after whom he patterns himself. Once the identification has occurred, the model does not have to be present for the behavior to be repeated. This is the difference between conformity motivated by identification and conformity motivated by fear. Richie slapped himself just as his mother had slapped him, even though, to his knowledge, no adult was present.[2]

Despite the inefficiency of identification in some cases, it does help to resolve conflicts and thus to reduce anxiety. The ways in which identification may resolve conflicts involving aggression have been summarized by Miller and Hutt (16, p. 22), who point out that people in all societies are subject to some prohibitions:

> Because these prohibitions are frustrating, hostile responses are inevitably elicited which are incompatible with the succorance needs of the child. By identifying with the prohibiting adult, he can resolve the conflict between his incompatible impulses and simultaneously obtain the much needed parental support. The latter is forthcoming when the child is enabled by his identification to conform to the imposed prohibitions.

[2] Some acts seem paradoxical until we see the models with whom the actors are identifying. The psychological literature contains some vivid examples. Some Jewish and socialist prisoners in German concentration camps resolved their conflicting reactions to the Nazi guards by identifying with them (1). So strong was the identification that the prisoners began to cut their clothing into the shapes of uniforms, to attack their friends in the camp, and to do rigorous exercises of the types practiced by the guards. Identification has also been invoked to explain the behavior of a young girl who, after an unpleasant dental treatment, began to cut up pieces of rubber with the motions of the dentist (7).

Identification is rewarding in still another way. It enables the child to bow to the parental will and still preserve his self-esteem. Since he had introjected parental injunctions as part of himself, he believes that he performs the acts on his "own accord." He has created a fictitious "free will" which saves him from experiencing the situation as one of coercion. Finally, by identifying with the parents and making their demands his own, the child partakes in their power. As a result, he is more able to tolerate the frustrations of obeying the rules of society.

### IDENTIFICATION, PSYCHOLOGICAL DISCIPLINE, AND REACTIONS TO CONFLICT

Now we can demonstrate how the concept of identification helped us to formulate some of our hypotheses relating discipline to our subjects' reactions to conflict. The threat of punishment often plunges children into conflict. They want to obey, but they are reluctant to forego the forbidden pleasures. To resolve the conflict, the children identify with their mothers. If two mothers differ in their methods of punishment, their children often differ accordingly.

*Psychological Manipulation.* Consider the contrasting practices of two mothers. One either spanks her son or threatens attack; the other manipulates her son psychologically by reasoning with him, shunning him, or implying that he is hurting her. As we shall see, middle-class parents are inclined to be conceptual and are concerned with self-control and responsibility. We anticipated that they would prefer psychological manipulation. If the boy whose mother prefers psychological tactics tries to hit her, she does not retaliate but acts hurt. In identifying with her, he becomes a nonfighter. To the extent that his behavior reflects this identification, he does not attack others, even in self-defense, since he has not patterned himself after an attacker. Instead, when he is in difficulty he controls himself just as his mother has done, and he shows that he is being hurt by the attacker.

Furthermore, because his mother defines his act as an attack on her and does not retaliate physically, the boy cannot, with any justice, be angry with her. If he accepts her definition, he has no focus for his anger other than himself. Then too, he may feel depressed because he has forfeited her love by his misbehavior. When he does blame himself, he may find that this earns her love. We predicted, therefore, that such a boy would defend himself against aggression by turning it inward.

The definition of misbehavior conveyed by a mother's disciplinary practices may also affect the kinds of moral standards that her son develops. It is not uncommon for a mother to present an idealized picture of herself to her child. She is careful never to lie, to swear, or to show any anger in his presence. If he does any of these, she appeals to his guilt. This double-barrelled attack usually results in the internalization of extensive prohibitions. We anticipated that later violations of these internalized prohibitions would create considerable guilt. We also thought that the larger the number of prohibitions, the more indirect the son would be in expressing his needs.

Psychological manipulation is apparently not restricted to members of our society. Whiting and Child (24) have conducted a cross-cultural study of a comparable type of manipulation: denial of love, threats of denial of reward, and threats of ostracism. They find that a preference for such "love-oriented techniques of disciplining" is associated with their measure of the guilt of their subjects.

### Some possible consequences of physical discipline

If a mother usually resorts to physical attack, her son is likely to favor a similar form of aggression. If he identifies with her, he is likely to seek direct outlets for his anger. If she often loses control while disciplining him, he, too, is likely to lose control. In general, he will probably express his anger both directly and motorically.

Unlike mothers who favor psychological methods, the woman who beats her son provides him with a target for his anger. He has someone to blame other than himself. This is compatible with a tendency to project. At any rate, the identification is probably not compatible with a tendency to turn aggression inward. Even if the mother's corporal punishment is mild, it may serve as a sign that the son has lost her love. In that event, he will probably conform to her definitions of misbehavior and internalize them as part of his conscience.

If the mother is prone to lose control of her emotions, she may prove to be an inconsistent model. She may tell her son not to fight, and then fight herself; she may tell him not to swear, and then swear at him when he misbehaves; she may tell him not to lie, and then tell lies which he discovers. Under such conditions, he internalizes an inconsistent set of rules.

If a woman's discipline is very harsh, it may signify an attack to her child rather than loss of love. Many such painful experiences may conceivably strengthen a tendency to deny the problem. If reality is frequently unpleasant, a boy cannot be blamed for wanting to run away or for escaping into his fantasy life. He is motivated to conform to the mother's proscriptions more by fear than by love. Because of the relative lack of reward, he may not internalize as many moral standards as the boy does who has not been mistreated. Since certain types of delinquents are said to have poorly developed consciences, we find indirect support of our prediction in the report (8) that parents of delinquents favor physical punishment while parents of matched nondelinquents try to reason with their children.

The possible association between harsh discipline and moral standards is illustrated by the results of another study. College students who cheat on a test when they think no one can find out have been most often punished physically as children; non-cheaters have been subject to "measures which seek to have a child feel that he has fallen short of some ideal or that he has hurt his parents and consequently is less loved by them because of what he has done" (15, p. 498).

### Classifying types of discipline

We obtained our information about child-rearing practices from interviews with the mothers of our adolescent subjects. Our studies were done in two time periods, and we used two populations of families. Chapter 4 contains a detailed description of our procedures. Our questions, which were tested in a pilot study, were phrased in such a manner as to encourage the mother to talk about her experiences in concrete terms. Each topic was introduced by a general question. After the mother answered, the interviewer asked her what she might do in specific instances and urged her to give examples.

In a typical question, we asked: "Suppose your son has just done something you feel is very wrong, something you have warned him against ever doing. What do you do at such times?" This item plus one other provided the primary basis for classifying the mothers.[3] The second was phrased as follows: "Parents have many different ways of getting their children to do what they want them to, or getting them to act the right way. They also have many different ways of getting their children to stop doing things they feel are wrong. What ways have you found most useful with your boy to get him to do right and keep him from doing wrong?" If the rater was doubtful, she also took into account the answer to the first question cited in this paragraph. In the few cases when the rater was uncertain, she read five other questions pertaining to child training.[4]

From each mother's responses, a ranking was made of the extent to which she employed four types of discipline. We list them here with examples of each:

a. Corporal: spanking, whipping, slapping, beating.
b. Scolding: threatening, bawling out, hollering.
c. Withdrawal of privileges or restriction of behavior: banishing the child to his room, preventing him from watching television, making him come home early, curtailing his allowance.
d. Psychological: manipulation by shaming, appeals to pride and to guilt, and expressions of disappointment.

All possible combinations of these types were too complicated to be analyzed statistically, so we divided the sample of mothers into three groups in terms of the most frequent type of discipline. In rating the first sample we decided to give disproportionate weighting to the methods in which we were most interested—psychological and corporal disciplines. To this end, we developed an arbitrary system of classifying mothers who favored scolding or the withdrawal of privileges as predominantly psychological or corporal in their methods, depending on the type they used most.

[3] This was done by Beverly B. Allinsmith.
[4] They may be found in Appendix B.

If psychological discipline was ranked third in frequency, and corporal fourth, we placed the parent in the psychological group, even though scolding and withdrawal of privileges were given the first two rankings. We gave special weighting to psychological discipline because parents found it hard to recall instances of it; where it was mentioned, we felt we should give it a greater weighting than references to the other three practices.[5] If psychological discipline was ranked second, and corporal discipline was not first, we assigned the mother to the psychological category. If corporal was second, and psychological not first, we assigned the mother to the corporal category. To be placed in the group that favored scolding or withdrawal of privileges, it was necessary that a mother be given a ranking of 4 on psychological discipline or a ranking of 3 on corporal discipline.

In order to test the reliability of the method of classification, an advanced undergraduate student in psychology, who was not acquainted with the hypotheses, was instructed by a staff member in the use of the code and given supervised practice with a few sample interviews.[6] Then the student coded forty interviews, an equal proportion of which were selected at random from within each of the four social sub-classes. The classifications of the mothers into the three categories of discipline agreed in 80 per cent of the cases.

## Requests for Obedience

Mothers vary markedly in the nature of their requests for obedience and in their methods of enforcing them. Some women make almost no attempt at explanation and expect their offspring to conform "just because I say so." Others carefully explain their purposes in the hope that the children, even if they do not comply, will not be confused. In our analysis of data, we refer to the former requests as *arbitrary* and the latter as *explained.*

Like discipline, a mother's requests have some obvious im-

[5] In rating the second sample we omitted this special criterion because it produced almost no cases.

[6] We are indebted to Mrs. Phylis Shire for her help in obtaining the reliabilities of our measures.

plications for her child's resolution of conflict. If she is arbitrary, he must obey without understanding. His world soon consists of high fences bounding many little spaces from which he can escape only by risking her disapproval. In new situations he cannot afford the risk of arriving at his own judgments. Because he often does not understand the purposes of his mother's regulations, he cannot tell whether she will condemn the actions that he takes on his own initiative. He can be sure only that following directions, whether or not they make sense, is the best way to keep out of trouble and win approval.

This picture of arbitrary requests is particularly relevant to our hypotheses about defenses. Given the difficulties that result from arbitrary requests, we anticipated that boys reared by this method would resort to such defenses as self-attack or denial as a means of obtaining relief from their confusing conflicts.

If, on the other hand, the mother tries to gain her son's co-operation by explaining the reasons for her requests, he often finds it easy to comply. He conforms not because of fear, but because he wants to help her in achieving a common goal. Since he knows the reasons for her rules, he can make his own judgments in new situations with some confidence that she will not disapprove of his subsequent behavior. He can thus take initiative when necessary. Compared to the child who constantly anticipates the unpredictable punishments of adults, the son of a mother who explains her requests usually has less need to alter his picture of ongoing events by means of defensive distortions.

### Classifying requests for obedience

To obtain information about a mother's requests for obedience, we asked her: "How important in general do you feel it is for a boy of (*son's name*)*'s* age to obey you when you tell him to do something?" If she requested further clarification, the interviewer was instructed to reply, "Just in general, how important do you feel it is for him to obey you?" In order to encourage the mother to elaborate, we asked her to give the reasons for her answer.

The responses were interpreted [7] in terms of a code with two parts. The first provided for a rating on a five-point scale of the

[7] By Betty J. Beardslee.

type of obedience expected by the mother. At one extreme of this scale was the category "mother expects blind obedience." There followed: "mother expects obedience on the basis that parents know what is right"; "mother expects obedience but makes some concessions to the child's needs"; "mother really insists on obedience in only a few things"; and, at the other extreme, "mother is willing to be swayed in all her expectations of obedience."

The second part of the code involved a rating of the mother's authoritarianism. Depending on her implied or expressed attitudes, we assigned her to one of three categories. A woman at the authoritarian extreme regards her child as subservient, assumes that it is his duty to obey, and appoints herself as supreme arbiter of all fundamental decisions in his everyday existence. At the nonauthoritarian extreme, the mother is most concerned about maintaining her son's integrity. She attempts to establish a practice of mutual participation in arriving at important decisions. Although she limits her child's behavior, she does not value conformity for its own sake. The middle category of the scale defines a position between the extremes.

Depending on a mother's ranking on both parts of the code, we classified her as favoring either explained or arbitrary requests. An assignment of a woman to the group that made reasonable requests for obedience required fulfillment of two criteria. It was necessary that she occupy one of the three more liberal positions on the code of concessions, and that she be classified in either of the two least authoritarian positions of the second code.

An assignment to the group that made arbitrary demands for obedience also required the fulfillment of two criteria. A mother had to be placed in either of the two strict categories of the first code and in either the authoritarian or the middle category on the second code. We also included in the group that made arbitrary demands those mothers who evaded the topic of obedience in the interview, but whose answers reflected an authoritarian attitude toward the child.

It was not possible to classify thirteen mothers from their descriptions of their methods. The two raters, working independently, agreed in 70 per cent of their classifications of the remaining mothers.

## Reward

*Qualitative Types.* There is much empirical evidence that reward affects learning (11). On first considering parental rewards, we assumed that their content would be congruent with other types of expression used by the members of a social class: that middle-class parents would offer symbolic rewards, such as signs of pride or kind words, that working-class mothers and fathers would offer concrete rewards, such as presents or new privileges. Should symbolic reward be the favored method of the middle class, we anticipated that it would be associated with a conceptual orientation and the indirect expression of anger. We also anticipated that concrete reward would be associated with motoric and direct expression. If this were true, concrete reward would be the favored method of the working class.

*Rate of Occurrence.* In the course of interviewing the mothers, we found that they did not always know when they were using symbolic rewards. An affectionate gesture may be very gratifying, but it may not be intended as a reward, and the mother may not recall it very readily. Because of this methodological difficulty, we shifted from type to frequency of reward in a second study. We had the impression that frequent rewards would be conducive to a warm and supportive atmosphere. Infrequent rewards often create remoteness in personal contacts, and may even help to maintain very hostile relationships. We were also invoking the association, well established by experimental psychologists, between frequency of reward, on one hand, and learning time and retention of certain skills on the other: With frequent reward, the skill is learned sooner and retained longer than with very infrequent reward. Since we assumed that denial is maximized by hardship, we postulated that it would be associated with minimal reward.

### Classifying types of reward

*Symbolic and Concrete.* In order to categorize women in the first sample with respect to type of reward, we asked: "Suppose your son has just done something that you feel is very good, or suppose that he has been particularly good. What do you usually do at those times?" We had considerable difficulty in classifying the mothers. Some parents were very uncertain. Many claimed that they did not reward their children. We interpreted this as a denial of bribery. With some qualms, we placed such mothers in the group who favored symbolic rewards. We did this on the assumption that they must have rewarded their boys in some nonconcrete, symbolic manner. More positive reasons for inclusion in the group favoring symbolic methods were the mothers' reports that they took pride in the child's achievements.

Many mothers gave almost no account of their reactions other than to say that they expected their sons to behave. We could assign such women only to an intermediate group who used neither symbolic nor concrete rewards. When mothers usually offered such objects as money and candy, we placed them in the group who favored concrete rewards.

*Frequency.* We asked two questions of mothers in a second sample to obtain data about frequency of rewards. The first was the same as the one we had used previously. Next we asked, "How often do you have occasion to do this?" Depending upon each woman's response to this second question, she was placed in one of two groups.[8] Those mothers who rewarded their children at least twice a week were placed in the first group. The second included those who rewarded their children less often. Eighteen mothers were eliminated from the sample because it was not possible to classify them on the basis of their answers.

## Early Socialization

In some of our studies we related topics like defenses or moral standards to procedures employed by parents early in the subjects' lives. According to psychoanalytic theory (4, 21), the child's early experiences in being trained to master his organ systems and to control the expression of his needs create a pattern of behavior and a set of values which he applies throughout life. His first decisive encounter with another person, his mother, occurs in the course of feeding; feeding is the focus of their rela-

[8] By Betty J. Beardslee.

tionship. To survive, he must learn how to ingest food. In the course of suckling the child gains much in addition to nourishment: He gets some of his first experiences of the world.

WEANING

If we assume that the feeding relationship provides the young child with some of his most frequent and important experiences with adults, then maternal practices and the timing and harshness of weaning should affect his picture of the people about him. For example, these practices should determine the frequency of some of his frustrations and conflicts, and should color his optimism about being helped by others. If he is weaned before he is ready to give up the breast or bottle, he may get the impression that adults are often frustrating, or that pleasure must be sacrificed in order to win his mother's love. Or he may learn that her love is available only if he fulfills her high standards of performance. If he is weaned harshly, before he has learned all the skills of the period of infancy, he may have difficulty in acquiring those skills of the following period that depend on a mastery of the earlier ones.

To date, empirical studies have usually related the child's age when weaning occurs to some test of his later personality adjustment.[9] It is often difficult to interpret the results because of the questionable validity of some of the techniques. One careful investigation which deserves special notice reports a significant relationship between severity of weaning and rigidity of feeding schedule, as reported by mothers, and dependent behavior of nursery-school children as rated by their teachers (18). Impressively positive results are also furnished by two anthropological papers. One reports a significant association between severity of weaning and the presence of oral explanations of illness in thirty-five societies (24). An oral explanation is one that attributes the illness to the ingestion of some food or poison, or to the magical effects of verbal spells and incantations performed by others. According to another analysis of cross-cultural practices in twenty-two societies, feeding on demand is positively related to amount of economic cooperation, which is defined by absence of hoarding, vague definitions of property within the family, sharing of

[9] These studies have been summarized by Child (2).

food, and lack of use of wealth for purposes of social mobility (3).

In our research we postulated that the middle-class mother would wean her child early because of her concern with his accomplishments. We also assumed that early weaning would be associated with guilt about moral violations. Finally, we explored the relationships of weaning to denial and to defenses in the second family.

### Toilet training

According to psychoanalytic theory, the timing and harshness of toilet training also provide the child with some of his most basic information about other people. If his mother makes demands before he is ready to sit up, or if she punishes him harshly for not meeting her demands, he may find it difficult to comply. If he resists her efforts to train him, a chronic battle may ensue. As a result, anal difficulties may become associated with anger. If defecating or retaining feces at the wrong time makes his mother angry, he may adopt either response as part of his repertory of attack. In that event, upon later repressing his aggression, he may develop chronic diarrhea or constipation. Observations of problem children (12) offer some corroborative evidence for these claims. Children whose toilet training was started before eight months of age, or was completed before eighteen months, manifest such symptoms as constipation, fear, and rage more often than do those whose mothers are less demanding. Other results of premature or overly harsh bowel training which are postulated in the psychoanalytic literature include an overemphasis on cleanliness, a tendency to retain objects other than feces, and the formation by the child of an impression that he earns parental love if he can obey arbitrary or meaningless demands.

The few empirical investigations of toilet training have not produced many positive results. One cross-cultural study (24) reveals that harsh anal training is not significantly related to any of a group of variables derived from the psychoanalytic literature. Although people who have been subjected to premature or coercive methods are supposed to be stingy and stubborn, toilet training is not associated with economic competition (3).

In American society a significant association has been reported between severity of toilet training and compulsive tendencies in five-year-old children (25), and contradictory results are reported for the relation between toilet training and aggression (19, 25).

In our research we anticipated that the middle-class mothers, because of their concern with teaching their children to perform well and take responsibility early, would wean earlier and use more coercive methods of toilet training than would the working-class mothers. Because of the children's resistances, we assumed that this early training and coerciveness would be associated with stringent moral standards concerning the expression of aggression. We also explored the associations of different kinds of weaning and toilet training with such defenses as denial and self-attack.

### Classifying harshness of weaning

Harshness was estimated on the basis of the child's age when weaned.[10] This was the age, in months, when, according to the mother's report, the child completely stopped nursing from the breast or bottle—whichever was later. We obtained the necessary information from two questions: "At what age did he stop breast feeding completely?" and "At what age did he stop bottle feeding completely?" We rejected age of onset as a criterion of oral frustration because many parents wean very gradually. No appreciable oral deprivation need result from the use of a cup or solid food if the child is allowed the breast or bottle at the same time.

We had no basis for determining how early the weaning would have to take place in order to constitute an unusual hardship. Therefore, we divided the sample of ages at the median. This created two groups of mothers: those who weaned their children before they were twelve months, and those who weaned their children at twelve months or later.

### Classifying coerciveness of bowel training

Both age of onset and duration in months were considered in evaluating the coerciveness of a mother's bowel training. The questions were: "Now, how old was (*son's name*) when you began

[10] The classifications of weaning and toilet training were done by W. Allinsmith.

bowel training?" and "How old was he when he was completely bowel trained?" Age of onset told us something about the earliness of the mother's demands. We assumed that very early onset would constitute a hardship. Duration gave us indirect evidence of pressure.

In terms of her coerciveness, each mother was assigned to an extreme, high, or low group. We included in the group using *extreme coerciveness* those mothers who started training their children between the ages of one and six months, and whose training period lasted less than six months.[11] We identified *high coerciveness* on the basis of three categories: initiation of toilet-training between one and six months and duration of six months or more; initiation at seven to nine months regardless of duration; initiation at ten to eleven months with a duration of one to six months. Low coerciveness meant that either the training had started at ten to eleven months and lasted more than six months, or that it was begun later regardless of the duration of training.

In establishing these groupings, we were guided by the opinions of authorities concerning the coerciveness of various ages of initiation and periods of duration in American society. Seven to nine months is the earliest acceptable starting age according to the consensus (12, 20). We realize that our groupings are very complex. In compensation for this, however, they have the advantage of being constructed in terms of empirical criteria.

## Sex Identity

We conclude our list of major antecedent variables with sex identity, a topic which helped us to make inferences about our subjects' backgrounds. From these inferences, we developed some of our most speculative, yet fruitful, predictions about the origins of certain reactions to conflict. The studies of sex identity enabled us to examine moral standards, defenses, and expressive styles with a new age group and in the context of conflicts centering about masculinity and femininity. We will now summarize our

[11] We separated the extreme and high groups because we developed different predictions concerning the effect of these methods on moral development.

conception of sex identity and show how we used it as an index of child-rearing experiences.

Sex identity is one aspect of self-identity, the continuity and sameness which we sense in ourselves and which others see in us. As a result of many social experiences, each man develops a sense of the special meaning that he has for others and for himself. His identity is what he stands for.

Part of everyone's total identity is the pattern of sex-linked characteristics, both learned and unlearned, that mark him as masculine or feminine. American men and women, for example, differ in physical strength, gait, vocal inflection, posture, initiative taken in courtship, types of interest, and the like. Depending on a particular man's characteristics in each of these areas, he may be classified as being predominantly masculine, or predominantly feminine, or in some intermediate group.

Regardless of his actual identity, each male who is at all sensitive to the values of his peers is inclined to view himself in as masculine a light as possible; this identity is most rewarded. If he is actually feminine, he may repress the signs of this identity, or he may acknowledge them but misinterpret their significance.

One of our primary purposes in the studies to be reported was to compare the reactions to conflict of three different kinds of men. One of our groups of subjects was feminine both unconsciously and consciously (we shall refer to this combination by the letters FF); a second was unconsciously feminine but consciously very masculine (FM); and a third was unconsciously and consciously masculine (MM).[12]

In arriving at the predicted associations between identity and conflict, our thinking took two directions. One was developmental; the second involved the making of direct inferences from the characteristics of the three groups about their probable reactions to conflict. We relied most on the first, which we now describe.

### Origins of sex identity

We made two assumptions about the origins of the three patterns in our developmental orientation. First, we assumed that

[12] We are indebted to R. Nevitt Sanford for his suggestions, made in a lecture at the University of Michigan, of techniques for identifying the three types.

each boy initially identifies with his mother and then transfers to his father. As an infant, he spends most of his time with his mother. He learns about objects, people, time, causality, social rules, and other such properties of his world through constant contact with her. He becomes very dependent on her because she feeds and cleans him, protects him from harm, and prevents him from misbehaving. He consequently comes to expect her to help him to overcome emergencies.

Later, the father usually becomes the more significant person. He becomes more visible as a source of discipline. He has certain unique abilities which the son admires. His life outside the home piques the child's curiosity. By identifying with his father, a son gradually acquires the expressive gestures, the habits, and the interests that are typical of males rather than females in our society. We thought that these earlier identifications would not be conscious, since they are embedded in a large number of activities and occur before events are labeled verbally.

A second assumption about identity involved fixation. We saw each stage of development as entailing the acquisition of skills that form the building blocks of the next stage. Hence, if some difficulty occurs at one stage, the child may not master all the requisite skills. He then remains more closely identified with the mother—and, therefore, more feminine—than another boy who can forge ahead. And, depending upon the degree of difficulty, he is correspondingly handicapped in learning the more complex skills of the next stage.

Whether he is masculine or feminine in his underlying identity, the average male child, as he matures and develops friendships, feels an increasing social pressure to act in a masculine manner. If his gestures are feminine, or he lacks an interest in machinery, he may become the object of ridicule. If he is proficient in sports played by boys, he gains considerable recognition from his friends.

Frequently, masculine values are acquired by identification with a great football player, a jet pilot, or some mythical hero. By patterning himself after Robin Hood or Tarzan, a young boy comes to idealize physical prowess, fairness, democracy, support of the weak and oppressed, and great courage which may at times verge on needless foolhardiness or cruelty. These values are quite different from the self-sacrifice, gentle sensitivity, and succorance that characterize such feminine ideal prototypes as Juliet or Florence Nightingale. In contrast to the earlier parental identifications, later ones with heroes, real or ideal, are probably matters of conscious concern for every normal boy. They are part of his conscious sex identity.

Some of the principles that we have just outlined cast light on the origins of our three types of sex identity. When both unconscious and conscious identities are predominantly feminine, the boy's identification with his mother cannot have been affected by the norms of his peers. He consciously accepts his feminine characteristics, although he may deny their significance. If the FF does not deny his femininity and accepts his traits as being feminine, he may engage in homosexual activities, or he may express himself in such activities as hair dressing or designing women's clothing.

The unconscious feminine identity may be defended against by a conscious masculine one. While the FM remains identified primarily with his mother, he aspires to be masculine, and consciously considers himself so. To convince himself and others that he is not feminine, a boy may engage in activities that appeal only to masculine men. For example, he may cultivate exceptional skill in weight-lifting or in wrestling. Yet, the unconscious femininity manifests itself too. The usual outlets are expressive styles, particularly those that are not considered meaningful. In special circumstances it is possible, for example, for a man to behave passively with a person in authority and still think that he is being masculine.

In the presumably mature boy, both unconscious and conscious identities are masculine. The MM has identified with his father, and there is no incompatibility between unconscious and conscious reactions.

### Developmental basis for predictions

In our studies we compared the three types, the FFs, FMs, and MMs, with respect to such variables as severity of guilt, control, first family of defense, turning against the self, and passivity. We used two types of reasoning in our predictions. One involved the issues which we have summarized in our developmental account of sex indentity. In general, we assumed that the less masculine the boy is, the earlier his developmental problems occurred. A boy with feminine identification who is relatively impervious to the meanings of his feminine traits to his peers must be fairly immature. A boy with feminine identification who wants to be masculine is more mature, since he is sensitive to the reactions of others and tries to conform. A boy with masculine identification on both levels is most mature. We thus inferred the stage at which a boy was fixated from the identities. We then deduced his probable reactions to conflict about aggression.

When a baby is identifying with his mother, he learns to discriminate reality from unreality and the tendency to appeal to others for help. If a man customarily reverts to the skills of this level, he may become unconsciously feminine because of his identification with his mother. We also thought of him as employing the unrealistic orientations of the baby. Since he is relatively immature, such a man may react even to mild conflicts with poor self-control and with displays of impetuous emotionality. Because he is inclined to be unrealistic and relatively insensitive to the pressures of others, he may not develop a compensating, overt masculinity. Since it is so hard for him to control his aggression, he may have difficulty in behaving according to his moral standards. It seemed to us that he would consequently be troubled by considerable guilt.

Once he becomes aware of his peers' values, the passive, feminine boy may, in time, come to repress his femininity. In that event, he becomes the man who is unconsciously feminine and consciously masculine. We thought that the FM, in contrast to the FF, has usually learned to control the direct expression of anger. Since the control has not yet become dependable, it may be applied to excess. In adjusting to adults, the FM has usually obtained considerable practice in employing such mechanisms as turning his anger against himself and reversing it. Since he has not adequately learned to inhibit his expression of anger, he, too, is inclined to be more disturbed by guilt than is the MM.

Compared to the first two types, the man who is predominantly masculine and does not have to reject some feminine components in his make-up has passed through the earlier stages with least difficulty. He has also had minimal difficulty in acquiring the interests, practices, and expressive styles of masculine boys.

Since he has realistic means at his disposal for resolving conflict, he does not have to resort to defense mechanisms as readily as the FF and FM do. Nor does he have to be passive or overcontrolled because he fears an outbreak of incomprehensible needs.

This summarizes our developmental approach. In our studies of sex identity we did not investigate the childhood of our subjects. From the early experiences which we assumed, we made inferences about moral standards, defenses, and expressive styles.

### Contemporaneous approach

It is important to note that we could have arrived at some of our predictions without considering the early childhood of our subjects. The FFs, for example, violate some critical social rules in their everyday behavior. To do this, these men must deny either the existence of the social pressures or their importance for self-esteem. The FFs must therefore be very unrealistic.

We can infer the greater realism of the FMs from their conscious masculine identification. Because they are at war with themselves, they must also deceive themselves, but about their own impulses and not about external events. The FMs thus cannot be as realistic about their own impulses as the MMs can be. From a purely contemporaneous point of view it would have been difficult to predict that the FMs express much passivity, favor the defense of turning against the self, or manifest little strong emotion. While it was not absolutely necessary to introduce conceptions about development in order to derive all of our predictions, we present such thinking because it provided suggestions for those of us who planned and conducted the study in its initial phases.

### Classifying unconscious sex identity: Franck's test [13]

Many responses that we might label as masculine or feminine evolve in connection with the practice of sex-linked activities. Because boys play baseball, for example, they are inclined to develop particular types of gestures and muscular coordination. Some of these styles of expression, such as the tendencies not to bend the wrist and to walk in long strides, are masculine. Girls are more likely to bend the wrist and to take smaller steps. Since few people realize the significance of such sex-linked styles of ex-

[13] Justin Aronfreed and Leonard Lansky classified the subjects.

pression, they provide us with a valuable index of unconscious sex identity.

One method of eliciting some expressive styles is to obtain subjects' drawings. This is the procedure used in the Franck Drawing Completion Test (6), our measure of unconscious identity. The test contains thirty-six simple geometric figures which the subject completes or elaborates in any way he chooses. Franck devised criteria for analyzing both style and content of drawings.

In her pretests of style she found that men are most likely to expand the area of the original figure, to close objects that are open, to draw angular shapes, protrusions, and unsupported lines, and to unify the figure. In contrast, women are more inclined to elaborate internal spaces, and to draw open objects, rounded and blunted shapes, and supported lines.

Franck also found marked sex differences in the objects that people draw. Her indicators of masculinity included "active containers," such as automobiles and fountains, caricatures, faces that fill most of the drawing space, tools, eyeglasses, and "engineered structures," such as bridges, tunnels and skyscrapers. Among feminine indicators were furniture and interiors of homes, fruit or flowers, and such passive containers as bowls or rowboats. In her scoring manual (5), Franck cites norms for citizens of eight countries. In all her samples the groups of men differed significantly and in the same direction from the groups of women. Independent ratings of drawings by three judges yielded intercorrelations that were all above .90.

Franck's technique appealed to us on two counts. If it is a test of unconscious identity, it should not correlate significantly with tests of conscious identity when administered to a large enough population to include a significant number of FMs. It is not significantly related to any of three popular, verbal tests of masculinity-femininity,[14] the Terman-Miles Attitude Interest Analysis test (23), the M-F Scale of the Strong Vocational Interest Blank (22), and the M-F scale of the Minnesota Multiphasic Personality Inventory (10). Each of the three calls for reports of attitudes and interests. We felt, therefore, that Franck's test must measure something other than conscious sex identity—something which also dis-

[14] This analysis was made by J. Heston, who reports it in *Educ. & Psychol. Measurement,* 1948, 8, 375–387.

criminates between males and females. A second virtue of Franck's test was its relative lack of relationship to the experiences of the two sexes. It would be hard, for example, to argue that men have less experience than women with sailboats and canoes, objects that are drawn more frequently by women. Nor can experience alone be used to explain the fact that men exceed women in the drawing of such domestic objects as candles and kitchen knives.

CLASSIFYING CONSCIOUS SEX IDENTITY: GOUGH'S TEST

A number of tests have been constructed to sample conscious reports of activities and interests relevant to sex identity. We selected the Gough scale, which discriminates significantly between men and women and has split-half reliabilities of .88 for females and .86 for males. It has the additional virtue of being a short test; it contains fifty-eight true-false items.

Like Terman and Miles, Gough (9) finds that women, unlike men, tend to emphasize clean, neat work, feelings of sensitivity, responsiveness to social nuances, and social timidity. Women also report a lack of confidence, a sense of compassion, a lack of interest in the abstract political and social world, a need for order, a moderate pettiness, and irritability in judgment.

## Summary

Each man develops a general orientation to his occupation which he is then likely to transfer to other spheres of activity. He performs his duties in his own individual manner; he develops a particular set of values; he relates to superiors and fellow workers in his own characteristic ways. In this chapter we have traced the relation between his orientation and the child-rearing practices used in his family: the reasonableness of requests for obedience, methods of enforcing requests, techniques of rewarding children, manner of weaning, and coerciveness of toilet training. We have also described an adult characteristic, sex identity, from which we inferred parent-child relationships and reactions to conflict. To illustrate the reasons for our interests in the parental practices and in sex identity, we have speculated on some of their possible relationships to moral needs, defenses, and expressive styles. We have also described our methods for classifying subjects with respect to sex identity and the child-rearing practices used by their parents.

## References


1. Bettlheim, B. Individual and mass behavior in extreme situations. *J. abnorm. soc. Psychol.*, 1943, *38*, 417–52.
2. Child, I. L. Socialization. In Lindzey, G. (Ed.), *Handbook of social psychology*. Cambridge: Addison-Wesley, 1954.
3. Cohen, Y. A. A study of interpersonal relations in a Jamaican community. Unpubl. Ph.D. dissertation, Yale Univ., 1953.
4. Erikson, E. H. *Childhood and society*. New York: Norton, 1950.
5. Franck, Kate. *Franck drawing completion test: preliminary manual.* Melbourne: Australian Council for Educational Research.
6. ———, & Rosen, E. A projective test of masculinity-femininity. *J. consult. Psychol.*, 1949, *13*, 247–56.
7. Freud, Anna. *The ego and the mechanisms of defence.* London: Hogarth, 1937.
8. Glueck, S., & Glueck, Eleanor. *Unraveling juvenile delinquency.* New York: Commonwealth Fund, 1950.
9. Gough, H. G. Identifying psychological femininity. *Educ. & Psychol. Measurement,* 1952, *12*, 427–39.
10. Hathaway, S. R., & McKinley, J. C. *Manual for the Minnesota Multiphasic Personality Inventory.* New York: Psychol. Corp., 1943.
11. Hilgard, E. R. *Theories of learning.* New York: Appleton-Century-Crofts, 1956.
12. Huschka, Mabel. The child's response to coercive bowel training. *Psychosom. Med.*, 1942, *4*, 301–28.
13. Inkeles, A., & Levinson, D. J. Natural character: the study of modal personality and sociocultural systems. In Lindzey, G. (Ed.), *Handbook of social psychology.* Cambridge: Addison-Wesley, 1954.
14. Knight, R. P. Introjection, projection, and identification. *Psychoanal. Quart.*, 1940, *9*, 334–41.
15. McKinnon, D. W. Violations of prohibitions. In Murray, H. A., *et al.*, *Explorations in personality.* New York: Oxford University Press, 1938.
16. Miller, D. R., & Hutt, M. L. Value interiorization and personality development. *J. soc. Issues,* 1949, *5*, 2–30.

17. Sanford, N. The dynamics of identification. *Psychol. Rev.*, 1955, *62*, 106–18.
18. Sears, R. R., Whiting, J. W. M., Nowlis, V., & Sears, Pauline S. Some child rearing antecedents of aggression and dependency in young children. *Genet. Psychol. Monogr.*, 1953, *47*, 135–234.
19. Sewell, W. H. Infant training and the personality of the child. *Amer. J. Sociol.*, 1952, *58*, 150–59.
20. Spock, B. *The pocket book of baby and child care.* New York: Pocket Books, 1946.
21. Sterba, R. *Introduction to the psychoanalytic theory of the libido.* New York: Nerv. & Ment. Dis. Monogr., 1947.
22. Strong, E. K. *Vocational interests of men and women.* Stanford: Stanford Univ. Press, 1945.
23. Terman, C. M., & Miles, C. C. *Sex and personality.* New York: McGraw-Hill, 1936.
24. Whiting, J. W. M., & Child, I. L. *Child training and personality: a cross-cultural study.* New Haven: Yale Univ. Press, 1953.
25. Wittenborn, J. R. *The development of adoptive children.* New York: Russell Sage Foundation.

PART THREE

# POPULATIONS STUDIED

# 4

## SELECTING SUBJECTS

The studies of reaction to conflict were the products of a continuing, long-range program. Throughout the program we attempted to explore different aspects of the broad topic of conflict. Our research may readily be divided into three stages, each focusing on its own particular problems and, therefore, requiring its own sample of subjects.

### The three stages of the program

During the initial stage we leaned toward the investigation of those problems that we could visualize most clearly. We were also biased toward concepts that did not raise serious methodological problems. Most important, we had to restrict ourselves to investigations that did not strain our limited budget. As a result of these pressures, we decided to concentrate on expressive style. We attempted to predict expressive style from social position and from types of maternal discipline and reward. We selected a group of boys in early adolescence to test our hypotheses.

When we planned a second set of investigations, we were able to profit from the results of our initial studies. We had more information about conflict, and we had gained considerably from the experience of designing our initial instruments. In addition, we could expand our activities because we had more funds. Consequently, we investigated the more complex topics of moral standards and defense mechanisms. We also included other parental methods in our analysis of child rearing. We added frequency of reward, the extent to which parents explained requests for obedience, and methods of regulating the children's oral and anal functions. We tried to get a second population of subjects who were comparable to the first in all respects that might have affected our results.

During the third stage we decided to study the moral standards, defenses, and expressive styles connected with patterns of conscious and unconscious masculinity and femininity. Our methods and problems dictated the selection of young, adult males as our subjects.

In this chapter we will describe our reasons and criteria for selecting each sample. Many of our reasons apply to all three samples and, for that matter, are requisite to good design in general. Since it would be needlessly repetitive to review them in detail, we will illustrate most of our points in terms of the first two samples. We will attempt to demonstrate how we were able to eliminate the possibility of certain alternative interpretations of our results by selecting boys with particular characteristics. We will then raise similar considerations in describing our criteria for selecting the final group.

## Controlling Sources of Error in Selecting the First Two Populations

We needed subjects whose different upbringings had reinforced contrasting methods of resolving conflict. This was our primary reason for selecting boys from two social classes. We were confident, from our reading of the literature on stratification, that samples from different social classes would provide us with many sizable differences in reactions to conflict. We also assumed that differences in social status might throw additional light on the associations between child-rearing practices and various reactions to conflict.

### Selection criteria

In selecting each population, we controlled conditions other than those associated with social class.[1] Otherwise, they might

[1] We described our method of determining social class in Chapter 2.

have affected our results in ways that we could not have interpreted. One such source of error, for example, might have arisen because of uncontrolled sex differences. We predicted that children from the working class would express their aggression more directly than would those from the middle class. But suppose most of the subjects were boys in one class and girls in the other. Common observations suggest that girls in our society are less direct than boys in expressing aggression. Had we included both girls and boys in the same study, we would not have been able to tell whether differences in directness of aggression had resulted from differences in sex, differences in social class, or both. For this reason and others described below, we restricted our samples to males. To control differences in sex and other possible sources of error, we required that all our subjects in the first two populations be in the seventh, eighth, or ninth grades of schools in Detroit or Highland Park, within one year of the median age for their grade, male, above borderline intelligence, without apparent personality disorders, white, Christian, born in the northern part of the United States, from unbroken homes, at least third generation Americans, in nonmobile families, the children of parents who were born in the northern part of the United States, and descendants of immigrants from northwest Europe.[2] We would like to discuss the reasons for these criteria.

*Age.* Our subjects were pupils in the seventh to ninth grades of schools in the general area of Detroit. Children in school are available as are no adult populations. Subjects in their early teens are sophisticated enough to cooperate intelligently in interviews and experiments, and experienced enough in their culture to reflect its influences. They are particularly valuable for a study of conflict because they are unsophisticated about tests and interviews. Because they do not realize the significance of their answers, they do not disguise their thoughts as much as adults do. In setting the ninth grade as an upper limit, we could be sure to have a large sample of working-class students from which to choose our subjects. Sons of manual laborers often drop out before finishing high school, but almost all of them complete the eighth grade and many finish the ninth. Children in junior high school also offered the advantage of being able to read and write well enough

[2] We had to violate this last criterion in a few instances. The exceptions are not disproportionate in any class.

to take some tests in groups. This saved our project the extra hundreds of hours of work which would have been necessary to give the tests individually.

*Area of Residence.* We deliberately chose subjects from a large urban area. Preliminary studies with public school children in Ann Arbor, Ypsilanti, and other small Michigan communities had given us results that generally supported our hypotheses but often fell short of significance. In talking with the children we gained the impression that there were no greatly marked cleavages in the ways of life associated with differences in their fathers' occupations. In small towns middle- and working-class children live near each other and may get to know each other well. They often attend the same schools. Differences in taste and temper between the classes are likely to blur in these intimate contacts. Child-rearing practices in both classes may be subjected to the same pressures. To find populations with greater differences in earlier experiences, we decided to work in the metropolitan area of the industrial city of Detroit where the forces of industry and city life accentuate the separation of occupational groups from each other.

*Sex.* We decided to restrict our sample to males. It was very expensive to obtain subjects and we could not be sure of getting many more than one hundred. If we had to divide this number in half in order to eliminate the effect of sex differences on our results, the small numbers in each group would force us to sacrifice the analyses of some of our most important hypotheses. We had two reasons for studying boys rather than girls. The psychoanalytic description of personality development is very incomplete for females. This lack of information is commonly explained by the greater complexity of the developmental sequence for females. Whatever the reason, the picture of the development of males is more comprehensive; it is complete enough to suggest testable hypotheses. Our second purpose in choosing boys was that they may be affected more distinctly than girls by the social influences which interested us. Boys are constantly guided toward an occupation. Existing research suggests that this occupational emphasis gives boys early and thorough training for participation in a given social class. The girls' preparation for marriage and motherhood does not give them as adequate a training in the values and styles of living in their social class.

*Intelligence: Group Tests.* Studies have shown that differences exist in the intelligence test scores of the two social classes (3, 4). Unless we controlled this characteristic, we would be uncertain whether or not it was the real source of any obtained differences between the classes or between boys subjected to different child-rearing practices. In order to be chosen, subjects had to be classified as having an intelligence score of C [3] or above on the schools' placement test, or an intelligence quotient of 75 or above on any of the several tests administered in the school system. This requirement, and the next two as well, were included to make certain that we did not select children with very low levels of intelligence.

*Intelligence: Age in Grade and Primary Mental Abilities.* As another method of eliminating very retarded and very advanced children, we required that a subject's age not deviate by more than one year from the median age for his grade in school. In addition, we administered three subtests from the Chicago Tests of Primary Mental Abilities—those for Verbal Meaning, Reasoning, and Spatial Ability (8). High scores on tests such as those given in the schools depend very much on the adroit use of words. This penalizes boys in the working class who place less value on verbal facility and have less opportunity to develop it than do boys in the middle class. The ability to use words skillfully gives the subjects less of an advantage on the spatial and reasoning sections of the Chicago battery than it does on many other intelligence tests.

*Personality Disorders.* It was necessary that our subjects not be so emotionally handicapped by personal problems as to render them incapable of following instructions adequately. To avoid this possibility, we eliminated children who seemed to their teachers to be emotionally disturbed, or conveyed an impression of severe personality disorder when they were being observed by the investigators.

*Ethnicity, Race, Descent, and Area of Birth.* Only by obtaining subjects from the same cultural background could we be confident that most of them within a particular social class had probably been raised in a similar manner. This led us to avoid choosing boys from special groups whose values and child-rearing

[3] There are five categories, A to E. A score of C signifies average intelligence.

practices may differ from those characteristic of most American families. It was also necessary to reject children from some groups containing drastically fewer families in one class than another. Thus we eliminated boys from Jewish and Negro families, from families descended from eastern and southern European immigrants, and from families in which the parents were born abroad or south of the Mason-Dixon line.[4] We rejected the southern born because most were rural and because we could not be sure that the methods with which they were reared were comparable in meaning to those used in northern states.

*Intactness of Family.* We required that a subject come from an unbroken home. This criterion was introduced to eliminate boys with special experiences resulting from divorce or from the death of a parent.

*Inter-generational Mobility.* Finally, in order to obtain maximal contrasts in child rearing we eliminated children from mobile families: those who live under the economic conditions of one class and emulate the characteristics of another. Such an inconsistency might have profoundly affected child training in various ways. We evaluated the families' mobility in terms of two criteria: inter-generational mobility, and discrepancy between actual and reported social class. The first referred to changes in social class position between our boys' parents and their grandparents. To evaluate the amount of change, we asked each mother for a detailed description of the occupations of her father and her husband's father. Information about the income and education of these men would also have been useful, but we found in early tests of our interview that too few wives knew these facts to justify our asking them. On the bases of information available for each grandfather with an urban occupation, we assigned him a social class placement by fitting him into the Yale classification of occupations. Then we grouped the occupational categories as we had for the fathers, to produce four social class types. Having done this, we compared the occupational levels of fathers with those of paternal and maternal grandfathers.

[4] This line, which can be thought of as running along the southern boundary of Pennsylvania and down the Ohio River to the Mississippi, has been used historically to define the border between the northern and southern states.

*Mobility: Discrepancy Between Actual and Reported Social Class.* At best, the index of inter-generational mobility was a crude one. We feared that it might not be sensitive enough to catch important differences in movement or desire for movement from one social class to another. Hence, we used the classes in which the mothers placed themselves as a supplementary measure of mobility. The second index was obtained from each mother's answers to two questions that we adapted from those of Centers (1). The first required her to identify her social class: "If you were asked to use one of these four names for your social class, in which would you say you belonged: the middle class, lower class, working class, or upper class?" Next we requested her to estimate whether her position was in the lower or upper half of that class. In analyzing the results, we considered "working class" and "lower class" to be synonymous.

For a boy to be included in the study, it was necessary that his mother's subjective estimate of the family's class be within one class level of the objective position, and that the objective status be within one level of the statuses of maternal and paternal grandfathers. By one level, we mean the difference, let us say, between upper middle and lower middle, or between lower middle and upper working classes.

The search for children meeting all of our qualifications was very costly. Once we identified our subjects, we went ahead with our studies with confidence that we had controlled many conditions other than social class which might affect our results. In the case of one condition, verbal intelligence, the control paid extra dividends. As we shall see in Chapter 9, intelligence varies with social class in a special manner which throws light on the origins of denial.

## Some Characteristics of the First Two Samples

This description of our primary criteria covers the highlights of our procedure. Further details about our major decisions and our reasons for making them may be found in Appendix A, which contains a short historical summary of our project, and a description of our methods of selecting subjects and interviewing mothers. We shall now address ourselves to two questions which follow from our listing of criteria: How well did we satisfy our standards, and what kinds of populations did we finally select?

### Social class

*Relative Sizes of the Four Subclasses.* In each sample we tried to obtain the same proportion of children from the upper middle, lower middle, upper working, and lower working classes. We found it was not possible to obtain equal proportions and also satisfy the various criteria. To illustrate our difficulty, let us consider the influence of the criteria of race and ethnicity on the relative proportions of subjects in the four subclasses. We limited our subjects to whites whose families originally came from northern and western Europe. In Detroit there is a sizable concentration of lower middle and upper working class families who fit our criteria, but relatively few upper middle and lower working class families. Although a 1951 survey by *The Detroit News* revealed this unequal distribution, we began our first study on the assumption that the many schools in a large urban area would provide us with enough subjects from each of the four social strata. The results showed that we were too optimistic. Once we had weeded out the children who did not meet all our criteria, we had 15 boys in the upper middle, 26 in the lower middle, 55 in the upper working, and 24 in the lower working categories. In the second year, we were able to increase the proportion of upper middles, but we did even less well than the first time in obtaining lower working-class subjects. Our totals in four strata were 24 in the upper middle, 35 in the lower middle, 34 in the upper working, and 19 in the lower working class.

While the numbers of boys in the upper middle and lower working class are disappointingly small, we find that the proportions of subjects in the four strata are very similar to each other in the two populations. In fact, there are no significant differences.

### Efficacy of controls within the samples

If we had not attempted to control certain variations in the subjects' attributes, they might have contributed to the differences we found between boys from the middle and working classes. The controls of some variables, like sex or race, did not have to be checked since they left no room for variation. The success with which we controlled other variables, like age and intelligence, did have to be determined. Had there been disproportionate numbers of older or brighter boys in the two classes, for example, we would not have been able to tell whether or not differences in age or intelligence accounted for the significant socio-economic difference in motoric orientation. While our results are reported in terms of differences between middle and working class, we tested the efficacy of our controls by making separate comparisons between the two major classes and also among the four subclasses.

According to Table 4-1, which contains a summary of our results, the four social subclasses in both samples contain very

**TABLE 4-1**

Comparisons of Selected Characteristics of Children in Different Social Classes: Controls within First and Second Samples

| | *Significance of Differences* [a] | | | |
|---|---|---|---|---|
| | *Among Four Social Subclasses* | | *Between Middle and Working Class* | |
| *Characteristics of Children* | *First Sample* | *Second Sample* | *First Sample* | *Second Sample* |
| Age [b] | .05 | ns | ns | ns |
| Grade in school | .02 | ns | .01 | ns |
| Verbal intelligence | .01 | .05 | ns | ns |
| Reasoning intelligence | .01 | .05 | ns | ns |
| Spatial intelligence | ns | .01 | ns | ns |
| Family's religious preference | ns | ns | ns | ns |

[a] The chi-square technique for testing independence in contingency tables was used to test the significance of the twenty-four associations. In each case, a test was made of the independence between social class and one of the six characteristics. The four columns list the probabilities that the obtained chi square values could have arisen by chance if there were no associations between social class and particular characteristics. When the probability of chance occurrence exceeds .10, we use the letters *ns* to indicate that the association is not significant and that any trend is negligible.

[b] In computing the significance of each of the six characteristics, we divided it into two or three categories. When there were two categories on a test we divided the population at the median for the entire sample. We divided each sample into two groups on the basis of age. One was thirteen years or less, and the other was fourteen years or more. Grades in school were either seventh, eighth, or ninth, and Verbal, Reasoning, and Spatial scores of intelligence were either high or low. The families' religious preferences were classified as Roman Catholic or Protestant.

similar proportions of Roman Catholics and Protestants. About 80 per cent of the boys in each social class come from Protestant homes and 20 per cent from Roman Catholic families. On each of the remaining controls, there is at least one significant difference. The four subclasses in the first population differ significantly in age, school grade, and scores on the Verbal and Reasoning tests of intelligence. The classes in the second population differ significantly in their performances on the three subtests of intelligence.

## Comparability of Boys in the Two Samples

How similar were boys obtained in different samples and categorized as being in the same social class? In particular, are there any outstanding differences between such populations on the conditions we tried to control? Such comparability was not absolutely necessary to interpret our results, since we did not combine samples nor did we ever do the same study with the two samples. We would have liked to repeat some studies, but the expense of collecting data prompted us to keep exploring new problems. Yet, comparability still seemed desirable since it would help us to make theoretical sense of different findings within the two populations. Furthermore, where we did not obtain comparability, this raised the possibility that some characteristic might not have been held constant in one or both samples. Our data are summarized in Table 4-2, which again contains analyses of differences between subclasses, as well as between total classes.

The most striking finding is the resemblance between the two samples of each social class. Of forty-eight comparisons between subclasses, five are at or beyond the .05 level of probability. By chance, we would expect 2.4. The two differences between total classes reaching an acceptable level of significance are also not far from the chance expectancy of 1.3 So close is the number of differences to the one that we might have expected by chance that we consider the two samples as possessing essentially the same characteristics. We shall now describe the conditions for which the differences are significant.

*Age on Last Birthday and Grade in School.* In the first sample our lower middle-class children were older than the lower middles chosen in 1953. We attributed this difference to the elimination of ninth-grade boys in the second year. This difference

**TABLE 4-2**

Comparisons of Selected Characteristics of Children in Different Social Classes: Controls Between Samples [a]

| Characteristics of Children | *Significance of Differences Between Sample I and Sample II* | | | | | |
|---|---|---|---|---|---|---|
| | *Within Each Social Subclass* | | | | *Within Each Social Class* | |
| | *Upper Middle* | *Lower Middle* | *Upper Working* | *Lower Working* | *Middle* | *Working* |
| Age | ns | .01 | ns | ns | .01 | ns |
| Grade in school | ns | .05 | ns | .01 | ns | ns |
| Verbal intelligence | ns | ns | ns | ns | ns | ns |
| Reasoning intelligence | ns | ns | ns | ns | ns | ns |
| Spatial intelligence | ns | ns | ns | ns | ns | ns |
| Family's religious preference | ns | ns | ns | ns | ns | ns |
| Father's education | ns | ns | ns | ns | ns | ns |
| Father's occupation (Yale index) | ns | ns | ns | ns | ns | ns |
| Father's occupation (census classification) | ns | .02 | ns | ns | .05 | ns |
| Mobility from maternal grandfather's objective social class | ns | ns | ns | ns | ns | ns |
| Mobility from paternal grandfather's objective social class | ns | ns | ns | ns | ns | ns |
| Mother's subjective social class | ns | ns | .05 | ns | ns | ns |

[a] Because of the high cost of reproduction, the seventy-two tables from which these results were derived are not included in the appendix. Interested readers may obtain them from the authors.

between the two samples probably accounts for the fact that the lower middle-class boys in our first population came from later school grades than boys in the second population. We find, in addition, that lower working-class boys in the former group were concentrated in the eighth as well as the ninth grade, while, in the latter, such boys were largely seventh graders. These differences between the samples do not appear to be serious. They probably would not have contributed any significant amount of error in comparisons between samples since we matched our groups for intelligence and chronological age, and applied a rough control for age-within-grade in selecting the children.

*Census Classification of Fathers' Occupations.* When we first examined the interview data, we got the impression that there was a difference in the distribution of fathers' occupations of our middle-class boys in the first and second samples, and that the Yale occupational index [5] was masking the difference by combining such diverse groups as managers and professionals. We found that our impression was correct when we retabulated fathers' occupations according to the categories of the United States Census. The significant difference between the two lower middle-class samples was produced by two factors: the presence of some semi-skilled laborers in the first group and their total absence in the second, and a sharp rise in the proportion of salesmen in the second. Since, for the total samples, the fathers' educations were very similar, the presence of blue-collar occupations among lower middle-class fathers in the first population indicates that some of these lower middles were not well established in their class. They probably resembled those in the upper working class more than did the lower middles in the second sample. If this atypical character of our first group of lower middles had any affect on our results, it probably made it harder to validate our predictions of difference between the lower middle and upper working classes, and between the entire middle and entire working classes. Since this difference between our first and second samples of lower middles minimizes the probable significance of our predictions, we were inclined to ignore it when our data revealed the trends we expected.

*Subjective Social Class.* As compared with the second sample, significantly more upper working-class mothers in the first group said that they were in the lower working class. If these judgments of the boys' mothers stood for real differences in hopes for future advancement in upper working-class homes of the two populations, they required special controls of our data. The judgments might, for example, have accentuated the differences be-

[5] This has been described in Chapter 2.

tween subjects in the upper working and lower middle classes or between all working and all middle class subjects in the first sample. In analyzing our results we have, therefore, gone back to examine the possible effect of this difference on our data. We have not found that its control had a significant effect.

## Methods of Child Rearing in the Middle and Working Class

Just how do parents in different social classes compare in their methods of rearing children? On this point the descriptive literature compiled by various students of society (2, 5, 7) is fairly clear. Parents in the working class are typically pictured as losing emotional control and as favoring corporal punishment, infrequent explanations of requests, but later and milder methods of oral and anal training. To our knowledge, methods of reward have not been described in the literature on child rearing, but we guessed that, in line with the reported predilections of blue-collar workers for concrete thinking and for harsh methods of discipline, the parents would give concrete and infrequent rewards.

Parents in the middle class are usually pictured as retaining emotional control even when very disturbed, favoring appeals to guilt, explaining requests for obedience, and initiating oral and anal training early and by harsh methods. We anticipated that rewards by these parents would be symbolic and frequent. The obtained differences between boys in the two social classes agree with the expectations. As indicated by the data reported in Table 4-3, all the associations are significant and in the predicted directions.

How independent is the class difference in a parental practice of the relation between that practice and others? If, for example, early weaning and psychological manipulation were done by the same women, then if one of the two practices were held constant, the other would no longer discriminate significantly between subjects in the middle and working classes. We determined the extent to which a class difference in one practice was independent of the effect of others by reanalyzing the relation within the categories of every other practice. Thus we separately analyzed the class differences in obedience within the groups giving frequent and occasional rewards; and we separately analyzed the class differences in control within the groups using different kinds of discipline. After reanalyzing all ten relations, we find that nine remain significant when other child-rearing practices are held constant. The exception is frequency of reward, which is no longer

TABLE 4-3

Social Class and Child-Rearing Practices

| *Child-Rearing Practice Related to Social Class* | *Trends: Boxes with Largest Frequencies* [a] | *N* | $\chi^2$ | *Probability* [b] |
|---|---|---|---|---|
| First sample | | | | |
| Discipline | WC and corporal discipline; MC and psychological discipline | 115 | 49.45 | <.001 |
| Type of reward | WC and no reward or concrete reward | 115 | 29.52 | <.001 |
| Mother's emotional control | WC and lack of control | 115 | 5.05 | .02 |
| Second sample | | | | |
| Type of discipline | MC and psychological discipline | 105 | 6.08 | <.05 |
| Frequency of reward | WC and occasional reward | 77 | 2.69 | .05 |
| Requests for obedience | WC and arbitrary requests | 81 | 9.40 | <.001 |
| Weaning | MC and early weaning | 103 | 5.26 | .01 |
| Toliet training | MC and coercive training | 104 | 2.83 | <.05 |

[a] WC and MC are the initials of working class and middle class.
[b] All probabilities were obtained by means of one-tailed tests.

significantly associated with social class when harshness of weaning is held constant. We are inclined to explain the lack of significance in terms of the fallibility of our measure of reward.

## The Third Population

A study of the association between sex identity and reactions to conflict required the selection of another population. For this research we decided to use male college students. We felt that it is not until late adolescence that a person's sex identity becomes crystallized. A younger group was also precluded by our plan to arouse the subjects sexually, a method which could not have been used in the secondary schools where the staffs are usually very sensitive to the possibility of parental criticism. College students are accustomed to unusual procedures. When asked not to discuss an experiment, they usually comply if they are promised a later explanation of the purposes and results of the study.

SELECTION OF SUBJECTS

We obtained most of our men from the Army, Air Force, and Navy R.O.T.C. program of the University of Michigan. We also recruited volunteers from two classes in the Department of Physical Education. Compared to the University population, our sample had proportionately almost three times as many freshmen and twice as many sophomores. In addition, it had approximately twice as many students in the schools of engineering and business administration. The ages of the men varied between sixteen and twenty-four years, and the majority fell between eighteen and twenty-one.

For reasons cited at the beginning of this chapter, we decided to restrict our population to men. This is why we chose subjects from classes in R.O.T.C. and Physical Education.

Non-whites were eliminated from our sample, because they differ from the population on whom tests of sex identity have been standardized. Other races may also differ from whites in their early experiences and, consequently, in their definition of masculinity and femininity. We also picked only men born in the United States because we wanted a group from one society.

Because we could not foretell the possible effect of marriage on expressions of femininity, we restricted our sample to unmarried students. Finally, we used only subjects who lived with both biological parents during at least four of the first six years of life. Constant contact with the same adults should have facilitated identification with a masculine and a feminine figure during the formative years. We obtained the necessary information about the subjects' backgrounds from a questionnaire that they filled out after taking the two tests of masculinity-femininity.

## Defining three patterns

Upon examining the test scores of the 522 men in the initial pool, we selected the MMs, FMs, and FFs.[6] To identify our two unconsciously feminine groups, we first chose all subjects in roughly the upper or feminine quartile [7] of the range of scores on the Franck Drawing Completion Test. Then we labeled as FFs all of these men who were also in the upper 32 per cent of the scores on the Gough Femininity scale. This group had the most feminine scores on both tests. We labeled as FMs those subjects who had scores in the highest or feminine quartile on the Franck tests and who were in the lowest 36 per cent of the Gough scale. Their unconscious scores were at the feminine extreme; their conscious scores at the masculine extreme.

Our conception of mature men led us to select the MMs on the basis of masculine scores that were not extreme on either test. In our society it is advantageous for the normal male to have some feminine traits, such as an interest in social nuances or a readiness to wait for others to take initiative. The mature man does not reject these, but integrates them with his other behavior. It does not threaten him to consider the interests of others or to be passive at the appropriate times. Only some FMs have to reject all traits that are not masculine. Since these men must make strenuous attempts to control their unconscious femininity, they cannot tolerate the display of interests, expressive gestures, or actions that may be characteristic of women. On the Franck test the MMs varied between the thirteenth and fiftieth percentiles. On the Gough test, they varied between the eighteenth and thirty-seventh percentiles. It would be more accurate to refer to this group as MfMf, to indicate that we selected them from the non-feminine end, but not the extreme of either range of scores. For convenience, we have shortened the code to the letters that are comparable to the labels of the other groups.

[6] Given the values of our society, we did not expect to find MFs except through some error in our tests or the unlikely condition that a boy was first raised by very mature parents and then shifted to a very neurotic pair after the first years of childhood. In a sample of 522 cases there were three MFs.

[7] Actually it was 28.5 per cent. Our cutting points were determined by the necessity of getting as many extreme cases as possible, as well as by the clustering of scores.

## Summary

In this chapter we have outlined our methods of selecting three samples, and have described their characteristics. In our first two, which were used in studies of social class and reactions to conflict, we tried, with only partial success, to obtain an equal number of cases from each of the social subclasses. To control conditions other than social class, we chose boys from the junior high school level who resided in the metropolitan area of Detroit. In order to be included in our samples, each boy had to be within one year of the median age for his grade, above borderline intelligence, free from serious emotional disturbance, white, Christian, descended from immigrants who came from northwestern Europe, born in the northern states, from a nonmobile family. In addition, his eligibility depended on his parents having been born in the northern part of the United States. On comparing the first two samples, we found them similar on most characteristics requiring control in a study of conflict. To be eligible for the last sample, which was used in investigations of sex identity and reactions to conflict, a person had to be a white, an unmarried male, an undergraduate at the University of Michigan, and an American by birth. It was also necessary for him to have lived with both of his biological parents during four of his first six years, and to have obtained certain combinations of scores on the Gough and Franck tests of masculinity-femininity.

## References

1. Centers, R. *The psychology of social classes.* Princeton: Princeton Univ. Press, 1949.
2. Davis, A. Child training and social class. In Barker, R. G., Kounin, I. S., & Wright, H. E. (Eds.), *Child behavior and development.* New York: McGraw-Hill, 1943.
3. Eells, K., Davis, A., *et al. Intelligence and cultural differences.* Chicago: Univ. of Chicago Press, 1951.
4. Havighurst, R. J., & Janke, Leota L. Relations between ability and social status in a midwestern community: I. ten-year-old children. *J. educ. Psychol.,* 1944, *35,* 357–68.

5. Miller, D. R., & Swanson, G. E. *The changing American parent.* New York: Wiley, 1958.
6. Osborn, R. C. How is intellectual performance related to social and economic background? *J. educ. Psychol.,* 1943, *34,* 215–28.
7. Sears, R. R., Maccoby, Eleanor, & Levin, H. *Patterns of child rearing.* New York: Row, Peterson, 1958.
8. Thurstone, L. L., & Thurstone, Thelma G. *The Chicago tests of primary mental abilities.* Chicago: Science Research Associates, 1943.

# PART FOUR

# RESULTS

# 5

## MORAL STANDARDS

### I. Needs and Moral Standards

How can one ever hope to describe adequately the network of forces that creates a conflict, and the endless variety of methods for resolving it? For purpose of description, the tools of the poet are sometimes far superior to those of the scientist. A far clearer picture of the guilts, of the overwhelming anxieties and anguish, and of the defensive self-deceptions associated with conflict may be gained by reading *Hamlet* than by reading an account of a controlled experiment. But the empirical investigator of personality is not interested solely in description. He seeks explanations. He tries to establish connections between various types of observation—between social class and a defense, or between a child-rearing practice and a moral need—so that he can predict how his subjects will act in similar circumstances in the future.

Before the investigator can make a prediction, he must decide on the definitions of his variables. This is a matter of no small importance, since the phrasing of hypotheses determines the form of the results.

As our first task, then, we had to decide on criteria for identifying our basic concepts. At the core of this task was the definition of need. Conflicts may involve incompatible needs. Internalized moral standards define the acceptability of various expressions of needs. Certain defenses facilitate self-deception about the nature of one's needs. Expressive styles often reflect particular ways of satisfying needs, and may affect the selection of substitutes when conflict occurs. In short, our primary concepts hinge, in great part, on the definition of need.

This chapter is divided into two sections. In the first section we will propose a set of categories for identifying and classifying needs. The categories provide us with a taxonomy which we will later use to classify morals and defenses. In the second section of the chapter we take up the topic of moral standards. As before, we will present somewhat more than we investigated in our studies because we wish to give a picture of the theoretical context within which our work has grown.

## Need

Having stressed the significance of need, we must now face the painful fact that there is no consensus among social scientists as to the meaning of the term. For that matter, there is not even a convention concerning a label. The literature on motivated behavior contains such varied words as *drive, need, motive, value, attitude,* and *role*. There are many others. While these terms have some overlapping meanings, they also point to important theoretical disagreements.

On first examination, the major motivational theories seem either so contradictory or so unrelated to each other as to discourage any attempt at a synthesis or a rational choice among them. A further study of the various points of view, however, indicates that they usually differ in only a limited number of ways. Certain differences refer to levels of discourse: If the problem is defined in physiological terms, the concepts are naturally integrated with others pertaining to organic functions; if the problem is defined in terms of personal experience, the concepts are integrated with others which are derived from subjects' reports.

These observations contain a lesson for any investigators who plan to study needs. Obviously, no systematic position has been supported by enough empirical data to convince most of the experts. Furthermore, the fact that many definitions of need seem to be unrelated to each other signifies that the proponents are working on different problems and not that they are in fundamental disagreement. Since there are no absolute criteria, the investigator must choose the theoretical position which is most helpful in clarifying the problems he hopes to study.

In its most general form, our problem was: What causes people who cannot express a need directly to differ in their choices of substitutes? We investigated three different processes which might explain the process of substitution: moral standards, defenses, and expressive styles. We thought that each would contribute to the selection of alternative expressions of a need.

If we were to benefit from the concept of need, it was necessary that our definition help us to visualize the components of conflict and their interrelationships more clearly than we might otherwise. In evaluating the different theoretical positions,[1] we found that some involved issues which were not crucial to the problems we intended to pursue. One such issue, for example, concerned the innate components of certain motivated acts. Another concerned the strengths of various needs. Some of the issues were very germane to our problems. They required decisions about the levels at which concepts are defined, assumptions about the concept of energy, and the choice between a contemporaneous and a historical orientation to one's problems.

### Some issues involved in defining needs

*Levels of Discourse.* Some theorists work with physiological concepts whose meanings are derived from organs and their functions. Other theorists phrase their problems in behavioral terms. Inferences are made from observable performance about the strength of a motive or of anxiety. A third group of theorists phrase their problems in experiential terms.[2] These investigators concentrate on the experience of the perceiver. Since information about percepts is derived from behavior, we do not regard experience as being on a level separate from behavior.

There are no inherent advantages or disadvantages in any of the three approaches, and a particular investigator's choice typically depends on his problems and theoretical predilections. From the

[1] The Achievement Motive (15) contains a summary of the issues and the different points of view.

[2] This approach is sometimes called phenomenology. We avoid this term only because it is often restricted to conscious awareness. Our interest in defenses involved us in research on the unconscious reactions of our subjects.

subject's behavior, we made inferences about his conscious and unconscious experiences.

*Energy.* A second issue that must be settled before a need can be defined concerns the nature of energy. Older theorists, like Freud (3) and McDougall (16), assumed that there is a moderate level of tension which is characteristic of an organism in balance. As they pictured the individual, he is usually quiescent, and he has available a reservoir of energy. A need arises when some sensory signals or stimuli upset the normal balance. According to Freud, for example, the stimuli open the sluice gates of the reservoir and liberate the power. It is then applied to activities which eliminate the stimuli.

In devising our studies, we were influenced more by theoretical systems which assume that energy is always available (11, 13, 18, 23). Hence, its arousal does not have to be explained. According to this point of view, stimuli do not transform potential to kinetic energy, but, rather, are selected by the organism. They then focus the effort of the individual in one direction rather than another. Given these assumptions, the emphasis in the phrasing of problems tends to shift from: "Where did the energy come from?" to "In what direction and to what ends is the energy being applied?" [3]

*The Contemporaneous versus the Historical Approach.* One other decision affected the definitions of our concepts. A prediction can be phrased in at least two ways. It can be phrased in

[3] It was necessary for us to take a position on the question of energy because it is so central to the psychoanalytic account of conflict. Substitution is usually viewed as a change in the distribution of energy. Some psychoanalysts regard defenses as mechanisms for changing the quantities of energy available to needs in conflict (20). Certain kinds of conflict are commonly explained as a damming up of the organism with the result that there are no adequate energy outlets (7). Some psychoanalysts (9, 10) view normality as the ability to "neutralize" the energy of forbidden needs. Contrary to the usual meaning of the word, in this case, neutralization does not seem to refer to a canceling of energy, but to its diversion from antisocial to approved and productive forms of expression. It is also assumed that the new outlets, unlike the usual indirect ones, permit the expression of as much energy as do the most direct outlets. The general conception of energy underlying these concepts of conflict is patterned after the homeostatic models developed in the early part of this century. Its inadequacies are being recognized by many specialists, among them some psychoanalysts (4, 12), and it requires modification to conform with the more recent findings of physiologists (11).

terms of the forces of the immediate situation, or in terms of antecedents. In other words, we can do a contemporaneous or a historical analysis. If we investigate the relation between denial and current popularity in school, our problem is a contemporaneous one. If we investigate the association between denial and earlier child-rearing practices, we are testing an historical hypothesis. While we paid considerable attention to contemporaneous events in our research, we phrased most of our hypotheses as relationships between our subjects' current reactions and indices which, while most of them were current, were significant because of what they indicated about past experiences. Representative of such indices are social class, child rearing, and sex identity.

## Classifying Needs

The problems of identifying needs and classifying them become paramount as soon as we prepare to interpret any sample of motivated behavior. Suppose we are trying to make sense of a child's imaginative story. Until we decide on the variables in which we are primarily interested, and define them in a manner that permits objective recording, we cannot identify the needs embedded in the story. Without criteria for identifying particular needs, we cannot determine whether a story about a dragon eating a man is an expression of hostility, hunger, guilt, passivity, possibly all four, or still other themes. Until we can establish a basis for identifying needs and for grouping them, we cannot begin to think of predicting alternative expressions of needs, of defining moral standards about needs, or of studying defenses against them. In our research we found that the most fruitful way to picture a need is as a system of *action tendencies,* all of which implement the same *goal state* or *end state.* Like the top of a mountain, the goal state can be reached by many pathways. If one path is blocked, another must be taken. While it may be more tortuous, it leads to the same terminus. In order for the end state to stimulate action, there must be a *discrepancy* between it and the *current state.* Let us assume that a man is hungry. Certain stimuli, either internal or external, in the present situation point up the contrast between hunger and satiety and create a disposition to eliminate it. Stimuli define the need in terms of the person's anticipated gains. In other words, hunger pangs or the sight of food stimulate the quest for a meal. Usually, the stimuli arouse affective reactions: the hunger pangs become upsetting. The affect elicits images of actions which can bridge the gap. From past experience, the man associates these actions with the achievement of the end state and a change in his affective state. In terms of our example if hunger pangs have begun to upset him, and he takes the steps necessary to obtain any of a variety of foods, he can end his unpleasant condition. Because the information about these steps is acquired, we think of the organization of all need systems, even those with certain built in structural components, as being learned. Since people are usually learning new ways to fulfill old needs, all needs may be viewed as constantly changing.

In summary, a need is a system of action tendencies all of which implement the same end state. The action tendencies are organized in an order of preference, but any one of them can be substituted for any other without changing the goal state. The goal state gives meaning to the interrelationships among the action tendencies. Hence, it is our basis for defining a particular need.

Many taxonomies have been proposed, and it may help to highlight the characteristics of ours if we stress the differences between it and others. The primary difference results from our disinclination to view need solely in terms of the characteristics of action tendencies. Unlike some investigators, we do not define it in terms of the act used to attain the end state: We do not speak of a need to expel or to hurt. We do not identify the need in terms of the object acted upon: We do not speak of a need for music or for clothes. We do not identify the need in terms of the stimulating condition, either internal or external: We do not speak of a hunger need. We define needs only by their end states, the goals of the action. Thus, for example, we do speak of needs to attain orgasm, to achieve increased social status, and to eliminate the source of irritation. These are commonly labeled as sexual, ambitious, and aggressive.

But how are we to recognize a need? We cannot answer the question by armchair reasoning. We must identify the goal or end state by empirical means. To do this, we require two kinds of information. We have to find the stimuli which initiate the striving for an end state. We must also locate the group of action tendencies, all of which serve the same end state and may be substituted for each other with reference to it.

These are not simple tasks. The number of possible actions which may be used to achieve an end state is usually very large. In addition, we know barely enough about the principles of substitution to estimate the ways in which such clusters are learned and in which the ordering of action tendencies develops. Some of these principles are described in Chapter 13. Until each system is established by empirical test, we cannot be confident about the identity of any particular need.

Despite our uncertainty, we have had to choose some needs arbitrarily in our studies of conflict. We have selected two needs, or clusters of action tendencies. For each there is some evidence of substitution within the cluster. To avoid confusion, we refer to these need systems by their conventional labels of "aggression" and "ambition." As we view the goal of the former, it is the annihilation of a certain class of noxious stimuli. The end state of ambition probably involves the attainment of a particular social status. We imagine that empirical studies will ultimately modify our pictures of both systems. We have some faith, however, that the action tendencies we have studied are interrelated in ways which satisfy our conception of need: The members of each system have an identical goal.

To illustrate the complexity of the systems that we have called needs, let us consider three examples. Even in the case of a relatively "simple" need, such as eliminating hunger pangs, the possible actions can vary considerably. The variety of edible objects is tremendous. So are the individual acts which may be involved in obtaining the food and in eating it. And many kinds of affective states may result from the appeal and meaning of the different foods and acts.

There is an even greater variety of alternate paths to sexual gratification. We may classify as sexual all the actions "which tend specifically to lead up to, and . . . to accompany the reproductive act or such substitutive acts as may give gratification of a kind that is usually associated with the act" (8). The range of possibilities includes most of the phenomena of courtship, of romantic love, of autoeroticism, and of perversion.

Still greater complexity may be found in needs which are not limited by man's inherent structure and functions. A man may implement a complex end state, such as increased social status, by buying an expensive car, improving his education, moving to a more prosperous part of town, and myriad other actions. And even within American society the potential expressions vary in different groups depending on their socio-economic, religious, and other characteristics. Some members of the working class, for example, buy television aerials or have gold caps put on their teeth. In other societies there are further variations. Despite this diversity, if we patiently consider a particular individual, we can determine the actions which may serve to increase his status.

While the variety of potential actions is very great, it usually is considerably reduced by the actualities of a real situation. Only some of the alternatives are available. This becomes obvious if we consider the anger of a pedestrian who has just been splashed by a passing motorist. Within the pedestrian's repertory are such possibilities as doing physical harm to the motorist, giving him constructive suggestions concerning his driving habits, calling him insulting names, and making sarcastic comments. In the actual encounter only some of these are feasible. Before the pedestrian can do more than take a breath, the motorist has departed; the victim may fulminate or fume to himself, but there is little he can do that involves the other person.

The resolution of conflict involves the substitution of certain action tendencies for others. The latter are higher on the hierarchy of preference, but they are proscribed by moral standards. Certain clusters are selected from among the acceptable alternatives because of a tendency to favor one defense over another or one expressive style over another. An explanation of the process of substitution requires some conception of the nature of action tendencies. In the remainder of this chapter we shall first elaborate the meaning of action tendencies, and then use them to define moral standards.

## Dimensions of Action Tendencies

All the action tendencies of a need have an order of preference with respect to the goal state. If he could, the pedestrian would probably prefer to punish the stranger who splashes mud as he unconcernedly rides by. Since this is not possible, the pedestrian must seek another outlet for his anger. If he is mature, he has little choice but to express himself privately or seek outlets in fantasy. If he is immature, he may displace his aggression to a child, or he may develop suspicions of the motives of all people who drive cars.

If we knew more about the characteristics of various action tendencies of a need, we might be able to describe the conditions under which they can be substituted for each other. Some dimensions of action tendencies may be found in the commonsense definitions of the layman. If asked to define an impulse, the average man would probably start by speaking of an inner urge or sense of want. If pressed further, he would then begin to speak in terms of the components of action tendencies. He might name an object required to terminate the urge, he might describe the acts necessary to attain the object, and he might discuss his feelings when the impulse is aroused. His descriptive terms would naturally fall into the three categories of *act, object,* and *affect*. We add the fourth category of *agent* to help us in analyzing moral standards and defenses. This refers to the person who is responsible for the action tendency. Certain moral standards permit us to be aware of an action tendency so long as it is not ours, and certain defenses help us to distort the awareness of our connection with forbidden objects, affects, acts, and agents.

The four categories are easily illustrated. Let us suppose that a manual laborer has suddenly become conscious of the higher social status and standard of living of a friend with more education. If, at this time, we ask the laborer to make up stories about events depicted in some vague pictures, he may recount a plot in which the hero (agent) wants to study (intended act) engineering (object). Associated with this theme may be an affective state like envy. At some level the laborer is aware that his end state is the improvement of social status, but he may not think in such terms. He can report the components of his action tendency. If asked, he can point out that the wish is his, he can describe what he would like to do, he can talk about the area of study, and he may be able to describe his feelings.

Each dimension consists of a number of elements, all of which are organized in an order of preference based on their relative efficiency in implementing the goal state of the need. It is the elements within dimensions which are the building blocks of action tendencies. If any element is selected from each of the different kinds of dimensions and then all four are combined, the result is an action tendency that can conceivably implement the goal state. The many possible combinations of individual agents, acts, affects, and objects show why a particular need can subsume so many action tendencies.

We have stated that the dimensions can be helpful in categorizing moral standards, defenses, and expressive styles. Before we can define such categories, however, we must examine certain aspects of action tendencies in greater detail.

### Intended act

The most obvious aspects of any action tendency is the urge to engage in some action that may achieve the goal state of the need—to eat, to hurt, to praise, to buy, to make love, and so forth. In fact, needs are sometimes classified in terms of actions: ". . . to reject, to exclude, to expel . . ." (19). But, as we have said, a need is a system which may be served by many acts. To illustrate this point, we consider the anger of a worker. He has just been transferred from a job requiring very fine visual discrimination to a lower paying one because his deteriorating eyesight was reported by a foreman. The employee thinks his work is as good as ever, and is very angry at the foreman. There is a range of possible acts that would express his need at the employee's disposal. One is physical attack. But this is hardly the only alternative. He can also insult his superior to his face, comment sarcastically on his loyalty, or spread malicious gossip about him. The employee can also express his anger very indirectly. For example, he can volunteer a helpful analysis of the organization's deficiencies. The different acts are elements in a dimension which is organized in terms of a need system of aggression. While the specific order of elements in a dimension of intended acts can be determined only empirically, it has certain general characteristics. Other things being equal, for example, the more efficient the element is in implementing the goal state, the more direct it seems, and the more it is preferred. If the employee does not fear retaliation or the pressure of his conscience, he probably expresses his anger most adequately by some attempt to inflict pain. In that event, he is not very inclined to insult the foreman, and constructive criticism is probably low in his order of preference. Other actions, such as reading a book about the feeding of dogs or the playing of the trumpet, are probably not in the employee's hierarchy of action tendencies since they are not relevant to the goal state of the need.[4]

### Object

In order to predict the action tendencies that an individual in conflict may substitute for those he most prefers, we must also take the dimensions of objects into account. Act and object are complementary. Neither can occur without the other. If the act is eating, there must be an edible object; if the act is hurting, the object must be capable of being damaged or suffering pain; if the act is purchasing, the object must be a commodity. Unless the man does something to an object, he cannot attain the end state. If the object is lacking, he keeps striving until he gains access to it or to a substitute. If the goal state requires avoidance, the need persists until the object is removed.

An act requires an object, but not a particular one. Any of a large number of objects can satisfy a need. The hungry man can eat a large variety of foods. The angry man can attack many objects. Like acts, the elements in a dimension of objects can be ranked in order of preference with respect to their appropriateness to the end state. The employee would most prefer to hurt his foreman. But if this object is too frightening or violates a moral standard, the aggression can be satisfied less directly by being shifted to another object, such as the employee's wife, or an enemy.

[4] It would have helped us to analyze expressive style if we had some method of classifying acts. However, we could find no fruitful system. Theorists have proposed a number of schemes for reducing all acts to a number of general categories. One popular method divides all acts into those that involve an approach and those that involve an avoidance of the object (14, 17). More ambitious systems divide acts in terms of relationships to the object: incorporation, elimination, retention, and bestowal (19, 22). In our research on expressive style we examined the origins of predilections for action within such categories as motoric-conceptual, directness of expression, and degree of passivity. They are discussed in Chapter 13.

### Affect

To satisfy a need, the act must produce a change in the affect. If an angry man strikes another, he stops being angry and feels gratified. If a fearful man runs away, he is no longer afraid and feels relieved. The anticipation of a desired change in the affective state arouses images of techniques for achieving the goal state. Whether or not they lead to action depends on a number of other conditions of which we cite two. The first is the presence of an appropriate object and the opportunity to engage in an act relevant to the goal state of the need. A man can imagine that he is kissing a beautiful actress, but he cannot do it unless she is actually present and cooperative. Second, the expression of the idea in action depends on the absence of conflicting needs. If the man who wants to kiss the actress cannot allow himself to picture the act because it would make him feel too guilty, he may not express his impulse even if the actress is present and cooperative.

Affect is another dimension which can vary and still implement the goal state. When he sees his foreman, the man who thinks he has been unfairly treated may express his anger in different ways: by livid hatred, irritation, or bland indifference. Under certain conditions, he may even satisfy the need by being very affectionate. Among members of the American middle class, the hierarchy is close to the order in which these affects have been listed. It may differ in members of particular religious, socioeconomic, and ethnic groups.

### Agent

The fourth dimension of action tendencies, the agent, is so obvious that it is often overlooked. It is the perceived origin, or location in space, of the action tendency. If a man is reporting his own impulse, he realizes, if he is not distorting it, that he is the agent. He thinks, "I want to do it."

The perception of agent is important to the psychology of conflict because some moral standards make it difficult to take responsibility for one's own forbidden action tendencies. In addition, some defenses facilitate the disowning of one's impulses. Just how this is done is easily understood if we examine the process whereby a child learns to discriminate between himself and others.

Most people do not have to think very much to decide whether a particular need is or is not one of theirs. The normal adult can tell this very easily. But this ability has to be learned. Observations of infants indicate that they are not born with the awareness of a self or even of a body with boundaries. These concepts require a number of complex skills which the child masters only after long months of practice. First he learns to distinguish among his various needs. Then he becomes acquainted with the parts of his body. As he uses his body, he gradually comes to discriminate events within him from those outside him. Social experience next teaches him that there are other people like himself, and that they have needs similar to his. Finally, he learns the concepts and words that contribute to his awareness of self and its distinction from nonself. Only then can he know that he is the agent of a particular impulse.

Given the appropriate conditions, any learned skill can be inhibited. As in the case of the intended act, affect, and object, the perceived agent can shift and still satisfy the goal state to some extent. A man may suffer so much from the awareness of an antisocial need that he unconsciously defends himself against the knowledge by falling back to a less differentiated stage of perception. Then he cannot discern the fact that he is the agent. If the employee is very guilty about his hatred, he can attribute it to any one of a possible group of people, including the foreman. Then he can disown it in himself. We will have more to say about this kind of distortion in the chapter on the classification of defenses.

## Moral Standards

As a child matures, he internalizes many kinds of standards. There are standards about aggression, accomplishment, efficiency, and many other aspects of behavior. Standards are often divided into moral and nonmoral categories. Standards about aggression, for example, are usually viewed in moral terms, but standards about accomplishment are seldom conceived in this manner. The principles discussed in the remainder of this chapter apply to all standards in most instances; for the sake of clarity, we confine our illustrations to the moral area. As we shall see, morality is inseparable from motivation and action, which is why standards are so readily categorized in terms of the dimensions of needs. In addition to classification, we shall also consider the meaning of concepts which enter into our research on internalized moral standards. The terms are *moral, guilt, extensity,* and *severity.*[5]

Were it not for moral standards, the most direct path to the goal state would usually be taken and there would be no conflict. But if the most direct action tendency is proscribed, another must be substituted. Moreover, the alternative must be morally acceptable. An explanation of substitutes is thus not possible without an analysis of a person's internalized standards. If they define many activities as immoral, for example, he suffers from more frequent conflict and has fewer available substitutes than the man whose standards define fewer activities as immoral.

### Definition of morality

Before we continue, we must define a *moral* standard. Our definition includes four criteria. First, the term involves obligations to act or to inhibit action. Ugliness is not immoral, but stealing from the poor is. Second, for an activity to be conceived in moral terms, it must be susceptible to deliberate choice or rejection. Undesirable behavior is not considered immoral if it is the product of coercion. Third, the choice must be relevant to the ultimate welfare of the community, or some large part of it. Fourth, the action is judged in terms of a scale of commonly shared values. Positive action that promotes the community's welfare, or the inhibition of acts or action tendencies that may endanger it, are labeled with words like "right" and "good." A man may be regarded as virtuous if he contributes a substantial portion of his income to the poor, or if he never says a harsh word to his neighbors. Actions that endanger the community's welfare are labeled "wrong" or "evil." Stealing money from a blind man elicits universal condemnation.

The same moral rule can often be phrased either positively or negatively: it is good to tell the truth, it is a sin to tell a lie; it is good to acquire property honestly, it is evil to acquire it dishonestly. Many mothers are inclined to phrase moral precepts

[5] Our formulations have been influenced by those of Allinsmith (2), who develops the implications of these concepts in greater detail, although in slightly different language.

more often as prohibitions than as positive ideals. The injunction "Don't be a tattletale" is more common than the offering of rewards for keeping confidences; the admonition "This is not yours" is more common than praise for self-control. When we discuss conflict in the following section, we use negative definitions to illustrate our ideas about classifying moral standards. We do this because so many conflicts are initiated by moral prohibitions. Since negative definitions are so pertinent to the arousal of conflict, we have also concentrated on them in our two investigations of internalized standards.

## Moral Standards and Dimensions of Action Tendencies

We have included acts and impulses in the province of moral norms. It is probably in the course of internalizing them that a child becomes sensitized to the dimensions of all action tendencies. Many moral standards define the adults' rules for rewarding and punishing behavior. If a little boy does not restrict his behavior to the acts, affects, agents, and objects which are idealized in these rules, he is in trouble.

We may illustrate the connections between moral standards and the learning of dimensions by citing some hypothetical experiences of the American middle-class child. If he hits his sister, the repeated phrase "Don't hurt your *sister,*" which accompanies his parents' punishment, soon makes him aware that female siblings are among the forbidden *objects* of direct aggression. Such questions as "Did you *tease* the cat?" similarly impress him with the importance of avoiding a particular class of *acts*. The sharp injunction "Stop that *temper tantrum!*" teaches him that, regardless of the provocation, a temper tantrum is a form of forbidden display of *affect*. And questions that stress responsibility—"Did *you* mark up this book?"—make him painfully aware that he would not have been punished if someone else had been the *agent* of the act. In short, he learns that certain acts, objects, and affects are forbidden. If any of these are discernible in his behavior, he is punished. If he resists them, he may be rewarded. Since the moral rules are usually applied with some consistency and over a long period of time, he finally internalizes them.

DIMENSIONS AND EXTENSITY

To account for the relationship between a moral standard and a substitution, we need information not only about the dimension of a need to which the standard applies, but also the range of morally proscribed elements within the dimension. We use the term *extensity* to describe the range of a standard. To illustrate the meaning of extensity, we now return to the employee who has been relieved of his job. We have noted that he can express his anger at the foreman in varied ways, that we can analyze each of his action tendencies in terms of four dimensions, and that we can arrange the elements of each dimension in an order of preference with respect to the goal state. We must analyze his moral standards in terms of relevant dimensions and extensity to understand his final action.

Some standards apply only to a single, most preferred act. Instances are the Commandments "Thou shalt not kill" and "Thou shalt not steal." More extensive standards forbid a range of acts rather than just the ultimate one. An example is the American middle-class standard that condemns any kind of physical attack unless another attacks first. If the employee has internalized this standard, he cannot engage in any kind of physical attack on the foreman without feeling guilty.

Standards can be even more extensive. If the employee becomes guilty when he undertakes any acts except those which do good for his enemies, he has no recourse but to help the foreman.

Extensity may also apply to objects and to affects. Some standards specify the object: "Do not covet thy neighbor's wife." Other standards proscribe an entire range of objects. "Thou shalt not kill" connotes "all living things." "Let him who is without sin cast the first stone" rules out the blaming of any person.

There are similar variations in ranges of prohibited affects. Sometimes, a moral standard applies to a particular emotional state such as envy or lust. At other times it covers a group of affects. If the angry employee has internalized the very extensive standard of loving his enemies, he cannot manifest such affects as hatred, irritation, or coldness without becoming guilty.

Finally, there is a range of prohibited agents. Sometimes

a child is told he may not engage in an act, such as telling a lie, even though it is done with impunity by older people or those in another social class. He may also discover that he can view only certain people as agents and not others. If he blames a forbidden childish act on an imaginary companion or a mature person, he is not believed; he may even be punished. Indeed, it is considered immoral in certain families to attribute a malicious intention to a relative even if the observation is correct. Usually, there are some legitimate scapegoats. One can always credit the enemies of his country with malicious thoughts.

## The Results of Violation

Violations of a moral standard may result in *shame* or *guilt*. To demonstrate the significance of these terms, it is necessary that we outline the sequence of events which occurs when standards are internalized. The process is a lengthy and complicated one, which starts when a child experiences pressures to curtail his sources of pleasurable expression. Some of these pressures take the form of parental prohibitions and threats of punishment. He cannot strike out whenever he feels angry; he must give up asking others to do things for him which he can do for himself; he must take turns. Other pressures are self-imposed because he seeks to establish an identity (6) as a cooperative and respected working member of a particular social group. He wants to resolve disagreements as constructively as possible; he wants to curb his expression of irritation; he wants to be masculine; he wants to learn socially valued skills.

Naturally, the child initially rebels against some restrictions, and he does not hold unswervingly to his resolutions. In time, however, his attempts to gain recognition and love and to avoid punishment begin to take precedence over his immediate pleasures. He gradually yields to the adults' blandishments, their punishments, and their seductive rewards.

### Shame and Guilt

At one period, when some of the parents' rules have been partially internalized, the avoidance of shame motivates the child's conformity. In order for him to become ashamed when he has violated a moral norm, his act must be observed by a real or imagined person (5). If, for example, some adults witness a child's loss of bladder control, he feels demeaned just as he has been demeaned for such failures in the past. He cannot force people not to look, nor can he really blame them for looking. Of course, shame is not restricted to immoral behavior. One can be ashamed of an unkempt appearance or of being a poor dancer.

Shame requires the witnessing or the potential detection of the forbidden act. This is not true for guilt. Once the child has completed the process of patterning himself after important adults, the external observer is replaced by an inner voice. Even when there is no danger of detection, the child is impelled not to steal; although no one can read his mind, he avoids certain evil thoughts. When he resists temptation, he experiences a self-approval similar to the approval that he once received from his parents. When he violates his internalized standards, he condemns himself in the manner once used by his parents.

Once a child has internalized moral standards, he takes a large stride in the direction of becoming a cooperative member of his community. Even in the absence of external pressures, he can inhibit his impulses for the common good. He is motivated to do this by the many gratifications he gains from conformity and constructive action. But he pays a price for the gratifications. He cannot turn off his antisocial needs simply because he has contradictory ones. As before, he often wishes to engage in acts like hurting friends, or taking objects which are not his. For the rest of his life he is destined to suffer from anxiety and the pangs of conscience at such times. Each generation thus re-experiences man's fall from grace.

## Moral Standards and the Resolution of Conflict [6]

We have already noted that moral standards often define the nature of the conflict. They also affect its frequency. In general, conflict occurs most often when standards are extensive. If the

[6] A more complete account of this topic may be found in Allinsmith's thesis (1) and in Flugel's monograph (8).

prohibitions against aggression, for instance, rule out most of the possible acts, then even unexpressed feelings of petty irritation may create considerable guilt.

In addition to affecting the frequency, type, and intensity of conflict, moral norms define the acceptability of the defenses and expressive styles that may be used to resolve the difficulty. To avoid guilt, a man's defenses must be compatible with his moral code. An American who is conscience stricken at even the thought of hurting others may find it more compatible with his range of prohibitions to reverse his wish to hurt a hated object rather than to project the aggression. If, however, he is a member of the primitive society of Ifaluk (21), where it is customary to attribute disapproved needs to evil spirits, it is a simple matter for him to project his anger onto demons. Withdrawal is a defense that is often precluded by the American ideal of persisting at a difficult task and the fear of regarding oneself as a quitter. With these values, which are particularly strong among white-collar workers, it is almost impossible to give up and run away from an important activity, even when it appears that failure is inevitable. In the studies reported in Chapters 9 and 11, we anticipated that boys in the middle class would be more inclined to employ defenses such as reversal and turning against the self, and that boys in the working class would be more inclined to employ defenses in the first family.

Finally, moral standards delimit the range of expressive styles. They cannot be used if they violate a particular standard. Let us assume that a boy is angry at his friend and his standards proscribe physical attack on any object. Although he is accustomed to expressing himself by means of the large muscles of the body, he cannot express his anger in this style. He must shift to a morally acceptable one. Our picture of the values held by people in the two classes influenced our anticipation of differences in degree of motoric expression and in frequency of the more direct forms of aggression.

### Variables in our research

In the investigation described in Chapter 6, we studied the origins of subjects' *resistance to temptation* and, when an immoral act was committed, the *severity* of their guilt. Severity refers to amount of guilt aroused by violation. Two people may both be troubled by pangs of conscience after committing the same act, but they may differ considerably in the severity of their guilt. Such a difference may reflect their contrasting experiences during childhood when their misdeeds were discovered by parents. Two boys may feel, for example, that it is immoral to slap one's sister in anger; yet if both commit the act, the one who grew up in a permissive household may become only temporarily depressed while the other, who was taught to idolize the sanctity of womanhood and punished severely for any disrespect to females may be quite disturbed for some time. In our research we initially anticipated, therefore, that the harsher child-rearing practices, or milder ones signifying appeals to guilt, would be associated with greatest severity.

In our tabulations we had to take into account the fact that guilt can be expressed directly, defended against, or expiated. For each subject we counted all forms of guilt, both conscious and unconscious. We also did some separate studies of *defenses against guilt.* In the studies reported in Chapters 6 and 7, we analyzed the frequencies with which subjects with different backgrounds resorted to different defenses, particularly *externalization.* This was the most frequent defense used by our subjects, and is a special form of projection. Externalization is a projection of the moral standard. Instead of blaming or hurting himself, the guilty person exaggerates the extent to which he is being blamed by other people.

## Summary

In this chapter we have discussed our reasons for stressing the subjective aspects of need and for our particular conceptualization. We define a need as a disposition to activate a system of action tendencies, all of which implement the same goal state and any one of which can be substituted for any other without changing the goal state. A need is initiated by a discrepancy between current state and end state. The discrepancy elicits images of past actions that have led to the goal state. Such images and their associations are usually concretized in a particular situation as action tendencies. An action tendency can be analyzed in terms of its dimensions of intended acts, objects, affects, and agents. Each dimension consists of a number of elements. These have a hierarchy of preference in terms of their efficiency in implementing the goal state. The elements of dimensions are units which, when combined in a manner that is appropriate to a situation, become action tendencies. Usually, there are many combinations of acts, objects, affects, and agents which can implement a particular goal state. Thus any need includes a large number of action tendencies.

The conflicts that we studied involve some internalized standard, which defines as unacceptable certain kinds of action. Because the standard precludes the expression of the most preferred action tendency, it must be displaced by a more remote one. The prediction of the substitute is the central problem of a theory of conflict. In part, the selection depends on the range of substitutes which violate the standard. Differences in moral standards are thus associated with contrasting choices of alternate action tendencies. Moral standards can be analyzed in terms of the same dimensions as were used in the classification of action tendencies. The extensity of a standard is defined in terms of the number of proscribed elements within the dimensions. The severity of a standard is inferred from the amount of guilt suffered after its violation.

## References

1. Allinsmith, W. The learning of moral standards. Unpubl. Ph.D. dissertation, Univ. of Michigan, 1954.
2. ———. Conscience and conflict: the moral force in personality. *Child Develop.*, 1957, *28*, 469–76.
3. Breuer, J., & Freud, S. Studies of hysteria. New York: *Nerv. and Ment. Dis. Monogr.*, 1936.
4. Colby, K. M. *Energy and structure in psychoanalysis.* New York: Ronald, 1955.
5. Erikson, E. H. *Childhood and society*. New York: Norton, 1950.
6. ———. On the sense of inner identity. In Knight, R. P., & Friedman, C. R. (Eds.), *Psychoanalytic psychiatry and psychology.* New York: International Universities Press, 1954.
7. Fenichel, O. *The psychoanalytic theory of neurosis.* New York: Norton, 1945.

8. Flugel, J. C. *Men and their motives.* New York: International Universities Press, 1947.
9. Hartmann, H. Comments on the psychoanalytic theory of the ego. In Eissler, Ruth S., Freud, Anna, *et al.* (Eds.), *Psychoanalytic study of the child,* Vol. 5. New York: International Universities Press, 1948.
10. ———, Kris, E., & Lowenstein, R. M. Notes on the theory of aggression. In Eissler, Ruth S., Freud, Anna, *et al.* (Eds.), *Psychoanalytic study of the child,* Vol. 3–4. New York: International Universities Press, 1947.
11. Hebb, D. O. *The organization of behavior.* New York: Wiley, 1949.
12. Kubie, L. S. The fallacious use of quantitative concepts in dynamic psychology. *Psychoanal. Quart.,* 1947, *16,* 507.
13. Lewin, K. *A dynamic theory of personality.* New York: McGraw-Hill, 1935.
14. ———. Environmental forces in child behavior and development. In Murchison, C. (Ed.), *A handbook of child psychology.* Worcester, Mass.: Clark Univ. Press, 1931.
15. McClelland, D. C., *et al. The achievement motive.* New York: Appleton-Century-Crofts, 1953.
16. McDougall, W. *Outline of psychology.* New York: Scribners, 1923.
17. Miller, N. E. Experimental studies of conflict. In Hunt, J. McV. (Ed.), *Personality and the behavior disorders.* New York: Ronald, 1944.
18. Murray, H. A., *et al. Explorations in personality.* New York: Oxford Univ. Press, 1938.
19. ———. Toward a classification of interaction. In Parsons, T., & Shils, E. A. (Eds.), *Toward a general theory of action.* Cambridge: Harvard Univ. Press, 1951.
20. Rapaport, D. (Ed.) *Organization and pathology of thought.* New York: Columbia Univ. Press, 1951.
21. Spiro, M. E. Ghosts, Ifaluk, and teleological functionalism. *Amer. Anthropol.,* 1952, *54,* 497–503.
22. Sterba, R. *Introduction to the psychoanalytic theory of libido.* New York: Nerv. and Ment. Dis. Monogr., 1947.
23. Strauss, A. (Ed.) *The social psychology of George Herbert Mead.* Chicago: Univ. of Chicago Press, 1956.

# 6

## MORAL STANDARDS

## II. The Learning of Moral Standards *

In this chapter we will describe a study of three reactions to conflict. One is severity of guilt about death wishes, theft, and disobedience; a second is defense against guilt by externalization; and a third is resistance to temptation.[1] We related each of these reactions to the parents' social positions, their timing of weaning and toilet training, their disciplinary procedures, and the extent to which they explain their requests for obedience. Somewhat more space is devoted to concepts and techniques in this chapter than in the others because the investigation helped us to develop some of the methods which we used in our subsequent work.

### Identifying Moral Responses

In planning an empirical study of moral responses, we first had to specify criteria for identifying them. Conscience comes into play when there is a temptation to violate an internalized moral standard. An examination of the possible reactions to such temptation suggests the kinds of evidence required to know whether a person is influenced by his moral standards. There are three possible reactions: The per-

* In the research team, Wesley Allinsmith was responsible for the research to be reported and for the preparation of the chapter, which is based in part on his doctoral dissertation (1). We are indebted to Harvard University for its support of part of the work reported in this chapter.

[1] The three concepts have been defined in Chapter 5.

son may resist temptation and conform to his moral requirement. He may, instead, violate the norm and experience feelings of guilt. There is then usually some evidence either of his remorse or of his methods of alleviating self-criticism and obtaining absolution. Finally, he may violate his standards and not experience guilt. He is then likely to be unaware of his remorse because he has distorted it by means of a defense mechanism. To obtain evidence of the operation of his moral standard, it is necessary to observe either this distortion or his attempts at absolution of the unconscious guilt.

The existence of internalized standards is not demonstrated merely by conformity to a norm. And internalization cannot be demonstrated merely by apparent guilt feelings, atonement, defense against guilt, or self-punishment following a misdeed. What looks like guilt may be partly or entirely fear, and, as will be shown, some behavior resulting from defense against guilt is hard to distinguish from fear. A man may resist temptation, not solely to avoid guilt, but to get approval or to avoid the disapproval of others.

How can manifestations of conscience be distinguished from the placating of others or the avoidance of their disapproval? The problem of identifying guilt is not solved by asking a subject how he feels after he yields to temptation. He may not be clear in his own mind about the relative strengths of his guilt feelings and of his fears of people's reactions. He may be sincerely confused because he has defensively distorted his self-reproach. Even the most sincere disavowal of guilt feelings cannot be accepted at face value. Before a response can be attributed to a moral standard, fear must first be ruled out as an explanation of the subject's behavior. The investigator must eliminate all chance of approval by others for resisting temptation, and all risk of disapproval or punishment. The subject must be confident that his infraction either cannot be detected or cannot be attributed to him. Then punishment by others can occur only if he has given himself up or betrayed himself, acts which are evidence of an internalized need for absolution.

The necessity of eliminating risk makes it very difficult to study conscience by observing subjects in actual life situations. In such situations there is usually a good chance that an immoral act will have social as well as internal repercussions. It is thus necessary to create experimentally a plausible circumstance which permits a tempted subject to violate his norm without fear of discovery. There must be neither an external advantage to him from conformity nor an external disadvantage for misconduct.

### Previous investigations of moral responses

A real life situation may be approached if the subject is tempted to engage in a moral violation when he is led to believe that he cannot be observed or found out. There have been a few studies in which risk was eliminated and subjects were successfully tempted to misbehave. Sometimes they were asked to take a test on which it was possible to cheat. Either the test itself was designed to reveal cheating in a way subjects would not suspect (9), or cheaters were detected by observations through a one-way screen (11). In one investigation each subject was left alone with a collaborator in the guise of a fellow subject (7). To tempt the subject to shun his duty, the collaborator abandoned a dull but required task and engaged in a pleasurable but forbidden activity.

While ingenious, these methods are not completely satisfactory. For one thing, they waste the responses of some subjects. Those who resist temptation are not guilty and cannot be included in research on the severity of guilt.[2] Second, such methods may lead to a mislabeling of some subjects. Certain investigators have assumed that subjects who resist temptation have more stringent standards than those who yield. However, instead of lacking strong moral prohibitions, some may have transgressed despite them and may feel guilty about their misconduct. In many studies temptation is not held constant: Some of the subjects who have yielded to temptation may have more severe standards than those who resist, but may have been more strongly tempted.

Even when a sample is restricted to those who violate the norm, a technique is still required to measure guilt. The use of the methods described would have to be accompanied by a pro-

[2] One way of causing all subjects to transgress is to create an unintentional misdeed. Aronfreed describes such a technique in Chapter 7. It is also possible to increase temptation to such an extent that all subjects violate their standards. We rejected this approach for fear it might seriously disturb some subjects (7).

cedure for assessing the subjects' conscious and unconscious feelings.

## The Story Completion Test

These considerations led us to use a type of projective test in which the subject is given a story beginning which describes a moral violation. He finishes the story in his own words. In so doing he expresses his reactions to the immoral act. To illustrate the problems in developing such a test, we consider the item: "Henry steals some money from a man asleep in the park."

### Criteria for constructing stories

The story beginning about Henry is inadequate as it stands; it does not rule out fear of detection. To eliminate risk, we may add: "Nobody sees him do it," and we may provide Henry with a safe way of disposing of the money or with a good excuse to account for his sudden wealth. Furthermore, the story does not specify the amount of the theft. If one subject imagines it to be fifty cents and another fifty dollars, differences in guilt may result from the two interpretations rather than from variations in the severity of standards. We have to specify the extent of the violation to obtain less equivocal results. Although any given amount may have differing values for various subjects, such variations are probably much narrower than those which would be gotten if this information were omitted.

Another type of error in judging severity can occur if the relationship of the victim to Henry is not described and extenuating factors made clear. A subject who visualizes the sleeping man as a drunken playboy may react differently from the subject who has a blind man in mind.

The content of the need expressed by the forbidden act must also be taken into account. Henry's motive for stealing must be made plain. Otherwise, some subjects may regard the theft as an expression of anger, while others may interpret the theft as an attempt to gain money.

To give a misdeed similar moral implications for all subjects, we included in each story beginning (a) a secret violation of a common moral teaching, (b) by a given act, (c) expressing a stated or evident motive, (d) directed at a specified category of person, and (e) in a defined situation. Once we had taken these precautions, we could assume with some confidence that the misdeed would have similar moral implications for all subjects.[3]

Here are the stories we used:

DEATH WISHES

> Dave likes his baseball coach. The other day the coach promised him privately that Dave could pitch in the big game on Saturday. When the team meets for final practice, the coach doesn't say anything to Dave about pitching. Dave is afraid he has forgotten or changed his mind. He keeps thinking to himself over and over again: "The coach isn't going to keep his promise. I hope he doesn't even make the game. I wish he'd drop dead!"
>
> When Dave arrives at the game on Saturday afternoon, . . .

We then terminated the story in two different ways. In the first version, "he sees from the scoreboard that he is scheduled to pitch." Dave thus discovers that his evil thought was not justified. The second version of the plot about death wishes closes as follows:

> he hears that the coach has just been in an accident and has been taken to the hospital. Everyone is worried. The game is about to begin. Dave sees from the scoreboard that he is scheduled to pitch.

[3] The assets of the story completion method were demonstrated in a previous study, which is described in Chapter 14. We departed from the previous method in two respects: In presenting the story beginnings, we omitted pictures because we found that a verbal description was sufficient to stimulate projective productions by our subjects. We wrote longer beginnings because we wished to define each moral transgression very carefully. After pretesting stories about hostile wishes, disobedience, and stealing, we revised them until they were comprehensible to all subjects and until we felt we had eliminated any reasonable possibility that the hero might be detected. In addition to the six stories we analyzed, some other story beginnings were administered as pilot measures or as warm-up items. The full set of stories is presented in the original report of this investigation (1). The stories were developed and pretested in collaboration with David A. Rhodes. Both he and William D. Winter contributed many ideas about the interpretation of subjects' story endings.

In this ending, the death wish, while unjustified, is partially realized. When we administered the test, we began with the first version; the second version came fourth in the series.

THEFT

Bill's friends have formed a baseball team. They promised Bill he could be their catcher if he could get a catcher's mitt. His father told him he could not buy him a catcher's mitt. Bill saved all the money he could. At last he had $10.00 saved up to get a really good glove. When he arrives at the sports store, he sees the sales-clerk going down the stairs to the cellar of the store. The clerk does not see Bill. Bill decides to look at the catcher's gloves himself before calling the clerk. He finds just the one he wants. Then he reaches for his money. It is gone. He realizes that he has lost it on the way downtown. Bill feels awful. He looks around. There is nobody in the store or near it outside. The clerk is still in the cellar. It occurs to Bill that the mitt would just fit under the bulge of his jacket.

In addition to this version, which enabled us to study resistance to temptation, we included an identical item which ended with two further sentences:

He hides the mitt under his jacket and walks out of the store. No one sees him leave.

The item about temptation was second in the series, and the version concerning transgression came fifth.

DISOBEDIENCE

One day Ted's mother goes visiting a friend of hers in another town. At noon just after his lunch Ted phones his mother and talks with her. She tells him to be a good boy and says she will be home at suppertime. Now Ted is all alone with nothing to do. He thinks of the boxes in the top of his mother's closet. She has told him *never* to take down the boxes. He knows that his mother won't be home till suppertime.

Thus ends the version about temptation, which came third. In the sixth and final item, concerning transgression, we added:

Ted climbs up and takes down the boxes.

ADMINISTRATION OF THE TEST

One male examiner administered the test to groups which varied between four and eight subjects. When the groups included twelve or more subjects, two examiners gave the test. A few boys who were absent were later seen individually.

The test was introduced with these instructions:

> We are interested in finding out what boys your age are like. I have some stories here for you to finish. I'll read each story aloud and you can follow it in your booklet. Then you finish the story, starting where the story here leaves off. This is not an English class. Don't worry about spelling. There are no right or wrong answers: you can say anything you want in your stories, and use any language you want. No one here at school will see your stories—we'll take them back to the University with us.

Then the examiner asked the boys to turn to the first item, which he read aloud as clearly and expressively as he could. Next he said: "Now you finish the story, telling what happens and how it turns out, and what the people in your story are thinking and feeling." The first three stories were administered in the early part of the session. Then there was a rest period during which each child ate a candy bar. When the testing recommenced, the examiner said that the next three stories would look like some in the earlier booklet, but that in each case the last part would be different.

CRITERIA FOR INTERPRETING THE TEST

It was necessary for us to identify guilt in all its forms, both conscious and unconscious. We used three general criteria to do this. One was direct acknowledgment of self-blame or guilt feeling. A second consisted of indirect manifestations of guilt, such as attempts at reparation. Finally, we tabulated defensive distortions. In some of these, the subject hides his remorse from himself by such methods as attributing the blame to others. In other defensive distortions, which we later discuss in more detail, the subject is punished by others. Such punishment may occur by accident or design. In identifying defensive distortion, we had to violate the criteria which we have listed in Chapter 8: We had no independent evidence of the unconscious guilt to which the defense was presumably applied. In the absence of this evidence, we may have incorrectly tabulated some reactions as defensive. This means that our obtained relationships between child-rearing practices and defense are probably minimal.

We counted punishment of the hero as a defensive distortion because the primary character in each story is in a risk-free situation. To write an ending about punishment, a subject had to externalize his own standards. He had to avoid awareness of his self-blame by projecting it. He consequently regarded others as wishing to blame or attack him. It is as though he changed the statement, "I want to punish me" to "They want to punish me."

In summary, our ratings of the different manifestations of guilt encompassed any kind of pain, anxiety, disadvantage, punishment, or threat of punishment experienced by the hero in the subject's story. By "disadvantage," we refer to efforts by the hero to make restitution or to confess. By threat of punishment, we mean events which almost happen to the hero, or contingencies which he fears. If, in a story about stealing, a detective catches the boy but lets him go, this threat is evidence of guilt even though the hero is not actually punished.

*Rating Severity of Guilt.* We evaluated the severity of each subject's guilt by means of a seven-point scale. Points of the scale were: (1) Very low, (2) Definitely low, (3) Definitely not high, (4) Doubtful high, (5) High, (6) Doubtful extreme, and (7) Extreme. In scoring a story, we divided the subjects into three categories. We labeled as *high* all subjects with an intensity of guilt ranging between 5 and 7. A second category, *medium,* included subjects whose intensity had been rated at 4.[4] We placed the remaining subjects in the *low* category.[5]

We evaluated a particular story for all the boys before we

[4] This category, as indicated in its label on the seven-point scale, was originally called *doubtful high* rather than *medium*. The stories seemed to the judges to be closer in intensity to high than to low guilt.

[5] We developed these groupings empirically. At first we intended to divide the sample in two, but we did not feel confident about including the many boys with ratings of 4 in either the high or low groups. We therefore created the medium group. There were a few extremely high cases, but because of their small number we did not separate them from the subjects with scores which were not extreme.

went on to the next. This prevented the rating of a given ending from being influenced by knowledge of the other endings written by the same boy. A few of our subjects wrote one or more endings that were too peculiar to be scored. We eliminated such endings from consideration.

It should be noted that in estimating severity, the rater made a subjective, over-all judgment. As an alternative method, we might have tabulated each separate manifestation of guilt and counted the number to arrive at the judgment of intensity.[6] Such a procedure would probably have yielded a very reliable code, but we eschewed it because it would have resulted in a lower score for a single drastic theme, such as suicide, than for two or more mild themes. With the over-all judgment, we were able to achieve a reliability quite satisfactory for the coding of projective stories.[7]

*Some Examples of the Scoring of Guilt.* To illustrate our scoring method, we cite some endings to the story about Dave and the coach. The rating of high guilt was given to endings in which the hero relinquishes the desired opportunity to pitch so he can rush to the hospital and see the coach, in which the hero explicitly expresses much remorse, or in which he pitches very badly. The rating of extreme guilt was given to instances of serious injury to the hero, long prison sentences, outlandish defensive distortions, and marked emotional upset, such as panic, expressions of terror, and suicidal inclinations. Guilt was rated as low if the hero pitches in the game and feels only slightly uncomfortable about the coach.[8]

[6] Meaningful findings with such an objective system were obtained in the study reported in Chapter 7.

[7] William D. Winter and Wesley Allinsmith independently judged twenty-five stories to establish the reliability of the coding procedure. A disagreement was tabulated when one of the raters differed from the other by more than one step on the seven-point scale of severity of guilt. In rating the stories both judges used six of the seven points in the scale. The percentage of agreement was 80. In the coding of externalization, the percentage of agreement was 88, and there was 100 per cent agreement in the coding of resistance to temptation.

[8] Occasionally an ending contained not even a mild indication of guilt. We combined such endings with those rated as low in severity. We did this to increase the small number of cases in which little guilt was expressed. Since the transgressions we studied are so universally forbidden in our society, we assumed that some parental prohibitions concerning these acts

*Rating Externalization.* The series of incomplete stories we developed to tap guilt enabled us to study not only its severity but also externalization, a type of defense against guilt. Defense mechanisms are often conceived as means by which a person may deceive himself about his forbidden action tendencies, but defenses may be applied to moral standards as well. When standards are experienced as alien or unpleasant they may be distorted as easily as hostile or sexual action tendencies. If a man then yields to temptation, he may silence the voice of conscience by defensive distortions of his guilt.[9]

According to Fenichel (4), ". . . the same mechanisms of defense which are used against discomfortable affects in general may also be brought into play against guilt feelings." Guilt can be isolated, so that a person is aware of self-criticism without experiencing the emotions which usually accompany it. Guilt can also be reversed, so that a man takes conscious pride in the immoral act. Several types of distortion can be accomplished by projection.[10] For instance, one may find fault in others instead of himself, or may incorrectly attribute his own guilt feelings to another person.

The form of projection we are calling *externalization* was the only defense that occurred with sufficient frequency to warrant analysis. We tabulated externalization when the hero in the story

---

had been communicated to all our subjects. If this were not so, we would be unable to include endings in which a subject gave no indication of guilt; absence of guilt in a person who has not been "taught" a standard reflects the lack of relevant experience rather than the variations in parental technique we seek to investigate.

[9] Mowrer (12) has made a valuable contribution by calling the attention of psychologists to the importance in personality of the repression of conscience. He implies that neurosis in our time is almost entirely a function of defense against guilt rather than defense against impulse. This is as one-sided a view as the position he attacks. Defense against guilt may well be a more prominent feature in current neuroses than it was in the neuroses treated by psychoanalysis at the turn of the century. But to suggest, as Mowrer does, that defense against impulse is not also a prominent feature in contemporary neuroses is to take a position we regard as untenable. Mowrer views psychoanalytic writers as being generally unaware of the significance of defense against guilt. Two authors who have written at length about the subject are Flugel (6) and Fenichel (4).

[10] Some implications of projection as a defense against guilt are discussed by Allinsmith (1, 2) and Flugel (6).

viewed the disapproval of his acts as coming from others rather than himself.

By locating a disapproving individual whom he fears and needs to placate, a man experiences the pressure of his conscience as an external rather than an internal force and avoids the pain of inner conflict. When there is a real basis for fearing external censure, externalization may well be the most frequent defense against guilt. The housewife who has gossiped about her neighbors becomes exaggeratedly afraid that they may learn the source of the gossip. The employee who has fallen short of his ideals of achievement is unrealistically afraid of his superior's condemnation.

When no discoverable offense has been committed, the mechanism of externalization is perhaps less often employed. At least, our subjects seldom resorted to this distortion in endings written about the death wish. Because there were so few ratings of this defense in such stories, we restricted our study of externalization to stories about the acts of theft and disobedience.

Our subjects used two major variations of externalization. In one, *pure externalization,* the hero is punished, or is afraid of being punished, by external forces which he cannot control. Ted's mother arrives and detects him, for instance, or a hand grenade in the boxes blows up. The externalized blame may be attributed to a human agent or to an inanimate force: A truck driver accidentally runs the hero down, or lightning strikes him.

In the second type of externalization, the punishment results from the hero's *provocation.* He delays the misdeed or continues his behavior until he is caught; he commits an additional infraction which makes punishment likely; or he gives himself away by a slip of the tongue.[11]

Using the transgression versions of the plots about theft and disobedience, we divided our subjects into those who showed externalization and those who did not.

*Rating Resistance to Temptation.* In our stories about theft

[11] We do not distinguish between the two types of externalization in presenting our findings. To increase the number of subjects categorized as using the defense, we combined boys with *pure externalization* and boys with *provocation.* When the two groups are studied separately they show similar trends in relation to child-rearing factors.

and disobedience we included not only a violation item but also a version in which the story beginning ends after the hero has been tempted but before he has committed the act. (The theme of death wishes permits no temptation beginning. There is no way to be "tempted to wish"; the wish itself constitutes the transgression.) We coded our subjects' endings as representing resistance to temptation when the hero abstains from the contemplated misdeed. If he commits the forbidden act of taking down the boxes or walks out of the store with the stolen mitt, yielding to temptation was scored.

*Rating Perceived Source of Standards.* In the hope of gaining some understanding of the subjects' pictures of their standards, we interviewed them about their moral feelings. We asked each boy, "How do you know whether a thing is right or wrong?" When necessary, this was followed with a clarifying question, "When you're tempted to do something wrong, how do you know whether to do it or not?" There were three kinds of replies. Some boys said, "I just know." A second group said they thought of other people's standards. For instance, some children said, "I think about what my mother would say." A few subjects said, "A little bird tells me," or "I hear a voice that tells me." The first type of answer was categorized as evidence of *inner certainty,* the second as *thinks of others,* and the last as *hears a voice*. We do not know how much faith to place in the children's replies, but the associations of their answers both with background variables and with other moral responses suggest that perceived source may possibly be an important attribute of personality.

## Sample and Controls

We obtained our 112 subjects from the second sample described in Chapter 4. Although we restricted the population to subjects who were no more than a year older or younger than their classmates, this precaution still did not rule out the possibility that differences in age might affect the boys' moral responses. The older subjects were presumably more mature than the younger ones. Age differences might have influenced guilt because of the upsurge of sexuality in adolescence or the shifts in patterns of defense which occur at puberty, according to psychoanalytic theorists. To determine the effect of age on our findings, we divided the distribution of ages at the median. In the younger group none of the boys had reached his thirteenth birthday. The other group included all who had passed it, plus three who were within a few days of that age. Taking each group by itself, we related our antecedent variables to our indices of conscience. In this way we tried to determine interactions of age with other background features. In addition, we compared the age groups directly with respect to each moral attribute. We shall describe the outcome of these procedures after mentioning the other controls.

To control intelligence, we split the distributions of the tests of Verbal Meaning, Reasoning, and Space Ability in Thurstone's battery of Primary Mental Abilities at the median and followed the same two steps we had followed with age. To control social position, we related antecedent variables to moral responses within each social class, within each integration setting, and within each class when divided by setting. (We later discuss indices of social position as antecedent rather than control variables.)

With the exception of social class, none of the control factors bears any interpretable relationship to the characteristics we studied. In a great number of distributions the frequency of significance is no greater than that to be expected on the basis of random error, and the pattern of findings appears haphazard. We concluded that intelligence, within the range represented in our sample, is unrelated to our indices of conscience, and that whatever bearing chronological age may have on the development of moral responses is obscured by the narrowness of the span of ages among our subjects. The interactions of social class with type of discipline are discussed when we present our findings.

## Hypotheses

### Severity of Guilt

One primary purpose of the research was to test some of the claims which link events in infancy and childhood with the intensity of moral responses. The two kinds of early events that we investigated were weaning and toilet training. The later parental practices included type of discipline, the extent to which requests for obedience were explained, and the frequency of reward.[12]

*Weaning.* We first divided our subjects into those weaned early and late. Taking as a basis the common assumption that early completion of weaning frustrates a child more than does late completion, we thought we would probably find that early weaning was associated with high guilt. For certain reasons, however, we felt unsure just what to expect. Clinical conceptions of severe guilt have been gained largely from observations of pathological depression, a disturbance which can be traced, in part, to guilt about aggression. It seemed possible that guilt about other types of moral transgression might have a different genesis. It can also be argued that late weaning, as represented in our sample, is as frustrating as early weaning. If so, severity of guilt may be enhanced with respect to whichever rules are being emphasized by the parents, or inferred by the offspring, at the time of weaning. Because of his comparatively advanced development, the child who is weaned late ordinarily experiences different parental demands from those which accompany early weaning. Our uncertainty about the probable associations between harshness of weaning and severity of guilt led us to take two precautions. First, we studied guilt not only about aggression, but also about theft and disobedience. In the story beginnings with the latter two themes, we made it clear that expression of anger was not the underlying motive of the protagonists. Second, we computed the probabilities of our results in terms of two-tailed tests.

*Toilet Training.* The possible relation between toilet training and severity of guilt has been described by Ferenczi (5) in his writing about "sphincter morality." It seemed to us that early and rapid training constitute a more difficult experience for the child than later and slower training. Yet, since we lacked confidence in the kind of association we would find between the severe method and severity of guilt, we again analyzed the associations between child rearing and three sources of guilt, and analyzed the significance in terms of two-tailed tests.

*Discipline.* It seemed to us that psychological discipline is an index both of parents' self-restraint about aggression and of

[12] Chapter 3 contains descriptions of our methods of classifying subjects in accordance with parental practices.

the manner in which they indicate disapproval. It appeared that each of these parental characteristics might make a child inhibited or guilty about his own hostile tendencies. We viewed the parent who favors corporal punishment as providing a model of aggression and as condoning it implicitly, if not explicitly. Therefore, we felt some assurance in expecting current discipline to be associated with remorse about hostility. We were not at all sure whether it would bear on remorse about other types of violation.

*Requests for Obedience.* Data concerning requests for obedience were coded from the interviews of subjects' mothers by another member of the project after we had tested our hypotheses about the relation to guilt of weaning, toilet training, and type of discipline. We had no clear rationale for adding obedience requests to the present study, but investigated their influence on guilt for exploratory purposes.

*Frequency of Reward.* This variable, like obedience, was added to our study later than the others. As we have indicated in Chapter 3, the method of measuring reward was not as satisfactory as those developed for other childhood antecedents. We studied its association with the different aspects of conscience but found no significant relations. Therefore we do not report the data.

*Social Class.* Our final background factor was the parents' social class.[13] We have already described our use of social class as a control. We examined its bearing as an antecedent factor in its own right even though we did not anticipate that boys in the two social classes would necessarily differ in severity of guilt. In almost all groups, parents enjoin their sons to obey adults, to respect property rights, and to restrain rage. It is true that in sociological accounts, members of the working class are often described as implementing their hostile thoughts by direct forms of aggression to a much greater extent than members of the middle class do. If such descriptions are correct, they may reflect differences other than in capacity for remorse following moral violations. A blue-collar worker may experience more temptation than the white-

[13] In order to explore the influence of integration setting we investigated differences between the middle and working classes when studied within the entrepreneurial and bureaucratic settings. We also used integration setting as a background factor. Finally, we examined its associations with moral responses when social class is held constant. The number of significant findings was no greater than chance, and so we do not report the data.

collar worker, or may be subject to fewer restraining influences from his social milieu. When he does not live up to his moral ideals, he may still feel guilty. Since we measured severity in terms of guilt following transgression, we did not feel we had a firm basis for predicting significant differences between boys in the two classes.

### Hypotheses about externalization, resistance to temptation, and perceived source of standards

We had no specific predictions about these three indices. We simply analyzed their associations with all of our antecedent variables. As in the case of the results we shall report about severity of guilt, we computed the probabilities of our findings in terms of two-tailed tests.

## Results: Severity of Guilt

### Guilt about death wishes

Many people experience no serious guilt when they have a hostile wish. If it were gratified, however, they might be overcome with remorse even if they were in no way responsible for the mishap. During the Second World War, when some soldiers' wishes about a companion were fulfilled in battle, their excessive guilt resulted in severe personality disorders. The soldiers felt they were to blame because they unconsciously felt that their wishes had caused the deaths.

In the second version of our story completion theme describing a death wish, the wish is partially realized when the coach is in an accident. Although Dave, the hero, is in no way responsible for the accident, we assumed that because of the tendency some subjects might have to equate wish with deed, this version would arouse vicarious responses of guilt more effectively than would the first version. Because of this assumption, we expected that responses to the second version would have more relation to the postulated childhood antecedents of guilt than would responses to the first. This is what we find. Neither the social backgrounds nor the parental training techniques are related to severity of guilt in story endings produced for the first version. But the early methods, weaning and toilet training, show significant associations with guilt expressed in response to the second version. These results for the story about the realized wish are reported in Table 6-1, which contains a summary of the major associations involving the severity of guilt. The detailed tables may be found in Appendix D.

The distributions for both weaning and toilet training have an unexpected characteristic. They are curvilinear, as may be seen from the tabulations in the appendix. Among the subjects who were weaned early, the proportion in the middle category on intensity of guilt exceeds the proportion in the high category. The curvilinearity of the distribution for toilet training is strikingly similar. So is that for discipline when only the psychological and corporal types are considered. Although the association between discipline and guilt does not approach significance for the sample as a whole, when it is analyzed within the middle and working classes it attains a probability of $<.07$ in the middle class and $<.90$ in the working class. Among middle-class subjects, the psychologically disciplined have medium and high guilt, the intermediately disciplined low guilt.[14]

If the curvilinearity represents the true state of affairs, we have no immediate explanation of it. It is possible to argue, however, that the true relationship may actually be linear. One suggestion, made by E. L. Walker, is that subjects who expressed only a medium amount of guilt in their stories were really the highest in guilt, but were inhibited by its very severity from expressing it adequately. Boys who were somewhat less guilty may have obtained the highest intensity scores because they were free to

[14] The marginal significance suggests that the results might have been different had the sample been larger. Allinsmith and Greening (3) retested the hypothesis with a sample of male university undergraduates, using indices of corporal and psychological discipline, but not intermediate discipline. The students rated the type of discipline favored by their parents, and completed the story items of the present study. The relation between intensity of guilt over death wishes and maternal discipline is significant at the .005 level. Psychological discipline is associated with high guilt.

It is of interest to note, parenthetically, that in our present data, weaning, toilet training, and discipline are not mere duplicates of one another; a study of the data reveals that each index controls part of the variance of severity.

**TABLE 6-1**

Background Conditions and Severity of Guilt

| | *Severity of Guilt about:* | | | | | | | | | | | |
|---|---|---|---|---|---|---|---|---|---|---|---|---|
| | *Death Wishes* | | | | *Theft (Revised)* | | | | *Disobedience* | | | |
| Condition | *Trends: Boxes with Largest Frequencies* | N | $\chi^2$ | *Probability* | *Trends: Boxes with Largest Frequencies* | N | $\chi^2$ | *Probability* | *Trends: Boxes with Largest Frequencies* | N | $\chi^2$ | *Probability* |
| Weaning | Early weaning & medium guilt (curv.) | 101 | 10.88 | $<.01$ | Early weaning & low guilt | 97 | 8.49 | $<.02$ | Early weaning & low guilt | 88 | 3.71 | .06 |
| Toilet training | Severe training & medium guilt (curv.) | 100 | 8.41 | $<.02$ | — | 97 | .18 | $<1.00$ | Severe training & low guilt | 89 | 3.74 | .05 |
| Discipline | — | 108 | 5.86 | $<.30$ | Mixed disc. & high guilt | 104 | 6.22 | .19 | — | 95 | .79 | $<.70$ |
| Obedience requests | — | 78 | .77 | $<.70$ | — | 76 | .63 | $<.80$ | — | 69 | .48 | $<.50$ |
| Social class | — | 108 | 1.09 | $<.60$ | Middle class & low guilt | 104 | 5.46 | .07 | — | 95 | .003 | $<1.00$ |

respond imaginatively to a guilt-inducing stimulus. If this explanation were correct, the medium group on the stories would be the actual high group and the association between weaning and guilt would no longer be curvilinear.

While we could not check this interpretation directly, we did obtain some indirect support for it from a comparison of the intensity of guilt expressed by boys with various combinations of

**TABLE 6-2**

Severity of Parental Practices and Guilt About Death Wishes

| *Number of Severe Parental Practices* | *Severity of Guilt* | | |
|---|---|---|---|
| | *Low* | *Medium* | *High* |
| Three | 1 | 15 | 6 |
| One or two | 16 | 9 | 22 |
| None | 6 | 1 | 2 |

"severe" scores on the three background conditions. By severe scores, we mean those which represent early weaning, severe toilet training, or psychological discipline. We combined the figures for those subjects who had one or two severe scores on these variables because they showed the same pattern. Table 6-2 contains the data.

When there are no severe scores on the rearing conditions, the intensity of guilt is generally low. When one or two of the background scores is severe, the frequencies of subjects with high or low severity of guilt exceeds the frequency of subjects with medium severity. When all three background conditions are severe, however, more subjects display a medium than high severity of guilt. In short, among boys who have experienced the greatest number of conditions likely to lead to high guilt, fewer subjects express high guilt than among subjects who have been subjected to an intermediate amount of pressure. This finding seems consistent with the speculation that the most guilt-ridden boys were more inclined to inhibit their feelings than were boys with an intermediate amount of guilt. Perhaps the kind of person who stifles his feelings may be produced through the teaching of self-abnegation and self-restraint by the child-rearing practices that we studied.

Another interpretation of the table, suggested by G. E. Swanson, is that one or two high scores may indicate marked parental inconsistency. Three may signify self-assurance in parents who are less violent and not so unreasonable in their demands.

Curvilinearity may also be interpreted as an artifact of the scoring of guilt. It is possible, for example, that boys rated as high in guilt were able to express conscious, overt remorse, whereas boys rated as medium were able to depict only atonement rather than conscious feelings. When we check the associations between child rearing and intensity of guilt within the two categories of conscious remorse and atonement, however, we find that the curvilinearity persists despite this control.

L. M. Lansky has suggested a second way of interpreting the curvilinearity as an artifact of scoring. He points out the improbability that boys like our subjects would be insensitive to the coach's plight. Possibly most or all of the subjects we rated as low in guilt were so upset that they denied or disguised their remorse drastically. If, in accordance with this interpretation, we combine subjects with low and high guilt, so that we compare those whose guilt is medium with all the other subjects, we find relations which are opposite in direction to those obtained when we follow Walker's suggestion. Early weaning and severe bowel training are associated with medium rather than the combination of low and high guilt, in each case at the .01 level. Later we discuss the possible meanings of these findings.[15]

GUILT ABOUT THEFT

In the endings which they produced for both versions of the story about theft, most of the subjects expressed high guilt. Medium and low ratings are very rare. The range of severity is, therefore,

[15] A fourth hypothesis about the curvilinearity stems from our control runs concerning age. Despite the restricted range of age among our subjects, there was a tendency in the distributions for weaning, toilet training, and discipline for the curvilinearity to lessen or disappear in the older groups. If confirmed by later research, this observation may enable us to account for the derivation, from work with patients in adulthood, of the hypothesis that the relationship is linear.

so narrow that there is little possibility of finding a relation with any background variable.

For exploratory purposes, we revised the cutting points of the guilt scores on the story containing the violation.[16] Then we divided the distribution at the natural points of separation between groups. This procedure added subjects with medium scores to the *low* group and reassigned subjects with high scores to the *medium* group. The new *high* group contained only those boys with previous scores of *doubtful extreme* or *extreme*. As indicated in Table 6-1, which summarizes the results concerning severity,[17] weaning is significantly related to severity of guilt expressed in the story endings. Low severity is associated with early weaning.[18]

GUILT ABOUT DISOBEDIENCE

In our third theme a son violates his mother's instruction not to take down some boxes in her closet. Upon examining the results, we found very similar associations between child rearing and guilt in endings written to the versions about temptation and transgression. In view of this outcome, we decided, in order to obtain a more reliable measure of the intensity of guilt, to combine the scores obtained from the two endings of each subject.[19]

[16] We chose the violation plot for the exploratory rescoring because we had more confidence in the judgments of guilt from this story than from the one about temptation. To be rated as severe in the case of subjects who resist temptation, the ending had to contain evidence, such as sharpness of the self-warning, of the amount of guilt that would presumably be experienced in the event of violation. Such inferences are tenuous at times. Later we analyzed the results for the temptation story and got no significant findings.

[17] The detailed tables may be found in Appendix D.

[18] Although the association between social class and guilt about stealing approaches significance, examination of the data reveals that the variance is attributable to the index of weaning. Whatever association social class has with guilt is a function of its correlation with age of weaning. There is a faint suggestion of a relation of discipline to guilt. Toilet training and obedience requests are unrelated to it.

[19] We did not combine the items about death wishes because there was a fundamental difference between the plots of those stories: The wish was realized in one version and not in the other. After combining the disobedience items, we returned to the two stealing versions and combined them, despite the fact that only one of the two stories showed any association with background variables. As expected, the combined score has no significant associations.

In combining the scores we arbitrarily assigned one point to a rating of *low* guilt and two points to a rating of *medium* for each ending. Because there was a preponderance of *high* scores, we split that group in two. We assigned three points to the lowest score in the high category—the ratings originally labeled as *high* —and four points to the higher scores—the ratings originally labeled as *doubtful extreme* and *extreme*. After adding each subject's points for the two stories, we divided the distribution of combined scores at the median.

Table 6-1 reveals that earliness of weaning and severity of toilet training are both significantly related to severity of guilt about disobedience. But, as foreshadowed in the case of theft, earliness and severity are associated with low rather than high guilt. Discipline, requests for obedience, and social class are unrelated to guilt over disobedience.[20]

## Interpretations of Our Findings Concerning Severity of Guilt

Because of some unanticipated complexities in the phenomena we investigated and our lack of foresight in controlling certain variables, our findings are equivocal in some respects. We outline below some of the resultant problems in interpreting our data.

### The differences in directions of association

In evaluating the different directions, and thus the specific meanings, of our findings about weaning, toilet training, and severity of guilt, we are faced with three main possibilities. We lack the evidence to choose among the three alternatives, but the speculations can be tested in future research. We will focus on disobedience as a means of illustrating them because our results for

[20] Both levels of probability are .04, according to the statistical method used when the data were originally reported (1). At that time chi squares for fourfold tables were corrected for continuity only when the expected frequencies were less than 10. Later in preparing this book a more conservative decision was made to apply the correction for continuity to all fourfold tables. The two probabilities to which we refer then became .06 and .05 as shown in Table 1. Since the text of this chapter was already set in galley, the interpretation of the .06 finding as significant has not been altered.

this source of guilt seem more reliable than those for theft; both weaning and toilet training give significant associations to guilt about disobedience and the judgment of guilt is based on two stories rather than one.

First, our findings may be valid as they stand, and the directions of the relations between guilt and child rearing may actually differ for disobedience and for death wishes. If the true association between parental practices and guilt about death wishes is curvilinear, we have no ready explanation for the discrepancy between such a trend and the one obtained for disobedience. If, in accordance with Walker's suggestion, we assume that the association for death wishes is linear, and therefore opposite in direction to the one for disobedience, we can speculate about this contradiction in trends. All restrictive or punitive parental practices—weaning is as good an example as any—may be frustrating to a child whether they occur early or late.[21] Perhaps the content of the guilt refers primarily to the behaviors which were subjected to discipline at the time weaning occurred. If a child was weaned at twelve months or later, for example, his standards may have become severe with reference to acts which were of great concern to his parents at that time. The acts may have included the exploration of strange surroundings and the testing of parental prohibitions concerning property rights. Very different acts may have become the sources of severe guilt if the child was weaned earlier, when he was less mobile, and his parents were more concerned with his tantrums or his lack of cooperation when he was dressed, diapered, or bathed.[22]

[21] Older children in our society who "voluntarily" give up the bottle must then be viewed either as having less sucking need than others or as having been subjected to unrecognized pressures and inducements to renounce sucking. Or perhaps those weaned very late are the only ones who are not frustrated. As anthropologists will testify, lateness of weaning in our sample is not lateness as far as many human societies go; in worldwide terms, virtually our entire sample was weaned early. One could therefore hold the view that weaning is frustrating only when it is early and still regard the late weaned in our sample as frustrated.

[22] We do not mean to suggest that rages do not have to be regulated during the second year when late weaning occurs. We do think that rage may be focal among the events which accompany early weaning. The young child associates parental disapproval with his *feelings* and *wishes* of rage. The older child has the necessary skills and mobility to express his aggression in action. When he becomes infuriated, he *acts* disobediently

These speculations suggest that internalizations in different moral areas do not necessarily have the same developmental origins. Early rearing factors may be important, but may have different meanings in different moral contexts. It also seems possible that internalizations in different moral areas are not necessarily alike in degree. A person may have very severe internalized prohibitions of stealing, but mild prohibitions of disobedience, or his severity may be high for disobedience and low for aggression. This interpretation is bolstered by our finding that our subjects' scores on intensity of guilt in one moral area are not significantly related to their scores in any other moral area.[23] The person with a generally severe conscience, then, may be rarer than has been thought.[24] Judging from our data, the person with a truly generalized conscience, either "punitive" or "psychopathic," is a statistical rarity.[25]

---

instead of merely flailing his arms and wishing to attack. The mother reacts with "Don't do that!" Since he now understands her words, he internalizes prohibitions of specific acts.

[23] Hartshorne and others (8–10) reached an analogous conclusion. They reported that children who cheat in one situation are not necessarily dishonest in another. But, as has been pointed out earlier, studies restricted to behavior do not indicate much about internalized standards. Subjects who cheat do not necessarily have less severe standards than honest subjects do. Subjects may transgress because they are sorely tempted, and they may feel guilty because of their actions.

[24] As part of our study we planned to compare the backgrounds of the group whose standards were all high with the group whose standards were all low. Of our 112 subjects, only three had high scores on all six stories, and five expressed high intensity on five of the six stories. When these eight are compared with fifteen subjects who had one or no high scores, we find that the two groups do not differ significantly with respect to any of the background conditions.

[25] Can this finding be reconciled with clinical observations of guilt-ridden people? It seems likely that whatever error or oversimplification may exist in clinicians' theoretical pictures of guilt is the result of their specialization in the guilts about aggression of psychiatric patients. Because parents cannot socialize children without provoking their rage, a tendency to become guilty about hostility perhaps permeates the fabric of everyone's personality. In certain psychiatric patients who have been unsuccessful in resolving their infantile conflicts, guilt about anger may be so prominent as to obscure other sources of troubled conscience. As far as we know, the boys in our sample are not psychiatric patients.

Two other factors may contribute to inferences about conscience which may be true only for guilt about anger. A person who has introjected prohibitions of aggression may enhance his guilts in other moral areas by turning his hostile feelings against himself. In addition, major guilts about

In sum, our results do not justify the inclination of some psychological researchers to make general statements about guilt and conscience from measures of a single moral reaction, or to take averages of scores applying to different moral reactions. It is necessary to speak of "guilts" rather than of "guilt," and to be sensitive to the complexities of moral learning.

From Lansky's viewpoint, it is possible to derive a second interpretation of the data: that the directions of association for death wishes and disobedience are not truly different. Perhaps some characteristics of late weaning and mild toilet training, or of the child rearing of which they are indices, reinforce defenses that make it difficult for boys with high guilt about death wishes to express their feelings. Thus subjects whose story endings we rated as low in guilt about death wishes actually may be high.

According to a third possibility, our findings for death wishes and disobedience appear different not because of the distinction between aggression and disobedience as contrasting types of transgression, but because of conditions we did not or could not control in our investigation. Some of these possible sources of error might include the following: [26]

*Wish versus Act.* The first interpretive problem arises because of uncontrolled differences in the contents of stories about disobedience and death wishes. The former involves an actual deed, while the latter involves an unexpressed action tendency. Concerns about the dangers of hostile wishes may originate at different periods of development from concerns about actual misdeeds. In short, the reversal in trends may have been caused by a difference between guilt about a wish and about an act rather than by a difference in guilt about death wishes and disobedience.[27]

---

aggression may be displaced onto irrelevant situations and thus create an impression of severe internalizations in all areas.

[26] A number of potential alternative explanations were ruled out by the design of the study, the procedure for selection of subjects, and the checks we made concerning the effects on our results of age, intelligence, and social position.

[27] Still other conditions should be held constant. To illustrate some of them, we begin with a hypothetical story about two men who are fishing in a row boat. One of them becomes furious at the other. The enraged man *wishes* to strangle his companion. Instead he aims a blow at the friend with the *intent* of giving him a black eye or bloody nose. The blow may or may not land. The *act* may thus differ from the intended one. If the blow lands,

*Fear versus Guilt.* The reversal in trends can also be attributed to the difference in the risks of punishment taken by the heroes in the stories about anger and disobedience. Hostile thoughts are not easily discerned, whereas an overt act of disobedience is usually a matter of public knowledge. We were not completely successful in eliminating risk. The fact that the mother is in another town, for example, does not prevent discovery of the misdeed by someone else. Moreover, we failed to specify how far away the other town was. In the future, "an hour's drive away" might well be added to the item about disobedience.

Themes of punishment and fear occur more often in the story endings written about disobedience than in response to the theme of death wishes, while the latter evokes more frequent self-blame and self-criticism. Assuming that risk was eliminated, we have interpreted fear as a defensive distortion or as a wish for absolution from guilt. But the fear may have been real rather than defensive. If this were so, our findings would signify that late weaning and bowel training are associated with high *fear* of discovery.

It is possible that even when risk is completely eliminated, some irrational fear is evoked. In that event, the scores for both disobedience and death wishes indicate strength of fear, and we related our childhood antecedents to differences in the perceived probability of being caught, not to differences in guilt. An examination of our data vitiates this contention. When we recompute the relations, separating the subjects who expressed conscious guilt about disobedience from those who described fear or punishment by others, the directions of associations are the same. Late weaning and mild bowel training go with severe guilt for both groups.

Rather than assume that risk has been eliminated, it may be

---

it may cause less injury than intended, or it may result in more injury—a broken nose or broken jaw. Even if the fist misses its mark, the friend, in dodging it, may fall out of the boat and drown. Thus the conditions of the *accomplishment* may be less or more extreme than the intended ones. The intention may be followed by accidental accomplishment when there is no act. Finally, the accomplishment may be unrelated to the intention. If, after events such as these in the fishing incident, we want to understand a man's remorse in detail, we have to be aware of the indicated differentiations. Only if we take each of them into account can we be sure that all subjects are responding to the same combination of wish, intention, act, and accomplishment.

sounder in future studies to vary systematically the amount of danger in a series of items and to relate these differences to the guilt in the story endings. While we originally thought in terms of the presence or total absence of risk, it seems plausible that people evaluate discovery more in terms of probability.

*Males versus Females.* Another aspect of the story content which we did not control was the sex of the adults. This variation may account for the contrasts in the directions of our findings. The object of the death wish is a paternal figure, the coach; the object of disobedience is the mother. If the parents' rearing practices have been nurturant, as late weaning is often conceived to be, the child may be more tied to his mother than to his father. As a result, he may find it very difficult to disobey her. Such a developmental sequence may explain the obtained connection between late weaning and high guilt about disobeying the mother. Very different results might have been obtained if the parental method had been harsh because it was premature. The child might then have become disappointed in his mother and formed a stronger attachment to his father. He would then have been more sensitive to rejection by his father than his mother, and when he became angry at his father, the prospect of losing his love would have been very threatening.

*Disobedience versus Sexuality.* An unsuspected problem in interpreting the results of the disobedience stories emerged when we analyzed some of the endings. For a number of subjects the entrance into the mother's closet and the investigation of her boxes seem to have had unconscious sexual significance. In quite a few stories the hero finds objects in the closet which pertain to the mother's love life or reproductive functions. It seemed possible that some subjects were reacting less to guilt about disobedience than to guilt about sexual interests. When we divide our subjects in accordance with the presence or absence of sexual content in their stories, however, we find that the two groups do not differ significantly with respect to weaning and the other parental practices, degree of guilt, or relations between parental practices and guilt.

*Order of Stories.* Our method was deficient in that it did not include the presentation of the items in different orders to various groups of subjects. We were not in a position, therefore, to determine the influence of the order of stories on our results. But if variations in order affected our findings markedly, not many of them would have been significant. It is our impression, therefore, that this source of error did not have a great influence on our data. Yet, because of the possible importance that the order of stories could have had, we controlled it in planning our later work.

CONCLUSIONS REGARDING SEVERITY OF GUILT

Severity of guilt in our junior high school boys is associated with the reported timing of their weaning and toilet training (or with unknown events in infancy and early childhood of which these rearing factors provide indices). The directions of the relations raise questions we have taken up in the discussion, but there is ample evidence of some kinds of associations. Intensity of moral response seems to be a function of experiences early in life. This conclusion applies to reactions concerning disobedience and perhaps theft, as well as concerning death wishes. It is probable that guilt about anger is also related to parental choice of disciplinary procedures, but only among middle-class subjects. Obedience requests and social class are unrelated to severity of guilt.

## Results: Externalization

*Externalization Following Theft.* We have described earlier our division of subjects into those who externalized and those who did not. As indicated in Table 6-3, type of discipline is significantly associated with externalization following theft. Externalization occurs least frequently among subjects whose discipline was mixed. Toilet training shows a nonsignificant trend, a finding that we shall discuss in the next section. Weaning, requests for obedience, and social class are unrelated to externalization.

*Externalization Following Disobedience.* No background condition is significantly associated with externalization. Type of discipline, however, shows a strong trend. The direction is the same as in the case of theft. Both weaning and toilet training show trends which do not reach significance. Examination of our data shows that the latter trends are primarily artifacts of the significant association of externalization with intensity of guilt, an association which is, of

**TABLE 6-3**

Background Conditions and Externalization

| Condition | Externalization of Guilt Following: Theft | | | | Disobedience | | | |
|---|---|---|---|---|---|---|---|---|
| | *Trends: Boxes with Largest Frequencies* | *N* | $\chi^2$ | *Probability* | *Trends: Boxes with Largest Frequencies* | *N* | $\chi^2$ | *Probability* |
| Weaning | — | 105 | .78 | $<.40$ | Early weaning & extern. absent | 105 | 2.15 | .14 |
| Toilet training | Severe training & extern. absent | 104 | 1.68 | .20 | Severe training & extern. absent | 104 | 2.86 | .09 |
| Discipline | Mixed disc. & extern. absent | 112 | 7.76 | .02 | Mixed disc. & extern. absent | 112 | 5.73 | .06 |
| Obedience requests | — | 81 | .18 | $<.70$ | — | 81 | .22 | $<.70$ |
| Social class | — | 112 | .003 | $<1.00$ | — | 112 | .16 | $<.70$ |

course, hardly surprising, since boys whose stories contain themes of punishment tend to receive ratings of high guilt.[28] Neither obedience requests nor social class is related to externalization following disobedience.

*Problems in Interpreting Our Findings about Externalization.* We have implied that externalization, as coded in our subjects' stories, is actually a defense against guilt. We cannot be certain that this is so, because we do not have independent evidence that our subjects were unaware of their inner conflict. Our data lend themselves to other interpretations as well. Punishment, or fear of it, in the stories may reflect an oversensitivity to danger on the part of some subjects. They may really be afraid or anticipating punishment, not just resorting to the defensive distortion of guilt. Danger to the hero in the stories may represent projection by our subjects of their hostility rather than an expression of their guilt. Finally, themes of fear and punishment in the stories may also reflect the desire for punishment that provides absolution.[29]

### Conclusions regarding externalization

While intensity of moral response is associated largely with factors early in life, the ways (rather than degrees to which) guilts are experienced by boys in early adolescence are primarily a function of current discipline. The intermediately disciplined have the least tendency to focus on external punishment or danger in response to secret acts of theft and of disobedience.

## Results: Resistance to Temptation

*Resistance to Temptation Concerning Theft.* Requests for obedience represent the one background condition significantly as-

[28] Assuming that externalization is, as we postulate, indeed a defense, we need to consider whether it is reasonable that those subjects resorting to externalization should be high in sèverity of guilt. In general, we think it is. People use defensive distortions when remorse becomes strong enough to be markedly unpleasant.

[29] The reader may wish to conjecture which of these explanations better fit the psychologically and which the corporally disciplined, both of whom tend to be externalizers in contrast to those treated intermediately.

**TABLE 6-4**

Background Conditions, Perceived Source of Standards, and Resistance to Temptation

| Condition | *Perceived Source of Standards* | | | | *Resistance to Temptation* | | | | | | | |
|---|---|---|---|---|---|---|---|---|---|---|---|---|
| | | | | | *Theft* | | | | *Disobedience* | | | |
| | *Trends: Boxes with Largest Frequencies* | N | $\chi^2$ | *Probability* | *Trends: Boxes with Largest Frequencies* | N | $\chi^2$ | *Probability* | *Trends: Boxes with Largest Frequencies* | N | $\chi^2$ | *Probability* |
| Weaning | — | 102 | 2.80 | <.30 | — | 105 | .09 | <.80 | Early weaning & resists tempt. | 105 | 2.69 | .10 |
| Toilet training | Severe training & inner certainty | 101 | 5.53 | .07 | — | 104 | .67 | <.50 | — | 104 | .08 | <.80 |
| Discipline | Mixed disc. & inner certainty | 109 | 7.89 | <.10 | — | 112 | .60 | <.80 | — | 112 | 2.83 | <.30 |
| Obedience requests | — | 78 | 1.72 | <.50 | Explained requests & resists tempt. | 81 | 4.24 | .04 | Explained requests & resists tempt. | 81 | 4.05 | <.05 |
| Social class | Middle class & inner certainty | 109 | 7.52 | .02 | — | 112 | .02 | <.90 | — | 112 | .32 | <.60 |

sociated with resistance to temptation about theft.[30] Table 6-4 depicts this finding. Subjects whose parents have made reasonable requests are inclined to resist temptation.

*Resistance to Temptation Concerning Disobedience.* Again it is the variable of requests for obedience which is significantly associated with resistance to temptation. Weaning shows a trend. Toilet training, discipline, and social class do not.[31]

Although we did not attempt to predict the direction of the association between obedience requests and resistance to temptation, in retrospect it seems a logical one. When parents have demonstrated their reasonableness, the child is likely to believe that there is a good reason for conforming to parental expectations.

*Problems in Interpreting Our Findings about Resistance to Temptation.* Our characterization of subjects' resistance to temptation is, naturally, valid only if we may assume that all subjects were tempted to the same degree. Were some more tempted than others, yielding to temptation would be a function of this fact rather than of a stable disposition to yield in such circumstances. If our assumption is unjustified, and those who yielded to temptation were the more intensely tempted, our finding means that parents who do not explain their demands have children who, more than other children, are tempted to disobey rather than being more inclined than the others to yield when equally tempted. In addition, we do not, at present, have the evidence to determine whether resistance to temptation in our stories mirrors the behavior of the authors in real life.

*Conclusion about Resistance to Temptation.* Like externalization, resistance to temptation in our data is associated with an index of current parental practice. Subjects whose parents have explained their requests are most inclined to write stories in which heroes resist temptation. Boys whose parents have been arbitrary are inclined to yield to temptation. In a later section we discuss our

[30] Within the middle class only, discipline is associated with resistance to temptation at the .05 level. Boys whose discipline has been mixed resist temptation. The probability is .50 for the working class. However, the association of discipline with resistance to temptation is largely a function of a correlation between externalization and resistance to temptation—an association we shall discuss shortly.

[31] Discipline shows a trend with a probability of .20 in the middle class. The probability is .90 for the working class.

notions of the psychological conditions under which subjects are likely to resist or yield.

## Results: Perceived Source of Standards

Table 6-4 contains our findings for perceived source of standards. Social class is significantly related to this index. More subjects from the middle class reveal inner certainty. Toilet training and discipline show trends: boys whose training has been severe and whose discipline has been mixed are inclined to express inner certainty. Each of these parental practices contributes to some of the variance of perceived source of standards: the trends are not solely a function of the correlation with social class of discipline and of toilet training. Weaning and obedience requests are not associated with perceived source.

Our information about perceived source was derived from the subjects' responses to the query, "How do you know whether a thing is right or wrong?" The fact that the answers are related chiefly to social class suggests that children's statements to an interviewer may represent conventional responses peculiar to certain social groups. We gain more confidence in the possibility that perceived source is a fundamental characteristic of personality when we discover certain interrelations among our indices of moral response. We now discuss these associations.

## Interrelations Among Our Variables

Externalization is significantly related to resistance to temptation. The externalizers give in to their impulses. Resistance to temptation, in turn, is significantly related to perceived source of standards. In judging what is right and wrong, boys who yield to temptation are inclined to rely on others rather than on their own feelings. Yet perceived source is not significantly associated with externalization. We imagine that the two variables are not related because inner certainty, as inferred from an interview, is valid primarily in instances of temptation rather than violation. When applied to a potential misdeed, reported standards about which there is inner certainty probably affect resistance to temptation. But after violation has occurred, many subjects who do not characteristically remain unaware of their standards may quell the pain of self-reproach by a defense such as externalization.

Resistance to temptation thus appears to us to be a function both of the tendency to be aware of one's standards before transgression and of the propensity not to defend against guilt following misconduct. People who are accustomed to disowning their moral needs, or to deceiving themselves about remorse after violation, are most likely to yield.

Additional interpretations of resistance to temptation are also possible. Some people may yield to temptation because of limited capacity to delay gratification: Even if they are able to estimate accurately the consequences of a contemplated act, they behave impulsively because their frustration tolerance is too low to enable them to control themselves. Others may misbehave in order to provoke punishment for some prior misdeed. Yielding may also reflect the ease with which a person has learned to obtain absolution from guilt. Perhaps a man with intense, overgeneralized fear may resist temptation even if there is neither risk of detection nor capacity for remorse. Finally, certain people may get masochistic gratification from the frustrating experiences connected with resistance. Anyone, of course, no matter how mature he is, probably yields when exposed to sufficient temptation. In the present study we have assumed temptation to be roughly equal for all subjects.

It has been suggested to us by R. L. Solomon and J. W. M. Whiting that the inclination to resist temptation may be learned quite independently of guilt. For instance, a spying parent who anticipates a child's misbehavior may teach him to inhibit himself. Yet, if such a parent treats violations lightly, the child may not become very remorseful when he does yield to temptation. We need more investigations of so-called "influence techniques" (13), which include attempts to prevent misbehavior as well as procedures for punishing the act.

The suggestion by Whiting and Solomon represents an interpretation of resistance to temptation different from the one we would have made before we began the study. It originally appeared to us that resisting temptation was a function of the severity of guilt: The more the guilt that accompanies misbehavior, the greater the resistance should be. We do not find such an association in our data. Instead, we find additional support for the assertion that resistance to temptation is a function of absence of defense. Subjects who write stories in which the heroes directly acknowledge their self-blame or guilt feelings following transgression—who defend against guilt neither by externalization nor in any other fashion—are significantly more inclined to depict heroes who resist temptation than are subjects who do not express conscious remorse.

Our final observation has to do with those subjects whose mothers report using intermediate discipline. These subjects are less inclined than others to externalize guilt, and our data suggest that they may also have more inner certainty about their moral needs. To the extent that absence of defense and awareness of one's needs are criteria of health, the emotional well-being of these boys may be greater than that of the boys whose parents use corporal or psychological techniques.

## Summary

In this chapter we first specified the conditions required to identify guilt. After describing the technique we developed in an effort to meet these conditions, we reported associations between child-rearing practices and social class, on the one hand, and eight indices of moral response on the other: severity of guilt about death wishes, theft, and disobedience; defense against guilt by externalization after theft and disobedience; resistance to temptation concerning theft and disobedience; and perceived source of standards. We found that the timing of weaning and toilet training are significantly related to severity of guilt about more than one type of transgression. Our results indicate that when we understand more about the direction of the associations, it may be possible to forecast from certain experiences in infancy the intensity of moral response in children twelve years later. While severity of guilt seems to be a function of experiences early in life, current disciplinary procedures are more effective in influencing the way guilt is now experienced—that is, whether or not it is externalized. Boys whose mothers use mixed discipline are least likely to externalize guilt. If we wish to predict resistance to temptation, we must turn to obedience requests, another index of current practice: Arbitrary requests are associated with yielding to temptation. Yielding is most frequent in subjects who defend against guilt after transgression or who rely on others' standards when contemplating a misdeed. Finally, it is middle-class rather than working-class children who show inner certainty about their standards.

## References

1. Allinsmith, W. The learning of moral standards. Unpublished Ph.D. dissertation, Univ. of Michigan, 1954.
2. ———. Conscience and conflict: the moral force in personality. *Child Develop.*, 1957, *28*, 469–76.
3. ———, & Greening, T. C. Guilt over anger as predicted from parental discipline: a study of superego development. *Amer. Psychol.* 1955, *10*, 320.
4. Fenichel, O. *The psychoanalytic theory of neurosis.* New York: Norton, 1945.
5. Ferenczi, S. Psycho-analysis of sexual habits. *Further contributions to the theory and techniques of psycho-analysis.* London: Hogarth, 1950.
6. Flugel, J. C. *Man, morals and society.* New York: International Universities Press, 1945.
7. Grosser, D., Polansky, N., & Lippitt, R. A laboratory study of behavioral contagion. *Human Relations,* 1951, *4,* 115–42.
8. Hartshorne, H., & Maller, J. B. *Studies in service and self-control.* New York: Macmillan, 1929.
9. ———, & May, M. A. *Studies in deceit.* New York: Macmillan, 1928.
10. ———, May, M. A., & Shuttleworth, F. K. *Studies in the organization of character.* New York: Macmillan, 1930.
11. MacKinnon, D. W. Violation of prohibitions. In Murray, H. A., *et al. Explorations in personality.* New York: Oxford Univ. Press, 1938.
12. Mowrer, O. H. *Learning theory and personality dynamics.* New York: Ronald Press, 1950.
13. Sigel, I. E., Hoffman, M., Dreyer, A., & Torgoff, I. Toward a theory of influence techniques: preliminary report. *Merrill-Palmer Quart.,* 1954, 4–17.

# 7

## MORAL STANDARDS

## III. Moral Behavior and Sex Identity *

An investigator can sometimes learn a great deal about a topic by approaching it from different vantage points. We have just described a study linking both conscience and defense against guilt with child-rearing practices. In the research we are about to report we investigated the associations between reactions to guilt, both direct and defensive, and various patterns of sex identity. We also explored loss of self-control, in this case over strong feelings aroused by the violation of standards.

We selected our subjects from the third population described in Chapter 4. From this group of white, undergraduate, unmarried college men, we chose three types of subjects. One was predominantly masculine, both consciously and unconsciously, one was unconsciously feminine but consciously very masculine, and one was feminine both unconsciously and consciously.[1] We arrived at our predictions by making a number of inferences about previous experiences which might have created the three types. As we stated earlier, these are not the only possible inferences. We cited them because they helped to illustrate the reasons for some of our hypotheses and our interpretations of results. In planning our research we speculated particularly about social backgrounds and

* In the research team, Justin Aronfreed was responsible for the research to be reported and for the preparation of the chapter, which is based in part on his doctoral dissertation (1).

[1] In Chapter 3 we outlined our methods of classifying the three types and some speculations about their possible origins.

earlier relationships with parents. From these speculations we derived hypotheses about reactions to guilt of subjects with different identities. We shall relate these speculations to the origins of different identities and to the severity of guilt. To clarify the meaning of our hypotheses, we must first describe our instruments and our techniques of using them.

## Method

### Projective test

To measure the severity of our subjects' moral standards, we administered a story completion test. We chose this method in preference to the interview because we felt that the average person is often unaware of, or unable to report, certain aspects of his moral standards and of his self-punitive behavior following their violation. The projective instrument was patterned after one developed by W. Allinsmith and described in Chapter 6. In adopting the basic features of this method, we wrote story themes which included aggression against a planned variety of objects. In each story beginning, the problem of the hero, a male, touches upon the conflicts and strivings ordinarily experienced by college students. The hero likes, and is in some way indebted to, the person who becomes the object of his aggression.

*Themes.* In a pilot study six themes were chosen from a larger number on the basis of stimulus effectiveness and of comparability in eliciting evidence of guilt and other self-punitive reactions.[2] We presented the six themes to each subject in two sets, each containing three stories. The plots in the two groups of tests were parallel with respect to content. In the first story of each set it is implied that an older woman interferes with the hero's sexual

[2] The stories may be found in Appendix C. For reasons cited in Chapter 6, each story theme involves a conflict and an actual violation of a moral standard. It is absolutely certain that no one else can know about the transgression. Only by inserting a violation into the risk-free plot could we be confident that the main character in the story was motivated by guilt rather than by an impulse to placate an authority or to avoid his punishment. Because no one else could know about the transgression, we could interpret as projections any endings which described other people as criticizing the hero.

interest in a young woman. By an expression of hostility, the hero unintentionally contributes to the death of the maternal figure. One story, for example, tells about Bruce who is very attached to his elderly teacher because she has helped him to write so well. He is driving in his car one day, sees her, and offers her a ride. She accepts. After they have been driving for a few minutes, he sees one of his class themes on the seat beside her. The theme is an account of his love for his girl friend, and he notices that the teacher has made some very critical comments. He is furious and wishes her dead. In his excitement he misses a stop sign and collides with another car. He is uninjured, but the teacher dies.

In the second pair of story beginnings, the hero is privately offended and then obtains revenge upon a sibling figure who has flaunted his superiority in the presence of a woman. The hero feels inadequate and gets his revenge by a dishonest victory in a competition with the offender. The last story in each set involves the criticism or belittlement of the hero by an older male authority figure. The hero expresses his resentment by attacking the source of the authority's power.

*Analysis of Story Endings.* Each subject's story endings were analyzed for evidence of severity of standards, defensiveness against a self-critical application of standards to one's own behavior, and loss of control. A subject's score for each set of stories was the total number of separate references to a particular variable. In a single story only those themes were counted which seemed independent of one another and distinct in content. If, for example, the hero felt bad and also criticized himself in the same sentence, only one tabulation was made. This scoring system was based, then, on the assumption that the severity of a person's standards is reflected in the frequency and variation of actions needed to relieve guilt aroused when the subject identifies with the hero of the story.

*Shift Scores.* The present study is one of a number in which we attempted to arouse a conflict as a means of intensifying the behaviors we wanted to observe. We tried to arouse guilt primarily because we felt that the stories in themselves might not be sufficient to provoke the subjects' characteristic responses to violations of standards. Three stories were administered before the arousal of guilt and three afterward. Shifts in the number of themes showing the various kinds of responses to violating standards were then used as measures of the dependent variables. This procedure made it possible to evaluate the effectiveness of the arousal technique and to compare the reactions of the three groups under the same conditions of guilt arousal.

Had the stories alone been used, there was a possibility that differences between the three groups might have occurred because of contrasting interpretations of the stories. If there were no differences between the three groups in the stories completed before arousal—showing that the stories had comparable stimulus values—differences in shift scores following arousal could be attributed to differences in the severity of standards concerning actions in the stories.

In order to control the possible effects on our results of the orders in which the two sets of stories were administered, we divided each of the three groups in half. To one half we assigned one set of stories before the arousal and the second set following the arousal. The other half of the subjects received the two sets in reverse order. We find that the orders of stories does not affect the significance of any of the results to be reported.

TECHNIQUE OF AROUSING GUILT

We first seated the subject before an "electronic" machine with a handle on the side. The panel of the machine contained a counter, a red light which flashed intermittently, and a small ammeter. Two wires attached to the back of the machine originated in an apparatus on another table. This apparatus consisted of a buzzer and a light, both of which were controlled by the examiner. Each time the subject saw a light or heard a buzz, he was to turn the handle of his machine. The examiner explained that the ammeter measured the lag between the signal and the turning of the handle.

According to the instructions, the examiner would combine the light and buzzer in complex patterns. It was necessary that the subject keep a steady rhythm in turning the handle: "If you fall a little bit behind, don't turn the handle jerkily, because the instruments inside are very delicate."

Then the task began. Each time the handle was turned, the dial on the ammeter swung to the other side, the red light flashed, and the counter clicked. The examiner used increasingly complicated patterns of lights and sounds which were finally very difficult to follow. Every subject seemed highly involved in the task. Then came the climax. Suddenly the subject heard a dull clanking inside the machine. The light, the counter, and the ammeter all stopped working.[3] When the subject tried to turn the handle, he found it was loose.

The examiner continued to operate the light and buzzer, apparently oblivious of the breakdown of the machine. When the breakdown was called to his attention, he rose in astonishment and tried the handle. He asked whether the subject had been able to maintain a steady rhythm. Then he looked up with an air of dawning realization and noted that the machine was, in fact, broken. He tried to make further adjustments, but gave up and said that the machine had to be repaired. Meanwhile, he asked whether the subject would be good enough to finish the second set of stories.

### Controls

We checked the possibility that a number of variables other than the ones we were studying might have affected our results. We reanalyzed the associations between sex identity and different reactions to guilt, while holding constant verbal productivity and scores on the intelligence test of the American Council on Education (4) to determine whether either of these could have accounted for some of the results. In no case was there a change in the significance of obtained differences. We also examined the results for the initial stories to see whether some subjects had reached a maximal score which they could not exceed in the second set of stories. We found no such instances. Furthermore, scores on the initial stories are not related to shifts in the variables under study.

[3] Inside the machine there was a battery in circuit with three instruments. Each turn of the handle closed this circuit by means of a revolving brush. The end of the handle inside the machine was threaded and screwed into a hole in a weight. By turning the handle, the subject was gradually detaching it from the weight. When the weight fell, the circuit was broken. Our method was modeled after one evolved by Klaus (2).

## Results

SEX IDENTITY AND SOCIAL POSITION [4]

The considerable cross-cultural variation in the forms of sex identity prompted us to investigate its relation to social position in our society. Because ours was a college population, we did not have enough subjects from the working class to permit a comparison of the two social strata. Fortunately, we did have enough representatives of the two types of integration, the entrepreneurial and bureaucratic.

*Entrepreneurial Families.* In postulating an association between type of integration and sex identity, we began with the observation that masculine traits are acquired slowly. A boy needs his parents' support throughout this process. If he is suddenly required to learn new and difficult skills, or if he is punished drastically, he may give up trying to develop masculine characteristics and adopt or retain simple techniques, some of which were learned earlier in life and are regarded as feminine in our society.

If parents are unduly concerned with developing an active, masculine son, they may, by premature or unreasonable demands, create many obstacles to masculinity. Even a cursory review reveals how much more inimical to feminine behavior in men are the pressures of the entrepreneurial setting than are those in the bureaucratic setting. When men are struggling for success in a competitive labor market, they prize initiative, aggressiveness, independence, and interest in the practical aspects of everyday life. Parents push their sons, often prematurely, toward all kinds of achievement, masculine and otherwise (3). If a boy can assert himself and assume adult responsibilities, he gains considerable recognition. If not, he can anticipate rejection. The entrepreneurial setting creates values that result in early and harsh parental pressures. Therefore, we anticipated that it would breed more unconsciously feminine men than would the bureaucratic setting.

*Bureaucratic Families.* In the bureaucratic setting mobility is available less to the talented individualist than to the man who

[4] The data discussed in this section on integration were collected and analyzed by Justin Aronfreed and Leonard Lansky.

can work well in a team. He, too, must take initiative, but to be successful he must be flexible, sensitive to the needs of others, and capable of winning acceptance. These qualities are much more highly prized than self-denial and the ability to achieve one's goals regardless of the means. Bureaucratic parents, consequently, encourage their children to develop social sensitivity. The youngsters are allowed a long period of dependence (3), and are rewarded less for surpassing others than for winning their acceptance. The bureaucratic setting provides more outlets for feminine traits than does the entrepreneurial setting, and imposes less pressure on boys to display masculine traits like initiative and independence. Hence we expected to find fewer unconsciously feminine men from bureaucratic families than from entrepreneurial ones.

*Predictions.* In view of these assumptions, we predicted that compared to entrepreneurial men, bureaucratic men would be less handicapped by premature parental pressures in developing masculine identities. Furthermore, we expected bureaucratic men to have much more leeway to explore and outgrow the expressive styles which might be labeled as feminine in the entrepreneurial setting.

In our analysis we compared entrepreneurial and bureaucratic college students from the middle class.[5] We predicted that the largest proportion of the two unconsciously feminine groups would come from entrepreneurial families and that most MMs would come from bureaucratic families. In Table 7-1 we summarize the results, not only for integration but also for the rest of the variables we studied.

The results support our prediction. Compared to the FFs and FMs, a much smaller proportion of MMs come from the entrepreneurial setting and a much larger proportion come from the bureaucratic setting. The MMs differ significantly from the combination of FFs and FMs and from the FMs as a group. The difference between the MMs and FFs is very close to significance. The two unconsciously feminine groups do not differ significantly from each other.

We cannot overlook the possibility that our results reflect

[5] Our criteria for social class and type of integration are contained in Chapter 2.

TABLE 7-1

Sex Identity, Integration, and Reactions to Violations of Standards

| | | *Direction of Shift* | | | | |
|---|---|---|---|---|---|---|
| *Condition* | *Sex Identity* | *No Increase* | *In-crease* | *Rate of Increase* | $\chi^2$ | *Proba-bility* |
| Severity of standards | MM | 30 | 5 | MM < nonMM | 27.97 | <.001 (1t) |
| | FM | 6 | 26 | MM < FM | 27.52 | <.001 (1t) |
| | FF | 15 | 25 | MM < FF | 16.13 | <.001 (1t) |
| | | | | FM < FF | 2.19 | .14 |
| Direct expression of guilt | MM | 23 | 12 | MM < nonMM | 4.01 | .02 (1t) |
| | FM | 14 | 18 | MM < FM | 2.43 | .06 (1t) |
| | FF | 16 | 22 | MM < FF | 3.19 | .04 (1t) |
| | | | | FM < FF | .01 | <1.00 |
| Defenses against guilt | MM | 23 | 12 | MM < nonMM | 2.54 | .06 (1t) |
| | FM | 14 | 18 | MM < FM | 2.43 | .06 (1t) |
| | FF | 20 | 20 | MM < FF | 1.30 | .13 (1t) |
| | | | | FM < FF | .08 | <.40 (1t) |
| Loss of control | MM | 33 | 2 | MM < nonMM | 9.02 | <.001 (1t) |
| | FM | 20 | 12 | MM < FM | 8.39 | <.001 (1t) |
| | FF | 27 | 13 | MM < FF | 6.78 | <.01 (1t) |
| | | | | FM < FF | .04 | <.90 |

| *Condition* | *Sex Identity* | *Entre-preneurial* | *Bureau-cratic* | *Relation: More Entrepreneurs* | $\chi^2$ | *Proba-bility* |
|---|---|---|---|---|---|---|
| Integration | MM | 16 | 13 | MM < nonMM | 7.56 | .01 |
| | FM | 24 | 3 | MM < FM | 6.22 | .01 |
| | FF | 26 | 6 | MM < FF | 3.68 | .06 |
| | | | | FM < FF | .20 | .70 |

the process whereby people are selected for a major university, rather than a true association between integration and sex identity in the general population. It might be claimed that the unconsciously feminine men who have sufficient academic success in secondary or preparatory schools and gain admissions to a university come mostly from the future-oriented, entrepreneurial families. If this were true, our obtained differences would apply only to a college population. To test our hypotheses more generally we would have to obtain a more representative sample of the general population. However, even if such a bias existed in our sample, it could affect only part of our results. It would not explain the differences within the bureaucratic group, since they all presumably have similar values about education. We see no convincing reasons to postulate that bureaucrats value education less than the entrepreneurs do. Hence, we think that we would have obtained the same differences in integration had we studied the sex identities of men with limited education.

### Severity of standards

In the previous chapter we defined and discussed severity of standards in some detail. As we view severity, it refers to all forms of pain or discomfort that a person feels or inflicts upon himself when he has violated an internalized standard. A man may express the punitiveness of his standards in a wide variety of ways. Feelings of guilt are probably the most common. He may also seek atonement by punishing himself, by apologizing, or by making reparations to the person whom he has wronged. Or he may engage in acts which deprive him of pleasure, cause him to fail in some important undertaking, or cause him physical pain.

*Predictions.* How is sex identity related to moral standards? At certain stages of development, the normal boy begins to explore his neighborhood, to engage in boisterous physical activity, to take initiative in many activities, to resist his parents' regulations, and to display sexual curiosity. If he is not free to try out some of these new kinds of behavior, it is very difficult for him to synthesize a masculine identity. Yet some parents react to these emerging behaviors with severe punishment and marked rejection. It is possible for the son to retain their love only if he follows their suggestions and passively seeks their help in overcoming various emergencies. Like anyone else, the boy adopts as his own the standards that his parents apply in restricting his attempts at self-assertion. He internalizes these norms. Later, when he violates them, the severity of his guilt is proportional to the intensity of his early punishment at his parents' hands. In sum, we anticipated that boys who had developed feminine identities would have more severe moral standards about aggression than the boys whose parents provided the opportunities to try out masculine behavior.

*Criteria.* In scoring the story endings we identified severity of standards in terms of attempts to relieve the pressure of guilt. Such attempts can take various forms. Most obvious are the instances in which the main character of the story expresses remorse and punishes himself, makes attempts at reparation, or tries to absolve himself of guilt by confession, apology, or the sacrifice of some source of pleasure. Two examples are: "Joe feels badly; he apologizes," and "Bill feels worthless, and he cannot face people." Such responses were classified as direct expressions of guilt.

We also tabulated three manifestations of defenses against guilt. One was the hero's projection of his critical or punitive feelings. The second defensive distortion was displacement of blame, and the third was denial of guilt. Our code for these defenses is contained in a later section of this chapter.

*Analysis of Results and Predictions.* Scores for total severity were computed by adding the separate scores for direct expression and for defenses. We compared the number of subjects in each group who increased any of the manifestations of guilt, direct or defensive, with the number who either did not change or who decreased their expression of guilt.[6]

We predicted that, following arousal, the two unconsciously feminine groups would show more of an increase in guilt than would the unconsciously masculine subjects. We had no prediction about the differences between the FMs and FFs.

To test the hypothesis we compared the frequency of the MMs' guilt themes with those of all other subjects. As indicated in Table 7-1, the difference is very significant. Fewer men with unconsciously masculine identification increase their references to

[6] To obtain a measure of reliability, J. Aronfreed and T. C. Greening independently coded the stories of twenty subjects chosen at random and in approximately equal proportions from each of three groups. The unit of analysis was the individual story ending, and a disagreement was tabulated whenever a theme involving any direct or indirect expression of guilt was tabulated by one judge and not the other. In their coding of 120 stories, the two judges agreed on 85 per cent of the themes coded for direct expression of guilt and on 76 per cent of the themes coded for defense.

guilt following the "breaking" of the machine than do men with unconscious feminine tendencies. When we compare the feminine groups, we find that the difference is not significant. The FFs have slightly less of a tendency to increase guilt than the FMs do.

DIRECT EXPRESSION OF GUILT

We began our study with the idea of comparing subjects with respect to the severity of their guilt. On considering the expression of severity, we realized that we would have to tabulate both direct and indirect forms. Having found that the three groups of subjects differed significantly with respect to total severity, we then made separate analyses of the associations with sex identity of direct expressions and the defenses. Only then could we know how these two manifestations of severity were related to each other, whether or not only one of them was actually responsible for the significant differences in total scores, and whether the relation of sex identity to each was independent of the other expression.

As indicated in Table 7-1, the MMs are significantly less inclined toward the direct expression of guilt than is the combination of the other two groups. The difference between the MMs and the FFs is significant; the difference between the MMs and FMs is very close to significance.

When we compare the direct expression of guilt in all subjects with the frequency of defenses, we find a significant negative relation. As we might expect, the more directly a man expresses guilt, the less he needs to defend himself against it. Conversely, the less directly he expresses his guilt, the more frequently he has to defend himself. This inverse relation is true for the FMs and FFs, but not for the MMs, who are disinclined to use defenses against guilt. We next determined the extent to which the association between sex identity and one of the manifestations of severity was independent of the other. To this end, we held one variable constant and reanalyzed the relation of the other manifestation of severity with sex identity. They remain significant when either variable is held constant and an analysis is made of the association between the other and sex identity. In short, direct expressions of guilt and frequency of defenses are negatively related to each other, and the relation of each to sex identity is independent of the other.

DEFENSES AGAINST GUILT

Some people cannot tolerate more than a certain amount of guilt. When it exceeds their threshold, they distort reality and defend themselves, not against the forbidden need, since its expression has already led to self-condemnation, but against the guilt itself.

Defenses against guilt involve the distortion of a person's self-critical application of his standards to his own actions or impulses. In a pilot study we found that three defenses were used most frequently in the story endings. They were projection of the punitive aspect of the standards, displacement of blame, and denial of the standard or violation. In using projection of criticism, subjects described heroes as attributing punishment or critical attitudes to other people or impersonal forces. A story hero might feel disliked by others, for example, or he might be accidentally hit by a truck.[7] Some of the heroes even provoked other people to attack or reject them, or interpreted as punishment either fortuitous misfortunes or the coincidental hostile behavior of other people.

Displacement of blame was easy to identify since the stories were written in such a manner that only the heroes could reasonably be blamed for the aggressive act. In endings involving displacement, the hero usually blamed other people for his behavior or justified his behavior by reference to theirs. References to the defense of denial occurred only rarely. It was coded when the hero energetically glossed over or minimized his behavior, but not when he seemed to be unaware of its moral implications. In one ending involving denial the hero said, "Why should I feel guilty? He's no good anyway. All's fair in love and war."

What kind of a person defends himself against the pressure of his conscience? He is often the type whose internalized

[7] We were very conservative in coding projection. We did not include, for example, criticisms of the hero for violations which were matters of public knowledge, since the subjects' responses could have been motivated less by guilt than by fear of punishment or by shame.

standards are so severe that they produce intolerable guilt when violated. As we have just indicated, excessive severity often results from excessively punitive parental discipline. It may also occur if the parents' standards are very restrictive. A child who internalizes such restrictive standards is deprived of many outlets for his aggression which most people can use freely. Because of his limited avenues of expression, he is more likely than most people to violate his standards. If his guilt is very intense or very frequent, he may find it easier to defend himself against it than to suffer the unpleasant consequences of his behavior.

*Predictions.* The early experiences of the male who is unconsciously passive and feminine often create extensive, severe standards. When he violates them, he is inclined to resort to some defense against his standards. In contrast, the man who has had an opportunity to acquire a variety of socially acceptable outlets for his aggressive needs is less likely to express his aggression in ways that violate his standards. He is also able to recognize his guilt, because it is not very intense.

*Predictions for Individual Defenses.* Originally, we planned to analyze each of the three defenses separately. For each, we had anticipated significant differences between the two unconsciously feminine groups as well as between them and the MMs. Every subject wrote some story endings containing references to defenses, but, unfortunately, the frequency of any particular type of defense was small. As a result, we could not compare the three groups with respect to any one defense. Had we been able to do so, we would have predicted that the FFs would exceed the other groups in their references to defenses in the first family.[8] The difficulties of the FMs should have led them to favor the second family of defenses.[9] Furthermore, we would have anticipated that, following the arousal of guilt, both the FFs and FMs would increase their defensiveness more than the MMs. The masculine identities of the latter could not have developed unless they had learned to judge their problems realistically.

*Predictions for Combined Defenses.* While the number of references to any one defense was small, it was possible to compare the three patterns of sex identity with respect to shifts in

[8, 9] These have been identified in the first chapter and will be discussed in detail in the next one.

total defensiveness. Although we expected the defenses of the two feminine groups to differ, we anticipated that their difference in defensiveness would not be significant. We predicted that the MMs would increase references to defenses less than the combined feminine sample would.

*Results.* As indicated in Table 7-1, changes in the defensiveness of the MMs do not differ significantly from the combined changes of the FFs and FMs. The 6 per cent probability that the difference could have occurred by chance is, however, very close to significance. The same probability is obtained for the difference between the MMs and FMs. As we expected, the two feminine groups do not differ significantly from each other. The MMs do not differ significantly from the FFs.

### Loss of control

Four assumptions were made about loss of control, all of which led to the same kind of prediction. We predicted that loss of control would occur if passivity had been reinforced, early difficulties had occurred, conflicts were numerous, or moral standards were extensive. We now consider each of these contributing factors in turn.

*Reinforcement of Passivity.* First we assumed that, as children, men with unconscious femininity were rewarded for passive reactions and punished for attempts to take initiative and to express aggression directly. A boy who is deprived of initiative has only a limited number of outlets for certain forms of aggression. Even these outlets may become foci of intense conflict. Some needs can be suppressed only for a limited time before they affect overt behavior, sometimes in violation of internalized standards.

*Early Difficulties.* A second and closely related assumption attributed loss of control to some difficulty which caused a retardation in personality development. Femininity was our index of such a difficulty. The unconscious femininity of the FFs and FMs suggests that they have more difficulties in childhood than the unconsciously masculine subjects do. Within the first few years, the child learns to inhibit, at least temporarily, the direct expression of certain needs. By developing this skill, he avoids the disapproval of adults as well as the pressures of his conscience. As we viewed the FFs and FMs they do not completely master some of these early interpersonal skills, one of which is self-control under stress.

*Frequency of Conflict.* The third assumption about loss of control was derived from our picture of conflict. Even if the unconsciously feminine subjects have learned to control themselves, they may be hard-pressed to exercise that skill because they are subject to frequent conflicts. At a minimum, the incompatibility between their own feminine and masculine standards, or between their feminine standards and those of other men, must create frequent anxiety. Unlike the unconsciously masculine subjects, the FMs cannot accept their unconscious sex identities. Although the FFs need not repress each feminine trait, they often try to hide it from others; they have to be on guard much of the time to avoid condemnation by some friends. In contrast to the unconsciously feminine subjects, the MMs are under little stress. They presumably suffer relatively few conflicts, are proficient in inhibiting their actions, and have available a wide variety of socially acceptable substitutes for forbidden outlets.

*Defenses against Standards.* The fourth assumption is a corollary of the third. Poor control on the part of unconsciously feminine men can also be derived from their extensive and punitive standards. If a person's standards are so harsh that he is frequently forced to distort them, it may be difficult for him to control unacceptable behavior.

*Criteria.* Control is lost if the hero cannot restrain himself from committing an act that he obviously wishes to avoid. There must be some evidence that he is critical of his own behavior or suffers discomfort as a result of it. The lack of acceptance shows that control, while weak, is directed at the inhibition of the proscribed acts. Violation of standards is not sufficient evidence of lack of control, since the act may be accompanied by feelings of justification rather than attempts at inhibition. Thus, sadistic behavior does not indicate loss of control unless there is evidence that the hero has committed the act despite efforts to restrain himself. If he becomes insane, for example, and then commits a sadistic act, this behavior indicates a loss of control. Other examples which we tabulated as loss of control included acts explained by the hero as losing his head, strong emotional outbursts, such as crying and screaming, and explosive, self-damaging behavior, such as wild alcoholic bouts or uncontrolled criminal acts.[10]

*Results.* Table 7-1 contains a comparison of the three groups. As predicted, unconscious femininity is associated with a greater increase in loss of control than is unconscious masculinity. The frequency of the loss of control shown by the MMs differs very significantly from the combined frequencies of the two feminine groups. Apparently, the unconscious feminine groups have the fewest realistic methods of resolving conflicts over guilt. The FFs do not differ significantly from the FMs.

In all three groups the proportions of stories about loss of control are small. This need not surprise us when we consider that our subjects were all men with sufficient control to have passed their courses in elementary and secondary schools, to have obtained good enough grades to be admitted to a major university, and then to have earned passing grades in their courses. Had we selected subjects in the first year of high school, we imagine that many more would have increased their number of references to loss of control following the arousal of guilt.

## Summary

In the study reported in this chapter we analyzed the relative frequencies of severe guilt, direct expression of guilt, defenses against standards, and loss of control in groups of men with different patterns of sex identity. To obtain these reactions, we administered one story completion test before, and another after, an attempt to arouse actual guilt in our subjects. In analyzing our results we compared the number of subjects in each group who increased references to a particular reaction following the arousal, with the number who did not increase their references. We find that both groups of unconsciously feminine men exceed the unconsciously masculine ones in the proportions who come from entrepreneurial settings. In addition, the FMs and FFs are more inclined than the MMs to write story endings which express

[10] The two independent raters agreed in 85 per cent of their ratings of loss of control.

very severe moral standards and refer to guilt, defenses against guilt, and loss of control.

## References

1. Aronfreed, Justin. Moral standards and defenses against guilt. Unpubl. Ph.D. dissertation, Univ. of Michigan, 1955.
2. Klaus, E. J. The effect of experimentally induced guilt on thematic apperception. Unpubl. honors thesis, Univ. of Michigan, 1951.
3. Miller, D. R., & Swanson, G. E. *The changing American parent.* New York: Wiley, 1958.
4. Thurstone, L. L., & Thurstone, Thelma G. Amer. Council on Education Psychological Examination. Princeton, N.J.: Cooperative Test Division, Educational Testing Service.

# 8

## MECHANISMS OF DEFENSE

### I. The Mechanisms of Defense

We now turn to the study of defense mechanisms. The planning of such research requires some critical theoretical decisions. To begin with, it is necessary to decide what is meant by defenses. Methods must be developed to identify different mechanisms; then their common properties can be studied. Certain similarities and differences among the mechanisms suggest that they can be divided into groups. Once these groups are located, it is possible to determine whether or not a person tends to favor defenses of only one group in resolving his problems. Information about the properties of different groups or "families" of defense will also facilitate the study of their origins.

### Identifying Mechanisms of Defense

In deciding on a definition one must first distinguish between defensive distortions and other kinds of mistakes. Do true errors ever occur? Of course they do. Then how can one determine whether or not a mistake results from a defensive distortion and is motivated by conflict? While there are many valuable references to the mechanisms of defense in the psychoanalytic literature, they provide no definitive answers to this question. Freud established defensive mechanisms as one of the cornerstones of psychoanalytic theory; sprinkled through many of his papers are instructive examples of defensive distortion. He had to delay a systematic examination of them, however, until he could first explore the content and organization of various types of conflict. Only in his final publications did he return to the mechanisms of defense and, even then, only incidentally.

Freud defines a defense as "a general designation for the techniques which the ego makes use of in conflicts which may lead to neurosis" (6). Such a definition is too general to be of help to the empirical worker.[1] It is amplified considerably by the comments of Anna Freud (5), who notes that the "ego's defensive operations" are unconscious and that they repudiate "the claims of instinct." The repudiation includes two processes. Defenses keep "ideational representatives of repressed instincts" from becoming conscious, and create a "transformation" in the affects associated with the need.

This definition applies primarily to the defenses seen most often by the psychoanalyst: those employed to distort the perception of needs whose direct expression would violate one's moral standards. To prevent guilt, for example, a boy may reverse his impulse to hurt a friend. Miss Freud also cites other problems to which the various mechanisms are often applied. Defenses may serve to regulate needs which, if expressed directly, would create a realistic problem: To avoid failing, a boy transfers his ambition to another field of endeavor. Defenses may also be used to alter needs with excessive strength. Even an appropriate sexual impulse may be inhibited when it threatens to overwhelm the individual. Finally, defenses may be applied to problems created by external events or static personal traits: A man who has lost his money, or is sensitive about his short stature, may never think about these facts.

To conduct research on a concept like defense, one must first decide on minimal criteria for defining it. The following example of behavior involving conflicting needs will illustrate the

[1] Given this generality, it is not surprising that the concept of defense is often used very loosely. The label of defense has been applied to neurotic symptoms (13), which are specific substitutes for forbidden needs rather than inferred mechanisms; to general personal characteristics, such as resistance to change (8); and to cultural products, such as myths (10), which are usually neither defenses nor products of defensive distortions.

criteria used in this study. A father sought therapeutic help because he was troubled by extreme anxiety. Within a short time, he discussed with the therapist his inability to impose firm restrictions on his young son's hostile acts. The father had fallen into a trap created by his misinterpretations of certain popular literature on child rearing. He feared that a firm disciplinary stand might hurt the child's personality and, probably more important, dry up the wellsprings of his love. The son, in order to test the limits of his father's tolerance, had become increasingly offensive. Despite his own resentment, the father had expressed only patience and love. In the event which engages our interest, he reported to a friend a depressing dream about the son's death.

Because of the man's "permissiveness," he was not able to retaliate against his son. In fact, he appears to have repressed his impotent fury. Why do we infer a defense from his behavior? If we interpret the dream as a wish, we see an aggressive goal state and a preferred action tendency: to kill the son. This action tendency is incompatible with the father's moral standard of supporting and loving his son. The contradiction between the manifest and latent content of the dream provides another ingredient, the distortion, which results from the conflict between the moral norm and the hostile action tendency. If the father were asked about the homicidal wish, he would indignantly deny it. Yet he reported it in a language whose real meaning he did not understand.

To identify repression or, for that matter, any other defense, one must be able to locate an event, usually an action tendency, which, if it were expressed directly, would create objective difficulties or violate the person's internal norms. Because this unconscious impulse engenders anxiety, the individual unconsciously substitutes some alternative for the original. Obviously, the father's moral compunctions would not permit him to commit murder. He repressed and reversed the impulse, so that he could act in such a manner as to help his son.

The dream provides us with evidence that the father was employing a defense. This is inferred from the discrepancy between the unconscious reaction and its conscious substitute. The particular mechanism is identified in terms of the nature of the discrepancy. If there were another kind of substitute, the defense would have another label. In this case the combination of repressed death wishes and conscious love suggests the defense of reversal. If the angry father killed a cat, a displacement of the object would be inferred from this substitute. If he developed a fear that his son was in danger of being attacked by a playmate, the defense would be labeled projection.

## Comparisons among the Defenses

Even a superficial examination of the various defense mechanisms suggests the feasibility of dividing them into certain general types. If a woman faints when confronted with the aggressive implications of an apparently innocent act, it is not surprising to find that she is inclined to defend herself at other times by running away. Both reactions are similar in that they completely remove her from her problems. It is less probable that a woman with such defenses will deflect her aggressive need from others onto herself. If she could tolerate the depression which results from self-blame, she would not have to resort to the socially handicapping method of blacking out. If such observations are correct, the defenses of turning against the self and of physical withdrawal belong to different categories and probably have different origins.

A system which permits the division of a large number of defenses into types provides some ready hypotheses and broadens considerably the implications of empirical findings. To what extent can the results which pertain to one specific mechanism be generalized to other defenses in the same category, and to the contrasts between defenses in different categories?

### Primary differences among defenses

How does one go about the job of grouping defenses? First, we examined all the defenses to locate their most obvious differences and similarities. We found that four major characteristics stood out. (1) Some defenses require almost no previous skills and depend on responses present shortly after birth, while others depend upon the previous mastery of complicated reactions; (2) some defenses help to transform a major part of the objective world, while others produce only slight distortions; (3) some defenses seem particularly suited to specific kinds of conflict, while others seems applicable to all types; (4) some defenses create social difficulties, while others do not. These characteristics are not mutually exclusive. In fact, it is in terms of their overlap that we arrived at our classification of defenses into two families. To show how we developed our final groupings from the four characteristics, we shall describe each of them in further detail.

*1. Simplicity-Complexity.* Some responses which may later be employed for purposes of defense appear very early in life and require little or no training. The infant reflexively withdraws his burned hand from the fire. Months later, he runs away from frightening objects. It is not long before he develops a general tendency to remove himself, physically or psychically, from any pain-inducing objects. This response becomes a psychological defense when he later applies it to the resolution of conflict. To avoid facing an unpleasant problem, the anxious person may remove himself from it. He can convince himself that all is well as long as he does not need to face the actual facts.

In contrast to withdrawal, projection requires a relatively advanced stage of development. Before the child can erroneously attribute his unwelcome anger to others, he must have assimilated some very complex information about the nature of his bodily boundaries, the moral standards of his group, the meaning of responsibility, and the cues that enable him to estimate the needs of others.

*2. Degree of Distortion.* Defenses like denial in fantasy may eliminate from awareness not only the conflicting needs, but whole ranges of related facts. Retreat to a wish-fulfilling realm of fantasy obliterates or reinterprets large sections of reality, much as a large cloud covers the face of the sky.

Other defenses pinpoint the specific source of the difficulty, distorting only the aspect of the conflict that is causing anxiety. An angry person who defends himself by displacing the object no longer wants to aim at the original target. Other than that, he can correctly appraise all other aspects of the action tendency. He does not have to distort the agent, act, or affect. Displacement of the object compares to denial as a rifle does to a shotgun.

*3. Specificity-Generality.* Some defenses seem equally effective with almost any conflict, while others are appropriate only to special types. As a defense, falling asleep alleviates almost any problem regardless of the sources of anxiety. The Balinese term "afraid-sleep" indicates a recognition of the defensive function sometimes served by this behavior. Bateson and Mead's monograph (1) contains some vivid photographs of a Balinese who goes to sleep while he is being tried for a crime. This is his means of reducing anxiety.

Other defenses are best suited to a specific class of difficulties and seem irrelevant to others. Reversal is a case in point. Reversal seems most appropriate to conflicts involving dichotomized moral categories: when a choice is between such contradictory alternatives as dishonesty and honesty, or homosexuality and heterosexuality. The alternatives are often painted in black and white with few or no shadings. One cannot be partly dishonest. By definition, the alternative to the opprobrious word "dirty" is "clean." Whether or not the categories are dichotomized, opposites are required before the mechanisms can be used. Without them, the forbidden original impulse cannot be "reversed."

*4. Social Effectiveness.* We considered not only the complexity, degree of distortion, and specificity of defenses, but also the extent to which their use produce social difficulties. Some mechanisms create social emergencies when applied excessively, while others may earn approbation. If an American has fits or trance states when he cannot tolerate a conflict, he may be hospitalized because of the potential threat to his fellow men.[2] The child who turns his anger on himself instead of trying to hurt his mother may be praised for his modesty. He may also gain approval if he reverses his intended act and is very solicitous about his mother's health.

## Two Families of Defenses

If defenses show similar patterns—if, for example, mechanisms whose use results in maximal distortion are also those which require minimal previous learning—we can assign them to the same category. When we compared the defenses in this manner, we

[2] Of course, the evaluation of any behavior of this sort varies considerably with the society. Some societies regard trance states as holy and honor the sufferer (1).

found we could divide all the mechanisms which we have considered into two families. Members of the first family share the characteristics of simplicity, maximal distortion, generality, and the creation of social difficulties. Denial is representative of such mechanisms. Almost anything can be denied, be it observable fact or motivational state, since the mechanism results in a blotting out or reinterpreting of the event. The defense is as easy as dreaming, and requires little previous practice. But while the stuff of which dreams are made is consoling, it provides few practical solutions. The man who denies his difficulties cannot take active steps to help himself. In fact, if he is frequently unable to estimate what is happening about him, he may not even be capable of carrying on normal social relationships.

The second family differs from the first on each of the four criteria. Its defenses are complex, they distort less of the perceptual field, and they are applicable only to specific kinds of conflict.

Turning against the self is a typical member of the second family. To develop this defense, one must have previously acquired the complex wish to belong to certain social groups, even to the extent of sacrificing freedom to express forbidden needs. The wish depends in turn on other skills. Among these are the perceptions of body image, of self, and of the distinction between self and others, the knowledge of approved and disapproved forms of aggression, and the understanding of the purposes and functions of social groups.

Instead of obliterating his problem completely, the person who turns his aggression inward is still aware of his hostility. He confines the displacement to the object. The mechanism tends to be specific and results in minimal distortion. We are inclined to broaden the definition of the defense so that it applies to the turning inward of any need. Thus we can explain autoeroticism as the turning inward of a sexual need. Even with this broad definition, however, the defense still does not begin to acquire the general applicability of any in the first family.

In American society the second family of defenses creates fewer social problems than the first. An adult who is angry and feels unworthy seems much less peculiar to his friends than the man who is angry and then has visions. In fact, blaming oneself for evil thoughts usually helps to inhibit aggression and gain social approval. Turning a sexual need inward results in a private expression which may prevent difficulties with others.[3]

## Defenses in the First Family and the Interpretation of Imagery

Of the primary differences among defenses, degree of distortion throws most light on the origins of mechanisms in the first family. We may evaluate any perception in terms of a continuum which defines degree of distortion. When accuracy is maximal, the event is recorded the way it actually occurs. We often gain information about the true event from the testimony of others or from certain instruments. If the event is an external one, such as an eclipse of the sun, it can also be observed and reported by a number of observers, and it can be photographed. If it is an internal condition, such as hunger, evidence of its occurrence can be gained from introspective reports, from an analysis of the blood, or from measurements of stomach contractions. We place our confidence in such observations because they are logically consistent with other facts that we have checked. They also follow certain physical principles which apply to any objects in time and space.

At the other extreme from objective perception is the image of fantasy—it has also been called "irreal" (12) and "primary process" (7). In our daydreams occurrences are often not related in a logical manner; they may even violate the physical properties of real objects in time and space. The same event may either precede or follow another or both, or an object like the Cheshire cat may become dematerialized.

[3] We may be inclined to question whether defenses in the first family create more social complications than defenses in the second family when we compare them with respect to the pathological symptoms they produce. After all, self-attack may contribute to a depressive psychosis and even suicide. To claim that such pathologies represent less serious problems than a disorder such as schizophrenia may seem to be stretching a point. In one sense, however, this claim seems defensible. Because the depressive is not likely to abandon the world of objective fact, he is accessible to verbal techniques of psychotherapy. Usually his prognosis is much better than that of a schizophrenic. The same is often true of the depressive who fails in his attempt at suicide.

Normally, if we are alert to the signals from external events, we find it very difficult to add to them from our world of fantasy. Conversely, when we are luxuriating in dreams of glory, our eyes may receive physical signals, but we seldom respond to the meaning of what we see. As a result, when images of actual events create too much anxiety, we can avoid them by substituting images of more pleasant events. This technique of extinguishing the perceptions of actual events is the distinguishing characteristic of defenses in the first family. Regardless of the mechanisms, they lead to the replacement of perceived actual events by fantasies constructed in accordance with coveted desires. The specific mechanism used to achieve the substitution is determined in part by the source of the anxiety. If it is elicited by external circumstances, the person may withdraw physically. If it is internal, so that he cannot run away from it, he may blot the experience out of awareness by fainting or going to sleep, or he may remain awake but retreat to his daydreams for a period of time. If the anxiety is caused by a personal attribute, such as ugliness, or by a conflict with someone from whom the person cannot flee, he may radically misinterpret the facts. He can then remain on the scene because he is blind to facts which are readily interpreted by most other people.

Because the defenses which facilitate some kind of total escape have not been viewed as a homogeneous group, they have not been explored to any degree. Of the mechanisms named in the literature, denial in act and in fantasy, withdrawal, and restriction of the ego probably belong to this family. As we have indicated, there are undoubtedly many more. Research on their characteristics is urgently needed.

### THE REINFORCEMENT OF DEFENSES IN THE FIRST FAMILY [4]

In our society the defenses in the first family are so handicapping that they are used mostly when other techniques are not available. According to the investigation described in Chapter 9, for example, if a boy's current relations with his parents exact

[4] This is an elaboration of a theory proposed by Ferenczi (4). We recognize that it is speculative—in fact we are not in total agreement among ourselves about its various aspects. Yet we include these observations because they treat an important aspect of perceptual development, and because they suggest a number of testable hypotheses.

too many penalties or offer too few rewards, he may have no alternative but to retreat into fantasy. Reports of behavior under such unsufferable conditions as the battlefield (9) and concentration camp (3) indicate that, given enough stress, anyone can be reduced to a state in which he favors defenses in the first family. But some men crack very early, while others can maintain their alertness to reality for much longer periods.

We imagine that the accumulation of extreme environmental pressure over a period of years creates a propensity for mechanisms in the first family. A man who has been subjected to many such pressures may be inclined to resort to denial even when his anxiety is not very great. Inherited characteristics and prenatal experiences may contribute to such propensities, but we will restrict our speculation to the possible effects of postnatal experiences.

Social scientists agree that the infant is not born with the ability to tell the difference between an imagined event and one that has actually occurred. How does he learn to make the necessary discrimination? We will consider the answer in some detail, because it provides us with a key to the learning of defenses in the first family.

We begin our exploration of imagery with an observation stressed by certain schools of epistemology in philosophy. When an event occurs, the person knows what is happening because he looks, he hears, he feels, he smells: His knowledge is derived from sensory impressions. Such messages seem to be registered in the nervous system so that, during recall, the images and sensations can be re-experienced, although less vividly. It is commonly assumed that everyone is born with this capacity to recapitulate perceptual events. Even in the infant they leave a "trace" (11) which permits a partial experiencing of the event at a later time.

Given this assumption, we may postulate that once an infant has been hungry and then fed, he should again have images of being fed the next time he becomes hungry. Since he has no inborn concepts about reality or fantasy, he cannot distinguish between his memory and the true occurrence. Nobody knows how he finally learns to tell them apart, but it is possible to speculate about the process. Our explanation requires four assumptions, which we can illustrate in terms of a hungry infant's perceptions.

First, images of the real feeding are more vivid than remembered ones. Second, the event is followed by actual satiety, which stops the sequence of images. In contrast, the wish-induced image is followed, not by satiety but by an initial period of solace and then feelings of distress and further images. Third, if the infant is usually fed within a short time after he becomes hungry, he has many experiences with the contrasting qualities of the two kinds of images. Finally, he learns to classify objects into two types, those that he still sees and those he does not see when he closes his eyes. He later learns to call the former imaginary and the latter real. Babies' fascination with the game of peek-a-boo may reflect their pleasure in making the first discriminations between the two kinds of perceptual experience.

These assumptions can help us to understand how painful events might delay the discrimination between the two kinds of imagery or cause the child to replace the image of a real event by a fantasied one. Let us suppose that a mother did not plan to have her child, and that she often neglects his care when it interferes with her social life. Sometimes when he is hungry, she may not even be at home. He will then cry, stop when he has a fantasy of suckling, and cry again until he has other fantasies. This chain of events continues until his mother returns and gratifies his need. Compared to a consistently fed infant, one who is fed inconsistently probably needs a longer time to distinguish between different types of images. We say this for a number of reasons. He has less opportunity to contrast the qualities of the two kinds of images. Instead of frequently experiencing them together, he has long sequences of fantasied images, interspersed with fits of crying. More important, instead of contrasting weak, need-induced images with the vivid ones of actual feeding, he more typically contrasts the relative gratification gained from the wishful images with the unpleasant experience of hunger. In addition, he gets more practice than the more consistently fed infant in gaining pleasure from the imagery of fantasy. Even if he learns to tell the difference between the two kinds of images, his world of real objects may provide him with so little pleasure or so much pain that he learns to avoid them by substituting the more gratifying wishful images. Both frequent gratification from wish-fulfilling imagery and many painful experiences may reinforce a readiness to substitute wishful images for the correct perception of one's real problems.[5]

In sum, excessive stress is our explanation for the use of defenses in the first family. We have referred to two kinds of stress. Either it has been very recent, so that the person was left no recourse but a final escape into fantasy, or it represents years of pain, anxiety, or hunger, so that he is likely to employ denial where others resolve conflicts in more mature ways. In our research we assumed that our subjects from the working class had much experience with both kinds of stress.

Judging from the living conditions of manual laborers, we anticipated that they would be more inclined than white-collar workers to resolve conflicts by defenses such as denial and withdrawal. Physical inconveniences like substandard shelters and crowded living conditions are still the lot of a segment of the working class. As reported in Chapter 4, blue-collar workers influence their children's behavior by such harsh methods as physical discipline and arbitrary requests for obedience. We anticipated that these practices would lead to denial.

## Defenses in the Second Family and Displacement

The normal child in our society outgrows the tendency to recast objective fact in accordance with his needs. Beyond a certain age he can no longer resort to imaginary companions or sincerely convince himself that something he has just seen or felt did not occur. He then begins to make increasing use of the sec-

[5] In this chapter we are concerned only with an inefficient use of wishful imagery: its substitution for the perception of a real problem. As a person matures, he gains increasing skill in implementing his actual problems by means of wishful imagery. As a child plays at being an aviator or fireman, he learns many occupational facts and physical skills. His fantasy in play is not inherently different from that which guides the brush of a painter or the speculations of a physicist. Adults differ from the infant primarily in the skills which enable them to select from different images those that help to solve an actual problem.

ond family of defenses. He resorts to this group of techniques, not to obliterate a need, but to reinterpret it by distorting one or more of its dimensions. Because the distortion is not a total one, he can tolerate awareness of some aspects of the need instead of being routed by his anxiety. The mechanism of displacing the object shows how slight his misperception may be. When an angry person employs this defense, he is aware of a wish to hurt, aware that it is his own, and aware that he feels angry. His only self-deception concerns the object of his anger. He wants to attack another object rather than the preferred one.

We do not usually realize how often normal adults avail themselves of defenses in the second family. It may seem improbable that our "mature" friends may be using a mechanism that distorts their motives as much as projection does, for example. Yet everyone is strongly motivated to disavow action tendencies whose expression would make him feel guilty or lead to social ostracism. Once the adult has committed an aggressive deed, he cannot usually pretend to himself that he did not do it. At best, he can engage in the complicated process of projecting the desire in retrospect and viewing his deed as a retaliation. But if the act has not been committed, he can readily deceive himself about his intentions. Unlike the act, the tendency is usually not betrayed by concrete evidence or by witnesses.

Projection requires not only the disowning of needs, but also their displacement to a substitute agent. This second step is easier than the first since the individual has less information about another's needs than his own. Let us assume that a man is talking to a woman. To get some idea of her thoughts and feelings, he puts himself in her place and makes some tentative guesses. Then he tries to verify his suppositions from her conversation, facial expressions, vocal quality, and gestures. This judgment may become very difficult if he is very disturbed by his own hostile impulses, so that he is overly sensitive to indications of irritation in her. His perception of her needs may be further complicated by his own reactions to his initial interpretation. If he suspects that she is angry, he may unintentionally verify his incorrect impression by becoming somewhat distant or even hostile so that she really becomes irritated.

DIMENSIONS OF NEEDS AND THE SECOND FAMILY OF DEFENSES

To illustrate the distortions created by some of the defenses in the second family, we return to the case of the man we discussed previously. He has lost his job and has the action tendency: "I wish to kill the foreman." If he does not misjudge his homicidal urge, he realizes that he is the agent, that the object is his erstwhile friend, that the content of his affect is one of hatred, and that the intensity of his feeling is so great that, if he does not control himself, he will engage in a destructive act.

Apart from his fears of the law and of social disapproval, the employee may be deterred by his conscience and his positive feelings for his superior. If his anger is very great, his anxiety may make it too difficult for him to resolve the conflict in a rational manner. Then he distorts the need.

Characteristic of defenses in the second family is the fact that they result in a displacement or shift within one or more dimensions of the need. An element which serves the end state most directly is displaced by one lower in the hierarchy of preference, but more compatible with the moral standard or feared consequence. The second or substitute element is sufficiently remote from the original that the connection between the two is not apparent.

Table 8-1 contains an analysis of displacement involved in five defenses commonly mentioned in psychoanalytic literature.

**TABLE 8-1**

Analyses of Five Defenses in the Second Family

| *Defense* | *Agent* | *Intended Act* | *Affect* | *Object* |
|---|---|---|---|---|
| Displacement of object and turning against the self | A | A | A | D |
| Isolation | A | A | D | A |
| Reversal | A | $D_r$ | $D_r$ | A |
| Projection | D | A | A | A |

In the table, the letter *A* signifies awareness of the most direct expression in a specific dimension of the need, *D* means displacement to a substitute element, and $D_r$ indicates a special case of displacement to a substitute which is the "reverse" or opposite in meaning to the original.

The first line describes displacements of the object. If the employee uses this mechanism, he knows that he is the agent, that the intended act is to kill, and that the feeling is hatred. Only the object is distorted. Instead of the original quarry, he substitutes a related one which does not violate his moral need. He may advocate the execution of ex-Nazis or capital punishment for peddlers of narcotics.

Still another object which he may substitute for the original is himself. Turning the aggression inward is a special case of the more generic defense of displacing the object. We have therefore diagrammed both defenses in the same way.

In the second line of the table we have analyzed the mechanism of isolation, which involves a shift in the original affect. If the laborer isolates his affect of hatred, he does not have to distort any other dimensions of his impulse to kill the foreman. He can then contemplate his intended act objectively without fear of his emotion. Or he may have an interesting daydream in which he "accidentally" kills the foreman. This fantasy need not create any anxiety so long as the laborer does not realize that the dream expresses a strong wish. Because of the absence of the usual emotion, he has little cause to fear that he will lose control.

The defense diagrammed on the third line is reversal: the displacement of the original intended act and affect by others which are opposite to them in meaning. Here, agent and object are accurately perceived. The employee may substitute love and a desire to help for the hatred and destructive wish toward the foreman.

In projection, which is depicted on the fourth line, the agent is distorted. There is no misinterpretation of the hatred, the wish to kill, or the target. But the laborer may attribute the wish to another discontented employee, or to a friend of the foreman with whom he often quarrels.

When we examine the table of the second family we find a number of defenses, some of which have been mentioned in the clinical literature but have not yet been labeled. There are, for example, no terms for the substitution of acts that are not opposite in meaning to the original. What mechanisms would the angry laborer be using if he replaced his original action tendency by a desire to gossip about the foreman, to play a practical joke on him, or to avoid him whenever possible?

There is some question in our minds about the extent to which defenses in the second family can operate without repression. At first, Freud regarded repression as a master defense. In this initial version of his theory repression is a necessary concomitant of all other mechanisms. Unless a man first eliminates his action tendency from awareness, he cannot turn his anger on himself, project, or reverse the act. Later Freud demoted repression to the same status as the other defenses. We lean to this latter point of view: Displacement is probably a sufficient explanation for the lack of awareness which accompanies defenses in the second family.

There seem to be two kinds of displacement: one with insight, the other without insight.[6] In the former case the laborer knows that he is angry, but kicks his dog while muttering furiously about the foreman. In the latter case the man kicks his dog, but complains bitterly about the animal; he is unaware that he is using it as a scapegoat for the foreman. In both instances the object is displaced, but while the second seems to involve lack of insight the first does not.[7] Whether or not displacement with insight can be considered a defense will ultimately be decided only after a larger system of classification has been developed which embraces more subtle defenses than those that were investigated in our studies and, in addition, thinking, certain physical skills, and other

[6] We are indebted to M. Brewster Smith for suggesting the two kinds of displacement.

[7] Another interpretive problem is raised by complex defenses like "altruistic surrender" (5). To illustrate this mechanism, Anna Freud cites the case of a young governess who encourages and helps others to gratify impulses which she herself cannot express. Although she repudiates her own sexuality, she is an enthusiastic matchmaker; although she is indifferent about her own clothes, she is very interested in having her friends dress well. In this manner she obtains vicarious gratifications. Her behavior obviously reflects a combination of defenses. Altruism does not seem to entail processes other than the kinds which we have discussed. Some of its unique characteristics result from complex combinations of these processes.

capacities which, while they have much in common with defense mechanisms, differ from them in terms of degree of self-awareness. We think that eventually all such responses will be regarded as variations of problem solving, and that a factor such as degree of awareness will be used to evaluate the amount of available information.

We are struck by the extent to which members of the second family of defenses facilitate self-control and the avoidance of social difficulties. To rob an aggressive action tendency of its potential danger, a man need only express it in an active sport. Or he may shift to a friendly act such as constructive criticism. Or he may project the forbidden action tendency. Since he cannot then acknowledge it as his own, he does not express it.

Such defenses are particularly adaptable to the pressures of middle-class life. If the child is ultimately to be rational and realistic, to work hard, to sacrifice for future gains, and to take responsibility for his own conduct, he must, at a minimum, learn to control the direct expression of his needs. This function is best implemented by such defenses as displacement, isolation, reversal, and turning on the self.

These conjectures led us to expect an association between social status and defenses in the second family. We hypothesized that boys in the middle class would be more likely to employ such mechanisms than boys in the working class. We also anticipated that certain child-rearing practices would be associated with a predilection for defenses in the second family. We reasoned that to encourage the development of skills required for the mastery of these defenses, parents would have to make their rules as clear as possible, be flexible in their discipline, and offer inducements for conformity. We therefore anticipated that such treatments as reasonable requests for obedience, mixed types of discipline, and frequent rewards would be associated with the inclination to favor defenses in the second family.

## Summary

Defenses facilitate the inhibition and selection of indirect outlets for needs whose direct expression would either create social difficulties, elicit guilt, or lead to an overwhelming emotional state. In addition, certain mechanisms permit the reduction of external sources of anxiety. To establish the existence of a defense, one must demonstrate the occurrence of discrepant unconscious and conscious reactions.

In this chapter we proposed a grouping of defenses into two families. Mechanisms in the first family require little previous experience, entail a maximal amount of distortion, may be applied to any source of anxiety, and create social difficulties. Defenses in the second family require the previous mastery of many complex skills, entail a minimal amount of distortion, are suited to specific types of conflict, and their use usually results in socially acceptable behavior.

Defenses in the first family help a person to escape, either physically or psychologically, from the source of his anxiety. In considering their origins we outlined a possible process whereby a child may learn to discriminate between fantasy and images induced by actual events. From the nature of his process we deduced the conditions which might facilitate the discrimination, delay it, or prevent it. We expected nonrewarding or harsh parental practices, such as corporal punishment and unexplained requests for obedience, to reinforce the inclination to employ defenses in the first family.

Substitution within dimensions of needs is the basic characteristic of defenses in the second family. These may be classified in terms of the dimensions within which the substitution takes place. We anticipated that mechanisms in the second family would be reinforced by conditions of middle-class living. It seemed to us that the values of the white-collar workers, and their inclinations to favor such child-rearing methods as making reasonable requests, using mixed kinds of discipline, and giving frequent rewards, would encourage the learning of the complex information and skills needed for the development of defenses in the second family.

## References

1. Bateson, G., & Mead, Margaret. *Balinese character: a photographic analysis*. New York: N.Y. Academy of Sciences, 1942.

2. Benedict, Ruth. *Patterns of culture.* New York: Houghton Mifflin, 1934.
3. Bettelheim, B. Individual and mass behavior in extreme situations. *J. abnorm. & soc. Psychol.,* 1943, *38,* 417–45.
4. Ferenczi, S. Stages in the development of a sense of reality. *Sex in psychoanalysis.* New York: Bruner, 1950.
5. Freud, Anna. *The ego and the mechanisms of defence.* London: Hogarth, 1937.
6. Freud, S. *The problem of anxiety.* New York: Norton, 1936.
7. ———. Two principles of mental functioning. *Collected Papers,* Vol. IV. London: Hogarth, 1949.
8. Horney, Karen. *New ways in psychoanalysis.* New York: Norton, 1939.
9. Kardiner, A. *The traumatic neuroses of war.* Menasha, Wisc.: George Banta, 1941.
10. Kluckhohn, C. Myths and rituals: a general theory. *Harvard Theol. Rev.,* 1942, *35,* 45–79.
11. Koffka, K. *Principles of gestalt psychology.* New York: Harcourt, Brace, 1935.
12. Lewin, K. *Field theory in social science.* New York: Harper, 1951.
13. Symonds, P. M. *The dynamics of human adjustment.* New York: Appleton-Century-Crofts, 1946.

# 9

## MECHANISMS OF DEFENSE

### II. Denial of Failure *

One way of responding to a source of severe anxiety is to behave as though it does not exist. Awareness of the difficulty can be extinguished by physical or psychic withdrawal from the situation. We have described such techniques and their origins in our discussion in Chapter 8 of the first family of defenses. As methods of relieving anxiety, such mechanisms are very efficient, but the efficiency is often earned at great cost. A problem cannot be solved when there is no awareness of it. Indeed, when the defenses preclude awareness, they prevent a realistic solution. Hence, use of defenses in the first family can aggravate a difficult problem. Like aspirin, they eliminate pain, but they have little effect on the underlying causes, which often become progressively troublesome.

We will now report a study of one such defense, denial in fantasy. Of course, the use of fantasy is not restricted to denial, and need not be defensive. In his play a child engages in fantasy to try out new experiences. Under conditions which he can control, he imagines different ways of behaving without concern for the consequences. Similarly, when the adult seeks solutions to his problems, he explores alternative plans of action in fantasy.

However, we were concerned with the use of fantasy as an

* In the research team, Betty J. Beardslee was responsible for the research to be reported and for the preparation of the chapter, which is based in part on her doctoral dissertation (1).

unrealistic method of escaping from one's problems. The term *denial in fantasy* (3) refers to a defense which substitutes a pleasant daydream for unpleasant events and aspects of reality. Such a substitution serves to deny frightening, depressing, or anxiety-arousing occurrences, thereby defending the person against disturbing feelings.

In times of crisis, fantasy is a seduction to which even the most realistic people may succumb. But adults differ markedly in the extent to which they abandon practical attempts to solve problems in favor of impractical daydreams. Our primary question in this chapter is: What causes a person to deny his problems? We shall answer it in terms of one basic premise. The greater the real gratification derived from a particular group of experiences, the stronger is the predilection to orient oneself realistically to comparable experiences. Conversely, the less the gratification or the greater the pain in the experiences, the stronger is the predilection to escape into another more reassuring world—a world of fantasy. If a child's efforts to explore his world have brought restriction and punishment, he has little alternative but to deny his difficulties. A satisfying relationship with his mother wherein physical and emotional needs are met will encourage the child to seek further experiences with people. If he is given freedom and support in his attempts to explore and master his environment, he will learn to tolerate life's inevitable frustrations, for past attempts to remedy them have usually been successful. Thus his past gratifications motivate him not to avoid problems but to find practical solutions to them. When he feels inadequate or threatened, he attempts to obtain security in real relationships and from real objects rather than through fantasy.

## Research Methods

To obtain empirical data we had to create an actual difficulty to which some of our subjects could adjust by an escape into fantasy. We had to find an important problem which creates much anxiety in everyone, a problem which is never solved by anyone with complete adequacy. We chose failure. We made reality painful by insuring that each subject would fail a series of problems which he was strongly motivated to solve successfully.

Failure is painful for a number of reasons. Primary among them is the loss of some measure of self-esteem. In our competitive society success and failure in the attainment of certain approved goals are often equated with notions of adequacy and inadequacy, with judgments of right and wrong. One is humiliated by his failure to measure up to the standards of others whose respect he wants. Often the goal is attainable by only a few. The race allows but one winner; the company has room for only one president. To the extent that they share in the ideal of victory and top achievement, most people seem destined to have some serious failures, and to suffer from acute anxieties in consequence.

People differ markedly in their reactions to failure because of contrasting standards, and also because of differences in methods of solving problems. Failure is often followed by intense conflict. Should one continue to strive, despite the threat of continued failure, or is it better to relieve the anxiety about one's adequacy by giving up, even though this may earn the condemnation of others? In planning his future action the realistic person usually re-examines the total situation, although such a review may be painful. Practical solutions require a recognition of the facts, unpleasant as well as pleasant, and a long-range approach to problems. Self-control and a sense of security must exist in order to overcome the panic and discouragement which follow failure. The threats to prestige and to self-esteem make the conflict between further aspiration and the impulse to retreat from the field of battle a painful one for everyone in our society.

Denial in fantasy is one means of reducing the anxiety created by failure. Some people abandon practical attempts to succeed and seek to counteract their low self-esteem by reconstructing their world in fantasy. They can satisfy their ambitions in daydreams much more fully than they ever can in reality.

### PROJECTIVE TEST

*Technique of Administration.* We obtained our subjects from the second sample described in Chapter 4. Our method of eliciting defensive distortions can be summarized very simply.

First we asked the boys to write imaginative endings for three story beginnings each of which described a series of events leading to failure. Then we motivated the subjects to do well on a group of tests which were so designed that no one could pass them. After the actual failure the subjects completed three new stories. Their endings could include realistic or improbable events.

We defined denial in terms of the change in the amount of unrealistic fantasy after exposure to failure. To simplify our exposition and to avoid tedious repetition of our definition, we shall refer, at times, to denial in fantasy. This term always means that defense was more frequent in the second set of endings than in the first.

The first set of stories were completed three weeks before the real experience of failure. The boys took the projective test in groups of eight. The examiner tried to keep the atmosphere as informal as possible. He emphasized that we were not testing intellectual ability, that there were no wrong or right answers, and that the results would not be graded. Then he instructed the subjects to finish each story: to tell how the hero thought and felt, what happened, and how things turned out.

*Content of the Test.* We devised the two sets of story beginnings [1] so that they were more or less parallel with respect to content. All story beginnings culminated in failure. The first story in each set was about failure in a particular area of achievement, the second about failure to gain social acceptance, and the third about failure on a job. By using the same types of events in the two sets, we hoped to eliminate some of the variations which might have resulted from differences in themes. To control further the effects of the stories' contents, we randomly selected for each subject one of eight different orders of the six stories.

In our pretests we repeatedly changed the projective stories until there was no obvious way for the subjects to convert failure into success. We may illustrate this point by citing a typical story. A boy named Pete cannot succeed at any sport even though he practices more than anyone else. He is short and neither strong nor fast. He finally manages to join the lightweight wrestling team. In his big match Pete is so anxious to do well that he gets rattled

[1] They may be found in Appendix C.

and is easily thrown. He is so angry that he bursts into tears in front of the crowd. After the match the coach tells him he should give up sports.

### Creating the experience of failure

After the boy completed the first three stories he was asked some standardized, open-ended questions about his aspirations. The questions were designed to arouse his anxieties about his goals and his capacities to achieve them. First the boy was asked to name his ideal job: "If you could have any job in the world, what job would you like to have?" Then the examiner inquired into the job he thought he might *really* have. This was followed by the question: "Do you think you would get along well in a job like that?" The examiner also initiated discussions about educational and social goals.

Following the interview the examiner said that he was going to administer a group of aptitude tests which would show whether the subject was being realistic in his plans. The object of the tests was to find out whether the boy was capable of doing well in the job he thought he would really get, and whether he had the kind of abilities that everyone needs to get along well, both on a job and with other people. These statements were intended to convince him that a poor performance would represent a serious failure.

The "aptitude" tests consisted of sixteen tasks, adapted from items in traditional instruments for measuring motor agility, verbal facility, perceptual skill, logical reasoning, ability to manipulate numbers, and the like. The tests were all short and their variety was intended to make them interesting to boys in both social classes. They are discussed in further detail in Chapter 10. The examiner commented that many of the tests would seem very simple, and that their difficulty resulted from the short time allowed for their completion. Then the examiner said that any subject with the kind of ability needed to make a success of himself had to pass fifteen of the sixteen tests.

To create failure we allowed each subject to complete only eight, or one half, of the tests. The sequence of successes and failures was randomized. Before the boy could finish certain tasks, he was told the time was up. At the end he realized that he had failed seven more than the allowable maximum of one. The subjects' reactions left little doubt in the examiners' minds about the genuineness of the experience of failure.

Following the completion of the second set of stories, we interviewed each subject to relieve him of the feelings of depression which resulted from failure. We told him that the experiment was really designed to find out how boys work under pressure, that we had created pressure by saying he should be able to finish fifteen tests, and that actually we knew this was impossible.

The examiner then informed the subject that he had done very well in this difficult situation. Material from his performance was cited to illustrate how adequately he had responded, and he was encouraged to express his feelings. Finally, the examiner requested the boy's cooperation in keeping the nature of the procedure secret. Interviews with boys later indicated that this confidence had been kept.

## Analyzing the Results

In a pretest of the stories we developed a code [2] for denial in fantasy. To be tabulated as expressing denial, an ending had to depict an unrealistic resolution of failure. This could occur only if the subject disregarded the limiting conditions in the story beginning or made up a sequence of events that was so improbable that it distorted the facts. For instance, one of our themes describes a boy who, having practiced his music very hard, is told by his teacher that he lacks talent. The ending was considered unrealistic if, without any intervening steps, the hero suddenly becomes very famous and is asked to play in Carnegie Hall. If the success seemed at all reasonable, we did not count the ending as unrealistic. In one ending, for example, the boy was described as changing his teacher, continuing to practice very hard, and, after years of effort, becoming a recognized musician. We had to accept this kind of ending as realistic, since it represented a conceivable course of action open to the aspiring musician.

[2] To establish the reliability of the code, we obtained the ratings of 120 stories by a second person who was not acquainted with our theory. The two judges agreed in 85 per cent of their ratings.

Thirteen of our 112 subjects wrote two sets of endings which contained neither unrealistic fantasy nor failure. Possibly these boys were concerned more with topics other than failure; possibly they were trying to remain uninvolved, or to reveal as little as possible of themselves. Because we were so uncertain about the meaning of their story endings, we omitted these subjects. We also had to omit three additional cases because they were absent during the last week of testing. We collected our data late in the research period and could not test these boys when they returned. After these eliminations, we had a pool of 96 subjects.

In analyzing the results we compared the boys who increased the number of endings involving denial with the boys whose stories contained the same number or fewer involving denial. We considered the former the defensive and the latter the nondefensive group. The defensive group consisted of 41 boys; the nondenying group contained 55 subjects. Of the latter, 27 expressed unrealistic fantasy less often after failure than before. The experience of failure tended to increase their attempts to solve their problem realistically. Another 18 showed no change in defensive endings. They had low denial scores in the endings they wrote both before and after failure. Finally, there were ten subjects whose stories did not contain denial either before or after failure, but who increased the number of endings expressing an acceptance of failure.

Unless a boy's story explicitly mentioned the acceptance of failure, we did not include him in the nondefensive group even though his stories lacked denial in fantasy. We took this precaution because we could not be sure whether the mere omission of denial signified a lack of preference for the defense. An increased acceptance of failure, however, was incompatible with an increased denial of failure. Hence, when omission of denial was accompanied by increased acceptance of failure, we included the subject in the nondefensive group.

Not all the subjects are included in every table. The tables relating the defense to child rearing, for example, lack some subjects because their mothers gave us information that we could not code.

Before analyzing our results, we investigated the possibility that some subjects who obtained very high scores on the first set of endings might, in effect, have reached a ceiling. In that event it would have been extremely difficult for them to increase the number of endings involving denial in the second set. Since our concern for the children made it necessary to invent a situation in which the threat of failure, although present, would not be excessive, we did not expect to find much denial in this group of relatively normal subjects. This expectation was fulfilled. More than 80 per cent of our subjects used denial only once or not at all in the initial set of three stories. All the subjects could have increased their scores considerably. We also found that the number of defenses in the initial stories was not significantly related to shifts in denial of failure.

## Verbal Intelligence

In reporting results we shall begin with our control variables because one of them, the score on verbal intelligence, has an unanticipated theoretical significance for some of the significant relations that we found.[3] On the Chicago Tests of Primary Mental Abilities (4), the Spatial and Reasoning scores are not significantly related to denial as a defense, but Verbal scores are.

As indicated in Table 9-1, which summarizes the primary results to be reported in this chapter, boys below the median in intelligence are significantly more inclined to increase denial after failure than are boys above the median.[4] This result lends itself

[3] We used two other controls—age and ego involvement. Neither is significantly related to denial. We measured ego involvement by means of a questionnaire we adapted from Calden's (2) questionnaire. This objective instrument, which requires the subject to check the items most descriptive of his reactions to the test, was administered after the second set of stories. The items consist of such terms as "tense," "bored," "tiring," "foolish," and "I didn't try to do well." The total score is the algebraic sum of the scores on the separate items. When we split the distribution of ego involvement scores at the median, we found that it was not significantly related to the shift in defense. Subjects who were very concerned with doing well on the test did not differ from those who were less strongly motivated in the defensive shifts following failure. It may be claimed that some subjects, thinking that they might earn approval from the examiner, exaggerated their ego involvement in the test. We are inclined to reject this interpretation because we promised the subjects anonymity. We derive our confidence in Calden's questionnaire from its previous validation with a group of boys slightly older than the ones in this study.

[4] The complete tables may be found in Appendix D.

to two possible interpretations: Boys with high verbal scores write realistic stories because of superior verbal skill, or bright boys react differently from boys of average intelligence to the threat of failure.

**TABLE 9-1**

Background Variables and Denial of Failure

| *Condition* | *Trends: Boxes with Largest Frequencies* | *N* | $\chi^2$ | *Probability* |
|---|---|---|---|---|
| Verbal intelligence | High intelligence & no increase | 96 | 4.52 | .03 |
| Social class | — | 96 | .003 | <1.00 |
| Social class & intelligence | MC: high intel. & no increase<br>WC: low intel. & increase | 96 | 11.83 | .01 |
| Obedience | Explained requests & no increase | 83 | 3.94 | .05 |
| Obedience & intelligence | Arbitrary requests: low intel. & increase<br>Explained requests: high intel. & no increase | 83 | 9.90 | .02 |
| Discipline | Mixed or psychol. discipline & no increase | 96 | 7.52 | .02 |
| Discipline & intelligence | Psychol. discipline: high intel. & no increase<br>Corporal discipline: low intel. & increase | 96 | 17.14 | <.01 |
| Reward | — | 78 | 1.18 | <.30 |
| Reward & intelligence | Frequent reward: high intel. & no increase<br>Occasional reward: low intelligence and increase | 78 | 11.30 | .01 |

If denial in story endings resulted from verbal facility, rather than from contrasting reactions to failure, scores on the intelligence test would have been significantly related to frequency of denial in the initial story endings, which were written when there was no real threat of failure. In analyzing those endings we found that references to denial were not significantly related to verbal intelligence. Hence, the difference in shifts cannot be explained solely as a function of verbal facility. It is only after experiencing failure that boys with superior verbal intelligence write more realistic endings than do boys with less verbal intelligence, and that the latter defend themselves by increasing denial in fantasy.

But what is the relation between verbal intelligence and denial? On one hand, it might be claimed that a boy whose unpleasant experiences have caused him to favor denial may, because of his frequent retreats into fantasy, find it difficult to acquire the verbal and conceptual skills needed for high intellectual capacity. On the other hand, it might be claimed that low intelligence is determined at birth, and that it enables a boy to accept uncritically distortions at which a brighter child would scoff. Or possibly a child's poor intellectual capacity causes him to be inadequate in so many situations that he is forced to use denial more often than would a brighter child. Our data cannot help us to choose between these alternatives.[5]

Because of the association between the defense and verbal intelligence we were particularly interested in the interactions involving verbal scores, background conditions, and denial. In computing the results, we made separate analyses of all associations, first, within the bright group, and then within the group of subjects below the median in intelligence.

## Child Rearing and Denial

In formulating predictions about the relationships between background variables and the defense of denial, we were guided by one general assumption. We thought that the more frequently the parents provided their child with actual gratifications, the less prone he would be to retreat into his world of fantasy. Conversely,

[5] If intelligence is inimicable to denial, why do we obtain a significant association only in the case of the verbal form of intelligence? If we conceive of it as a highly socialized form of intellectual functioning, one in which there is a strong interpersonal factor, we may not be surprised by the finding. High verbal intelligence requires the capacities to communicate one's own experiences to others and to conceptualize one's awareness of environmental events. Such capacities are developed in meaningful interpersonal experiences which foster self-awareness and sensitivity to social events, abilities which probably promote a tendency to favor realistic self-appraisals and practical attempts to solve conflicts.

the harsher the methods and the fewer the gratifications provided by the parents, the more prone he would be to retreat into his world of fantasy as a method of escaping from his problems. On the basis of this assumption we predicted that children would be least inclined to increase denial in story endings if they came from middle-class families, or if their parents explained the reasons for their requests, used frequent rewards, or administered the milder forms of punishment. Conversely, we predicted that children would be most inclined to increase denial if they came from working-class families, or if their parents made arbitrary demands for obedience, provided only occasional rewards, or preferred severe methods of discipline. We now recapitulate our results and show how they supported our general assumption.

## Social Class [6]

Various descriptions of living conditions in the two social classes highlight the superior material comfort, the careful parental supervision, the many economic opportunities, and the socially privileged position of the middle-class child. Some of the contrasts between the classes are often overdrawn, because much of the information about them dates back to the depression years. Yet the fact that boys from the working class probably suffer greater hardships than boys from the middle class was helpful in suggesting our first specific hypothesis. Because of our general assumption about the connection between hardship and defenses in the first family, we anticipated a significant association between social class and denial. Table 9-1 indicates that our data do not corroborate our prediction. There is not even a slight trend, either for the differences between the two total classes or for the socio-economic differences within the entrepreneurial and bureaucratic settings. It is possible that we minimized our results by eliminating children from broken homes, a criterion which excluded the lower, more socially deteriorated portion of the working class.

[6] We described our method of determining each family's socio-economic status in Chapter 2.

### Social class and intelligence

We get the anticipated association between denial and social class when we analyze it separately within the groups with high and with average intelligence. As reported in Table 9-1, boys in the working class who are below average in intelligence show a significantly greater inclination than do boys with high scores to increase denial of failure. Despite their poor living conditions, intelligent sons of manual laborers can often make their own opportunities. Since they can gain many rewards for striving, they do not have to employ denial. Regardless of their levels of intelligence, sons of white-collar workers do not have to resort to denial. Their social status provides gratifications and opens the doors to many opportunities.

## Individual Child-Rearing Methods

### Obedience [7]

It seemed to us that unexplained parental requests would create hardships for any child. Arbitrary submission to authority is unpleasant because it places the child in a vulnerable and often humiliating position. His security depends on his obeying orders. Since the rules have not been explained to him, he is reluctant to risk independent action for fear of doing something wrong. The parent who sets himself up as a supreme authority thus deprives the child of initiative and handicaps his adjustment to novel situations. In view of these observations, we anticipated that arbitrary requests would be associated with an increase in denial in the second set of story endings, and that explained requests would not. As our table shows, the significant association between requests for obedience and shifts in denial supports our prediction. When we make separate analyses of the relations between obedience and the defense for subjects above and below the median for intelligence, we again find significant results. The tendency to in-

[7] In Chapter 3 we described our method of classifying mothers in accordance with their requests for obedience. Because the answers of thirteen mothers were too vague to be classified, our sample in this analysis was reduced to eighty-three.

crease denial is minimal among boys who have high verbal scores and whose mothers have made reasonable requests for obedience. Increase in denial is maximal among boys whose intellectual resources are limited and who have had to adjust to arbitrary parental requests.

### Discipline

In line with our general assumption about the origin of denial, we expected that the harsher the discipline employed by the parents, the greater would be the boys' defensive shifts. Of the three types of discipline that we coded,[8] physical punishment seemed to us to be the harshest. It also seemed to us that psychological manipulation could be quite painful: appeals to guilt, expressions of disappointment, and threats of love deprivation can rob a child of his self-respect. Unlike the third, or mixed, method, corporal and psychological techniques are associated with a tendency to increase instances of denial in story endings. When discipline is mixed, it is varied in accordance with the specific misbehavior, and the child is not subjected to frequent threat of pain or disapproval. Our results indicate that children who are accustomed to this mixed discipline are least likely to deny failure.

The combination of discipline and intelligence is also significantly related to defensive shifts. Subjects whose intelligence is only average, and who have been exposed to corporal punishment, display the greatest tendency to increase denial. They do not have the intellectual resources to overcome the difficulties created by harsh parental methods. Among subjects with low verbal scores, we find a similar, but weaker, association between psychological discipline and denial. In the group whose discipline has been mixed, however, the boys show little increase in denial after failure, regardless of their levels of intelligence. These children do not need to fall back on a handicapping defense when their parents are using relatively supporting disciplinary methods.

### Frequency of reward

Since frequent rewards usually make reality gratifying and enable the child to win the adults' approval, we expected this

[8] In Chapter 3 we described our method of classifying mothers in accordance with their preferred types of discipline.

method to be associated with fewer shifts in denial than occasional rewards.[9] Although the trend is in the expected direction, the association is not significant at the 5 per cent level. In a separate analysis of reward and denial for subjects of high and of average verbal intelligence we find the over-all association significant. Verbal intelligence, however, accounts for most of the variation.

## Combinations of Child-Rearing Methods

Thus far we have reported the associations with denial of individual parental practices. On the assumption that any single treatment might have had a different relation to denial, depending on the others with which it was combined, we analyzed the association with defensive shifts of various combinations of parental practices.

### Obedience and Reward

On the basis of the hardship that we thought would result from each of the individual parental practices, we predicted an order in the severity of the different combinations of obedience and reward. As combinations varied from most to least severe, we expected a concomitant diminution in the proportion of the group who increased denial after failure. To test this association between denial and the combination of obedience and reward, with the ordering taken into account, we used the tau derived in terms of the modification of Kendall's method.[10] In Table 9-2, which contains a summary of all the findings for combinations of practices, we find that our prediction is supported by the results.

Subjects whose parents have made arbitrary requests for obedience and used only occasional rewards are most inclined to increase their references to denial in story endings written after experiencing a real failure. Such parental methods discourage practical attempts at the solutions of conflict. Next in order are

[9] We described our method of classifying mothers in accordance with the frequency of their rewards in Chapter 3. Of the ninety-six mothers, eighteen gave answers which we could not code. Some of the eighteen could not say how often they rewarded their sons. Others qualified their answers to such an extent that they could not be interpreted.

[10] The technique and its interpretation were explained in Chapter 1.

boys whose parents have accompanied the arbitrary requests with frequent rewards. Still fewer subjects increase references to denial in the group who have been subjected to reasonable requests and relatively infrequent rewards. Subjects whose parents have en-

**TABLE 9-2**

Combinations of Background Variables and Denial of Failure

| Conditions | Trends: Boxes with Largest Frequencies | N | Relation | Probability |
|---|---|---|---|---|
| Obedience & reward | Arbitrary requests: occasional reward & increase<br>Explained requests: frequent reward & no increase | 65 | .28 $\tau$ | <.01 (1t) |
| Discipline & reward | Psychol. discipline: frequent reward & no increase | 78 | 18.05 $\chi^2$ | <.01 |
| Within psychological discipline: reward & intelligence | Frequent reward: high intel. & no increase<br>Occasional reward and increase | 46 | 14.41 $\chi^2$ | <.01 |
| Discipline & obedience | Arbitrary requests: psychol. discipline and increase | 83 | 8.87 $\chi^2$ | .12 |

forced reasonable requests with frequent rewards show the least amount of denial. This final combination of methods provides the least interference with the children's attempts at practical action.[11]

### Discipline and Reward

We did not analyze the association between denial and the combination of discipline and reward in terms of Kendall's method, primarily because we had no basis for ordering the probable associations with denial of different combinations of corporal and psychological discipline. We therefore used the usual chi square method. As indicated in the second table, shifts in denial are significantly associated with the different combinations of dis-

[11] We had hoped to add verbal intelligence to the combination of reward and obedience, but the frequencies in some of the cells were too small to permit this type of analysis.

cipline and reward. We have already noted that mixed discipline is least conducive to denial. This relation remains the same when reward has been frequent or only occasional. The frequency of reward also makes little difference in determining the amount of denial shown by boys who have been subjected to frequent physical discipline. Frequency of reward does seem to make a difference, however, to children whose parents have used psychological manipulation. A separate analysis of this psychologically disciplined group of boys reveals a very significant association between denial and reward. Boys who have received frequent rewards are much less inclined to increase fantasy following failure than those who have been given only occasional rewards. Most of the latter increase denial after threat. If mothers have disciplined their children by such psychological methods as appeals to guilt, the stressing of their inadequacies, or threats of love deprivation, the resultant guilt and negative self-evaluation may leave the children with few resources when confronted with a serious failure. If mothers who have made psychological appeals have relieved their pressure with frequent rewards, their sons are inclined to solve their problems by means of realistic methods. Within groups of psychologically disciplined subjects, the combination of reward and verbal intelligence is significantly related to shifts in denial.[12] If there are no incentives—if discipline has been psychological and rewards infrequent—even the most intelligent boys are inclined to retreat from failure to unrealistic fantasy. But with frequent rewards, the group with high verbal scores seem to capitalize on their capacities to obtain gratification by realistic methods; few of these boys deny their failures.

### Discipline and obedience

Although obedience and discipline, by themselves, are significantly related to denial, the combination of these parental practices is not. In general, the obtained trend could have been predicted from a knowledge of obedience alone.

[12] A tripling of the number of categories would have been required to control the effects of intelligence for all the combinations of discipline and reward. As a result, the number of cases in each category would have become extremely small. Since the primary source of the interaction involved the combination of psychological manipulation and reward, we had to be content with an analysis of the association between this combination and the shifts in defense of subjects with high and with average intelligence.

## Weaning and Toilet Training

We did exploratory analyses of the relationship to denial of weaning and toilet training, on the assumption that the early introduction of either practice might be sufficiently painful to reinforce a withdrawal from realistic pressures.[13] It was difficult to choose between this hypothesis and two equally plausible alternatives: Timing may be important only if it is consistent with the severity of later experiences; timing alone may be less relevant to denial than the quality of the child's emotional relationship with his mother when she initiates a practice. An analysis of our data reveals that neither weaning nor toilet training is significantly associated with increased denial after failure. To determine whether socio-economic status might have affected these relations, we retabulated them separately within the middle and working class. The results are still not significant.

## Summary

In predicting the relationships to denial of the various indices of our subjects' backgrounds, we anticipated that unrewarding experiences and harsh parental methods would reinforce the defense, and that gratifying experiences and benign methods would not. Our findings support this general hypothesis.

*Individual Background Variables.* When parents have made arbitrary demands for obedience, or have favored either corporal or psychological discipline, their children are inclined to employ denial. Membership in a social class, frequency of reward, and the harshness of weaning or toilet training are not significantly associated with increase in denial. The former two become significantly related to the defense when verbal intelligence is controlled.

*Discipline and Reward.* The combination of discipline and reward is significantly associated with an increase in denial. When discipline has been psychological and incentives sparse, denial in-

[13] We have described our methods of classifying the mothers according to the harshness of their practices in Chapter 3.

creases; when discipline has been psychological and rewards frequent, denial does not increase. When disciplinary methods have been mixed, denial does not increase regardless of the frequency of reward.

*Obedience and Reward.* The various combinations of reward and obedience indicate how negative pressures and incentives operate together to promote a realistic orientation or a propensity for denial. When parental practices have been most severe—when requests have been unexplained and rewards occasional—the proportion of subjects utilizing denial is maximal. When parental practices have been benign—when requests for obedience have been explained and rewards frequent—the proportion of subjects who deny failure is minimal.

*Discipline and Obedience.* While, by itself, each of these parental practices is significantly related to the boys' shifts in denial, the combination is not.

## References

1. Beardslee, Betty J. The learning of two mechanisms of defense. Unpubl. Ph.D. dissertation, Univ. of Michigan, 1955.
2. Calden, G. The relationship of varied test definitions and degrees of ego involvement to Rorschach test performance. Unpubl. Ph.D. dissertation, Univ. of Michigan, 1951.
3. Freud, Anna. *The ego and the mechanisms of defense.* New York: International Universities Press, 1946.
4. Thurstone, L. L., & Thurstone, Thelma G. *The Chicago tests of primary mental abilities.* Chicago: Science Research Associates, 1943.

# 10

## MECHANISMS OF DEFENSE

### III. Repression of Failure *

Certain failures pose a serious problem for every individual. They represent serious blows to one's prestige and self-esteem, and they create much anxiety and depression. Since they represent past events, the facts can be remembered or forgotten, but they cannot be changed by any practical endeavor. Because failures are so unpleasant, memory of them is often altered in retrospect, even by very stable and realistic people. There are different kinds of alteration; all of them require some obliteration of fact, but they differ in the resultant degree of distortion and in their social consequences.

Denial in fantasy is one method, and not a socially advantageous one, of reducing the anxiety created by an irremediable failure. In this chapter we will report a study of a second defense, repression. Repression can accomplish the same results as denial and is usually less damaging to one's interpersonal relationships. As in the previous study, we traced individual differences in the tendency to favor this defense to social class and to various child-rearing practices.

* We are indebted to Betty J. Beardslee for collecting the data and assisting in the design of the study.

## A Comparison of Denial and Repression

Denial and repression are similar in that the use of either modifies the awareness of unpleasant events. But they have different consequences. The denial of an event leads to a particular kind of false belief whose incompatibility with readily verifiable facts is often apparent even to the casual observer. If a man feels demeaned by a failure and then denies it, he alters his interpretation and memory of many facts. He substitutes a wishful version of events for the actual ones; as a result, he believes that he has been successful. Repression, in contrast, creates a relatively circumscribed hiatus in conscious experience. The automatic inhibition of perception creates blind spots, but does not usually create an untenable interpretation of a series of events. Often this mechanism facilitates socially adjustive behavior. If a man is more inclined to repress rather than deny failure, he is likely to blot out some key fact. But he does not have to alter his conception of most of the happenings. If he represses a failure, he does not think he has succeeded. He may forget that he once wanted to succeed very badly.

### An illustrative case

These rather general descriptions of the two mechanisms can be made more specific with the help of a hypothetical case. A young man was very attracted to a girl who lived in his neighborhood, and invited her to social events on seven occasions. Each time she declined, saying that she had a previous engagement. She was also evasive about times when she might be free. Finally, she accepted an eighth invitation and went to a dance with him. There she was polite but reserved, and she insisted on going home early. After that evening she accepted no further invitations.

It does not seem farfetched to infer from these facts that the girl did not return the young man's affection. Naturally, any man would be unhappy about this turn of events, and might even lose confidence in himself. In fact, the lowered self-esteem might be too painful to bear. Then he might begin to deceive himself about the failure of his suit. What would he believe if he adjusted to his unpleasant emotional state by denying its causes? Denial might be manifested by a belief that he had succeeded, that the girl loved him. To arrive at this conclusion, he would have to alter his recollection of numerous facts. He might omit a few, alter the meanings of others, and then reorganize the totality, so as to arrive at a new interpretation. He might, for example, forget that the young lady first refused a number of invitations, and he might accept the excuses she had given. The fact that she went to the dance and was polite on that occasion might be viewed as signs of strong affection. He might decide that she had wanted to see him later, but that her father forced her not to see him. Or he might forget her later refusals in favor of fantasies about her being passionately in love with him. He might even develop the conviction that it was he who had lost interest in her. In short, the distortions and reorganization of facts would lead to an alteration of a failure into a wishful face-saving version of all the events.

What if the young man had resorted to repression instead of denying the causes of his unhappy feelings? He would probably obliterate from awareness one or two key facts; then he could be quite accurate in evaluating most of the others. He might forget, for example, that he had once loved the girl. With the passage of time, he might even forget exactly who she was. In either case, he would not have to make the false assumption that she returned his love, and he would not have to buttress his defensive distortion by altering his recollection of many other facts. He might still remember that she refused all his invitations but one, and that she was not very warm at that time. Such memories could be tolerated, however, once he obliterated the recall of his own need for her or of her identity.[1]

### Defenses and the alteration of perception

Psychologists do not yet understand just how denial and repression affect perception. Denial seems to involve obliteration from consciousness, or distortion, of all cues pointing to events that have elicited anxiety. Some of the distortion is apparently

[1] We assume that either denial or repression can be used to relieve the distress created by a serious failure. This assumption is not shared by some psychoanalysts, who postulate that external events are denied and that repression is suitable only to internal events, such as action tendencies. It seems to us that either defense is applicable to both external and internal events, although we have the impression that, statistically speaking, external or past events tend to be denied rather than repressed, and that action tendencies tend to be repressed rather than denied.

accomplished by the substitution of wish-fulfilling fantasies for actual events. The content of the fantasy is usually connected with the sources of anxiety by nonlogical associations. As a result, the interpretation of events acquires a quality not unlike that of a pleasant dream. Actual meanings tend to be changed into their opposites: Failures are converted into successes, weaknesses into strengths, and hostile actions into well-meaning attempts to help people.

As was indicated in Chapter 9, an inclination to favor denial in fantasy is probably reinforced by early, and probably lengthy, experience with harsh parental techniques. To avoid the resultant pain, the child learns to retreat from the world of actual events into his private world of fantasy. Repression also results in avoidance, but does not signify a total retreat. Only a few specific facts are altered, and there is no gross reinterpretation of total events. According to Freud (5), there are two phases in the development of repression. The initial phase, "primal repression," consists of a denial of entry into consciousness of a perceived event. But primal repression is not sufficient to prevent awareness of a "mental presentation" for very long, since any experience that is associated with the repressed material creates an inclination to "remember" it. Conscious recall of the painful event that has been the subject of primary repression is then prevented by "repression proper." This mechanism involves an "after expulsion," or an elimination from awareness of new percepts, although these do not originally elicit anxiety. They come to do so because they are associated with the repressed material. The closer the association, the greater is the anxiety aroused by these new percepts, and the greater is the inclination to repress them.

"Repression acts . . . in a highly specific manner . . . a little more or a little less distortion alters the whole issue." Freud notes that idealization and joking permit even those events which are very closely associated with repressed material to become conscious. Then they can be reported accurately. The circumscribed scotoma that result from repression permit far more realistic behavior in many instances than is possible when a group of facts are altered by the mechanism of denial.

### Repression and the second family of defenses

Into which family of defenses does repression best fit? Repression is similar to defenses in the first family in that it seems to provide a total escape from a problem. Repression is similar to defenses in the second family in that its alterations depend on displacements within dimensions, its use facilitates inhibition of action tendencies, and it does not create gross distortions of meaning.

Like defense mechanisms in the second family, repression requires a rather protracted period of education. Before a child can repress the fact that he has had a serious failure, for example, he must have developed a body image and a conception of self, he must have learned different standards of accomplishment, and he must have identified with individuals to whom such standards are very important for maintaining self-esteem. Once these are acquired, only the specific information immediately associated with the repressed material has to be eliminated from consciousness. The child does not have to retreat into his private world of fantasy or radically reinterpret what he sees in order to overcome his anxiety.

There are probably more than two families of defense, and repression may not be a member of either of the ones we have investigated. But even if repression fits neither constellation, it may still have a special relation to defenses in the second family. As mentioned earlier, it may be required for their operation. Reversal of hatred, for example, may entail first a repression of the affect and then its displacement. And projection may entail first a repression of the fact that the agent is oneself and then a displacement of the agent. Repression may or may not be required for the successful distortion of an action tendency by means of defenses in the second family; we think we can conceive of instances in which the mechanism is not necessary. Yet, it probably facilitates the operations of such defenses, and is combined with them quite frequently.

## Method

In our investigation we tried to satisfy four criteria in identifying an instance of repression. It was first necessary that the subject be aware of an event. Second, the event had to be an unwelcome one which caused him anxiety. Third, he had to give evidence that he could not voluntarily recall the event once he became anxious. Fourth, we required indirect evidence that the lack of memory was not a true case of forgetting. This criterion was satisfied by evidence of the more efficient recall of other events which took place at the same time as the unpleasant ones.

A consideration of these criteria readily revealed that the story completion test, the technique used in most of our studies, was not suited to the measurement of repression. Such a method requires free association rather than recall. In the projective test we typically introduced intolerable events in story beginnings and inferred defenses from the substitutes described in the story endings. The omission of topics did not necessarily signify repression.

### DIRECTIONS FOR ADMINISTERING TESTS OF REPRESSION

The test of repression was given in connection with the study that has been reported in Chapter 9. Sixteen short, timed tests were administered under conditions which made it very important to succeed. The subjects were informed that a passing score required the completion of fifteen tests. The tests were so designed that only half of them could be finished in the allotted time. Before and after this procedure we administed story completion tests with themes about failure. Finally, following the method first used by Zeigarnik (9), we asked the boys to recall as many of the sixteen tests as they could. Our measure of repression was the difference between the number of incompleted and completed tests that were recalled. We now describe in greater detail the procedure for testing selective recall.

Each boy was seen individually. First, he was asked a series of standardized, open-ended questions about his aspirations. The examiner said, "If you could be anything in the world you wanted to be, if you could have any job in the world, what job would you like to have?" Then he asked, "What do you really think you will be?" and "What kind of a job do you really expect you will have twenty years from now?" There followed other questions about the requirements for the dream job and the more probable one, the reasons for the choices, and the subject's qualifications. The interview was designed to make the subject think about and doubt his own capacities.

Next the examiner said that he was going to administer an aptitude test that would show how realistic the boy was being in his plans and aspirations. In the instructions we tried to convey the impression that the test would provide a real indication of the boy's ability to succeed. Our object was to maximize his motivation to do very well on the test. First the examiner said, "We are interested in finding out how realistic boys are in their ambitions for themselves . . . whether they are really capable of doing well on the kinds of things they want to do, and whether they have the . . . abilities that everybody needs to get along well, both on the job and with other people." Then he mentioned the job to which the subject aspired and said, "Probably you wonder just how well you're going to make out. Undoubtedly you are not sure of yourself." He described the tests the subject was about to take as being short and as representing various aptitudes and abilities. ". . . so that we can find out in a short time just how well you can do in lots of different things." He added that the tests would sample some of the skills required for the job in which the subject was interested. While the tests would seem very simple, he said, it was important to remember that they were timed. Thus, those that were not completed within a certain period would count as failures, even if the subject could have completed them if he took a longer time.

KINDS OF TESTS

We used two criteria in selecting tests. They had to be short, because our time was very limited. They also had to contain as many different kinds of items as possible. The variety supported our claim that many skills were being tested. It also increased the probability that some of the tests would appeal to children with different kinds of interests. Had all the tests been similar, they might have appealed to special interests that were more common in one social class than in another. Had we restricted the tasks to verbal ones, for example, the middle-class subjects might have become more interested, and more confident in their abilities, than subjects from the working class. In addition to tests of verbal skills, we also included tests requiring skills in drawing, motor speed, perceptual quickness, and attention.

All of the final sixteen tasks were adapted from various laboratory techniques and standard psychological tests. The time limits varied between one and three minutes. We now list and describe each of the sixteen tests in order. We shall first give the title of the test and then summarize its instructions.

1. *Following Directions:* Put a circle around all the curved figures and a line through all the straight line figures. Put a large X through all numbers. Start at the beginning and take each figure in order.

2. *Parts and Wholes:* Each of the words below names a part of something. After each word, write the name of the object of which it is a part. For example, nose is a part of . . .

3. *Speed Test:* Put a dot in each of the circles. When you finish, go back and make sure that each of your dots is clearly marked.

4. *Scrambled Sentences:* Rearrange the words in the sentence below so that the sentence makes sense.

5. *Missing Parts:* This is a test of how well you observe people. In each of the figures and faces below, there is something missing. Finish each of the drawings so that it is complete.

6. *Same and Opposite:* Find a word for each of the spaces below. Example: A word that means the opposite of hate is . . .

7. *Maze:* On the next page, you will find a maze. Put your pencil in the starting box, and from there find your way out to the exit. Do not go into any blind alleys because two such mistakes mean that you automatically fail. Once you have begun, do not lift your pencil from the paper.

8. *Making Words:* From the letters P S A I L T E make three words of four letters each.

9. *Coordination:* Draw a line that goes over each of the straight lines, and circles each of the X's. Be sure that your line does not touch any of the figures.

10. *Counting with Subtraction:* Beginning with the number 30,

count backwards alternately skipping 4 and then 3 until you get to 0. Write the numbers on this paper.

11. *Guides:* Each circle on the page below has either a number or a letter in it. Start with the first letter of the alphabet, A. Draw a line from there to the first number, 1. Then continue to the next letter, B; then to the next number, 2. Continue to the stop circle, alternating letters and numbers.

12. *Coding:* If the following sentence (sample code) means "It was found under a peach tree," what does this mean? (test code)

13. *Ba Words:* Beside each number (there were five), write a word that begins with the letters *ba.*

14. *Pursuit:* Pursue each of the lines starting in a numbered box at the left to its end in a box at the right. Then write the starting number in the box at the right.

15. *Fruits and Vegetables:* Rearrange the letters to form the name of a fruit or vegetable. For example, A P E is pea.

16. *Number Series:* In each of the number series below, the last two numbers are missing. Complete each series by filling in the spaces with the correct numbers.

To make sure that all the subjects failed, the examiner first said that no one with the ability needed to make a success of himself would fail more than one of the sixteen tests. We had arranged the time limits to guarantee that only eight, or one half, of the sixteen tests would be completed. An announcement that "time is up" prevented the other half from being finished. Then the examiner said he would figure out the subject's score while he wrote endings for a number of stories like the ones he had completed previously. After those story endings were written, the subject was asked to recall as many of the sixteen short tests as he could. He was told to mention them in the order they came to his mind, and to describe them clearly enough to convey their nature. When he could no longer think of any, he was urged to try once more.

### Analysis of results

Depending on the kinds of tests the subjects remembered most, we divided them into three categories. One recalled more incompleted than completed tasks, one recalled the same number of incompleted and completed tasks, and one recalled more completed than incompleted tasks. The tendency to recall completed tasks was our definition of repression. This definition was suggested by previous studies (1, 7) demonstrating that when subjects are eager to do well and are placed under stress, they are inclined to forget their failures and to recall their successes.

The recall of completed tasks satisfies our original definition of a defense. To begin with, each of the tests was used by all boys for a period of at least three minutes, so there was a sufficient opportunity to become acquainted with it. In addition, all the subjects failed to meet the minimal standard of performance for a task on which they were highly motivated to excel. Their failure then presumably became a source of anxiety. Subjects were given the same amount of time with interrupted and completed tests. From the fact that more passed tests were remembered than failed ones, we inferred an inclination to repress the latter.

## Individual Background Conditions

It was difficult to predict the conditions that might create a predilection for repression. Our uncertainty stemmed, in part, from the stress in the psychoanalytic literature on the possible relation between extensive repression and psychosis (4). Since psychosis often involves denial, it seemed possible that denial and repression might occasionally go together. We were inclined to consider repression a more mature defense than any of the ones requiring a pathological break with reality. Consequently, we anticipated that the tendency to recall completed tasks would be associated with predominantly benign experiences. In our group these were indicated by membership in the middle class and by the gentler parental practices. Since the research was exploratory, we tested the significance of results by means of two-tailed tests.

### Social class [2]

Why might boys in the middle class be more inclined toward repression than their peers in the working class? First we assumed that repression creates relatively little distortion of one's total field

[2] The methods of classifying families with respect to social class and type of integration have been described in Chapter 2.

of awareness, and that it facilitates socially conforming behavior. Few facts are eliminated from consciousness, and the tolerable ones can be reported accurately. Their meaning does not have to be denied. As reported in Chapter 2, people in the middle class place a high value on accurate perception, since it helps to evaluate the probable outcomes of certain economic risks, and to indicate the kinds of impulses that must be inhibited for the sake of future gratifications. Lack of accurate perception can interfere with the learning of the social skills needed for the manipulation of symbols. It seemed probable to us that repression, because it implements the goal of inhibiting the direct expression of certain needs, might be reinforced by certain experiences and child-rearing practices that are common to people in the middle class.

**TABLE 10-1**

**Individual Background Conditions and Memory for Tasks**

| *Conditions* | *Trends: Boxes with Largest Frequencies* | *N* | $\chi^2$ | *Probability* |
|---|---|---|---|---|
| Social class | MC and completed tasks | 106 | 5.90 | .05 |
| Discipline | — | 106 | 5.60 | $<.30$ |
| Obedience requests | Reasonable requests and completed tasks | 92 | 6.72 | .04 |
| Frequency of reward | — | 84 | 1.59 | $<.50$ |
| Weaning | Harsh weaning and completed tasks | 99 | 5.43 | .07 |
| Toilet training | Coercive training and completed tasks | 102 | 4.25 | .12 |

We have noted in the previous chapter that denial of failure is most characteristic of boys from the working class who are in the lower half of the distribution of verbal intelligence, and that boys from the middle class are very disinclined to resort to denial in fantasy. As indicated in Table 10-1,[3] which summarizes the relations between background variables and repression, boys from the middle class are significantly more inclined to repress their failures than are boys from the working class. Middle-class back-

[3] The detailed tables may be found in Appendix D.

grounds are associated with the inclination to remember completed rather than incompleted tasks.

INTEGRATION

In all our studies we have made separate analyses of class differences within the entrepreneurial and the bureaucratic settings. Since so little is known about these two types of integration, we had no basis for anticipating whether they might affect an inclination to repress failure. On analyzing the difference between the two social classes within the entrepreneurial group, we find that there is a very slight tendency for boys from the working class to exceed boys in the middle class in the proportion who remember more incompleted than completed tasks. But the chi square is not significant. Among subjects from bureaucratic families the difference between the classes is significant and in the anticipated direction. Sons of white-collar workers significantly exceed the sons of blue-collar workers in the proportion who remember more completed than incompleted tasks.[4] Sons of blue-collar workers show some inclination to remember more incompleted than completed tasks.

Any explanation of the reasons for the significance of class differences within the bureaucratic group and not the entrepreneurial one can only be speculative. People in the entrepreneurial setting must maintain the faith that sufficient skill in taking risks and in capitalizing on one's opportunities will ultimately be climaxed by success. According to the accepted ideology, temporary failure should be viewed as a valuable lesson rather than a source of despair. If boys from entrepreneurial families are taught to make realistic evaluations of failure, they may be disinclined to repress it. Since the son of the manual laborer in the entrepreneurial setting can often cultivate a faith in future mobility, even he may learn to take the bitter with the sweet.

If these assumptions about the two social classes are correct, they explain the lack of a significant difference. It is difficult for the white-collar worker within the bureaucratic organization to consider himself the master of his own fate. He, too, strives to improve his lot and to improve his economic position. Yet, be-

[4] The chi-square of 9.34 is significant at the .01 level of probability.

cause he is often impotent to rectify the causes of failure, he may sometimes have no alternative but repression. As for the bureaucratic blue-collar worker, curtailed mobility and job security may leave him relatively contented with his lot, or, at any rate, disinclined to put forth the effort needed to hurdle the barriers to advancement. If he is not very concerned with relative status, he may not experience sufficient anxiety to repress his failures. Hence, he resorts to the defense less frequently than does the white-collar worker.

### Discipline [5]

The fact that harsh discipline was associated with an inclination toward denial suggested the possibility that benign discipline might be associated with repression. But as before, we were not very certain about the kind of discipline that was most benign. Originally, we were inclined to choose psychological discipline, because it usually signifies an absence of physical pain. Yet, it was difficult to consider such a technique very supportive in view of the lengthy periods of guilt to which it can lead. The findings of a number of our studies all point to the fact that mixed, and apparently more flexible, discipline is most benign. There is a very slight tendency for children to remember completed tasks if their parents have favored mixed kinds of discipline, but, as indicated in Table 10-1, the association between type of punishment and memory for tasks is not significant.

### Requests for obedience

We anticipated that the requests would have to be reasonable in order for the children to favor repression, a defense which restricts the distortion to painful events but does not require a total retreat from the situation. Explanations of parental requests clarify some of the principles behind them. The children can then react to specific causes of anxiety and do not have to develop an incorrect interpretation of a total problem.

Our anticipation is supported by the results reported in Table 10-1. Requests for obedience are significantly associated with the

[5] The methods of classifying mothers with respect to techniques of child rearing have been described in Chapter 3.

recall of tests. If the parents have usually been reasonable, the boys are likely to remember completed tasks. If the requests have been arbitrary, the boys are likely to remember more incompleted tasks or an equal number of incompleted and completed ones.

### Frequency of reward

As was stated in Chapter 3, we were somewhat dissatisfied with the index of reward. It was based only on the answer to one question, and many mothers were not sure whether or not to count certain affectionate gestures or statements of pride as instances of reward. Since we expected the more supportive techniques to be associated with a tendency to favor repression, we anticipated that the frequently rewarded boys would exceed the infrequently rewarded boys in the proportion who recalled more completed than incompleted tasks. The results, summarized in Table 10-1, reveal no trend.

### Weaning and toilet training

Early weaning and coercive toilet training are the methods preferred by parents in the middle class. It seemed possible that these methods might be associated with repression, the defense used most frequently by sons of white-collar workers. But early weaning and coercive toilet training are relatively harsh methods. According to our conception of the origins of repression, it is not reinforced by such techniques. It also seemed possible that while they may be somewhat unpleasant, they are not as harsh as methods like unexplained requests or corporal discipline, and that they may even motivate a child to please his mother. In view of the contradictory implications of the alternative interpretations, we had no anticipations about the kinds of associations we might find between these early child-rearing methods and repression. Table 10-1 reveals that the associations with the boys' recall of both weaning and toilet training are not far from significance. Early weaning and coercive bowel training tend to go with the recall of completed tasks. These parental techniques, which are relatively harsh and are used most often by mothers in the middle class, apparently do not interfere with the children's learning of rules and may actually facilitate it by setting relatively high but attainable standards of performance.

## Combinations of Social Class and Child Rearing

Social class may be viewed as a general context which defines the meanings of different parental practices. We have noted, for example, that boys from the middle class are more inclined to repress their failures than are boys from the working class. This finding suggests that adults in the middle class may place a greater value on being realistic, even in the face of anxiety, than do adults in the working class. If this is a true difference, the inclination to repress rather than to deny failure may be associated with intense parental pressures only in the middle class and not in the working class.

### Social class and discipline

By itself, type of discipline was not significantly related to the recall of tasks. Yet, as indicated in Table 10-2, when the relation between the two is recomputed within the middle- and working-class groups, the over-all association is very significant. In the middle, but not the working class, psychological discipline is associated with the recall of completed tasks. In the working class the only trend, and it is a weak one, pairs corporal discipline with the recall of interrupted tasks. Actually, the primary source of variation occurs in the corporally disciplined and mixed groups. Among the corporally disciplined, boys from the working class display a tendency to recall incompleted tasks, while boys from the middle class are more inclined to recall completed tasks. Among subjects who have been treated with the relatively benign mixed discipline, there is a strong tendency to recall completed tasks in the middle class, and no trend in the working class.

### Social class and requests for obedience

The over-all association involving social class, requests for obedience, and recall of tasks is very close to significance. The probability of chance occurrence is .06. It might have been lower had there not been a paucity of parents in the middle class who made arbitrary requests for obedience. The primary source of the

**TABLE 10-2**

Combinations of Background Conditions and Memory for Tasks

| *Background Conditions* | *Trends: Boxes with Largest Frequencies* | *N* | $\chi^2$ | *Probability* |
|---|---|---|---|---|
| Social class & discipline | MC, psychological discipline and completed tasks; WC, corporal discipline and incompleted tasks | 106 | 23.68 | .01 |
| Social class & obedience requests | MC, explained requests, and completed tasks; WC, arbitrary requests and same number of completed and incompleted tasks | 92 | 12.18 | .06 |
| Social class & frequency of reward | MC, frequent reward and completed tasks; WC, frequent reward and incompleted tasks | 84 | 9.09 | .17 |
| Social class & weaning | MC, early weaning and completed tasks; WC, late weaning and incompleted tasks | 99 | 9.02 | .17 |
| Social class & toilet training | MC, coercive and completed tasks; WC, coercive and incompleted tasks | 102 | 15.15 | .02 |
| Obedience requests & discipline | Explained requests, psychological discipline, and completed tasks; arbitrary requests, psychological discipline, and the same number of completed and incompleted tasks | 93 | 17.54 | .07 |
| Reward & discipline | Frequent reward, psychological discipline, and completed tasks; infrequent reward, psychological discipline, and same number of completed and incompleted tasks | 85 | 15.17 | .13 |
| Reward & obedience requests | Explained requests, frequent reward, and completed tasks; arbitrary requests, frequent reward, and incompleted tasks; arbitrary requests, infrequent reward, and the same number of completed and incompleted tasks | 74 | 13.32 | .04 |

variation in recall is provided by the difference between boys in the two social classes within the group whose parents have usually explained their requests for obedience.[6] Within the middle class, this technique is associated with the recall of completed tasks; within the working class, it is associated with the recall of incompleted tasks.

[6] The chi-square of 4.35 has a probability of only .12.

### Social class and frequency of reward

Only a very weak trend is characteristic of the relationship involving social class, reward, and the recall of tasks. Again, the reinforcement affects the rate of repression primarily in the class most concerned with the results of the defense. Within the group whose parents have favored frequent rewards, boys in the middle class show a significant tendency to recall more completed tasks, while boys in the working class are more inclined to recall incompleted tasks.[7]

### Social class and weaning

Since the associations with repression of weaning and of toilet training were not far from significance, it seemed fruitful to reanalyze separately the results for each practice within the middle- and working-class groups. We had found that coercive methods were associated with the defense. For reasons already cited, we anticipated that such trends would be stronger in the middle class than in the working class. Table 10-2 does not support our prediction for weaning. When class is taken into account, the relation between weaning and repression does not become significant. We do get the anticipated trends: Boys in the middle class who were weaned early are inclined to remember completed tasks, and boys in the working class who were weaned later are inclined to remember more of the interrupted ones.

### Social class and toilet training

When class is taken into account, the association between toilet training and repression becomes significant, and in the anticipated direction. The primary source of variation occurs among boys who have been raised by coercive methods. Within that group, boys in the middle class remember more of the completed tasks and boys in the working class remember more of the interrupted ones.[8] The defense is affected by pressure only within the group which probably places a high value on the results of repression.

[7] The chi-square of 6.49 is significant at the .05 level.

[8] Within the group who were subjected to coercive methods, the chi-square for the association between social class and repression is 10.56 and is significant at the .01 level.

## Combinations of Parental Practices

The same parental practice may have different associations with defenses, depending on the other practices with which it is combined. We anticipated that repression would be associated more with combinations of benign techniques than harsh ones.

### Requests for obedience and discipline

The association involving obedience requests, discipline, and recall of tasks is almost significant. The probability of chance occurrence is .07. The marginal significance may have been caused by the small number of cases in some boxes. Groups who have been subjected to psychological or to mixed discipline seem to be contributing the primary source of variance. When the method has been predominantly psychological, boys for whom requests for obedience have been explained are significantly more inclined to remember completed tasks than are boys whose parents have used arbitrary requests.[9] Such boys are most likely to remember an equal number of completed and incompleted tasks. When the method has involved mixed discipline, the group raised with reasonable requests for obedience are most inclined to remember completed tasks, while the group raised with arbitrary requests are inclined to remember incompleted tasks.

### Reward and punishment

The over-all chi-square, involving frequency of reward, punishment, and repression, shows a mild trend in the predicted direction, but is far from significant. The primary source of the trend is provided by the psychologically disciplined group. When this method has been combined with reasonable requests, the boys are most inclined to remember completed tasks. If requests have been arbitrary, the boys are likely to remember an equal number of completed and interrupted tasks. Even within the psychologically disciplined group, however, the relation between reward and recall is not significant.

[9] The chi-square of 6.81 is significant at the .05 level.

REWARD AND REQUESTS FOR OBEDIENCE

The relation involving obedience, reward, and recall of tasks is significant. As anticipated, the benign combination of reasonable requests and frequent reward is associated with the recall of completed tasks. When reward has been frequent, but requests unexplained, boys are more inclined to recall incompleted tasks.[10]

## Discussion

We have been investigating defensive distortions of a problem with consequences which are obvious to most people and very damaging to one's self-esteem. Hence, we have assumed that the resultant anxiety is particularly amenable to the kind of defense that obliterates some facts. Mechanisms which operate in this manner are not the most efficient or mature ones; they must obliterate observable facts to some extent. They can be ranked with respect to relative degree of obliteration and the seriousness of social problems that their use may help to create. On the basis of such rankings, we have concluded that the inclination to repress failure results in more mature behavior than does the inclination to deny failure. Throughout this volume we have postulated that the learning of complex skills necessary for socially acceptable behavior is reinforced most strongly by benign and stimulating methods. In the present study we anticipated that relatively benign antecedent conditions—membership in the middle rather than the working class, mixed rather than corporal discipline, explained rather than arbitrary requests, and frequent rather than infrequent rewards—would be associated with repression rather than denial.

Our assumptions about the nature of repression gain support, not only from our empirical data, but also from some congruent findings reported by other investigators. We shall now summarize some of the studies that are relevant to our design and the interpretations of our results.

[10] Within the group who have been rewarded frequently, the association between requests for obedience and recall of tasks has a chi square of 8.75 and is significant at the .01 level.

INSTRUCTIONS AND RECALL

In planning our method we were influenced by Rosenzweig's (8) and Alper's (1) findings that the relative recall of completed and incompleted tasks varies with the degree of threat in the instructions. Rosenzweig gave nonthreatening, task-oriented instructions to one group of subjects. He said he was constructing some puzzles for future research and needed to know how good they were. In general he tried to act in a manner that would make the subjects feel comfortable. He explained interruption, for example, not as failure, but as an indication that he had gotten sufficient information. When the instructions were intended to be threatening and ego-involving, he defined the task as an intelligence test. In addition, he tried to arouse as much anxiety as possible by devices like holding a stop watch and defining interruption as a failure to complete the puzzle within the allotted time.

Alper used very similar procedures. In the nonthreatening situation the subject worked alone in the presence of the examiner, who said he was testing some materials for a later experiment. He was very friendly and informal, and explained interruptions as indications that materials were difficult. In the threatening, and presumably ego-involving, situation the subject worked in the presence of the examiner, an attractive young female accomplice who served as a second recorder, and a male accomplice who acted as another subject. The task was defined as a brief intelligence test that the Army had found useful in selecting candidates for Officer Training School. In each session, the real subject was allowed to finish only half the tasks while the accomplice, acting as a subject, completed all of them. Lack of completion thus represented a failure in actual competition to do well on a very important test.

Depending in part on the nature of the instructions, subjects varied in their recall of completed and incompleted tasks. When instructions were task oriented, most subjects were inclined to recall incompleted tasks; when instructions were ego-oriented, most subjects were inclined to recall completed tasks.

These results of Alper and Rosenzweig, in addition to our conception of the conditions required to elicit a defense, made it imperative for us to choose between task-oriented and ego-oriented instructions. In view of the requirements for eliciting defenses, we chose instructions calculated to maximize ego-involvement in the task. Our primary reason, which we discuss in further detail in Chapter 16, was the assumption that anxiety must reach a particular level of intensity before serving as a stimulus for defensive distortion. In all our investigations of defense we attempted to create maximal threat or conflict, depending on the kind of mechanisms we hoped to elicit. Like Rosenzweig and Mason, we labeled as repression the inclination to forget experiences "that are unpleasant because they wound self-respect . . ." more than "experiences that are gratifying to the ego" (8).

PERSONAL TRAITS AND REPRESSION

Most relevant to the interpretations of our results are the findings reported by Rosenzweig and Mason (8) and by Alper (2), since both studies concentrated on the significance of recall for individual differences in personality. Rosenzweig and Mason used ego-involving instructions: They offered a prize to a group of crippled children for the best solution to a group of puzzles. The investigators were interested in the relation of recall to ratings of the children's pride. This trait was defined as the "desire to stand well with the group, and pleasure in one's own achievement." The data revealed an association between repression and pride. High ratings of pride, or concern with achievement, went with recall of completed tasks; low ratings went with recall of incompleted tasks. High intelligence was also associated with recall of completed tasks.

In an initial study of ten draft-age, male undergraduates Alper found two major patterns of selective recall. One entailed the recall of a preponderance of incompleted tasks when instructions were task oriented, and of a preponderance of completed tasks when instructions were threatening to self-esteem. Correlations with personality ratings made in terms of Murray's (6) dimensions of personality identified this pattern with "high tolerance of failure (ego strength)." Subjects high in tolerance of failure were also rated high on the inclinations to seek prestige and to lead others, the tendency to know what one wants to do and to do it, and the ability to organize one's efforts. These men got low ratings on pessimism about life and feelings of inferiority.

The second primary pattern entailed a recall of a preponderance of completed tasks when instructions were task oriented and of incompleted tasks when instructions were threatening to self-esteem. Men with this were rated high on pessimism about life and feelings of inferiority, and low on the inclinations to seek prestige, to defend oneself against blame, to set difficult goals and to try to reach them, and to perceive the world from a personal viewpoint and with self-satisfaction. In Alper's opinion, the inclination of subjects with weak ego to recall interrupted tasks when instructions are threatening signifies an eagerness to admit failure before one can be accused of it by other people.

In a validating study Alper (3) selected nine subjects with strong egos and nine with weak egos from a pool of eighty-six undergraduate males. The choice of each subject required agreement between independent ratings of him and his self-description on a "psychological insight test." This test consisted primarily of the nine variables that had discriminated between the two kinds of ego strength in the first investigation. Of the different measures of recall used in the second study, the one that was most comparable to the calculations of the present research involved a subtraction of the number of completed tasks from the number of incompleted tasks. Alper found a significant tendency for the subjects with strong egos to exceed the subjects with weak egos in the recall of a preponderance of completed tasks.

It is tempting to speculate on the parallels between the results of the present study and those of Alper and of Rosenzweig and Mason. Subjects in their researches who were inclined to recall completed tasks were concerned with prestige and seemed ambitious. In addition, Alper's subjects, who favored what we have called repression, might be described as knowing what to do and doing it, as being confident, optimistic, and capable of organizing their efforts. These are socially desirable traits, involving complex skills.

Now we make the questionable assumption that subjects and methods in the three studies were comparable; then we become very speculative. Suppose one asks what kinds of backgrounds would be most reinforcing for the traits of subjects who favored the recall of completed tasks. The backgrounds of our subjects who repressed failure seem very pertinent to such traits. Our boys came mostly from the middle class, and it is the white-collar workers who are most concerned with ambition and prestige. They receive a combination of explained requests and frequent reward, which is likely to build confidence and teach the skills required for successful effort. The parents of subjects from the middle class have favored psychological manipulation, a method that is likely to reinforce the internalization of high standards of accomplishment. In short, the backgrounds of our group who recalled completed tasks are congruent with the personality traits of subjects who performed in the same manner in the other two studies. Such backgrounds and traits are also congruent with the relative capacity to tolerate certain anxieties and to avoid a total retreat into the world of fantasy—traits which seem required for the development of a predilection for repression.

And what are the antecedents of the recall of incompleted tasks? Variables related either singly or in combination to lack of repression include membership in the working class, corporal punishment, and arbitrary requests for obedience. The pattern of background conditions associated with recall of failures is similar to that found for the antecedents of denial. This observation leads us to question the obvious assumption that the recall of failure is relatively realistic, since it signifies a facing of unwelcome information.

The fact that some boys remembered as many or more failures than successes does not necessarily signify a realistic reaction. To reduce the anxiety caused by the unpleasant event, some boys may have resorted to defenses other than repression. Denial, for example, because it alters the meaning of a failure, may not interfere with its recall. These speculations suggest the possibility of an inverse relation between the two defenses. In testing the relation we held social class and intelligence constant, since both were involved in associations with either of the mechanisms. We found that middle-class boys who are above average in intelligence are inclined to repress failure and not to deny it. Working-class boys who are below average in intelligence are inclined to deny failure and not to repress it. The trend indicates an inverse relation between the defenses when social status and intelligence are controlled, but the probability that the relation occurred by chance does not attain significance. It is .10. Possibly the figure would have been closer to .05 were it not for the small number of cases in each of the twelve boxes and the relative lack of spread in the scores on the test of verbal intelligence.

## Summary

Repression and denial are relatively extreme defenses which are used to relieve anxiety about intolerable events. We assumed that the former was the more mature defense, and that it would be reinforced by benign background conditions. Repression was defined in terms of the tendency to remember more successes, or completed tasks, than failures, or incompleted tasks, on a test in which the subjects were highly motivated to succeed. The disinclination to remember failures is found most often in boys who are from the middle class, or whose parents have explained their requests for obedience. It also occurs frequently among boys in the middle class whose parents have explained their requests, favored psychological discipline, or been coercive in toilet training, and among boys whose parents have combined explanations of requests with either psychological discipline or with frequent rewards. Combinations of benign methods seem most conducive to repression. Harsher ones seem more conducive to denial.

## References

1. Alper, Thelma G. Memory for completed and incompleted tasks as a function of personality: an analysis of group data. *J. abnorm. soc. Psychol.*, 1946, *41*, 403–20.
2. ———. Memory for completed and incompleted tasks as a function of personality: correlation between experimental and personality data. *J. Pers.*, 1948, *17*, 104–37.
3. ———. Predicting the direction of selective recall: its relation to ego strength and achievement. *J. abnorm. soc. Psychol.*, 1957, *55*, 149–65.
4. Freud, Anna. *The ego and the mechanisms of defence.* London: Hogarth, 1937.
5. Freud, S. Repression. *Collected Papers,* Vol. IV. London: Hogarth, 1925.

6. Murray, H. A., *et al. Explorations in personality*. New York: Oxford Univ. Press, 1938.
7. Rosenzweig, S. An experimental study of "repression" with special reference to need-persistive and ego-defensive reactions. *J. exp. Psychol.*, 1943, *32*, 64–94.
8. ——— & Mason, Gwendolyn A. An experimental study of memory in relation to the theory of repression. *Brit. J. Psychol.*, 1934, *24*, 247–65.
9. Zeigarnik, Bluma. On finished and unfinished tasks. In Ellis, W. D. (Ed.), *A source book of gestalt psychology*. New York: Harcourt Brace, 1938.

# 11

## MECHANISMS OF DEFENSE

## IV. Aggression and the Second Family of Defenses *

In Chapter 8 we proposed a division of the mechanisms of defense into two families. Defenses in the first family facilitate an escape from conflict by distortions which violate physical principles or the rules of probability. Defenses in the second family are directed against the person's awareness of needs: They help him to modify the unacceptable parts of himself. For this reason, we shall refer to them as the self-modifying defenses. Although the mechanisms in the second family are usually less efficient than are those in the first in dispelling anxiety, they have one major asset: They are particularly effective in resolving conflicts involving aggression and guilt. By means of these defenses, one can substitute socially acceptable tendencies for the forbidden ones.

A child learns very early in life that he can get along best with his parents if he inhibits his socially disapproved action tendencies and expresses only those that are approved. Defenses in the second family help him to conform without awareness of the necessary distortions in his action tendencies. By reversing a desire to hurt his sister, he helps her and then gains a reward from

* In the research team, Betty J. Beardslee was responsible for the research to be reported and for the preparation of the chapter, which is based in part on her doctoral dissertation (1).

his mother. If he turns his anger at his father inward, he becomes depressed, but he also avoids the difficulty that would follow the direct expression of his aggression and may even receive some paternal expressions of solace.

The study to be reported concerns the contrasting backgrounds that predispose children to differ in their predilections for mechanisms in the second family of defenses. To elicit the defenses, we attempted to create a real conflict between aggression and guilt. The predilections for self-modifying defenses were related to such aspects of background as social position and the mothers' child-rearing practices. The latter included methods of discipline, frequency of reward, demands for obedience, and severity of weaning and toilet training.

## Method

Our objects of study were the conflicts that involve aggressive needs. To arouse such conflicts, we created a situation designed to make the subjects angry, and then guilty about their anger. In order to gain information about the subjects' defenses, we gave them projective tests before and after the presumed conflict. Each projective test consisted of a series of story beginnings about people in conflict. The subjects were instructed to complete the stories. We held the story sequence constant by assigning eight different sequences at random to different groups of subjects. On the basis of their written endings, we divided the sample into one group who wrote more defensive endings after conflict, and another group who did not write more defensive endings.

### Arousal of conflict

We presented the first story completion test individually before making any attempt to create an actual conflict. The examiner read each story beginning aloud while the subject read it to himself. Then the subject wrote his ending.

After three stories were completed, the examiner suggested a rest. At this point he introduced the material designed to make the subject both angry and guilty. On the pretext of discussing some of the studies, he mentioned that we had been interviewing mothers. He said that mothers as a group reported many nice things about their boys, but that they also admitted some negative feelings which they would not divulge even to their own sons. According to the examiner's account, such confidences included the mothers' loss of patience with silly humor, boredom with childish interests, impatience with immaturity, embarrassment by clumsy and tactless behavior, inability to respect certain impulsive judgments, difficulty in knowing how to react to adolescent "crushes," and the impression that their sons were once attractive children with bright futures and were now neither providing the pleasures of the past nor fulfilling their early promise. Then the examiner said that while he knew the subject would want to talk about the mothers' opinions later, it was first necessary to get back to another set of stories.

After the boys had completed the second set of story endings, the examiner initiated a further discussion of the mothers' reactions which was designed to alleviate the feelings created by the earlier report. This time he said he should have mentioned that the opinions about boys being disappointing were obtained not from mothers in Detroit but from a group in California. "Detroit mothers don't seem to feel this way at all." He invited the subject to comment on the alleged statements of some of the California mothers and to speculate on the differences between them and the mothers in Detroit. Later the interviewer remarked that all women, even those in California, registered more approval than complaints. He added that the members of our project had a high opinion of the boys with whom they had worked. It was the examiner's impression that almost all the subjects became very involved in the discussion and reacted to the comments with considerable emotion.

In deciding on the type of conflict we would try to create, we were guided by our concern for the welfare of our subjects. It was necessary that they not be left with guilts and anxieties after the study was completed. It was equally important that we not create needless worry for the parents and teachers. Pretests of a number of techniques helped us to choose one that fulfilled our purpose, yet did not make the subjects excessively anxious.

In the final study the boys accepted the report about the differences between mothers in California and Detroit, took the conflict in stride, and showed no discernible aftereffects. The examiners all felt that they had successfully allayed any remaining anxieties during the interviews. Both the boys and their mothers were invited to consult with us if they had any questions about the research, or if any difficulties arose. Not one mother or son complained. School authorities reported only that the boys seemed to enjoy the tests.

### Story completion test

The boys wrote endings for three stories before arousal of conflict, and for three stories after arousal.[1] Each theme describes a boy's conflicting reactions to an adult whom he likes. The adult does something which, while well-intentioned, is very frustrating to the boy and tends to make him angry. A typical story describes an incident involving a boy named Harry and his aunt. While Harry's mother is away on a long trip, the aunt, who has previously helped him in many ways, stays with him. Harry has saved all his money for a ticket to a big football game, and has managed to buy the last ticket available. On the morning of the game the aunt becomes impatient with Harry's neglect of his room, cleans it up, and burns some papers she thinks are useless. That afternoon Harry cannot find his ticket. When the aunt describes what she has done, Harry realizes that she has burned his ticket. In their endings our subjects described Harry's method of resolving the presumed conflict between his anger with his aunt and his affection for her.

In another story Don, whose teacher has helped him to become a skilled artist, does an exceptionally good painting in preparation for a contest. The teacher has always criticized him for his sloppiness, yet she puts the painting on a table covered with glue and it rips beyond repair.

### Interpreting the story endings

We used three criteria in identifying the self-modifying defenses. It was necessary that the main character in the story not express his anger directly, that he distort his interpretation of the intended act or object, and that the distortion result in socially acceptable behavior. Four types of themes met our criteria. We

[1] The six stories may be found in Appendix C.

considered any one of these themes as instance of a defense in the second family.

*1. Turning against the Self.* One of the most common endings involves a displacement of anger from the original object to the self. When the displacement occurs, the hero feels guilty and exonerates the adult who is really responsible for the difficulty. For example, in one ending about Harry and his aunt he "did not say anything to her because it was his own fault. He did not clean up his room and he left papers where they should not be. From then on he left his room clean."

*2. Reversal.* Another ending that we tabulated as an instance of the second family of defenses describes the reversal of the presumed wish to hurt the adult: The main character in the story substitutes an act or affect which is opposite in meaning to the original. An example of this defense occurs in one ending to the story about Don and his careless art teacher: "Don feels very bad and he tells her it was all right and that without her help he would never had got it done and all goes well." We did not tabulate those themes in which the affection is a response to a realistic change in the plot, such as a successful attempt on the part of the teacher to win Don's affection by a new act of kindness.

*3. Diminishing the Forbidden Affect.* Another type of defense that meets the original criteria involves a self-deception about the attractiveness or unattractiveness of certain acts or objects involved in the conflict. It is a self-deception that eliminates the reason for the hero's anger at the adult. In one ending, for instance, Harry listens to the radio, hears that the game is a poor one, and is glad he did not go. Since he has not missed much, we presume that there is no longer any reason for him to dislike his aunt. The defense may also emphasize the good intentions behind the adult's damaging act, thus making it seem less destructive than it really was. In one such ending the teacher is trying to help Don when she accidentally rips the picture.

*4. Enhancing the Positive Affect.* Rather than diminish the loss, some defenses can be distorted in several ways which emphasize the good motives of the adult whose behavior has angered the hero: "Don thinks of all he has learned from her and is appreciative of all she has done for him." The distortion sometimes results from an identification with the frustrating adult. In completing a story about an anxious mother who is too concerned about her son's safety to allow him to play football, one subject said that the son begins to see the problem from her point of view and then feels solicitude rather than anger. Since he does not want to worry her, he no longer wishes to play. In another distortion the hero resolves the conflict by shifting from the disapproved act or object to one that the adult approves; then he convinces himself that the socially approved act is more beneficial than the forbidden one.

### THE SAMPLE AND CONTROLS

We selected our subjects from the second sample described in Chapter 4. Seven cases of the original 112 were not available for the investigation. From the remaining 105 boys, we had to eliminate 17 others who did not write defensive endings either before or after arousal. Without codeable endings, we could not classify these subjects. We could not know whether they were unaffected by our interviews or were defending themselves against becoming aroused. This group included almost equal numbers of boys from the middle and working classes. After coding all the story endings we assigned each of the final 88 subjects to one of two groups. The first group of 38 included all the boys who increased the number of defensive endings after the arousal of conflict. The second group of 50 contained 3 who stayed the same; 16 who decreased defensive endings; and 31 who never employed defenses in any of their stories, but whose endings after arousal of conflict described the direct expression of anger. We added the last group on the assumption that direct expression could not have taken place if the subjects had become more defensive about their anger after the conflict.

In addition to problems of classification, we were also concerned with the associations with mechanisms of defense of such variables as age, intelligence, "ceiling effects," and story order. Had these variables not been controlled, they, rather than the background variables, might have been the underlying causes of some of our significant results. We found that significant differences involving shifts in defense did not change when we held constant differences in age and the Verbal, Spatial, and Reasoning scores of *The Chicago Tests of Primary Mental Abilities* (3).

Nor were shifts significantly related to levels of initial scores in defense. As for a possible ceiling, no subject obtained an initial score that he could not increase in the second set of stories: No one reached a limiting score beyond which he could not go.

## Social Class

Under what conditions can a child resort to self-modifying defenses as a means of resolving his conflicts about aggression? First, of course, he must learn that particular action tendencies are socially unacceptable, and that their expression leads to unpleasant consequences, such as the parents' withholding of love or administering corporal punishment. Second, he must develop a concept of self that would be violated if he expressed the forbidden tendencies. Third, substitutes for these tendencies have to be compatible with his self-concept. If he acknowledges an incompatible tendency, such as an impulse to hurt an adult, he must turn it against himself. To avoid awareness of his hostility, and thus maintain an acceptable picture of himself, the child often employs distortions which minimize the affect connected with his impulse and enhance the possibilities of engaging in socially approved behavior. The resultant substitutes may then even be a source of increased self-esteem.

No single influence can produce such complex mechanisms. A child's picture of his current identity and of the kind of a person he should become develops within a total context of parental and social pressures. In making predictions we took into account ways in which child-rearing practices might define the prohibitions of direct aggression and affect the selection of defenses. We explored the influence of the social context on the associations between child-rearing practices and an increase in defensiveness by analyzing each separately within the middle- and working-class groups.

### The middle class

The mechanisms whereby a boy modifies the expression of aggression are in accord with the values of the middle class. According to Miller and Swanson (2), middle-class parents, particularly those in the entrepreneurial setting, begin to teach their children to control their expression of anger earlier than do working-class parents. Inhibition of direct forms of aggression is stressed, and penalties for violations are often severe. As a result, the young child learns very early to regard certain action tendencies as inner, but alien, sources of danger. By being "nice," seeing the other person's point of view, and behaving in an acceptable manner, particularly with authorities, the son of the white-collar worker can win the respect of parents and friends. He takes responsibility for avoiding the forbidden acts, and he blames himself when he loses control. Middle-class parents are very concerned with the teaching of these skills, because the child's future economic security may depend on their acquisition. A mother often evaluates her son's traits, not only in terms of adequacy in the present, but also in terms of prognostic significance for future success: "You can't act that way if you want to get ahead."

THE WORKING CLASS

Control of aggression is not necessarily a touchstone to success in families of manual laborers. Poor control of aggression may have little relevance to social position. Often the mother works and cannot supervise her son's activities. His emergencies arise from the vicissitudes of a difficult environment, vicissitudes which cannot be ameliorated by self-blame or by the reversal of resentment. Even if such a boy were to realize that control is required for social advancement, it would be difficult for him to learn the necessary skills. In the working class direct expression of aggression is typical of the adults from whom the child learns his pattern of acceptable behavior.

We predicted, therefore, that following the arousal of conflict, sons of white-collar workers would exceed sons of blue-collar workers in increased use of the self-modifying defenses. Table 11-1, which contains a summary of the major results to be reported in this chapter, indicates that the two classes differ significantly and in the anticipated direction.[2]

[2] The detailed tables may be found in Appendix D.

TABLE 11-1

Background Conditions and Defenses in the Second Family

| *Conditions* | *Trends: Boxes with Largest Frequencies* | *N* | *Relation* | *Probability* |
|---|---|---|---|---|
| Social class | WC and no increase | 88 | 5.04 $(\chi^2)$ | .03 |
| Obedience requests | — | 77 | .32 $(\chi^2)$ | <.60 |
| Social class and obedience requests | WC: explained requests and no increase | 77 | 28 $(\tau)$ | <.01 |
| Discipline | — | 88 | .02 $(\chi^2)$ | <1.00 |
| Discipline and social class | WC: psychological and no increase | 88 | 7.67 $(\chi^2)$ | .18 |
| Frequency of reward | — | 68 | .01 $(\chi^2)$ | <1.00 |
| Reward and social class | — | 68 | 4.53 $(\chi^2)$ | <.30 |
| Reward and discipline | — | 68 | 5.76 $(\chi^2)$ | <.40 |
| Obedience requests and reward | Arbitrary requests: frequent reward and no increase<br>Explained: occasional reward and no increase | 60 | 7.99 $(\chi^2)$ | .05 |
| Obedience requests and discipline | — | 77 | 2.32 $(\chi^2)$ | <.90 |

SOCIAL CLASS AND TYPE OF INTEGRATION

In Chapter 2 we proposed a division of subjects into entrepreneurial and bureaucratic categories. We noted that entrepreneurial fathers, particularly in the middle class, train their sons in control, responsibility, and traditional morality—goals which can implement the use of defenses in the second family. Such mechanisms are less functional for members of the working class who are in the entrepreneurial setting. Until recently, these people have had little economic security and have lacked a sense of controlling their own futures.

In the bureaucratic setting the sources of mobility have changed, and white-collar workers cannot gain as much from self-sacrifice and conformity to high standards as can their counterparts in the entrepreneurial setting. The same is true for the blue-collar workers, who have been helped by the progress of unionism within the last quarter century to earn increased tenure and higher incomes. Furthermore, since the blue-collar workers in a bureaucracy have been developing the motives and values appropriate to group participation, they are beginning to resemble the white-collar workers.

Our picture of the two types of integration thus led us to postulate that differences between subjects in the two social classes would be strongest in the entrepreneurial setting. When we compare the two classes within the entrepreneurial setting, we find a trend in the predicted direction, but the probability of .08 does not quite reach significance. As we anticipated, class differences within the bureaucratic setting are far from significant. Boys in the working class are slightly less inclined than boys in the middle class to use the self-modifying defenses, but the trend is a weak one.

## Obedience

In thinking about the relationships between parental demands for obedience and defenses in the second family, we found ourselves weighing two alternative predictions.[3] First, arbitrary requests may reinforce a tendency to favor the self-modifying mechanisms. When parents are authoritarian, they must frustrate their son frequently. Yet, because of the child's vulnerable and subservient position, he cannot express his irritation openly. Being trained to feel that adults are always right may cause the son to become guilty about his anger and to blame himself.

In the alternate hypothesis, we postulated that, by themselves, arbitrary requests may not be sufficient to reinforce defenses in the second family. Before he can develop the anxiety that elicits any defenses, a child must first have internalized standards proscribing hostile thoughts and acts. Because the meanings or purposes of arbitrary requests are often unclear, their frequent use may interfere with the child's internalization.

As the summary table shows, the association between de-

[3] In Chapter 3 we described our method of classifying the mothers in terms of their demands for obedience. Of the original 88 cases, 11 mothers gave answers which could not be coded. Therefore this analysis involves 77 cases.

mands for obedience and the second family of defenses is not significant. The results thus support the second hypothesis.

SOCIAL CLASS AND REQUESTS FOR OBEDIENCE

We next reanalyzed the relation between obedience and shifts in defense within the middle- and working-class groups. We anticipated a greater association between obedience and defense within the middle class than within the working class. Direct aggression is very unacceptable to the white-collar worker. Compatible with this value are mechanisms that cause him to blame himself for unacceptable impulses and to take responsibility for making amends. Within a particular class, the more severe the parental authority, the more anxious the child becomes about his angry feelings, and the greater is his inclination to resort to a defense mechanism.

We anticipated, therefore, that the differences between classes would be maximal when boys have usually been subjected to arbitrary requests for obedience. Accordingly, we analyzed the relation between defensive shifts and pairs of four background factors: (1) arbitrary and (2) explained demands for obedience in the (3) middle and (4) working classes. In terms of our judgment of the relative severity of the pairs, we predicted an order in their association with defensive shifts. The combination of middle class and arbitrary parental authority would be most severe, we thought, because the moral values of the middle class reinforce defenses in the second family more than do the values of the working class. Considering the postulated differences in the values of the two classes, we expected the combination of middle-class status and reasonable parental authority would be next highest in severity. Within the working class, arbitrary demands for obedience are more frequent than demands which are explained to the child. To analyze the significance of the anticipated trend in proportions, we employed Smith's modification of Kendall's test.[4]

As indicated in Table 11-1, we obtained the anticipated progression, and the over-all relationship is very significant. While the type of obedience, by itself, is not significantly related to shifts in defense, we obtain significance when type of obedience is

[4] We described the method of analysis and the interpretation of tau in Chapter 1.

combined with social class; a significance which is a function of the interaction among the variables. We assume that membership in a social class defines the actual content of the prohibitions, while the kind of requests indicates the methods with which the prohibitions are reinforced. Both kinds of information are needed to explain the origins of defenses in the second family.

## Type of Discipline

According to the summary table, discipline, like obedience, is not associated with variations in defensive shifts.[5] The association does not become significant when we take into account other child-rearing practices or social class. We had anticipated a possible association between the self-modifying defenses and psychological manipulation. Appeals to guilt, for example, create unpleasant feelings, but give the child no object against which to direct his anger. In contrast, corporal punishment provides the child with an aggressive model and an object for retaliation. Apparently, the effects of discipline on the learning of defenses is more involved than we originally thought. A particular method of discipline may convey many meanings. One boy may experience psychological manipulation as a form of rejection. Another, who feels thoroughly accepted by his mother, may not interpret maternal statements of disappointment as rejections, but rather as expressions of confidence in the offspring's capacities to improve.

Corporal punishment, too, can communicate different messages, depending on the relationship between mother and child. A spanking, for example, may be experienced as a painful attack, an act of retribution or vengeance, a withdrawal of love, or an appeal to guilt. Even discipline that produces guilt may be related to defense only indirectly. If all children inhibited their forbidden needs when suffering guilt, our prediction might have been verified. Some children, instead, express their needs, and then defend themselves against their guilt.

[5] In Chapter 3 we described our method of classifying the mothers in terms of their disciplinary techniques.

## Frequency of Reward

In view of our failure to obtain significant associations between the self-modifying mechanisms and single child-rearing variables, we were not surprised to find that frequency of reward is not significantly associated with defense.[6] Again, we attempted to view the relation between the child-rearing practice and the mechanisms in the context of the actions and values of a particular social class. As indicated in Table 11-1, this relation is still not significant.

Next we explored the relation between reward and defense in the contexts of types of discipline and of requests for obedience. We reasoned that the meaning, and thus the effect, of reward might vary with other pressures. It seemed possible, for example, that a mother who has used psychological appeals and given frequent rewards would be viewed by her son as a more approving authority than a mother whose psychological appeals have been unrelieved by incentives. Such patterns of practice might thus have differential effects on a tendency to employ defenses in the second family.

According to the results, the association involving reward, discipline, and defense is not significant. The combination of reward and obedience, however, is significantly related to the subjects' defensive response to our experimentally induced conflict. In analyzing the data we compared four groups. Each type of reward, frequent and occasional, was placed in the context of each type of obedience, arbitrary and explained. Since we were not confident of the possible relation to defense of all the different combinations of parental practice, we could not establish the ordered classification required for Kendall's test of significance. We find that the combination of arbitrary requests for obedience and occasional reward is most conducive to increases of defenses in the second family. This combination may be considered most severe. Parents who have usually employed such methods demand

[6] We described our method of classifying mothers according to frequency of reward in Chapter 3. Twenty mothers could not give us information about their methods of reward, so that our number of cases was reduced to sixty-eight.

the greatest conformity, yet withhold approbation, leaving the child with unrelieved anxiety and no alternative but to increase his efforts to control impulses which might get him into trouble. Frequent rewards and explained requests for obedience are associated with the next highest proportion of increased defenses. Apparently, explained goals that are positively enforced can constitute almost as much pressure as arbitrary demands made in the relative absence of any signs of recognition. In Chapter 9 we noted that the combination of frequent rewards and reasonable requests for obedience is associated with active, reality-oriented strivings: a decrease of defenses in the first family. Now we find that this combination of practices, possibly because it reinforces a desire to feel and do the "right things," is associated with an increase of defenses in the second family.

Subjects whose parents have made arbitrary demands for obedience, but have given frequent rewards are among the least defensive. Evidently the signs of approval enable the child to feel he has lived up to his parents' expectations. The sons of parents who have made reasonable requests for obedience and have given occasional rewards show the weakest tendency to increase their use of mechanisms in the second family. This combination of practices apparently represents the mildest parental pressure.

## Weaning and Toilet Training

It seemed to us that any possible associations of either weaning or toilet training with shifts in the self-modifying defenses following the arousal of conflict would depend on the consistency of these parental practices with other, more recent practices.[7] As in the cases of discipline and obedience, it seemed probable that methods of psychosexual regulation would reinforce a desire to conform, but not necessarily by means of the second family of defenses.

A tabular summary of our own results is not needed, since they can easily be summarized verbally. There are no significant associations between shifts in defense and either the time of wean-

[7] In Chapter 4 we described our method of classifying the parents according to the severity of their methods of weaning and toilet training.

ing or the severity of toilet training. On recomputing the association between shifts in defense and parental practices within each social class, we obtain chi squares with probabilities of less than .10. In the case of weaning the trend seems attributable predominantly to the relation between social class and defense. A comparison of the coercively toilet-trained individuals within the two classes, however, reveals another trend, which is only suggestive since it is not quite significant. The coercively trained within the middle class are inclined to increase their defenses, and the coercively trained in the working class are not so inclined. Possibly, coerciveness affects defense shifts only when it is combined with the concomitant values and practices of the social class in which the defense occurs most frequently.

## Summary

The self-modifying defenses in the second family help a person to change his awareness and expression of unacceptable action tendencies and to select socially acceptable substitutes. To elicit the defenses, we attempted to create a real conflict for our subjects between aggression and guilt. We tabulated discrepancies between the frequencies of defensive endings written for stories presented before and after the arousal of conflict. In analyzing the story endings written by the subjects, we tabulated turning on the self, reversal, and distortions that minimized the need for anger.

*Combinations of Practices.* The most vivid impression we get from the results is that no single child-rearing technique is sufficient to explain an inclination to favor mechanisms in the second family. Each parental practice seems to vary in its relation to defense in terms of other practices with which it is combined. Obedience alone, for example, is not related to shifts in defense; neither is reward so related. In combination with other practices, however, both are associated with variations in defensiveness.

*Social Position.* Socio-economic status, the best indicator of the general background of values and acts within which all the various practices are employed, is significantly related to shifts in the second family of defense following experimentally induced conflict. When made anxious about aggressive needs, boys in the middle class increase defenses against aggression; boys in the working class tend not to do so. These differences are more pronounced in the entrepreneurial setting than in the bureaucratic setting.

*Obedience and Social Class.* In the middle class, whose members presumably value the inhibition of direct attack, arbitrary parental requests for obedience are associated with increases in defense. Working-class boys are less inclined to increase their defenses, regardless of the type of obedience demands.

*Obedience and Reward.* The relation to defense of the combination of obedience and reward is also significant. When rewards have been occasional, and requests for obedience arbitrary, most boys increase their use of defenses in the second family. When rewards have been occasional, but requests for obedience have been explained, the pressure has been minimal and there is little necessity to modify one's reactions defensively.

*Discipline, Weaning, and Toilet Training.* Type of discipline, both by itself and in combination with other conditions, is not significantly associated with shifts in defense. Nor are weaning and toilet training significantly related to defense, either alone or in combination with social class. Among boys who have been coercively toilet trained, however, those in the middle class are somewhat more inclined than boys in the working class to respond to aggressive conflicts by increasing the self-modifying defenses.

## References


1. Beardslee, Betty J. The learning of two mechanisms of defense. Unpubl. Ph.D. dissertation, Univ. of Michigan, 1955.
2. Miller, D. R., & Swanson, G. E. *The changing American parent.* New York: Wiley, 1958.
3. Thurstone, L. L., & Thurstone, Thelma G. *The Chicago tests of primary mental abilities.* Chicago: Science Research Associates, 1943.

# 12

# MECHANISMS OF DEFENSE

## V. Sex Identity and Defenses against Aggression *

In this chapter we report an investigation of the methods used by college men who differ in sex identity to resolve their conflicts about aggression. The reactions to conflict included three defenses and two expressive styles. We compared differences in these reactions among three types of subjects. One type was unconsciously and consciously feminine (FF), another unconsciously feminine and consciously masculine (FM), and the third unconsciously and consciously masculine (MM).[1]

### Sex Identity

By sex identity, we refer to the total pattern of sex-linked characteristics that mark a person as masculine or feminine, both to himself and to others. They are exemplified by interests in such topics as clothing, sports, politics, and homemaking, by such spe-

* In the research team, Leonard M. Lansky was responsible for the research to be reported and for the preparation of the chapter, which is based in part on his doctoral dissertation (7). We are indebted to Fels Research Institute (Ohio) for supporting part of the research reported in this chapter.

[1] These classifications are described in Chapter 3.

cific skills as sewing, cooking, and fixing motors, and by such styles of expression as gait, inflection of voice, and gesture.

We have been primarily interested in the learned components of sex identity. In Chapter 3 we speculated about the ways in which people acquire the interests, skills, and gestures that differentiate males from females. These acquisitions are reinforced by the rewards and punishments of parents, peers, relatives, teachers, and chance acquaintances, and by each person's identifications with significant people, real or imagined. We now recapitulate the reasoning that helped us to predict the reactions to conflicts of men with different sex identities. As we have stated previously, our study was not a developmental one, and we could have made our predictions from observations of current behavior.

## Stages of Development

*Initial Stage.* In the first few months of life a child is distinguished by his relative helplessness and his dependence on others. When he is under stress, he can avail himself of only a limited number of reactions. He can cry and express his extreme tension, and he can withdraw by closing his eyes or by sleeping. These withdrawing responses serve to obliterate the painful reality.

Babies of both sexes are raised quite similarly during the first year. Yet, in the improbable event that a boy and a girl were to learn no subsequent skills, the boy would have the greater difficulty in our society because he would be less prepared to act like a male. Normally, in this period, children cry, they solicit the help of others, and they are very much interested in their own bodies. In our society, such behavior is considered feminine when exhibited at a later age.

*Second Stage.* In the next stage, which overlaps considerably with the first, the child learns to take initiative. First he seizes objects, then he sits, creeps, crawls, stands, and walks. He also begins to understand some of the differences between himself and others, and his relationships with people become increasingly complicated.

During this phase the child learns many standards of behavior.

He must inhibit his expression of anger by tantrums or physical attacks. When he loses control, he is often punished. After a while he learns that passive appeals provide one means of avoiding direct aggression and gaining the approval of adults. Because of his parents' constraints, blandishments, and rewards, he gradually internalizes their standards and begins to turn his aggression inward. If they reward him for behaving in a manner that is opposite to what he feels, the boy may also begin to reverse his feelings. Self-blame and reversal of his true feelings both help him to express his aggression in a socially acceptable manner.

*Third Stage.* Just as the healthy boy outgrows the early passive stage, so he outgrows the period when the problem of self-control is a salient one. As he matures, he begins to perform complex acts with ease. He gets to know many new kinds of people—other boys his age, storekeepers, teachers, and policemen. He acquires many masculine interests by identifying with such figures as aviators and locomotive engineers.

A mature boy retains the skills of earlier stages, but integrates them as part of a behavioral pattern that is appropriate for a person of his age. When necessary, he can ask for help or retreat from an impossible situation. More typically, he tries to resolve his conflicts in a rational manner. When he disagrees with friends, he may consult with them in order to develop compromise solutions. In general, he finds little difficulty in expressing many needs in socially acceptable ways.

## Immature Personality Structure

If an adult has had some difficulties in the earlier stages of life, he may develop a relatively immature personality structure. That is, he may be troubled by many conflicts because of his poor control, or inadequate tolerance of stress. Even mild conflicts may cause him to regress and to solve problems with techniques learned in earlier stages of development. If he reverts to the first stage, he may try to solve his problems in an unrealistic manner. If he reverts to the second, he may resolve conflicts involving aggression by turning the need inward. Because self-control is so important an issue at this stage, he is not likely to break out in displays of excessive emotion. This is particularly true if he has grown up in a middle-class family. He may also favor a passive adjustment to pressures of other people, because this facilitates conformity.

In short, we view the sex identity of an adult as a partial index of the kinds and degrees of difficulty he had during his early stages of development. Before describing our research procedures and results, we will outline our speculations about the development of the three different sex identities mentioned above.

## The Origin of Different Sex Identities

*The FF Pattern.* It is our impression that a boy can become an FF by at least two means. First, he may be forced to be unquestioningly compliant during the later stages of development. Perhaps the parents demand this compliance as a price for their love. Any attempt by the child to satisfy his growing need for initiative may be punished so severely that he begins to avoid it. He is therefore deprived of an opportunity to acquire some of the masculine skills and modes of expression, and he is inclined to favor some reactions that he learned during the first stage of development.

Premature pressures to behave in a masculine manner constitute a second possible reason for rejecting masculinity. Among the Dakota Indians, a man who cannot meet the stringent standards of masculinity may become "berdache" or a transvestite (1). Femininity in males sometimes signifies a similar retreat in our society. The boy gives up trying to be masculine. Whatever the sequence of events leading to the FF's identity, and we have not mentioned the complex problems of identification with the parents, we expected him to prefer defenses in the first family [2] and to express his feelings directly when in extreme conflict about aggressive wishes.

*The FM Pattern.* It is probably difficult to distinguish the FM from the FF during the initial stage of development. We imagine that both of these types are more strongly attached to their mothers during the very first stage of life than are the MMs. Pos-

[2] The families of defense are described in Chapter 8.

sibly, the unconsciously feminine males are kept dependent on adults for a longer period of time. Later on their parents probably treat them differently. We imagine that parents of a boy who becomes an FM make masculinity attractive and reward him if he develops in the desired direction. Since the growing child usually finds it difficult to integrate his strong feminine tendencies with the new masculine ones, he often has to renounce his feminine side. Because of his conflicts, he may be unable to master completely the more mature techniques of a larger stage. When under stress, he may favor control of his feelings, passivity, and defenses in the second family.[3]

*The MM Pattern.* The MMs have not been handicapped by any serious developmental problems. While the defenses of the earlier stages are available to these men, they are likely to favor mature techniques in resolving conflict about aggressive needs. These men are not unduly upset when an event does not turn out as they expect. We think that they are able to delay gratification, and that they can use socially acceptable substitutes for action tendencies blocked by conflict.

## Method

The subjects used in this study were selected from the third population described in Chapter 4.[4] There were 98 men in all, 29 FMs, 37 FFs, and 32 MMs. Each subject was seen individually. To obtain a record of his defenses and expressive styles, we administered a story completion test before and after a task designed to create conflict. He was interviewed after the final projective test in order to give him an opportunity to express any remaining anxiety. Then the examiner explained the importance of maintaining secrecy about the study.[5] From a further

[3] The families of defense are described in Chapter 8.

[4] They were unmarried, white, undergraduate men from the University of Michigan who, for at least four of their first six years of life, had lived with both their parents. In addition, their scores on the Franck (4) and Gough (5) tests of masculinity-femininity met the criteria, described in Chapter 3, for inclusion in one of the three groups.

[5] He said that new subjects with definite expectations about the tasks might respond differently to the initial set of stories from men who had no previous information about our methods. He gave a brief and somewhat

inquiry by Aronfreed, and from our observations during the testing of subjects, we got the strong impression that they had not talked to each other about the project.

THE PROJECTIVE STORIES [6]

The plot of each story concerned the frustration of a boy by a well-meaning adult to whom the hero is very attached. In many of their endings the subjects expressed the conflict between the impulse to hurt the adult and the desire to retain his approval or to avoid guilt. The themes of the first three stories were matched for content with the themes of the second three stories. In a typical plot, Russ, who is fatherless and has always been close to his mother, seeks her written permission for him to play football. He has played very well in the initial competition for positions on the squad, and has been accepted enthusiastically by the coach. The mother, who worries a lot about her son, thinks of a boy who was almost killed playing football, and refuses to sign the permission slip despite the pleas of her son and the coach.

To permit an analysis of the effects of story content on results, we randomly divided each of the three groups of subjects into two parts. We gave half the subjects the first set of stories before arousal and the second set after arousal. The remaining subjects were given the stories in the reverse order. We found that the order of stories did not significantly affect the relation between sex identity and any of the reactions to conflict.

CREATING CONFLICT

After completing the first set of stories, each subject was given an intervening task that was calculated to create conflict about sexual impulses. The decision to arouse unacceptable sexual wishes instead of aggressive ones was a compromise dictated by several considerations.[7] We had originally planned to do two

---

vague description of our purpose at the time, because the subjects were soon to participate in the study of moral standards reported in Chapter 7, and he did not want to affect their performance.

[6] Since we were interested in testing the same methods with subjects of different ages, we used some of the themes developed by Beardslee and described in Chapters 9 and 11. The stories can be found in Appendix C.

[7] We did not try to arouse aggressive needs, so we must limit our generalizations to conflict about such needs following sexual arousal.

separate studies, one with sexual arousal and stories about sex, and one with arousal of anger and stories about aggression.[8] Unfortunately, we only had enough subjects for one part of the design. Unsolved methodological problems concerning the arousal of aggression and the writing of stories about sexual conflict led us to choose the present design. We were also influenced by the result of a preliminary study in which we employed sexual arousal and stories with aggressive themes. The subjects did not see any connection between the two, and provided us with marked shifts in reactions to conflict.

To arouse a subject's sexual wishes, the examiner asked him to judge the aesthetic values of paintings and photographs of nude females.[9] The subject was told that the ratings would help us to find out whether photographers or painters do a better job of portraying the beauty of the human figure. A scientific answer, according to the explanation, necessitated a scale which would provide consistent ratings of artistic appeal. We were asking the subjects to judge the attractiveness of each portrait to help us in standardizing an instrument. When he made a rating, he could help us to understand it by referring to such features as face, skin texture, figure, limbs, and pose.[10]

The examiner stayed in the room while the pictures were being rated. We anticipated that the presence of a strange adult would inhibit the subject from expressing his sexual feeling in fantasy and would maximize his anxiety. We hoped that, with other outlets eliminated, he would express his defenses against this anxiety in his story endings.

The examiner also made subjective estimates of the presence or absence of sexual arousal. From these estimates of the subjects' reactions, we are fairly confident that our technique accomplished

[8] In the pilot studies in which we tried to arouse conflict about anger, many of our subjects were quick to see the relationship between the method of arousal and the themes of the stories. It appears that Feshbach (3) has since solved the problem of disguising the connection.

[9] The procedure is similar to one used by Clark (2), who found that the stimulation elicited symbolic expressions of sexuality on the Thematic Apperception Test.

[10] There were five pictures. Two were reproductions of famous paintings: Renoir's "Gabrielle in an Open Blouse" and Velásquez's "Venus and Cupid." The other portraits, which were photographs of nudes, were taken from a volume (6) on figure photography.

the desired result. During the rating procedure all the men showed such signs of anxiety as vocal tension, strained postures, and the dropping of pencils. The ratings of the five pictures took fifteen minutes on the average.

### Analyzing the results [11]

The reactions to conflict that we coded include realistic problem solving, the first family of defenses, the mechanism of turning against the self, and the expressive styles of emotional dilation and passivity. After coding each variable, we subtracted the sum of the tabulations for stories written before arousal from the sum for stories written after arousal. Then, for each variable, we compared the three types of sex identity with respect to the proportions who did and who did not increase their scores. When a subject did not use a particular reaction to conflict either before or after arousal, we had no basis for classifying him and had to eliminate him from that analysis. We reasoned that his omission could have reflected a lack of involvement or a general defense against expressing anxiety-producing material. Because some subjects wrote endings relevant to some variables and not to others, the total numbers are not the same in the different tables. It is important to note that our conclusions apply only to those FMs, FFs, and MMs who could express their reactions to conflict about aggression on a projective test.

### Controls

As a control of intelligence, we first divided the subjects in terms of the median of their scores [12] on the test of the American Council on Education (9). None of the significant associations between sex identity and reactions to conflict change when recomputed within the upper and lower halves of the distribution of intelligence. To determine whether our results might be

[11] The judge evaluated one story for all subjects before he went on to the next one. When he coded a story, he did not know whether it had been given before or after arousal; nor did he know the group to which the writer belonged. We are grateful to Mrs. Virginia Douglas who independently coded the stories of forty-six subjects selected in approximately equal proportions from the three groups. The proportions of agreement for the different codes varied from 74 to 98 per cent.

[12] We used the *T* scores obtained by the Evaluations and Examination Division of the University of Michigan.

attributed to lengths of stories, we compared the three groups with respect to the number of words in each ending. There are no significant differences. We also investigated the extent to which our results depended on a "ceiling" in the initial sets of stories. Of the five reactions to conflict that we analyzed, there is only one, emotional dilation, on which one subject obtained a maximal score in the first set of stories. Finally, we find that levels of initial scores are not significantly related to changes in reacting to conflict after arousal.

## Realistic Problem-Solving

### Criteria

Our first variable, realistic problem-solving, refers to the selection of substitutes that are relatively direct and also socially acceptable. We scored four kinds of endings as realistic: (1) substitution of reasonable alternative goals: Russ, the boy who cannot get his mother's permission to play football, becomes the manager of the team; (2) realistic conformity to the adult's pressure: Russ realizes that his playing football would worry his mother a lot, and decides that it is to their mutual benefit for him to give up the sport; (3) appreciation of the benefits provided by conformity: Russ is very impressed with his mother's concern for him and is very thankful for her love; (4) a successful challenge of the authority's views: Russ argues objectively and cogently until his mother gives her permission; he becomes a good player, is not hurt, and she admits she was wrong.

The subject got one point for each realistic theme in a story ending. Certain combinations of themes were possible, but since the first three codes precluded the fourth, the highest possible score for each story was three points.

### Predictions and results

We expected that the MMs, unlike the unconsciously feminine subjects, would be most likely to increase references to realistic techniques when made anxious by sexual arousal. From our picture of the FFs, we inferred that they would be least realistic, but we were not certain whether they would differ from the FMs.

While we thought that the unconsciously feminine groups would differ from each other in kinds of distortion, we felt that the anxiety of both groups would hamper them in their attempts to develop practical solutions to conflict. The results in Table 12-1, which

TABLE 12-1

Sex Identity and Shifts in Defenses and Expressive Styles

| | | *Direction of Shift* | | | | | |
|---|---|---|---|---|---|---|---|
| *Reaction to Conflict* | *Sex Identity* | *No Increase* | *Increase* | *Relations* | *N* | $\chi^2$ | *Probability* |
| Realistic problem-solving | MM | 10 | 13 | MM > nonMM | 85 | 7.40 | .001 (1t) |
| | FM | 20 | 8 | MM > FM | 51 | 3.00 | .04 (1t) |
| | FF | 28 | 6 | MM > FF | 57 | 7.66 | .01 (1t) |
| | | | | FM > FF | 62 | .51 | <.50 |
| Defenses in first family | MM | 9 | 5 | FF > nonFF | 46 | 3.96 | .03 (1t) |
| | FM | 10 | 4 | FF > FM | 32 | Exact Test | .04 (1t) |
| | FF | 6 | 12 | FF > MM | 32 | Exact Test | ns |
| | | | | FM > MM | 28 | Exact Test | ns |
| Turning against the self | MM | 8 | 9 | FM > nonFM | 42 | 2.26 | .07 (1t) |
| | FM | 2 | 7 | FM > FF | 25 | Exact Test | .05 (1t) |
| | FF | 11 | 5 | FM > MM | 26 | Exact Test | ns |
| | | | | MM > FF | 33 | Exact Test | ns |
| Emotional dilation | MM | 15 | 14 | FM < nonFM | 85 | 2.20 | .07 (1t) |
| | FM | 16 | 8 | FM < MM | 53 | .67 | .30 (1t) |
| | FF | 13 | 19 | FM < FF | 56 | 2.76 | .05 (1t) |
| | | | | MM < FF | 61 | .38 | <.60 |
| Passivity | MM | 17 | 8 | FM > nonFM | 63 | 4.60 | .03 (1t) |
| | FM | 5 | 10 | FM > MM | 40 | 3.26 | .03 (1t) |
| | FF | 16 | 7 | FM > FF | 38 | 3.47 | .03 (1t) |
| | | | | MM > FF | 48 | .01 | <1.00 |

contains a summary of all the data to be reported in the chapter, support our predictions.

As anticipated, the MMs increase realistic endings more than do the combination of the two feminine groups. The MMs also differ significantly from these groups individually. The FFs and FMs are least likely to increase realistic endings after sexual arousal. The difference between them is not significant.

## First Family of Defenses

### Criteria

In analyzing defenses in the first family we tabulated references to denial and withdrawal. We attributed an ending to denial if it was obviously incompatible with one of the facts in the story beginning. An ending to the story about Russ contains a denial of the facts if it permits him to play football although his mother does not give her permission. By the nature of the story, such events are not possible.

Withdrawal is a physical retreat from the scene of the conflict. In an ending illustrating such a retreat, Russ decides that he no longer has anything in common with his mother. To escape from the anxiety caused by his conflicting reactions to her, he leaves home and goes to work in another town.

### Predictions and results

While we predicted that under stress the two unconsciously feminine types would increase their defensive distortion of aggressive impulses, we did not believe these men would employ similar mechanisms. Whatever the source of the FFs' regression—whether it was severe stress very early in life or difficulty in the second stage of development—we thought these men would favor defenses in the first family. This prediction also followed from the observation that, as adults, the FFs express their femininity overtly, despite their knowledge that the society expects them to be masculine. It is difficult for them to reconcile such incompatible pressures. The FFs can either deny their rejection by masculine men, or withdraw to the exclusive company of people with feminine identities. We anticipated that the same methods might also be applied to conflicts involving aggressive needs. We predicted, therefore, that the FFs would use denial and withdrawal, mechanisms which help to obliterate or distort events whose characteristics are readily verified. We thought that as a group and individually FMs and MMs would be much less likely to employ these defenses.

The results summarized in Table 12-1 corroborate two of our predictions. The FFs show a significantly greater tendency than the FMs and MMs, as a combined group, to increase references to mechanisms in the first family. The difference between the FMs and the FFs is also significant. Since the FM's conflicts are not with others, but between his own internal needs, he benefits less than the FF from mechanisms in the first family. The difference between the FFs and MMs, while in the predicted direction, is not significant.

## Turning Aggression against the Self[13]

### Criteria

We tabulated turning against the self when the subject wrote either of two types of endings. In one, the hero ignores the authority's wise counsel and suffers the consequences. For example, Russ secretly plays football with local clubs. He devotes so much time to the sport that he fails in school. In addition he turns out to be a second-rate player. Finally, he is forced to take a full time job in a factory.

The second theme which we scored as turning against the self describes an injury to the hero. He is crippled or killed, or becomes sick, a delinquent, or a psychotic. In a representative story the hero is killed by a reckless driver while leaving the school. Since such events do not follow from the story beginning, we interpreted them as signifying a punishment for the hero's aggressive wishes.

### Predictions and results

In our developmental picture of middle-class males, we postulated that self-attack is a highly rewarded means of inhibiting aggressive action tendencies during the period when the FMs have their greatest difficulty. To insure control, these boys overlearn the middle class skills. We predicted that after sexual arousal the FMs would increase references to self-attack more than would boys in the other two groups. We had no reason to expect that the latter would differ significantly from each other. The

[13] This reaction is representative of the second family of defenses. We attempted to code reversal, another mechanism in the second family, but found too few instances to make an analysis.

MMs have more socially adequate means of resolving conflicts about aggression, and the FFs can always resort to denial or withdrawal.

When the FMs are compared to the other two groups taken together, the chi square is not quite significant, although, as anticipated, the FMs show the strongest tendency to increase turning against the self. The analyses of the data are summarized in Table 12-1. The lack of significance is caused primarily by the MMs, who increase self-attack more than we expected. Hence, they do not differ significantly from the FMs. The FMs do differ significantly from the FFs.

It seems that the FFs are least inclined to defend themselves against aggression by turning it inward. They need only ignore or reinterpret the facts to diminish anxiety. In frequency of self-blame the unconsciously masculine subjects fall between the other groups. The MMs can be realistic, but only when this approach helps to resolve conflict. When the problem does not lend itself to realistic methods, some MMs, like FMs, defend themselves by self-attack.

## Emotional Dilation and Constriction

### Criteria

We tabulated emotional dilation if in the story ending the hero attacks an authority physically, yells at him, makes such statements as "I hate you," or weeps, pouts, or sulks for some time in order to convey to others how upset he is. These responses are all direct ways of expressing feeling.

### Prediction and results

We anticipated that the FMs would be an emotionally constricted group. Unlike the FFs, the FMs cannot deceive themselves about external events. Unlike the MMs, the FMs often seem too torn by conflict, and too lacking in initiative, to employ the more realistic types of substitutes. These men often convey the impression that they cannot afford to relax and express themselves freely for fear of opening a Pandora's box filled with aggression and femininity. Because of this picture, we expected them to be less dilated than the MMs or FFs. We anticipated that the FMs would be significantly exceeded by the other two groups in increased emotionality, and, furthermore, that the FFs would differ significantly from the MMs. Emotion need not be threatening to FFs, because their defenses permit them to evade social pressures. While the MMs can be relatively uninhibited, because they do not have to suppress an underlying femininity, they are sufficiently realistic to be concerned with the social significance of emotional expression.

As indicated in Table 12-1, the three groups do not quite differ in the ways we predicted. The directions of results support our predictions, but there is only one significant finding. Compared to the MMs and FFs as a group, a larger proportion of the FMs are emotionally constricted, but the difference is not significant. Similarly, the FFs do not increase dilation significantly more than the MMs, although the trend supports our hypothesis.

The FMs do differ significantly from the FFs, but not from the MMs. The latter are midway between the two other groups. We imagine that the MMs, while they do not fear their affect, can inhibit themselves when necessary. They regulate their emotions more than the consciously feminine men do, but do not have to maintain the continuous vigil of the FMs. We seem to have underestimated the dilation the MMs would show under stress.

## Passivity

### Criteria

The other expressive style that we investigated was degree of passivity. We tabulated passivity when the problem in the story ending was resolved by the efforts of someone other than the hero. In a typical instance the principal and the other students intercede with the mother and convince her to permit Russ to play football. This ending is quite different from one in which Russ pleads his own case and convinces her that her fears are irrational.

### Predictions and results

During what we have called the first two stages of development the child gets continual practice in relating passively to others.

By "passive," we do not mean the absence of activity, which is the layman's definition, but a person's attempts to have others do something for or to him, which is the psychoanalytic definition. A child is passive when he cries in order to get his mother to feed him or carry him. He is also passive when he asks for her help in doing a task that he feels is a bit too difficult for him.

There is an important difference between these two examples. Crying illustrates the passivity of the first stage, when the infant is extremely helpless. Only later, when the child becomes aware of his lack of power and of his parents' capabilities, does he begin to make requests for help. This second kind of passivity is most prevalent during the period when the child is under pressure to inhibit his aggressive wishes. Some forms of independent action are then labeled as aggressive, and compliance with parental wishes is rewarded. By asking for help, the child can simultaneously placate his parents, control his aggressive feelings, and achieve his objective goals.[14]

We postulated that a passive style is learned at a time when the child begins to turn aggression inward or to reverse his feelings. Since asking for help is often a very realistic solution of a problem, we expected the FMs to increase their use of this response when under stress.

The FFs need not favor the kind of passivity we are talking about, because they customarily resort to an easier but more unrealistic solution. Under stress the FFs tend to reinterpret the facts. As we have seen, they are likely to fulfill their wishes in fantasy, or to express their impulses in direct action. We did not expect the MMs to increase passivity, since they have learned more socially acceptable ways of resolving conflict than asking for help. Even under stress they can be self-sufficient. We predicted, therefore, that the FMs would significantly exceed the other types of sex identity, both individually and as a group, in expressing increased passivity after sexual arousal. We had no reason to expect any differences between the FFs and MMs.

As anticipated, the FMs have a significantly greater tendency to increase passivity than the two other types of sex identity taken together. In general, the MMs and FFs are not inclined to increase

[14] We do not mean to imply here that the expressive style or the learning of it is conscious.

passivity following sexual arousal. As indicated by Table 1, we obtain significant differences when we make separate comparisons of the FMs with the MMs and FFs. The latter do not differ significantly from each other.

## Summary

We inferred differences in early parent-child relationships from three patterns of conscious and unconscious masculinity and femininity. On the basis of these inferred differences, we then predicted contrasting reactions to conflict involving unacceptable aggressive needs. We tested these predictions by comparing the proportions of the three groups who shifted their scores on a projective test following sexual arousal. The projective test required the subjects to complete unfinished stories about conflicts involving aggressive wishes.

Our subjects were undergraduate men in a large university. We employed Franck's Drawing Completion Test (4) as a measure of unconscious identity, and Gough's Femininity Scale (5) as a measure of conscious identity. We now list our major findings for each of our three types of sex identity:

*Unconsciously and Consciously Feminine Men (FF).* Instead of resolving conflicts about aggression by realistic means, the FFs are more inclined than the other subjects to favor the defense mechanisms of denial and withdrawal. The FFs also show the greatest inclination to be emotionally dilated when under stress. Unlike the FMs, the FFs do not attempt to resolve their conflicts by such techniques as self-attack or passivity.

*Unconsciously Feminine and Consciously Masculine Men (FM).* The FMs, unlike the FFs, are likely to turn their anger against themselves in resolving conflicts involving aggression, and to substitute passive action for the original action tendency. Like the MMs, the FMs are not inclined to employ mechanisms in the first family. Of the three groups, the FMs are most constricted, although this result did not attain statistical significance.

*Unconsciously and Consciously Masculine Men (MM).* When sexually aroused, the MMs, unlike the FFs and FMs, are most apt to increase their realistic attempts to resolve conflicts.

The MMs are also less likely than the FMs to use passive forms of expression. Contrary to our anticipations, the MMs are mid-way between the other two groups in self-attack and emotional dilation.

## References

1. Benedict, Ruth. *Patterns of culture.* New York: Houghton Mifflin, 1934.
2. Clark, R. A. Projective measurement of sexual motivation. *J. exper. Psychol.,* 1952, *44,* 391–99.
3. Feshbach, S. The drive-reducing function of fantasy behavior. *J. abnorm. soc. Psychol.,* 1955, *50,* 3–11.
4. Franck, Kate, & Rosen, E. A projective test of masculinity-femininity. *J. consult. Psychol.,* 1949, *13,* 247–56.
5. Gough, H. G. Identifying psychological femininity. *Educ. Psychol. Measurement,* 1952, *12,* 427–39.
6. Gowland, F. *Figure photography.* New York: Fawcett, 1954.
7. Lansky, L. M. Patterns of defense against conflict. Unpubl. Ph.D. dissertation, Univ. of Michigan, 1955.
8. Latscha, R. Tests of significance in a $2 \times 2$ contingency table. Extension of Finney's table. *Biometrika,* 1953, *40,* 74–86.
9. Thurstone, L. L., & Thurstone, Thelma G. *Amer. Council on Education Psychological Examination.* Princeton, N.J.: Cooperative Test Division, Educational Testing Service, 1949.

# 13

# EXPRESSIVE STYLES

## I. Substitution and Expressive Style

Originally we set out to explore the processes by which a person in conflict unconsciously arrives at alternate expressions of needs. Both moral standards and defense mechanisms limit the range of possible substitutes. Moral standards do this by defining certain alternatives as unacceptable. (Their expression then leads to guilt.) Defense mechanisms restrict the acceptable group of substitutes to certain components of the forbidden impulse, such as the object or the act.

Information about a man's moral standards and defenses permits only a limited prediction about the nature of his substitutes. The fact that he resolves a particular conflict by means of projection, for instance, reveals that he displaces the agent but does not indicate the specific substitute. Information about his moral standards helps to identify the alternative agents which would stir up his conscience; he avoids them if he can. This usually leaves a broad range of alternatives. To narrow the range further, we consider expressive style, a third source of restriction.

Expressive style, the subject of studies to be reported in the next two chapters, refers to individual variations in the manner of performing adaptive acts. In common parlance, styles are usually conceived in terms of dichotomous alternatives. People are described, for example, as inhibited or spontaneous, emotional or flat, rhythmic or jerky. Like moral standards and defenses, expressive styles create predispositions to favor certain types of displacement over others. To gain further insight into this process, we must first examine the nature of displacement in some detail.

## Displacement

Substitutes are sometimes so remote from the original elements of the impulse that at first it would seem as though any alternative might serve. Yet, for the person in conflict, the substituted elements must be related to the original ones in some way. What do the two have in common? And what determines the particular choice of substitute? To phrase our questions more specifically, we shall examine the displacements in two clinical cases.

### Two examples of substitution

We take our first illustration from the case history of a four-year-old boy whom Freud (11) calls "little Hans." Hans could not leave his house for fear that a horse might bite him. In psychotherapy an unconscious hostility toward the father was revealed as the root of the symptom. A well-socialized child, Hans was prevented by his conscience and his love for his father from trying to hurt him. Freud thinks that there may also have been a fear of retaliation from the powerful adult, whose potential rage was exaggerated by the boy's projections. Once the fear of harm was transferred to the horse, Hans felt unmixed love for his father. The boy's only difficulty was with horses, and he could avoid them by staying out of the streets. Now the original problem about displacement can be phrased more specifically. Why did Hans substitute a horse for the feared object? Why not a cat, or a train, or any of the other conceivable alternatives?

Before we attempt to answer this question, it is necessary to consider another example of displacement (10). A young girl, whose conscience prevented her from acknowledging to herself her fierce anger at her mother, was very naughty and anxious for a short period. Then she displaced her hostility onto another woman. Once she found another important female to hate, she could love her mother. But the hatred of another woman was incompatible with the girl's moral standards. Consequently, she shifted her anger onto still another object, herself. She became preoccupied with tormenting self-accusations, and she impulsively engaged in acts that lowered her in the esteem of others. Self-punishment was too painful a method of relieving her guilt, so she finally resorted to the projection of her aggression. Once she became convinced that others were persecuting her, she felt justified in expressing her hostility more directly.

Again we return to the initial question. The substitution of another woman for the mother seems more reasonable than the substitution of a horse for a father. But why another woman? Might the girl have chosen a man, or a more remote substitute like a horse or a dog?

The answer to our question requires the classification of substitutes into dimensions. The elements within each are homogeneous with respect to some characteristic. Freud's account conveys the impression, for example, that if Hans had not chosen a horse he would have substituted some other animal for his father. In contrast, the angry girl would probably have selected alternatives from categories of people. Both these patients displaced their hostility onto other objects, but these objects were of very different dimensions.

It thus appears that the displacement of an affect, act, or agent may occur within a number of dimensions. Successful research on the properties of most dimensions used by people in our society would represent a long step in the direction of developing a theory of displacement. As yet, the necessary information is not available. However, although few specific dimensions are known, it is possible to divide them into categories that suggest the nature of the ultimate theory.[1] Some dimensions are unlearned; others are learned. Within the learned dimensions, some substitutions depend on similarities among the elements; others depend on the fact that the elements have occurred together previously in the past. We now examine each of these instances.

### Unlearned dimensions

Once a response to certain kinds of stimuli is learned, there seems to be an inborn tendency to repeat it upon the occurrence of any of a particular group of other stimuli that are discernibly dif-

[1] These categories were proposed by Hilgard and Marquis (13).

ferent from the original. This principle is illustrated by a study in which a rat was placed in a two-chambered box and taught to run for food from one chamber to another whenever he heard a pure musical tone with a specific pitch (4). He also ran for food the first time he heard a tone an octave lower, but he was less inclined to move when the tone was only four steps above the original. A response that equates tones an octave apart is apparently determined by the structure of the nervous system. Both musically untrained animals and musically sophisticated men react in the same way. Unlearned equivalences may account for other displacements, such as the substitution of a red object for a yellow one, because both have warm colors.

Sometimes two objects are equated because they resemble each other, and the observer is either a child who has not yet learned to tell them apart or an older person who has reverted to the child's misperceptions. Hans seems to have undergone such a reversion when he substituted a white horse for his father. It was easy for an anxious boy to equate animal and parent, both of whom were large, had great strength, and were light-skinned. In addition, they both had attachments near their eyes: The horse wore blinders, the father glasses. Finally, they both had black areas around their mouths: The horse had a dark muzzle, and the father a dark beard. Obviously, Hans knew the difference between the horse and his father. His inability to discriminate between them appear to have been a reversion to an earlier way of perceiving the world, a reversion that sometimes occurs when excessive anxiety prevents a rational evaluation of events.

### Learned dimensions based on similarity of meaning

In most cases the associations that weld a group of elements into a dimension are learned. Some dimensions depend on meaningful connections among the elements; others depend only on the fact that the elements have often occurred together in the past. We begin with the first kind. The girl who hated her mother probably displaced the object within a group of dimensions. These seem to have included dimensions of females, of people with some power, and of people with responsibility for their actions. Suitable substitutes for the original object therefore included older females with authority and the girl herself.

A recent study by Lacey and Smith (20) sheds considerable light on the origins of such dimensions. The investigators presented each subject with a list of forty words, half with rural meanings and half with nonrural meanings. Eight words, such as *plow* and *chicken,* had obvious rural meanings; eight, such as *clock* and *smooth,* had no specific rural connotations. Upon hearing a word over a loudspeaker, the subject was asked to say all the single words that came to his mind. At the same time he was instructed to tap a telegraph key as evenly as possible. Four of the words were repeated six times. The crucial words, *cow* and *paper,* were presented an equal number of times. Half of the subjects were given an electric shock on the upper left arm when they heard the word *cow,* and half were shocked when they heard the word *paper.* During the experiment recordings were made of plantar skin resistance, digital blood flow, and heart rate, three indices of autonomic change.

As might be expected, subjects who were shocked upon hearing *cow* soon exhibited greater autonomic changes upon responding to that word than they did when responding to *paper.* Subjects shocked upon hearing *paper* did the reverse. This differential reaction appeared soon after the word was presented but before the shock occurred. When the thirty-one subjects were questioned, twenty-two did not know which word led to shock even though they anticipated the connections correctly in their autonomic reactions. More important, the unconscious anxiety spread to words associated with those originally paired with shock. Subjects for whom *cow* had become a source of anxiety also increased their autonomic responses upon presentation of other rural words. Subjects for whom *paper* had become a source of anxiety became tense when they saw other nonrural words. In short, a person who has learned a response to one concept may generalize the same response to other meaningfully associated concepts without being aware of either connection.

In summarizing the results of a follow-up study, Lacey, Smith, and Green (21) report that, in contrast to the informed subjects, the naive subjects showed greater autonomic change in reaction to rural words other than the ones leading to shock, and required a long time to lose their tensions when critical words were later presented without shock. In addition, subjects who were low on the Taylor Manifest Anxiety Scale exceeded those with high scores in the accuracy of their discriminations: Those with low anxiety gave larger emergency responses to the conditioned word stimulus during the initial shocking period and showed less generalization than did those with high anxiety.

From these experiments we infer that a person who develops an emotional reaction to a particular object may generalize the reaction to all objects that are similar to it in meaning. Probably, the greater his general anxiety, or the similarity between the two elements, the stronger is his emotional response. The affect occurs even if the original experience has been forgotten and there is no insight into the dimension of similarity. It is not surprising, therefore, that a forbidden original object or act may be unconsciously displaced by another in the same dimension.

### Learned dimensions based on contiguity

Not all the elements of a dimension need have common meanings. An individual may associate certain acts with each other or certain affects with each other simply because a nonmeaningful but consistent condition has reinforced their connections: They have always occurred at the same time or in the same place. Ordinarily, no one would connect a bell with food. Yet, if a bell rings whenever a dog is fed, he soon begins to salivate at the sound of the bell alone (2).

To the extent that the members of a society, or of particular subgroups, share a common set of experiences, they probably learn a common set of elements within any specific dimension and develop very similar dimensions of objects, acts, affects, and agents. Men in very different societies probably differ in their dimensions and the elements within them. Of course, even people in the same society may make relatively unique associations between elements because of special experiences. Such an experience may be illustrated by the pinning of a child's arm to his sides whenever he becomes angry. Naturally, he tries to free his arms and is likely to express his anger with his eyes. In later years when he cannot express anger directly, he may substitute wild gesticulations and a bulging of the eyes.

In the psychoanalytic theory of psychosexual development (34) the origins of certain dimensions of acts and of objects are explained in terms of culturally determined coincidences in parental behaviors. These and their elicited responses are connected only temporally and not in any way that is meaningful to either parent or child. For example, parents in some societies take great care to keep their infants warm and comfortable, to gratify their passive appeals, to allow them to suck whenever they are unhappy, and to hold and stroke them. Although mothers do not intend to teach their infants to associate their passive requests with being fed or with the expression of love, the fact that such connections are reinforced by pleasure many thousands of times may forge an equivalence that lasts throughout life. At one time or another everyone expresses friendship by feeding others. When some people are not able to gratify their passive needs, they may substitute overeating (8).

Another association elaborated within psychosexual theory is the one between aggression and dirtiness. If the child's mother becomes very disturbed each time he wets his bed, he may develop a tendency to express his anger by losing urinary control. The stubborn struggle over cleanliness between many an American parent and child sometimes lasts several years. In the course of the campaign the antagonists fight numerous skirmishes. As a result, some children equate attacking with being dirty. This association throws some light on the use of symbolic handwashing for the purpose of canceling hostile needs or acts. "Dirty" thoughts are often aggressive ones; the expression "to do one dirt" describes an aggressive act.

Dirt and sex are connected in the minds of some children because of the anatomical proximity of the organs used for sexual and excretory purposes, and because the bathroom is often the place where autoerotic practices occur and dirt is removed. If this association is made, the child may wash his hands to cancel symbolically his "dirty" wishes to masturbate.

What determines the choice of the dimensions from which substitutes are selected, and of the elements within the dimensions?

Only a speculative answer can be made to this question. To our knowledge, no one has investigated this aspect of substitution. Certain investigators have gathered sufficient data about some of the concepts we have investigated to give us some faith in their probable relevance to displacement. We also feel some confidence in our viewpoint because of the studies that we report in the next two chapters. Of course, we cannot ever hope to explain a specific substitution made by a particular person. Such a unique event depends too much on the special properties of the individual and the situation. If Hans had not seen many horses, for example, he could conceivably have displaced his aggression onto another animal.

## Expressive Style

As mentioned earlier, to account for unconscious choices of dimensions and elements, we have invoked, in addition to morals and defenses, a third group of personal characteristics which we shall call *expressive style.* In part, we derived the term from Allport and Vernon's (1) *expressive movement.* These authors use this concept to refer to "individual differences in the manner of performing adaptive acts, considered as dependent less upon external and temporary conditions than upon enduring qualities of personality." Referring to a similar concept, Reich (26) says it describes *how* a person behaves rather than *what* he does. We have substituted *style* for *movement* because we wish to cover individual differences, not only in physical reaction but also in perception and in the interpretation of what one perceives. In other words, our term includes more than the tendency to move in a particular way, such as spontaneously or tensely. It also includes a person's way of organizing his percepts—whether he is likely to see wholes or parts—and the nature of his concepts—whether they are more often abstract or concrete.

### Definitions

Expressive style is closely related to the psychoanalytic concept of *character.* According to Reich (26), the psychosexual stage at which a person is fixated and the patterning of his defenses create stabilized dispositions which are expressed even when he is not in conflict. Working in the same theoretical tradition, Klein and his associates (14, 16, 17) have investigated a number of *perceptual* and *cognitive attitudes,* which they view as "regulatory principles of the organism." Such principles express individual differences in the formal operation of adaptive properties and "have enduring effects on the way in which adaptive properties function."

The literature on personality contains descriptions of many characteristics which might be regarded as indicative of expressive style. In surveying the literature, we will divide styles into *perceptual, conceptual,* and *motoric* types. Most types have been defined dichotomously. Fairly representative of perceptual styles are *color* and *form dominance* (33), *extratension* and *introversion* (29), and *plastic* and *rigid eidetic* imagery (15). Among the categories that have been proposed for classifying concepts are *concrete* and *abstract* (12), *diffuse* and *articulated* (37), *synthetic* and *abstractive* (19), and *objective* and *subjective* (3). The literature abounds with categories of physical expression. *Dilated* and *constricted* (1), *rigid* and *flexible* (15), *undercontrolled, controlled,* and *overcontrolled* (5), and *oral, anal,* and *genital* (34) are a few of the types that have been proposed.

### Expressive styles and substitution

Each category of expressive style describes an aspect of behavior so integrally a part of the total pattern that it emerges without deliberation. A person is seldom aware that his gestures are expansive rather than constrictive, or that his concepts are concrete rather than abstract. If asked to analyze his style, he can sometimes do so but he does not usually think in such terms.

The lack of self-consciousness in expressive style is one reason why we think it may have an important place in the unconscious selection of substitute expressions of needs. The relevance of style to substitution may be illustrated by the case of a man who, having been hurt by a friend, is deterred from retaliating because of his affection and conscience. If he is accustomed to working with his body, he may unthinkingly displace the original act by one that permits physical expression: He may challenge the friend to a game of tennis. If the man is predominantly conceptual, he may try to talk the problem over with his friend. Such a style is likely to eliminate the motoric alternatives even if they are perfectly consonant with his moral standards and his mechanisms of defense.

INTERDEPENDENCE AMONG STYLES

The division of expressive styles into perceptual, conceptual, and motoric categories is misleading if it conveys the impression that the three kinds of style are basically independent or even easily distinguished from each other. In fact, they are so intimately related that they are almost impossible to separate. Reich (26), for example, attributes perceptual and conceptual styles to muscular orientations which regulate the receptivity and organization of various stimuli. The extent to which a style of physical expression may be linked to perception has been vividly demonstrated by Werner, Wapner, and their associates. In one study (39) they investigated conditions which caused subjects to differ in the amount of movement they attributed to a stationary point of light. People who were strapped to a chair saw more apparent movement than did others who kept their arms in continuous motion while making the judgments.

In another study, conducted in a dark room (38), each subject gave the experimenter directions as to how to adjust a tilted rod so as to make it vertical. During an initial control series of trials the rod was usually tilted to the left. In an experimental trial each subject received electrical stimulation on one side of his neck before he gave his instructions. As a result, he usually tilted the rod from the control position and in a direction opposite to the stimulated side. Apparently, the electrical stimulation increased muscle tonus in the neck; the resultant sensation affected the perception of the vertical position. In the opinion of the experimenters, such a result demonstrates the functional interdependence of the sensory and motor areas of the cerebral cortex. The manner in which people express themselves with their bodies cannot be separated from their perceptual styles.

In the following sections we shall first describe a number of different styles whose characteristics have been somewhat clarified by various empirical investigations. Then we shall cite evidence about the origins of variations in each of the styles. We shall concentrate on certain perceptual and motoric styles, the studies of which suggest the trends of future theories about the nature and origins of different kinds of expression. Finally, we shall introduce the two styles that are the topics of the next two chapters.

### Preferences for perceptual dimensions

Most investigators of perceptual styles have concentrated on the inclination to respond in terms of one dimension rather than another. There are many reports of marked individual differences in responsiveness to visual, postural, auditory, and kinesthetic stimuli. Such tendencies have even been observed in animals. According to Krech, *et al.* (18), some rats consistently react to the visual cues provided by a lighted pathway in a maze. Other rats orient themselves more in terms of a spatial pattern: They aim at a particular place, regardless of where the light is.

Human subjects provide the most abundant evidence of contrasting perceptual styles. Roe (27) reports that biologists and experimental physicists are inclined to define their problems in visual terms. This style is much less common among anthropologists and psychologists, who are more likely to formulate their problems in verbal terms.

In studying the artistic activities of children at a school for the blind, Lowenfeld (22) finds that this group of children includes both visual and haptic perceivers. The former subordinate other sensory reactions to the visual; the latter stress tactile perception. According to Lowenfeld, "Some weaksighted people immediately apply their eyes closely to anything which attracts their attention, even if they have only the most rudimentary vision. Others, even though they possess considerable visual power, approach everything through the sense of touch. . . ." Observations of children with normal vision reveal similar styles.

While most investigations of perceptual style have not been planned with a view to casting light on the resolution of conflict, they provide information which clarifies the selection of certain types of substitutes. Visual perceivers probably select alternative objects because they look something like the originals. Haptic perceivers may be more sensitive to tactile associations, and auditory perceivers may choose substitutes primarily because they sound like the originals. When people favor verbal imagery, it is likely that they displace within dimensions created by meaningful verbal associations. In short, it is possible to predict from the order of dominance in a person's perceptual orientation the dimensions from which he will select his alternate expressions of a blocked action tendency.

### Two types of perceptual style

Perceptual styles that may influence the choice of elements within a perceptual dimension have also been studied. Two such styles are suggested by factors that Thurstone (35) obtains from an analysis of perceptual tasks. One factor is defined as the "ability to shake off one set in order to take a new one." When tasks require this flexibility of sets, the subject must manipulate two configurations either simultaneously or in succession. In a typical test he follows two different patterns at the same time, each with a different hand. The second factor represents the ability "to form a perceptual closure against some distraction," or "to hold a closure against distraction." In one test requiring this ability, the subject is shown a simple figure, like a cross, and asked to locate it within a more complex figure. To perform this task well, he must disregard the configuration of the complex figure. The ability to find objects embedded in a large picture is also high on this factor.

Studies by other investigators further illuminate the nature of these two factors. In one of the first tests of an ability to shake off a set Frenkel-Brunswik (9) asked children to name the objects pictured on each of a series of cards. The first picture was that of a dog. As the series progressed, the animal's shape became increasingly feline so that the final card contained the picture of a cat. Some subjects thought they saw canine characteristics in many cards. When their labels became very inappropriate, these children guessed haphazardly or became blocked. Frenkel-Brunswik attributes this nonrational behavior to low tolerance of ambiguity. It is her opinion that some people must have clarity at all costs. They therefore organize the perceptual materials prematurely, generalizing on the basis of inadequate information. Then they carry over old, sometimes irrelevant, sets. Such subjects also have high scores on tests of religious prejudices.

The ability to shake off a perceptual set also seems necessary for the solution of Rokeach's (28) puzzles. In each puzzle the subject was asked how one would obtain a particular amount of water, say three quarts, by shifting the available quantity among three jars, which might hold seven, five, and one quarts, so that none of them held the necessary amount. After assigning a group of problems which could be solved only by a long and complicated method, Rokeach then changed to a second group which could be solved in either the first way or with a newer, simpler approach. Children who clung to the old method obtained high scores on a test of ethnic prejudices; children who were more flexible had low scores on the test. The inability to shift was also associated with a tendency to see issues in black and white.

A task very similar to Frenkel-Brunswik's changing series of animal pictures was used by Schlesinger (32) to identify *focusers* and *nonfocusers.* First he gave his subjects practice in judging weights in comparison with a standard series. Then, without warning, he made the series much heavier. He identified as focusers subjects who kept making estimates with reference to the earlier series. Focusers not only clung to a set, but also had ". . . an underlying preference for experiencing the work in a narrowed discriminating way, even when the task does not demand such an approach." To determine the extent of their reluctance to commit themselves, Schlesinger asked these subjects to state whether they liked, disliked, or were indifferent to a group of pictures. Compared to nonfocusers, focusers reported more instances of indifference. Contrary to his prediction, however, focusers were not unduly distracted by variations in color, weight, texture, and the like in estimating the sizes of discs.

To identify *levelers* and *sharpeners,* Holzman and Klein (14) used a technique which resembled Frenkel-Brunswik's even more than Schlesinger's did. First they asked their subjects to rate the absolute sizes of five squares shown in random order. Then, without warning the subjects, the experimenters removed the smallest square and added one larger than any of the other five. They did this a number of times. As a result of these changes, a square which was the largest in one series ultimately became the smallest in another. The investigators labeled as levelers those subjects who were very inaccurate in detecting the position of a square within a group. Such subjects were typically most inaccurate when the largest squares in one series became the smallest in another.

Levelers were inclined to give similar estimates for all squares in the middle position of a series. Subjects were labeled as sharpeners if they were able to discriminate between squares in the middle positions of different series. Such subjects were usually quite accurate throughout the test. These two groups were selected from the upper and lower 27 per cent of the distribution of scores for accuracy and for loss of accuracy.

Once the subjects had been classified, they were asked to compare two lights with equal intensities, the second appearing after an intervening light. It has been shown that an intervening light creates errors in judgment. As Klein and Holzman predicted, the sharpeners, who had been more accurate than the levelers in judging the sizes of squares, also made more accurate comparisons of the lights. This difference was significant when the intervening light was dim, but not when it was bright, however. Apparently, sharpeners took the intervening light into account, and corrected their estimates in terms of the apparent differences in brightness.

In the opinion of Holzman and Klein (14) leveling leads to a "difficulty in extracting embedded stimuli from larger, more cohesive stimulus organizations." This language is reminiscent of Thurstone's description of his second perceptual factor (35).

Scores on Thurstone's test of embedded figures are significantly related to two perceptual styles described by Witkin (40). In one study the subject sat in a chair within a room, both of which could be tilted at various angles. After the investigator tilted both, the subject was required to adjust either the chair or the room to the upright position. In another study the subject sat in a dark room and looked at a rod within a frame, both of which were luminous. Either or both were inclined at different angles, and the subject was asked to change either one to the vertical position. Individuals who had difficulty in locating the embedded figures in Thurstone's test were most inclined to rely on cues from the background in estimating the vertical position: They depended mostly on the frame in adjusting the rod and on the tilt of the room in adjusting the chair. Other people, who were more adept at locating the hidden shapes in Thurstone's test, relied more on figural cues: They depended mostly on their own bodily positions or on the angle of the rod.

A review of the findings that have been cited indicates that there is a cluster of related perceptual and conceptual responses. First, the ability to adjust one's estimates to changes in a series is related to the ability to see embedded figures. Second, the former is inversely related to racial prejudice, the tendency to make black and white judgments, the reluctance to commit oneself, and difficulty in making rational corrections of perceptual distortions. Frenkel-Brunswik (9) has included prejudice and extreme judgments in the cluster of traits that she calls representative of "intolerance of ambiguity." The reluctance to commit oneself and the difficulty in making rational corrections of distortions also appear to fit into her proposed cluster, which might be viewed as an index of conceptual flexibility.

### Motoric styles

Style of physical expression has been the object of very few investigations. Allport and Vernon's (1) important pioneering effort suggests the richness of the topic. These investigators were particularly interested in the internal consistency of each individual's expressive acts. A man who is shy, for example, reveals it not only in what he says, but even more in his facial expression, his handshake, his pattern of speech, his posture, and his manner of walking.

In their investigations of expressive gestures Allport and Vernon found clusters of related gestures rather than a general consistency. They found a consistent speed of reaction, for example, when the same act was carried out with different muscle groups—as in drawings of the same object made by foot and by hand—and when different acts were carried out by different muscle groups—as in writing and rhythmic leg tapping.

Allport and Vernon report three such clusters or group factors. One, the area of a man's expressive gestures, is manifested by the size of his writing and the length of his stride in walking. A second factor, the tendency toward centrifugality, is illustrated by overestimation of the distances of objects from one's body and by the spread of cubes that a subject lays on a table. A third factor, emphasis, is revealed by the intensity of vocal expression, the pressure in writing, and the number of lines a subject draws when instructed to fill a space with parallel lines.

Unfortunately, these findings have not received the attention they deserve, and few attempts have been made to relate the categories of expressive movements to traits of personality. One convincing study (7) suggests some of the possibilities. It reveals a significant relation between area of expressive behavior and a test of dominance. Subjects who took up a large space in expressing themselves were usually dominant in their behavior with the investigator. They were inclined to be late for their appointments. When they were, they made no apology. Some did not knock when they entered the investigator's office; some criticized the study. Quite the reverse was true of the diffident persons who used little space to express themselves. They usually came early, knocked when entering, and asked deferential questions.

## Classification of Expressive Styles

When a psychological term is coined to describe a trait, it frequently refers to a style or some of its aspects. In view of the tremendous number of styles, their complex interactions, and the fact that so little is known about the field, it is not surprising that a system of classification that would embrace all of them has not yet been proposed. Is it possible to suggest a method of classifying styles which would facilitate the prediction of individual differences in the substitution of action tendencies? We can suggest an approach in terms of a system that we have discussed in the fifth chapter of this book. There we proposed that needs be analyzed in terms of the dimensions of act, object, affect, and agent. These components of needs enabled us to develop categories for moral standards and for defense mechanisms in the second family. We think that the system may also prove helpful in classifying styles, since so many of them reflect moral norms or are generalizations of predilections for certain defenses.

We can clarify this proposal by some illustrations of expressive styles and substitutions. Passivity and initiative refer to the extremes of a continuum that may be used to describe *acts*. If a man is passive, he is likely to substitute a passive act for the more preferred one proscribed by his moral standards. Strength of the motoric orientation and the continuum of dilation-constriction, as it is conceived by Allport and Vernon, are also styles referring to acts. If a man is very motoric, he is likely to select his substitutes for acts blocked by conflict from the ones involving the use of the large muscles. If he is also constricted, the substituted act will probably be one performed in a small space.

We have already given some examples of preferences for different dimensions of objects. Some people are predominantly auditory; others are more visual or verbal. There are no good psychological terms for the inclinations to favor the dimension of objects rather than acts or affects, but the popular term "scapegoating" expresses this style rather vividly. Styles of expressing affects have been characterized by such terms as "flat-excitable," "hostile-friendly," and, possibly, "color-form." Among the styles pertaining to dimensions of agents are degree of responsibility, litigiousness, suspiciousness, and self-abnegation.

A surprisingly large number of expressive styles can be classified in terms of the components of needs. Yet, when this is done, there are still some styles that we cannot classify. Most of them are so general that they may be applied to any component of a need. The continuum of directness is a good example. Substitutes may range from the direct to the indirect within the dimensions of acts, objects, affects, and agents. The same is true for concrete-abstract, and for infantile-mature, a style indicating stages of development when dimensions were established.

In sum, we propose two categories of expressive styles. In one category they are classified in terms of the dimensions of needs, and in the other they are classified in more general terms which are applicable to any dimension. The two categories may not enable us to classify all styles, but we can make considerable progress in conceptualizing those which affect substitution in instances of conflict.

## Sources of Difference in Expressive Styles

Thus far we have confined ourselves to the issues involved in describing expressive styles. In our studies of this topic we concentrated on the backgrounds which create individual differences. Since the varieties of expression are so great, it is not surprising that many different sources have been proposed. We shall now summarize some of those which seem most pertinent to the resolution of conflict. We again start with perceptual styles.

A tendency to favor a particular sensory modality can have a number of roots. Krech (18) offers a hereditary account of the variations in his rats. Explanations of differences in perceptual orientation among humans usually stress cultural variations. In Schachtel's opinion (30), reliance on vision and audition is most common in our society, but not necessarily in others. American parents are inclined to ignore or punish their children for certain olfactory and gustatory interests, and are more likely to reward their responses to events at a distance. As a result, the offspring develop great sensitivity to such subtle cues as the frown and smile, as well as to verbal requests. American training may help to account for Schlaegel's (31) finding that both sighted and blind subjects have the same order of sensory preference: first visual, then auditory, next tactile-temperature, and finally olfactory-gustatory.

Balinese parents respond more to kinesthetic reactions and to plastic behavior than do Americans, and they give verbal directions to their children only infrequently. According to Mead (24), Balinese children "learn from the feel of other people's bodies and from watching, although this watching itself has a kinesthetic quality."

Environmental influences on perceptual styles include much more than cultural differences in parental practices. Special experiences may help to make a particular modality very important. Roe (27) reports that boys' imagery is related to their fathers' occupations. In his study of associations to words and phrases Schlaegel (31) finds that the semi-blind whose infirmity was acquired after the age of six produced the most visual imagery of all his subjects. Apparently they place exceptional value on their sight.

Sex and age differences contribute to some marked variations in expressive style. In Witkin's study, women exceeded men in responses to visual cues in the field; men responded more to internal experiences. He suggests that these contrasting reactions reflect corresponding differences in the basic psychological organizations of the sexes. The abilities of men and women to adjust an object to the vertical position varied with age: Older subjects were generally superior to younger ones. The differences between males and females diminished between the ages of eight and thirteen years, but increased again in adulthood.

Differences in chronological age also determine the capacity to develop various types of concepts (36). The child progresses from the concrete to the abstract. Concepts of form, such as triangularity and roundness, are usually manifested within the first three years. A number of additional years must elapse, however, before a child makes sophisticated use of such concepts as time, cause and effect, and constancy of volume. In addition to age, other characteristics, such as intelligence (23), vocabulary (6), and socio-economic status (25), have all been reported as being associated, to some extent, with the frequencies of various kinds of concepts. It seems to us that people who differ with respect to these characteristics probably have different dimensions of acts, affects, objects, and agents.

Experiences in the family seem to have a profound effect on a person's expressive style. According to Frenkel-Brunswik, children with a marked intolerance of ambiguity are usually reared by many rigid and unexplained rules. Their parents are likely to define relations in terms of dominance and submission and to enforce their authority by severe discipline. Often these parents are in socially or economically marginal groups and are upwardly mobile, which explains some of their concern with rules of conduct. To relieve their insecurity and to rise in the social hierarchy, they require rigid obedience to these rules by both themselves and their children (9).

One of the most comprehensive attempts to explain the origins of expressive styles is Reich's (26) theory of character. Reich accounts for differences in character structure primarily in terms of degree of regression. A person who is extremely fearful of expressing his anger directly, for example, may develop any of a number of character traits. He may become passive or inactive, he may become seductive, or he may try to be polite at all costs. He may also become preoccupied with orderliness as a means of guaranteeing that he will retain control of himself, he may develop an incapacity to feel his emotions, thus assuring that he will not be overwhelmed by them, or he may become convinced that he is stupid, thus robbing himself of the conviction necessary for direct action. The various forms of behavior that he substitutes for the aggressive act depend on the stage at which he is fixated. If he is orally fixated, he is predisposed to favor incorporative and passive modes of expression. If his character structure is anal, he is more inclined to engage in repetitive, meaningless behavior, or to engage in sadistic activities. If his character structure is phallic, he may develop hysterical symptoms, or seek out adventurous activities which reassure him of his masculinity.

### Expressive styles that we investigated

In this volume we recapitulate studies of five expressive styles. Investigations of three of them, passivity, emotional dilation, and control, have been described in the seventh and twelfth chapters. If a man is very passive, he is strongly inclined to provoke others to do things to or for him. When direct expression of an action tendency is blocked by conflict, he is likely to substitute either an act which motivates supportive activity by others, or an object capable of providing the required support. The object may have such traits as maturity, authoritativeness, and strength. If a man is emotionally constricted in his substitutes, he is likely to be limited to acts and objects requiring little expression of strong affect; if his control is poor, he may choose some substitutes impulsively, despite an effort to avoid them.

In the first few years of life passive appeals are of most service to the child, and he is very inclined to be emotionally dilated and lacking in control. To become constricted, he must learn to inhibit the expression of certain emotions. To develop control, he must learn to evaluate the characteristics of the adults' reactions, to inhibit his first impulse, and to choose substitutes deliberately. The FMs [2] have acquired these skills. Because of certain developmental difficulties, it is possible that the FMs do not possess sufficient mastery of some of the more mature skills of later stages. For this reason, among others, we anticipated that the FMs would favor the substitution of passive alternatives more than would the more unrealistic FFs or the more socially skilled unconsciously

[2] The symbols on this page are defined in Chapter 12.

masculine men. Because the FMs are overtrained to inhibit the direct expression of anger, we anticipated that they would not lose control and that they would favor the substitution of emotionally constricted alternatives. The results have supported our predictions.

In the next two chapters we shall report studies of two other expressive styles. The first is the directness with which a person customarily expresses his aggressive needs: the degree of remoteness of his substituted acts and objects from those in the most preferred action tendency. The second style refers to the inclinations to communicate and to approach one's problems with a conceptual rather than a motoric orientation. Each of these styles is relatively independent of the other and of predilections for certain defenses. Regardless of the defense, a man can displace the object by a very dissimilar or a very similar one. And substitutions may be either motoric or conceptual, or both. In the following descriptions of our studies, we elaborate further on the meanings of the styles.

In formulating our hypotheses about the origins of expressive styles we were impressed both by their visibility and their salience in interpersonal communication. The fact that a mother expresses herself conceptually, directly, and in an emotionally dilated manner when disciplining her son is significant to him because these are the styles used by adults when they are trying to change his behavior. Underlying a number of our hypotheses is the assumption that in identifying with an adult, a child selects the traits most evident in the adult's methods of using power. The older a boy becomes, the more he internalizes his parents' expressive characteristics, since they are such integral aspects of the methods whereby his behavior is regulated. If the father strikes people in order to get his way, the son is inclined to strike people; if the father appeals to guilt feelings in others, the son expresses himself less directly.

From our observations of white- and blue-collar workers we inferred the existence of marked contrasts in their expressive styles. Consistent with the pressures within the middle class to develop conceptual skills, to exert self-control, to plan for the future, and to conserve valuable property are the tendencies to express aggression indirectly and conceptually. Consistent with the pressures within the working class to develop manual skills, to live in the present, and to influence people by physical means are the tendencies to express aggression directly and by means of the large muscles of the body.

Most field workers have not thought in terms of expressive style, so their descriptions only suggested the socio-economic groups in which we might find specific styles. We were influenced primarily by the evidence of unequal proportions of certain personality disorders in the two social classes. Such disorders also reveal differences in the expression of aggression. In middle-class disturbances, such as depression and obsession, anger is expressed by tortuous indirection. The depressive suffers from internal torment, but is predominantly passive in his reaction to other people. Obsessional neurosis is expressed by ritual, but almost never by physical attack. In contrast, pathologies like conversion hysteria and catatonic schizophrenia, which are common among working-class patients, often entail direct expression of aggressive needs. The hysteric may have fits during which he unconsciously follows his first impulses; the aggressive catatonic may even become homicidal.

Other characteristics of the disorders most common in the two socio-economic groups suggest differences in conceptual and motoric styles. Patients with middle-class disorders try to solve their problems conceptually. The obsessive ruminates; he may worry that he has not performed his ritual of checking the records in his office in just the right way, or he may fear that he has unintentionally offended a friend. In his brooding he tries to recall all the events which led to the imagined offense so he can do something to straighten things out. The depressive is similarly preoccupied. He feels bowed down by the weight of his guilt; he constantly reviews his past sins; he wonders how he could have been so evil; he wishes he could undo some of his impulses or acts.

In the pathologies of the middle class, disfunctions of the voluntary muscles are conspicuous by their relative absence. Disturbed patients seem to inhibit muscular expression. The obsessive is noted for his relative lack of gesture; the depressive's muscles are often flaccid.

Quite a different picture is conveyed by the disorders that are most prevalent among members of the working class. Disturbances in the functions of the voluntary muscles are fairly common. In hysteria the muscular disorder can often be traced to an early experience which created a fear of sexuality or aggression. Because of the fear, the hysteric represses his sexual need. He may implement the repression by unconsciously distorting some sensory or muscular function that is usually under voluntary control. If his trunk is paralyzed, for example, he cannot make love. Sometimes the symptom expresses the need symbolically. If a limb is rigid, it may unconsciously symbolize tumescence.

Catatonic schizophrenics, who also tend to come from the working class, resolve some of their conflicts about aggression by immobilizing in rigid positions certain sets of muscles that might be used to express the forbidden need. In extreme cases catatonics can maintain a physical position for hours—long past the time when pain would force the average adult to abandon his stance.

## Summary

Expressive style refers to individual variations in the manner of performing adaptive acts. To explain the possible effects of expressive style on the selection of substitutes by a person in conflict, we began the chapter with an examination of displacement. First we considered unlearned dimensions, then those which are learned. We showed how an organization of dimensions may take place because the elements have occurred together in the past, or because the elements are related in terms of some common meanings.

With regard to conflict, an expressive style may be viewed as an inclination to select substitutes from a particular dimension or from particular elements within a dimension. To illustrate these predilections and their possible origins, we cited studies of perceptual, conceptual, and motoric behavior. Then we proposed a tentative method of classifying styles with respect to the resolution of conflict. We concluded with an examination of the expressive styles that we studied and some speculations about their origins.

## References

1. Allport, G. W., & Vernon, P. E. *Studies in expressive movements.* New York: Macmillan, 1933.
2. Anrep, G. V. Pitch discrimination in the dog. *J. Physiol.,* 1920, *53,* 367–85.
3. Binet, A. Attention et adaptation. *L'Annee Psychol.,* 1900, *6,* 248–404.
4. Blackwell, H. R., & Schlosberg, H. Octave generalization, pitch discrimination, and loudness thresholds in the white rat. *J. exp. Psychol.,* 1943, *33,* 407–19.
5. Block, J., & Block, Jeanne. An investigation of the relationship between intolerance of ambiguity and ethnoclatism. *J. Pers.,* 1951, *19,* 303–11.
6. Deutsche, J. M. The development of children's concepts of causal relations. Minneapolis: *Univ. Minn. Inst. Child Welf. Monogr.,* 1937.
7. Eisenberg, P. Expressive movements related to feelings of dominance. *Arch. Psychol.* New York: Columbia Univ. Press, 1937.
8. Fenichel, O. *Psychoanalytic theory of neurosis.* New York: Norton, 1945.
9. Frenkel-Brunswik, Else. Intolerance of ambiguity as an emotional and perceptual variable. In Bruner, J. S., & Krech, D. (Eds.), *Perception and personality.* Durham, N. C.: Duke Univ. Press, 1949.
10. Freud, Anna. *The ego and the mechanisms of defence.* London: Hogarth, 1937.
11. Freud, S. *Collected Papers,* Vol. III. London: Hogarth, 1925.
12. Goldstein, K., & Scheerer, M. Abstract and concrete behavior. *Psychol. Monogr.,* 1941, *53,* No. 239, 1–151.
13. Hilgard, E. R., & Marquis, D. G. *Conditioning and learning.* New York: Appleton-Century, 1940.
14. Holzman, P. S., & Klein, G. S. Cognitive system principles of leveling and sharpening: Individual differences in assimilation effects in visual time-error. *J. Psychol.,* 1954, *37,* 105–22.
15. Jaensch, W. *Grundzuge einer Physiologie und Klinik der Psychophysischen Personlichkeit.* Berlin: Springer, 1926.
16. Klein, G. S., & Saloman, Anne. Cognitive style and regulation of need. *Amer. Psychol.,* 1952, *7,* 321–22.
17. ———, & Schlesinger, H. Perceptual attitudes toward instability:

I. Prediction of apparent movement experiences from Rorschach responses. *J. Pers.*, 1951, *19,* 289–302.

18. Krech, D., Rosenzweig, M. R., Bennett, E. L., & Kruechel, B. Enzyme concentration in the brain and adjustive behavior patterns. *Science,* 1954, *120,* 994–96.
19. Kretchmer, E. *Physique and character.* New York: Harcourt, Brace, 1926.
20. Lacey, J. I., & Smith, R. L. Conditioning and generalization of unconscious anxiety. *Science,* 1954, *120,* 1045–52.
21. ———, ———, & Green, A. Use of conditioned autonomic responses in the study of anxiety. *Psychosom. Med.,* 1955, *17,* 208–17.
22. Lowenfeld, V. The nature of creative activity. New York: Harcourt, Brace, 1939.
23. Long, L., & Welch, L. Influence of levels of abstractness on reasoning ability. *J. Psychol.,* 1942, *13,* 41–59.
24. Mead, Margaret, & Wolfenstein, Martha (Eds.). *Childhood in contemporary cultures.* Chicago: Univ. of Chicago Press, 1955.
25. Ordan, H. *Social concepts and the child mind.* New York: King's Crown Press, 1945.
26. Reich, W. *Character analysis.* New York: Orgone Press, 1949.
27. Roe, Anne. A study of imagery in research scientists. *J. Pers.,* 1951, *19,* 459–70.
28. Rokeach, M. Generalized mental rigidity as a factor in ethnocentrism. *J. abnorm. soc. Psychol.,* 1943, *48,* 259–78.
29. Rorschach, H. *Psychodiagnostics.* Berne, Switzerland: Huber, 1942.
30. Schachtel, E. On memory and childhood amnesia. In Mullahy, P. (Ed.), *A study of interpersonal relations.* New York: Hermitage, 1949
31. Schlaegel, T. F. The dominant method of imagery in blind as compared to sighted adolescents. *J. genet. Psychol.,* 1953, *83,* 265–77.
32. Schlesinger, H. Cognitive attitudes in relation to susceptibility to interference. *J. Pers.,* 1954, *22,* 354–74.
33. Scholl, R. Zur Theorie und Typology der teilinhaltlichen Beachtung von Form und Farbe. *Ztsch. Psychol.,* 1927, *101,* 281–320.
34. Sterba, R. *Introduction to the psychoanalytic theory of the libido.* New York: Nerv. and Ment. Dis. Monogr., 1947.
35. Thurstone, L. L. *A factorial study of perception.* Chicago: Univ. of Chicago Press, 1944.
36. Welch, L. A preliminary investigation of some aspects of the

hierarchical development of concepts. *J. genet. Psychol.,* 1940, *22,* 359–79.

37. Werner, H. *Comparative psychology of mental development.* Chicago: Follet, 1948.
38. ———, Wapner, S., & Chandler, K. A. Experiments on sensory-tonic field theory of perception: II. Effect of supported and unsupported tilt of the body on the visual perception of verticality. *J. exp. Psychol.,* 1951, *42,* 346–50.
39. ———, & ———. Toward a general theory of perception. *Psychol. Rev.,* 1952, *58,* 324–38.
40. Witkin, H. A. The nature and importance of individual differences in perception. *J. Pers.,* 1949, *18,* 145–70.

# 14

## EXPRESSIVE STYLES

### II. Directness with which Anger Is Expressed *

Nowhere is the significance of expressive style more evident than in a person's reactions to conflict. We were primarily concerned with a particular style: the directness with which boys express aggression. To explore the origins of differences in directness, we investigated such aspects of our subjects' backgrounds as their parents' social positions and methods of discipline and reward. We will examine some contrasting solutions of a hypothetical conflict in order to illustrate our concept of directness of expression.

*An Illustrative Case.* School was out for the day. Joe and Ted were taking their favorite route home across an empty lot when they heard an angry voice from the far side. An enraged old woman shook her fist at them and told them never to trespass on her property again. She cursed them and all the other boys who tramped on her land. Joe and Ted were startled. Joe exclaimed angrily: "Why that old battle-ax! Who does she think she is anyway? *Her* lot! Why, kids have been using this path for a hundred years." At this he swore at the old woman, picked up a rock, and threatened her with it. Instead of joining his friend, Ted grabbed his arm and said, "Hey, take it easy, there's no use in starting

* In the research team, Beverly B. Allinsmith was responsible for the research to be reported and for the preparation of the chapter, which is based in part on her doctoral dissertation (2).

anything. It probably is her lot. Let's skip it." When he left Ted, Joe was still bursting with anger. First he muttered to himself that he would stone her dog. Later he had a daydream about her house being destroyed by a hurricane. The daydream was succeeded by other hostile ruminations, such as plans to deface her house on the next Halloween and ideas of organizing a citizens' committee to deprive her of her land and to donate it to the town for a children's park.

In contrast to Joe, Ted seemed calm. When he returned home, he greeted his younger sister with a broad smile, and asked her about the game she was playing. She impatiently cautioned him to watch where he was walking, and said that he might mess up her toys if he were not careful. At this, Ted exploded with: "I'll walk where I darn well please, and don't you tell me what to do!" His sister stared at him in amazement.

We presume that Joe and Ted were both angry. Yet, they felt and acted quite differently. Joe expressed his aggression much more directly than Ted did.

*Some Further Examples of Differences in Directness.* Although the more direct types of expression take many forms, they are not hard to recognize. Some men are ruthless, shoving aside obstacles in their path, even if they have to hurt friends in the process. Some men instantly retort, or even strike out without provocation. Some develop into demanding, resentful supplicants. Some express anger by criminal behavior, and some become aggressive crusaders for just causes.

The less direct expressions of aggression are more difficult to recognize, because they are often calculated to deceive not only the observer but the angry person himself. We find the clearest examples of indirect expression in the clinical literature. The man who seems unruffled in the face of unfair treatment may, while he is unconsciously very distressed, feel sincerely affectionate toward his tormentor. The polished, gentlemanly little boy in the sixth grade may love his ambitious and intellectual parents, but by not learning to read he is unconsciously punishing them for their stringent demands. A shy six-year-old girl becomes panicked when she has to go to school. When questioned, she says she is worried about leaving her mother alone at home. In therapy the origin of her school phobia is finally traced to unconscious fantasies about killing the mother. The girl must always be in a position to assure herself that she has not committed murder.

Many years of training are necessary before a child can control his anger and express it indirectly. Any nursery teacher can vouch for the fact that young children do not control themselves with the same success as do older ones. Savage blows and violent battles are often the rule. Fights may even culminate in bitten fingers, ears, or arms. Yet, in a short time, most of these same children take turns, share their toys with each other, and are reasonably polite to adults. However, some children remain physically aggressive and lose control readily, while others suffer from excessive inhibitions. What has happened to the once unfettered feelings? [1] How can we account for the differences in the expression of anger? These problems prompted our study.

## Method

### SUBJECTS

We obtained our subjects from the first sample described in Chapter 4. We chose male adolescents in part because in our culture boys at this stage of development experience considerable conflict about expressing aggressive needs, particularly toward authority figures. Boys who are entering their teens also seemed appropriate because they are mature enough to have developed characteristic styles of expressing anger. In short, we chose adolescents because we were trying to study relatively characteristic expressive styles that were sufficiently fraught with conflict to be readily elicited in our subjects.

[1] The existence of innate components in aggression is a moot point which has been considered mostly by members of the psychoanalytic movement. In *Beyond the Pleasure Principle* (10) Freud proposed an unlearned aggressive force with many of the same properties as the erotic one. According to his description, this force presses for expression and becomes tamed in the course of early socialization. Subsequently, aggression may be expressed either constructively (8, 9), as in the striving for socially approved goals, or destructively, as in physical attacks on others. Recent psychoanalytic writers (3, 11, 12) accept Freud's premise although they are inclined to reject his philosophic assumption of a "Death Instinct."

THE PROJECTIVE TECHNIQUE

We rejected the interview as a method for studying the directness with which boys express aggression, because children have a natural reluctance to discuss their antisocial impulses with adult interviewers. In addition, people are not always aware of their expressive styles. To obtain reactions which our subjects probably could not describe in an interview, we decided on a projective test involving the completion of a group of stories. Since everyone finished the same stories, the endings were all relevant to the same conflicts. This control would not have been available had the subjects been asked to describe incidents in their own lives.

We constructed six story beginnings.[2] In each, a boy either loves or fears an older or more powerful person who is unfair or who is an unintentional source of frustration. Hence, the boy is in conflict. He wants both to retaliate and to seek the adult's love or protection. In a typical story beginning Jack, who admires the baseball coach and cherishes his approval, is rejected when he tries out for the team. He feels the coach has not given him a fair chance.

We administered the test to groups of from four to seven boys. Every effort was made to create a relaxed atmosphere. We promised the subjects anonymity. We also said that correctness of spelling did not matter, that there were no right or wrong answers, and that no one outside our project would see the stories. After booklets were distributed, a picture depicting the situation in the first story was flashed on a screen.[3] The examiner read the beginning of the story aloud while the subjects read it to themselves from their record booklets. Timing was flexible, and anyone who had trouble getting started was given individual encouragement.

*Rating the Subjects on Directness of Expression.* An aggressive person can express his need in many possible ways. As indicated in Chapter 5, we can order these action tendencies on a dimension varying from most to least direct. The hypothetical cases

[2] These may be found in Appendix C.

[3] We selected pictures from the Thematic Apperception Test (14) or Symonds' Picture Story Test (16, 17).

with which we began this chapter suggests some possible alternatives within this continuum.

Joe and Ted were both angry at the old woman, even though Ted seemed overtly unaffected and tried to stop his friend from retaliating.[4] If Ted had not expressed his anger in the outburst at his little sister, it would certainly, we think, have taken some other form. He could have easily turned his aggression against himself, so that he became guilty about his illegal trespassing. Or he might later have misinterpreted an elderly teacher's facial expression as an indication of her dislike for him. He might also have bitten his nails more than usual, or he might have lost his appetite.

As for Joe, even he was not maximally direct in his hostility to the old woman. He did not actually hurt her; he was too afraid of others or of his conscience. But unlike Ted, Joe knew he was angry. Some substitutes were available to him which were more direct than those that Ted could use. Joe could tolerate the thought of throwing rocks at the woman's dog; he could fume about meddlesome old ladies, and make plans for revenge. He could imagine a citizens' committee taking her land by force and donating it to the children of the town.

*Defining a Continuum.* The variety of possible substitutes raises the vexing methodological problem of defining a continuum of directness. Without such a continuum, we could not compare Ted's anger at his sister with Joe's fantasy of hurting the old woman's dog. In constructing our scale of directness with which anger is expressed, it was necessary to take into account the displacements both of objects and of acts. We took an empirical approach in developing criteria for ranking the various substitute expressions of anger. First, we analyzed and classified the story

[4] Dollard, Doob, *et al.* (7) also consider this question of alternative action tendencies. In their analyses of aggression they stress such topics as nature of instigation, strength of frustration, amount of interference, possibilities of substitute reactions offered by the situation, and efficiency of such substitutes in reducing the original frustration. Upon finding that some of their subjects did not manifest direct aggression, these authors assumed that such subjects have not been sufficiently frustrated. We think that frustration does not always lead to overt aggressive behavior. Given evidences of frustration, we assume that aggression that is not directly expressed has been blocked and will emerge indirectly.

endings written by a preliminary group of subjects. Our analysis enabled us to code the substitute reactions in terms of eighteen categories, ranging from most to least direct expression of the hostile need. Then we combined the eighteen categories into the four which we finally used. To illustrate the range, we list all of the refined categories here and then tell how we chose the final four.

*A Range of Directness.* The first two themes in order of directness were physical attack and flight. The third category, which included attacks in the future or in the company of other participants, was slightly less direct than the first two. Still relatively direct were steps four to eight in our scale: verbal attacks, mild blaming, improbable means of attack or accidental ones, verbal attempts to get the object into trouble with others, and flight in the future or with little reference to the object.

Inhibition of action or a shift from the original object characterized the ninth to the thirteenth categories. They included attacks upon displaced objects, unexpressed aggressive thoughts about the original object, unexpressed mildly critical thoughts about the original object, unexpressed aggressive thoughts about a displaced object, and unexpressed, mildly unpleasant feelings with no mention of an object.

In the five most indirect endings, the hero is not aware that he is angry. In category fourteen, he is aware of aggressive motives, feelings, or acts, but he attributes them to the object. The remaining parts of the code required that aggression not be seen in anyone. In order, steps fifteen to eighteen included solutions of conflicts by unaggressive means, feelings of depression or sacrifice of one's rights, unawareness or denial of any aggressive thoughts or feelings, and finally, very positive behavior toward the frustrating object.

*Analyzing the Results.* We coded the endings written by all subjects for each story before we began with the next. The coding was done with the eighteen-point scale.[5] Then we added the six scores of each subject. Two natural breaking points in the distribution of total scores enabled us to define groups of subjects who were most direct and most indirect. The middle range of scores still contained nearly 60 per cent of our subjects. We arbi-

[5] The detailed definitions of categories may be obtained from the writer.

trarily established a cutting point which divided this group into equal halves.[6] We then had four categories of directness with which aggression was expressed in the story endings.

To determine whether degree of directness might be a function of productivity, we counted the average number of words per story written by each subject and then computed the mean for each coding category. There is no association between length of story and directness of expression. When we controlled scores on the three subtests from Thurstones' *The Chicago Tests of Primary Mental Abilities* (18), there were no changes in the significances of relations obtained between directness of aggression and children's backgrounds.

## Results

### Hypotheses: social position and directness of aggression [7]

*Middle Class.* We begin our report of results by describing the relations to directness of aggression of two variables, social class and maternal discipline. Observation of the American middle and working classes indicates marked contrasts in the acceptable degree of directness. The achievement of a respectable position in middle-class society is contingent on the individual's control of direct aggression. When he is only a few years old a boy is taught:

> (1) to fight when attacked by another boy, (2) not to attack a boy unless he has been struck, (3) not to attack girls or supervisory adults under any circumstances, but also (4) not to withdraw when in a normal, approved, competitive situation (5, p. 143).

[6] To test the reliability of the procedure, a person who was unfamiliar with the theory and hypotheses of the study scored thirty-five protocols selected at random from each of the four social classes. The raters agreed in 88 per cent of their assignments of stories to the four categories. We are indebted to Mrs. Phyllis Shire for her help in computing reliabilities.

[7] Chapter 2 contains a description of the methods of determining social class.

In addition, he must follow rules restricting physical attack to certain sizes of opponents and to certain acts. If a boy is to fight at all, he cannot "hit below the belt." He must select a person his own size or larger. He may attack a smaller boy only in retaliation. So uncomfortable are many members of the middle class made by physical aggression that, when it occurs, they often force themselves not to recognize it (1, 4).

Indirect forms of aggression among the middle class, such as teasing, are not punished as frequently as the direct forms. The victim can rarely retaliate without being labeled as humorless and a "spoilsport." He is "expected to deny his recognition of the true feelings of the aggressor and his own anger and frustration" (4, p. 85).

*Working Class.* Compared to members of the middle class, working-class people have less to gain from self-control and sacrifice. According to one observer, the children are:

> . . . taught to fight. They experience more open exhibition of aggression in their homes, where father may beat up mother, the children are whipped frequently, and the child's own aggressive impulses are not much restrained by his parents. . . . As a generalization it might be said that (working) class children have fewer and less rigid controls on the free play of their impulses . . . (13, pp. 33–34).

While differences in the directness of aggression have been observed in both social classes, we must not forget that aggression is subject to considerable socialization in all segments of the society. Since working-class boys, in particular, are often subject to both positive and negative inducements to avoid direct attack and to engage in it, we were not sure how these subjects would treat the physical expression of anger in their story endings.

Another problem that complicates the prediction of differences between classes is created by pressures other than socioeconomic ones. Standards of the family, neighborhood, and school, are also pertinent to the socialization of aggression. Some of these standards are probably consistent with those of one's social class and some are not. Finally, the contrasts between the classes in their expressions of anger are probably overdrawn in the literature, which usually overemphasizes the lower half of the working class in describing the total group, and often reports information collected during the economic depression. Thus, while we anticipated class differences, we were not certain about the form they would take.

### HYPOTHESES: DISCIPLINE AND DIRECTNESS OF AGGRESSION

Parents vary widely in their disciplinary techniques: in timing, in the consistency of requests, and in the models the parents themselves provide for their offspring. As models, some adults are self-controlled and reveal few of their hostile wishes; others seem to erupt as frequently as Old Faithful. Apart from specific acts, the parents' tolerance for the expression of feeling creates a general atmosphere which is probably important in understanding how children learn to express anger.[8]

One might expect, on first consideration, that the amount of maternal discipline will have a profound effect on the directness with which a child vents his anger. The methods by which the discipline is imposed, however, seem more crucial. Display of overt aggression in doll play, for example, is related to severity, but not frequency, of punishment (15). The more severe the discipline, the more overt is the aggression displayed by the children.

In our study we assigned each mother to one of four groups, depending on whether she favored (a) corporal methods, such as spanking or slapping, (b) harsh verbal techniques, such as scolding, threatening, and yelling, (c) the restriction of privileges such as time allowed for television or the child's allowance, or (d) psychological discipline, such as shaming and appeals to guilt.[9] Since a woman who usually resorts to spanking provides her son with the

[8] Of course, parental expression is hardly the only determinant of children's habitual ways of expressing aggression. Many inhibited mothers have children who often engage in physical attacks. Occasionally, a parent encourages this behavior because of an unconscious need to experience it vicariously. Sometimes the child cooperates in the collusion because he wants to behave in a manner different from that of his parents. A discrepancy between the aggressive behavior of child and parent may also result from the latter's inability to enforce discipline. This may be caused by a mother's fear to express her own, possibly repressed, hostility toward her offspring.

[9] In Chapter 3 we described the method of classifying mothers according to their types of discipline.

model of an attacker, we anticipated that he would probably be very direct in his aggression. When a mother expresses her hostility overtly, she may become a target for her son's retaliation. It is also easy for the attacking boy, in his excitement, to convince himself that he is fighting injustice. As a result, his action may cover up his guilt and help him to deceive himself about his fear. Behind the mask of a bully, the coward often quakes.

Quite a contrasting picture can be drawn of the child whose parents, instead of punishing him physically, use reasonable appeals, appear calm, act hurt if he misbehaves, and patiently plead with him to control himself. Sometimes, neither the parents nor the boy know they are angry; often, it is only his guilt of which the boy is painfully aware. He feels he has no one to blame but himself, and he has few methods of atoning. If he wishes to please his mother, who so clearly wants to help rather than hurt him, he must vow to improve his behavior. Since she reveals no anger, she provides no focus for his hostility.

Because of the foregoing speculations, we anticipated that children whose parents favored corporal discipline would express aggression most directly in their story endings, and that children who were manipulated psychologically would seek indirect substitutes. We also predicted that boys whose parents scolded them or deprived them of privileges would express aggression less directly than the corporally punished and more directly than the psychologically manipulated.

DATA: SOCIAL CLASS, DISCIPLINE, AND DIRECTNESS OF AGGRESSION

The associations with directness of aggression of both social class and discipline are reported in Table 14-1, which contains a summary of all the primary results concerning the directness of aggression.[10] Discipline is significantly associated with the directness of expression, but social class is not.

We had not anticipated that the association between social class and the projective measure would be so small. The results are not improved when we compare the middle and working classes within the entrepreneurial and bureaucratic settings. Social positions alone, despite the impression we gain from sociological descriptions, are just not adequate to predict directness of aggres-

[10] The detailed data tables may be found in Appendix D.

**TABLE 14-1**

Background Conditions and Directness With Which Aggression is Expressed

| *Conditions* | *Trends: Boxes with Largest Frequencies* | *N* | *Relation* | *Probability* |
|---|---|---|---|---|
| Social class | — | 115 | .07 ($\tau$) | $<.30$ (1t) |
| Discipline | Direct aggression & corporal discipline | 115 | .30 ($\tau$) | $<.001$ (1t) |
| Within MC: discipline & directness of aggression | Indirect aggression & psychological discipline | 38 | .35 ($\tau$) | .02 (1t) |
| Within WC: discipline & directness of aggression | Direct aggression & corporal discipline | 77 | .37 ($\tau$) | $<.001$ (1t) |
| Type of reward | — | 115 | 1.44 ($\chi^2$) | .50 |
| Mothers' attitudes about control | — | 115 | .16 ($\chi^2$) | $<.70$ |
| Mothers' affective control | Direct aggression & lack of control | 115 | .26 ($\tau$) | $<.001$ (1t) |

sion in story endings. We probably cannot attribute this lack of significance solely to a deficiency in our measurement of social status, since social class is related to quite a few other variables which we investigated. Similarly, it is hard to explain the negative result in terms of some drawback in the test of directness of aggression, since this variable is also significantly related to certain other background variables, some of which are significantly associated with social class. The very complex association between class and the expression of anger is one we shall continue to explore throughout this chapter.

As anticipated, the aggression in story endings of children whose parents have favored psychological techniques is predominantly indirect. The aggression in story endings of the corporally punished youngsters is predominantly direct. Groups disciplined by less extreme techniques are intermediate in the directness with which they express aggression in the stories.

DISCIPLINE AND SOCIAL CLASS

It was difficult to reject completely the descriptions which link social position with the expression of anger. Relevant to these descriptions is one finding that we have reported in Chapter 4: Social position and type of discipline are significantly related. Middle-class mothers tend to favor psychological techniques, and working-class mothers favor the corporal methods.[11] This result raises an interesting problem. To phrase the issue most simply: working-class mothers beat their sons, boys who are beaten express their aggression directly, yet working-class children do not necessarily express themselves directly. Correspondingly, middle-class mothers manipulate their sons psychologically, psychologically manipulated boys use indirect methods to express their aggression, yet middle-class children are not always indirect. These results make sense if we assume that neither class tends to have a monopoly on any method, although each class may have its typical method.

These speculations led to an analysis of the relation between aggression and discipline within each social class. We were particularly concerned with the reactions to the projective test of children whose disciplinary experiences were and were not characteristic of their social class.

When computed separately within the middle class and within the working class, the association between discipline and the directness with which aggression is expressed remains significant. As indicated in Table 14-2, the trends are the same for both classes: Psychological discipline tends to go with indirect expression, corporal with direct expression. Since we anticipated a progression, we used the modification of Kendall's method described in the first chapter.

It seems that if the working class mother has used psychological methods, in part or whole, her son expresses himself indirectly, like the middle-class boy whose mother has used psychological methods. And if a middle-class mother has used corporal methods, her son tends to express himself directly. Eleven of the

[11] Of the 33 mothers rated as using intermediate disciplinary techniques, 18 are members of the upper working class, 10 of the lower working class, 4 of the lower middle class, and 1 of the upper middle class.

**TABLE 14-2**

Social Class, Parental Discipline, and Directness of Aggression in Story Endings

| | *Social Class* | | | | | |
|---|---|---|---|---|---|---|
| | *Middle* | | | *Working* | | |
| *Directness of Aggression* | *Psychol. Discipline* | *Intermed. Discipline* | *Corporal Discipline* | *Psychol. Discipline* | *Intermed. Discipline* | *Corporal Discipline* |
| Indirect | 19 | 1 | 1 | 8 | 17 | 13 |
| Direct | 10 | 4 | 3 | 1 | 11 | 27 |
| Proportion (indirect) | .66 | .20 | .25 | .89 | .61 | .33 |
| *N* | 38 | | | 77 | | |
| $\tau$ | .35 | | | .37 | | |
| *P* | .02 (1t) | | | <.001 (1t) | | |

thirteen boys disciplined in ways not typical of their social class respond to the story completion test in accordance with expectations derived from the kinds of discipline, not in accordance with expectations derived from social class backgrounds. When children in one social class have been subjected to the discipline most characteristic of the other class, the directness with which anger is expressed is determined more by discipline than by socio-economic status.

Although the association between social class and directness is not significant, different results might still have occurred within each disciplinary group. If the trends differed in direction, they might have been masked when the three types of discipline were ignored in the analysis of social class and projective endings. However, we find no significant associations between class and directness within the disciplinary groups. From this result and the previous one, we conclude that type of discipline, rather than membership in a particular social class, is the predominant determinant of the directness with which anger is expressed.

### Reward

Descriptions of child-rearing practices in American society (6, 13) led us to expect the class differences in type of reward reported in Chapter 2. According to the literature, middle-class parents favor verbal recognition and anticipate that their sons will be rewarded by the internal satisfactions they gain from behaving well. In comparison, the working classes tend to employ concrete rewards such as money or candy, rather than praise or expressions of affection.

To gain information concerning rewards, we asked each mother how she acted when her son had just done something she felt was very good. Depending on her answers, we classified her method as being predominantly symbolic, intermediate, or predominantly concrete.[12] Type of reward or recognition is significantly related to social class, but, as indicated in Table 14-1, it is not significantly related to directness with which aggression is expressed in the story endings.[13]

### Loss of control

How does a boy behave when a mother who usually loses control of herself tells him to control himself? Or when a mother who is always controlled tells him to fight when attacked? In discussing identification in Chapter 3 we predicted that, in cases of contradiction, the sons would follow their mothers' practices rather than their preachings. To test our prediction, we first asked the mothers the question: "Some parents feel it is all right to let a child know when they are angry and upset at him, since these feelings can't be hidden from him. Others find it best to remain calm and collected and never punish a child in anger. How do you feel about this?" In terms of the replies, we divided the mothers into two groups, one favoring free expression and one stressing control.[14] Approximately two-thirds of the mothers feel they should

[12] Chapter 3 contains a more detailed description of the method.

[13] We also explored the possibility that middle-class mothers give their children more recognition than do mothers in the working class. To obtain data relevant to this hypothesis, we asked mothers to select from a list of six possible reactions to good deeds the three that they used most often. Three of the responses signify strong recognition. A typical item is: "Tell him what a good boy he is and praise him for doing well." Three other responses describe less enthusiastic recognition. A typical item is: "Show him you expected it of him." Compared to working-class mothers, those from the middle class select more items from the list that signify an attempt to give their children a sense of importance. Like rewards, amount of recognition is not significantly related to projective scores.

[14] There is 90 per cent agreement between the two judges in their coding of responses.

control themselves. As we expected, most American mothers value self-control. This attitude, because it is so widespread, is not significantly related to social class. As indicated in Table 14-1, the reported attitudes about the importance of maintaining emotional control do not shed any light on the directness with which the children express aggressive needs.

We get quite another picture when we shift from mothers' opinions to actions. In terms of their responses to the total interview, we rated the women's actual self-control while punishing their sons. We again divided the mothers into two groups, one displaying a lack of emotional control, and the other some control.[15] Like discipline and reward, the amount of actual control is significantly related to social class. Middle-class mothers are more controlled than those from the working class. The association between actual control and preferred type of discipline is also very significant. Mothers who exert control over their own emotions favor psychological techniques; mothers who lack control employ corporal methods. We imagine that they lose their tempers and then strike out without thinking of the consequences. The intermediate disciplinary group is almost equally divided with respect to the two kinds of control.

The critical comparison involves the parents' self-control and their sons' responses to the projective test. If the direction of aggression is a product of identification, a son should not necessarily follow his mother's admonitions, but should model himself after the picture of her that he gets from her actions. He should control himself only if she controls herself. Our measure of the sons' control is, of course, the directness with which the major characters in the stories express aggression.

Table 14-1 reveals that absence of control is associated with very direct expression of anger, and that presence of control is associated with indirect expression of anger. In fact, the degree of maternal control decreases progressively as the directness of aggression varies from very indirect to very direct.

### The most direct forms of aggression

A second group of analyses was performed to explore further the common impression that members of the working class

[15] There is 87 per cent agreement between the two judges in their coding of responses.

differ from members of the middle class in the directness with which they express anger. We reasoned that the blue- and white-collar workers may actually differ, but only in the extent to which they favor the most extreme forms of direct aggression. Such a trend might have been hidden in the analysis of the total range of directness.

To obtain extreme reactions, we selected direct attack and flight for separate analysis. We categorized a boy as using the most direct attack if, in at least one of his story endings, he described the main character as physically attacking the frustrating object, expressing open defiance, attacking the object, but by some slightly modified means, or attacking a displaced object.

Flight is closely related to direct attack. Both reactions involve a recognition of the source of frustration, and both involve physical movement. They may even occur together: A hero flees while he plans an act of retaliation. For reasons that we have cited, we expected to find physical attack and flight most often in the story endings by working-class boys and boys who had been primarily subjected to corporal discipline. Table 14-3 reveals that all four predictions are supported by our data.

**TABLE 14-3**

Background Conditions and the Most Direct Forms of Aggression

| *Form of Aggression* | *Condition* | *Trends: Boxes with Largest Frequencies* | *N* | *Relation* | *Probability* |
|---|---|---|---|---|---|
| Direct attack | Social class | WC & attack present | 115 | 2.52 ($\chi^2$) | .06 (1t) |
| | Discipline | Corporal & attack present | 115 | .25 ($\tau$) | .001 (1t) |
| Flight | Social class | MC & flight absent | 115 | 5.82 ($\chi^2$) | .01 (1t) |
| | Discipline | Psychological & flight absent | 115 | .32 ($\tau$) | .001 (1t) |

*Social Class.* Working-class boys exceed the middle-class group in themes of attack and of flight. The classes must overlap considerably in their use of other direct endings and those which we call *somewhat direct.* We imagine that the small number of boys who mentioned flight reflects the American fear of being regarded as a "quitter" or a "coward." Not uncommonly, sons of working-class parents see themselves as evading responsibility. Such boys sometimes learn to cope with the pressures of middle-class authorities by retreating.

*Discipline.* As anticipated, it is the corporally disciplined boys who most commonly write story endings containing themes of direct attack and flight. Such themes are significantly less frequent in the endings by boys who have been disciplined by psychological means. Also infrequent is the recourse to flight by subjects whose punishment has been evenly divided between the two disciplines. Twenty-eight members of this group come from the working class. Yet, despite their origins, most of these subjects respond like the psychologically disciplined, middle-class boys. Apparently, even a mixed type of discipline involving some psychological appeals is enough to dispel a tendency toward flight. The conditions of corporal discipline and working-class background maximize the references to flight.

### Boys' opinions about the necessity of corporal discipline

If disciplinary methods favored by parents are transmitted by identification, then when the children mature they should also favor the same types of methods. We explored this hypothesis indirectly by obtaining the associations with social class of disciplinary methods and of the subjects' attitudes concerning the necessity of corporal punishment. We asked, "Do you think that boys sometimes need to be whipped or get a licking?" We next asked the boys detailed questions about their most recent experiences.[16]

*Social Class and Discipline.* Table 14-4 shows that the classes differ very significantly. The proportion of middle-class subjects increases progressively as opinion about corporal discipline varies from "Necessary" to "Qualified" to "Not Necessary"; conversely, the proportion of working-class boys increases progressively as opinion is varied in the opposite direction. The attitude toward "lickings" is also significantly related to type of discipline. Most of the psychologically manipulated boys consider beatings unnecessary or give qualified answers, while most of the boys whose

[16] We are indebted to Miss Elaine Platsky for her assistance with the interviews.

**TABLE 14-4**

*Boys' Opinions About the Necessity of Corporal Discipline*

| Background Conditions | Trends: Boxes with Greatest Frequencies | N | $\tau$ | Probability |
|---|---|---|---|---|
| Social class | WC favor corporal punishment | 107 | .37 | .001 (1t) |
| Discipline | Psychologically disciplined do not favor corporal punishment | 107 | .25 | .001 (1t) |
| Intelligence within working class | Boys with low intelligence favor corporal punishment | 57 | .32 | .01 (1t) |
| Intelligence within corporally disciplined | Boys with low intelligence favor corporal punishment | 36 | .33 | .03 (1t) |

parents have resorted to corporal discipline advocate beatings. It seems that the children whose mothers have beaten them to discourage them from beating others, will, when they are fathers, probably beat their own sons to discourage them from beating others.

*Intelligence.* It will be recalled that directness of aggression in story endings was not significantly associated with any of the subtests of intelligence. Among the working-class subjects, however, the verbal subtest is related to boys' opinions about the necessity of corporal punishment. The middle-class group does not have a sufficient range of scores on the test of verbal intelligence to warrant an analysis. As indicated in Table 14-4, those working-class boys with average intelligence are most inclined to favor corporal discipline. The brighter boys in the corporally disciplined group qualify their opinions or oppose corporal methods.

The results suggest an interesting conclusion, if we can assume that the subjects all interpreted the word "licking" in the same way,[17] and that boys with average verbal facility were stat-

[17] Our interviews with boys indicate that the same word, "licking," can mean grossly different things to different children. When asked to describe in detail the most recent punishments they had experienced, the corporally disciplined boys said that their parents used boards, sticks, knives, paddles, or "anything handy," and struck on the head, face, neck, and limbs. Nearly two thirds of this group said that they had received lickings within the

ing their true beliefs about corporal discipline, rather than merely giving unconsidered impulsive answers to the questions. Perhaps high verbal intelligence tends to liberate children from the determinism which transmits disciplinary methods from one generation to another. In other words, corporal punishment may remain a family habit only if intelligence is limited.

### AGGRESSIVE BEHAVIOR TOWARD TEACHERS

We found that children's expressions of anger on a projective test reflect their parents' methods of discipline. Would directness of aggression in actual behavior show the same results? We measured aggressive behavior toward teachers by having four peers of each subject describe him in terms of one of two alternatives: (1) When he gets scolded by the teacher or some other adult, does he: (a) feel bad, or (b) get mad at the teacher, and (2) He would talk back to the teacher if he thought he were right: (a) yes, or (b) no.[18,19]

Table 14-5 shows that the projective test is a good predictor of these ratings of behavior toward teachers. Peers of the corporally disciplined children say that these youngsters "get mad at" and "talk back" to the teacher. Unlike directness in the stories, ratings of aggressive behavior are significantly related to socioeconomic differences. As viewed by their peers, middle-class boys are most likely to "feel bad" when scolded and not to "talk back" to their teachers, while working-class boys are inclined to act aggressively. We imagine that the boys' ratings of their friends placed a heavier weighting on the more direct forms of aggression than did the rankings of story endings.

---

past year. The psychologically disciplined group reported lickings as being very rare. Even then, they were usually depicted in terms of a mild spanking on the buttocks.

[18] The alternatives selected by the four judges were pooled for each subject and he was then placed in one of three categories: aggressive in 66–100 per cent of the ratings (most aggressive); aggressive in 20–65 per cent of the ratings (moderate); or aggressive in 0–19 per cent of the ratings (least aggressive).

[19] We are grateful to J. E. Keller for formulating these questions and collecting these data.

**TABLE 14-5**

**Aggressive Behavior Toward Teachers** [a]

| *Variables Associated with Aggressive Behavior* | *Trends: Boxes with Greatest Frequencies* | *N* | $\tau$ | *Probability* |
|---|---|---|---|---|
| Directness of aggression in story endings | Direct endings in stories and aggressive behavior | 95 | .28 | .01 (1t) |
| Discipline | Corporal discipline & aggressive behavior | 95 | .25 | .01 (1t) |
| Social class | WC and aggressive behavior | 96 | .17 | .05 (1t) |

[a] The distributions may be found in Appendix D.

## Summary

While the total range of aggression expressed in a story completion test is not related to socio-economic status, the most direct forms, attack and flight, are significantly related or close to significance. The directness with which aggression is expressed, either in story endings or in behavior toward teachers, is significantly associated with discipline employed in the home. Mothers who have used corporal discipline have children who express their aggressive needs directly, and mothers who have manipulated their sons psychologically have children who express anger indirectly. Mothers who have favored mixed techniques have sons who are neither very direct nor very indirect in their aggression.

Our subjects act as their parents act, but not necessarily in accordance with their parents' requests. Women from the working class lose control of themselves, punish corporally, and have sons who, while they do not necessarily express anger directly, are inclined to favor fighting or fleeing. Their sons also advocate spanking, particularly if they are of low verbal intelligence. Women from middle-class backgrounds retain control of themselves while disciplining their children, employ psychological manipulation, and have sons who, while they do not necessarily express anger indirectly, are least likely to attack, to flee, or to advocate spanking.

## References

1. Aberle, D. F., & Naegele, K. D. Middle-class fathers' occupational role and attitudes toward children. *Amer. J. Orthopsychiat.*, 1952, *22*, 366–78.
2. Allinsmith, Beverly B. Parental discipline and children's aggression in two social classes. Unpubl. Ph.D. dissertation. Univ. of Michigan, 1954.
3. Beres, D. Clinical notes on aggression in children. In Eissler, Ruth S., Freud, Anna, *et al.* (Eds.), *Psychoanalytic study of the child,* Vol. 7. New York: International Universities Press, 1947, pp. 241–63.
4. Bettlheim, B. Mental health and current mores. *Amer. J. Orthopsychiat.*, 1952, *22*, 76–88.
5. Davis, A. Socialization and adolescent personality. In T. M. Newcomb and E. L. Hartley (Eds.), *Readings in social psychology.* New York: Holt, 1947.
6. Davis, A. American status systems and the socialization of the child. In C. Kluckhohn and H. A. Murray (Eds.), *Personality in nature, society and culture.* New York: Alfred A. Knopf, 1948, pp. 459–68.
7. Dollard, J., Doob, L. W., Miller, N. E., Mower, O. H., & Sears, R. R. *Frustration and aggression.* New Haven: Yale Univ. Press, 1939.
8. Erikson, E. H. *Childhood and society.* New York: Norton, 1950.
9. Freud, Anna. Notes on aggression. In Lorand, S., *et al.* (Eds.), *Yearbook of Psychoanalysis,* Vol. 6, New York: International Universities Press, 1950.
10. Freud, S. *Beyond the pleasure principle.* London: Hogarth Press, 1922.
11. Hartmann, H. Psychoanalytic theory of the ego. In Eissler, Ruth S., Freud, Anna, *et al.* (Eds.), *Psychoanalytic study of the child,* Vol. 5. New York: International Universities Press, 1950.
12. ———, Kris, E., & Lowenstein, R. M. Notes on the theory of aggression. In Eissler, Ruth S., Freud, Anna *et al.* (Eds.), *Psychoanalytic Study of the Child,* Vols. 3/4, New York: International Universities Press, 1949.
13. Havighurst, R. J., & Taba, H. *Adolescent character and personality.* New York: Wiley, 1949.
14. Murray, H. A. *Thematic apperception test.* Cambridge, Massachusetts: Harvard Univ. Press, 1943.

15. Sears, R. R. Symposium on genetic psychology: 3. Effects of frustration and anxiety on fantasy aggression. *Amer. J. Orthopsychiat.*, 1951, *21*, 498–505.
16. Symonds, P. M. *Picture story test.* New York: Bureau of Publications, Teachers College, Columbia University, 1948.
17. ———. *Adolescent fantasy.* New York: Columbia Univ. Press, 1949.
18. Thurstone, L. L., & Thurstone, Thelma G. *The Chicago tests of primary mental abilities.* Single booklet edition for ages 11 to 17. Chicago: Science Research Associates, 1943.

# 15

## EXPRESSIVE STYLES

## III. Two Styles of Expression: Motoric and Conceptual *

By definition, an expressive style is a trait; it is discernible in many different kinds of behavior patterns. We may sometimes observe the same expressive style, not only in a person's reactions to conflict, but in such varied forms of expression as his manner of walking, his attempts to solve conceptual problems, and his values with regard to different topics. So accustomed is each man to his own particular way of doing things that he is seldom aware of his style unless someone points it out to him. Even then, he may be unable to visualize his customary arm movements, or the extent to which he lets others take the initiative in social contacts. But the lack of conscious purpose is no indicator of the importance of expressive style, which is part of all our social behavior. We shall now describe an investigation of two expressive styles—*motoric* and *conceptual.*

### Examples of styles

A person's physical expression is frequently more indicative of his intended meaning than is his verbal statement. Let us con-

* In the research team, Elton B. McNeil was responsible for the research to be reported and for the preparation of the chapter, which is based in part on his doctoral dissertation (7).

sider two hypothetical men who are both seeing a psychotherapist. The therapist asks each about his difficulties. A transcript of the first man's remarks would reveal very little. He says that he just feels badly; he sincerely tries to cooperate, but he cannot think of much to say. This does not mean, however, that he is not communicating. He may do so very successfully, if unintentionally, not with words but with the signals of another language, the language of gesture. By movements of his eyebrows, mouth, hands, and shoulders, he conveys some of his message more clearly than he could with words.

The second man behaves quite differently when asked about his troubles. He gives what amounts to an analysis of his difficulties. In fact, he even delivers a short talk from prepared notes. In addition, in contrast to the first man, his face looks impassive, and his body is almost motionless, although his tension is betrayed by an occasional tremor in his voice.

Such expressive approaches reflect distinct styles of life. In referring to them as styles we imply that they are evident in many different kinds of activities. As we shall see, the man who unconsciously conveys his needs with his body typically earns his living by skillful use of his muscles and enjoys hobbies that afford him physical expression. He is often at a loss if he has to use concepts or symbols. The man who can paint a picture expressively and solve an abstract problem efficiently is seldom a laborer. He may even become uncomfortable on the unavoidable occasion when he has to work something out with his muscles.

We refer to the first expressive style, which makes such heavy use of the voluntary, and particularly the large muscles of the body as *motoric*. The second style, which involves the manipulation of ideas, is called *conceptual*. These styles are the topics of the research reported in this chapter. Because we have just begun to explore their characteristics, we have not yet tried to demonstrate their relation to the resolution of conflict. We have explored their generality by sampling such different kinds of activities as solving a problem, mimicking an emotion, choosing an occupation, and painting a picture. We have, in addition, examined their antecedents in different social positions and child-rearing practices.

## Predictions Concerning Expressive Style and Social Position

### SOCIAL CLASS

*Evidence From Patients.* As we indicated in Chapter 13, our interest in motoric and conceptual styles of expression was first kindled by the unequal occurrence of certain personality disorders in different social classes. Symptoms such as conversion hysteria and catatonia, which are more frequent in patients from the working than the middle class, often involve malfunctions of the voluntary muscles. Symptoms such as obsessions and depressions, which are more common in patients from the middle class, are often accompanied by an inhibition of many voluntary movements and by ruminative attempts to figure out the solutions of conflicts.

Since expressive styles are learned early in life, we concluded that normal members of the working class would show the same styles of expression as mental patients from that class. Normal working-class people would resolve their conflicts motorically, while normal middle-class people would substitute conceptual outlets.

*Literature on the Styles of Normal Children.* Many theorists have referred to the connections between social class and *motoric* and *conceptual* styles without using these labels. McCarthy (6) quotes an observer in nineteenth century Spain as commenting that: "The child of the rich understands more words and less actions and the child of the poor less words and more actions." This observation is not very different from the statements of a twentieth century American researcher (3) that ". . . the middle class handles chiefly symbols for a living, the working class handles chiefly things . . . ," that the middle-class child "learns that his language is a mark of his station in life. . . ." (4) and that ". . . the child of the working-class family is allowed a deeper physical enjoyment of his body during the first three or four years than is the middle class child." [1]

[1] Members of the two social classes differ in others ways which are not necessarily caused by, but are consistent with, predilections for particular expressive styles. Most professional boxers come from the working class.

INTEGRATION

We were more confident that differences between classes would be significant within entrepreneurial than within bureaucratic organizations. When organizations become bureaucratic, and their functions are divided into many interdependent specialties, the manual laborer seldom has the kind of job that permits him to take the drayman's pride in his brawn or the toolmaker's interest in his craftsmanship. The worker in a bureaucratic organization works on only a small part of the total product, and must meet only minimal standards of quality to hold his job. He may engage in some physical activity, but much of his work is done by machine. We therefore expected the working-class bureaucrat to be motoric, but not to the same extent as the laborer in the entrepreneurial organization.

The white-collar member of both entrepreneurial and bureaucratic organizations must be able to manipulate concepts with ease. But a conceptual orientation is not sufficient to insure advancement in a large modern enterprise. Because jobs are so specialized, reaching the next rung in the ladder usually requires special, and sometimes lengthy, training. Among the skills that facilitate advancement, the social may be even more salient than the conceptual. Since so many people work in teams, it is usually very important to be sensitive to people's needs. For all these reasons, we anticipated that the differences between motoric and conceptual styles of expression would be less marked within bureaucratic than within entrepreneurial organizations. So little is known, however, about the psychology of personnel in large corporate enterprises that we could not make our predictions with confidence.

---

While economic instability and the low social status of the occupation probably contribute to the differences between classes, we should not overlook a special qualification that sons of manual laborers possess for boxing: their motoric expressiveness. Also congruent with expressive styles are class differences in emotional expression at church services. In middle-class congregations, the sermon on theology or moral philosophy is the norm; seldom are there physical manifestations of emotion. In certain working-class churches emotional tension sometimes increases to such a pitch that hands clap, eyes roll, and bodies jerk (1).

The split by social class in styles of expression may also contribute to changes in the gestures of immigrants after they have been in this country for a while (5). Though their styles of expression are likely to be very similar at first, they gradually begin to differ, depending, in part, on whether or not the people are moving into the middle class.

## Social Class and Motoric Orientation

We chose our subjects from the first sample described in Chapter 4.[2] In general, we predicted that boys from the working class would convey ideas most naturally by means of their bodies, but be comparatively inept when asked to express the same ideas conceptually. We thought that middle-class subjects would use conceptual approaches very comfortably, but be relatively inept when required to communicate by physical means.

### The Game of Statues

*Instructions.* To create a natural situation requiring motoric communication, we first saw each boy individually and asked him to play a modified version of the children's game of "statues." First the boy would be turned around. Then he would "freeze" in a pose that depicted an assigned theme. He was not to move outside a circle which had been drawn on the floor. We asked him to hold each pose until his picture had been taken.

In a practice session the child was asked to freeze like the statue of a policeman directing traffic. For the experiment proper he portrayed four emotional states: happiness, fear, anger, and sorrow.[3] To make sure that he understood the meaning of each emotion, we illustrated it in terms of a concrete situation. First the boy was told to act "as if you are very, very happy: as if you had just won a million dollars or got the one thing in the world you have always wanted." Next, he was instructed to behave "as if you are very, very frightened: as if the wall of a building is falling over on you or a tiger is just jumping at you." Then he was told to freeze "as if you were very, very angry: as if you see a boy beating up your little dog, or as if a reckless driver has just missed you with his car." Finally, he was instructed to "behave as if you are in a great deal of sorrow—very, very sad: as if you saved a long time for something you wanted very badly

[2] Our method of classifying subjects according to social class is described in Chapter 2.

[3] We chose these emotional states, rather than concrete jobs like swimmer, dancer, or carpenter, because we feared that the latter might be much more familiar to, or have different meanings for, boys in different social classes. Emotional states are well known to everyone.

and then lost the money, or as if you just lost your best friend."

*Analyzing Shifts in Position.* We tabulated the frequencies of dilated movements in each child's photographs. Such movements were inferred from shifts from the original position in which he stood upright, facing forward, with his hands at his sides and his feet together. The signs of dilation included a raising of either hand to the height of the waist, both hands to the waist, or one hand to the shoulder. In addition, we tabulated a spreading of the legs, a shifting of the trunk from the vertical position, or a turning from the camera.[4]

*Results.* A person who was unacquainted with our theory and predictions rated each photograph in terms of the six criteria. An analysis of our data reveals that all the differences between middle- and working-class children are in the anticipated direction, and, with one exception, are significant for all criteria of dilation.[5] The exception, which is very close to significance, involves the criterion of vertical position of the body. Table 15-1, which contains a summary of the major findings concerning social status, reveals that the boys in the two classes also differ on an over-all index of a motoric tendency.[6] There is little question that in the game of statues boys from the working class are more motorically dilated than are our middle-class subjects.

## Social Class and Conceptual Orientation

We predicted that a task requiring a conceptual approach would produce a reversal of the previous results. We thought that boys in the middle class would manipulate concepts more easily than would boys in the working class. Before we could test this

[4] In the order in which the last three were presented, they were identified by the following criteria: Spread is greater than that required for normal stance and balance; the line perpendicular to the floor does not divide the subject into symmetrical halves; greater parts of top and bottom halves of body are turned from the camera.

[5] The complete tables for all results reported in this chapter may be found in Appendix D.

[6] To construct the over-all index, we first obtained a distribution of subjects in terms of the number of signs of motoric dilation. Then we divided the boys into three groups. Criteria for membership in the different groups were five signs or more, between two and four signs, and one or no signs.

hypothesis, we had to solve a difficult methodological problem. Most concepts are expressed by means of verbal symbols, but we could not use a verbal test because of the superiority of the middle-class subjects on such instruments. After examining many tasks, we chose two different types. We shall describe the first task, painting,[7] in this section; the second, manual problem solving, is described in the next section.

THE PAINTING OF ABSTRACTIONS

*Instructions.* We assembled the children in groups of ten or less in special testing rooms. Each boy sat at a desk on which there were five pots of poster paint—red, orange, blue, green, and black, five sheets of 11½ x 16½-inch newsprint, some paint brushes, heavy drawing pencils, a box of crayons, some toothpicks, a toothbrush, and a cup of water. First, we gave him five minutes to paint or draw a theme of his choice. This practice session was intended to familiarize him with the materials and to show him that we would not object to noise or free play during the painting period. After the introductory five-minute period he was told:

> Now we are going to do something a little bit different. We are going to do some painting, but you can use the other materials in addition to the paint if you feel like it. I am going to name some things I would like you to paint for me. Paint what you *think* and *feel* about these things. Just use the materials to express the idea or feeling behind the topic. It is not important whether or not anyone will be able to recognize what's in your

[7] The choice of painting raised four difficult problems concerning the interpretation of results. First, the middle-class boys might have been trained to paint in nursery school, or they might have had some special instruction elsewhere. Second, we were concerned about the extent to which painting is a motoric act. Upon investigating these two possibilities, we were inclined to dismiss them. We found no differences in training, and observations of the boys during the painting session revealed that almost all movement was confined to digital manipulation of the artistic materials.

It was also possible that boys in the two social classes differed in their information about abstract art. Finally, it could be claimed that middle-class boys have had previous experience with abstraction, so that even if they do not think conceptually, they can grasp the instructions to draw abstractly more readily than can working-class boys. All information pertinent to these interpretations tended to refute them, but we could not reject them with confidence. This is one reason why we later used an additional technique for eliciting a conceptual approach.

> paintings. It will be like an abstract painting. You don't have to paint the thing the way it may actually look to people. Use the materials to express the feeling or idea behind it.

Then he was asked to portray the same four emotional themes he had expressed in the game of statues.

In what sense can we claim that such a task requires a conceptual orientation? We thought that such an orientation was elicited by the instructions to express the ideas or feelings abstractly. Before the subjects would portray the assigned theme, they had to develop a pictorial concept.

*Analysis.* Guided by literature on the interpretation of artistic productions, we developed six criteria of dilation and constriction. We assumed that an unconstricted person would employ paint only, portray unrecognizable objects, use four or more colors, and cover most of the paper.[8] If he were constricted, we thought he would outline his shapes with black paint, and that his composition would occupy a small area.[9] A judge with no knowledge of our theory or predictions rated all paintings.

*Results.* With one exception, the differences are in the predicted directions, although the trends are not so marked as those obtained for motoric expression. Two of the six differences are significant, and one is close to significance. Contrary to the prediction, the association between expressive style and the criterion of *paint only* is in the opposite direction from the one predicted. It would have been significant if we had not predicted direction and made two-tailed tests. Whether this result reflects a poor criterion or a contradiction of our hypothesis we cannot say at this point. Boys in the two classes differ very significantly on an over-all index of conceptual orientation.[10]

While the statistics reveal marked differences in motoric and conceptual style, they do not convey the extent of the contrasts

[8] The minimal size involved a vertical dimension of at least eight inches and a horizontal dimension of at least ten inches.

[9] The maximal size involved a vertical dimension of five inches and a horizontal dimension of six inches.

[10] To construct this index, we first obtained a distribution of subjects based on the number of signs of conceptual orientation. Then we assigned each boy to one of the three groups. Criteria for membership in these groups were five signs or more, between two and four signs, and one or no signs.

**TABLE 15-1**

Social Class and Expressive Styles of Children and Parents

| *Expressive Style* | *Trends: Boxes with Greatest Frequencies* | *N* | *Relation* | *Probability* |
|---|---|---|---|---|
| Over-all motoric tendency in game of statues | WC & most motoric | 99 | .29 ($\tau$) | <.01 (1t) |
| Over-all conceptual tendency in paintings | MC & most conceptual | 99 | .26 ($\tau$) | <.01 (1t) |
| Conceptual tendency in spatial problem | MC & most conceptual | 85 | 8.61 ($\chi^2$) | <.001 (1t) |
| Over-all conceptual-motoric tendency | WC & most motoric; MC & most conceptual | 83 | .37 ($\tau$) | <.001 (1t) |
| Conceptual and motoric tendencies in mothers' reasons for leisure activities | WC & intermediate; MC & conceptual | 117 | .19 ($\tau$) | .02 (1t) |
| Conceptual and motoric tendencies in mothers' lists of satisfactions in jobs | WC & motoric; MC & conceptual | 102 | .37 ($\tau$) | <.001 (1t) |

observed by members of our staff. In the game of statues the typical working-class boy threw himself into the task with great spontaneity. The middle-class subject, even when his pose was muscular, was often self-conscious. His halting gestures conveyed the impression that he was not accustomed to communicating with his body. Yet once he began to paint, his motoric hesitancy and awkwardness usually vanished. When the working-class boy painted he became tentative or complained that he just could not get started.

A SPATIAL PROBLEM [11]

We decided to construct one other conceptual instrument, because we felt that the painting test did not have the apparent validity of the game of statues. We also sought another kind of activity, so that we could test the generality of the conceptual orienta-

[11] This part of the study was done with the second sample of subjects whose characteristics are described in Chapter 4. We are indebted to Harold M. Herman for his assistance in designing the study and collecting the data.

tion. Spatial problems seemed to be the most promising, and we finally decided on a modified version of the Carl Hollow Square Test (2), an instrument for measuring the subject's speed in fitting three or four blocks into a square frame. There are several problems, each requiring its own combination of blocks. The blocks are triangular, and two of their three dimensions are cut at either 45- or 90-degree angles. Even when given the correct blocks, most boys find them much harder to fit together than they seem at first glance. We increased their difficulty by asking each boy to choose the blocks from a larger group of sixteen.

In giving instructions for the Carl Hollow Square Test, we emphasized the goal of solving the problem: "Now, let's see if you can put the blocks into the square correctly." The score was the total number of different patterns a boy attempted in fifteen minutes. We tabulated an attempt at a pattern if the subject first combined two or more blocks and then inserted them together in the square. We expected that boys from the middle class would assemble more patterns than would boys from the working class.

The results parallel those obtained from the paintings. As indicated in Table 15-1, boys in the middle class are significantly more conceptual than are boys in the working class. The difference does not result simply from the greater activity of the middle-class subjects. The groups do not differ in the number of blocks picked up. However, in approaching the problem, working-class subjects are likely to fit one block at a time, while middle class boys are more inclined to work with combinations of two or three.[12]

[12] While we were conducting this part of the study we became curious about the extent to which styles of expressive behavior can be deliberately controlled. We anticipated that class differences might disappear if the boys were directed to orient themselves either conceptually or motorically. We used two sets of instructions. One encouraged the subjects to take a conceptual approach: ". . . it helps to work these problems if you spend some time trying to figure out what is the best way to do them . . . this time as long as you are not actually touching the blocks the time won't be up as fast." Another set of instructions encouraged the subjects to be motoric: ". . . you can solve the problem better by trying all the possible ways to fit these together that you can in the time allowed."

On the first trial all the subjects took the test under the goal-oriented condition. On the second trial one half received the instructions emphasizing a conceptual orientation and the other half received the instructions emphasizing a motoric orientation. The results confirm our predictions. When all the subjects attempted to figure out solutions, and when they were trying every combination manually, the differences between classes were no longer significant.

## Social Class and Interests

We had to obtain class differences in many different kinds of activities to test the generality of expressive styles. In addition to statues, painting, and problem solving, we chose interests in hobbies, games, and occupations as our final topics.

### INTERVIEWS

We gathered our information by interviewing each child in the initial sample. First, we asked him to name his most preferred activities and hobbies and then to pick from a list of reasons regarding leisure time activity the three he thought were most important. There were eight reasons, four conceptual and four motoric, and they were placed in alternating order. Examples of reasons are: "gives me plenty of exercise" and "develops my mind."

In a second part of the interview the subject chose from a list of ten hobbies the three he preferred most, and then picked the three most attractive games from a list of ten. Equal numbers of conceptual and motoric items were arranged in alternating order. Some of the choices among the hobbies and games were "collecting stamps," "body building club," "guessing games," and "tug of war."

Next, the subject selected from a group of eight job characteristics the three he deemed most important about the job he would like to have in adulthood. Half of the list was motoric and half conceptual. Among the alternatives were "involves writing at a desk," "keeps me in good physical shape," and "gives me complex problems to solve." He was instructed to evaluate each job, not in terms of its status or the level of income provided but rather in terms of those aspects that seemed most important. Then we showed him a list of jobs which had been judged by a national sample of adolescents as being very similar to each other in status and income. Half of the jobs were motoric and half conceptual.[13]

[13] Questions in the interview required a number of preliminary revisions before we were confident that the alternatives were approximately equal in attractiveness. We discarded Automobile Repairman from the list of jobs, for example, because we found that most parents disapproved of it and nearly all the children chose it first or second.

From the list of jobs he chose three that he would most like to have if he could have any job he wanted. We inserted this question as a control. We did not expect any differences between social classes in the ideal jobs boys dream about. Finally, he selected the three jobs in the list that were most like the ones he would probably get.

#### Analysis and results

On the basis of his response to each item, a subject was classified as being predominantly conceptual, intermediate, or motoric. In order to be labeled as *conceptual* or *motoric* within a particular category, it was necessary that he make the choice both first and most frequently. He was classified as *intermediate* if he selected an equal number of conceptual and motoric items, or if the majority of his selections did not agree with his first choice.

On all five comparisons, which are described in Appendix D, boys from the working-class express more motoric preferences than do boys in the middle class. Only three of the five results have a probability of less than 5 per cent. In both classes the motoric reasons for leisure activities and games outweigh the conceptual ones. This makes sense in view of the subjects' ages. In early adolescence boys are very concerned with developing physical prowess because it establishes their masculine status. But when the boys list the jobs they expect, or describe reasons for choosing occupations, they make judgments in terms of actual probabilities.[14]

## Social Class, Parental Reactions, and Expressive Styles

Thus far we have found the anticipated differences between boys in the two social classes when they played statues, painted pictures, took a block test, and expressed attitudes toward leisure activities and jobs. Furthermore, the association between social class and expressive style is the same as the type that we observed

[14] As we anticipated, there is no significant difference between the classes with regard to the most desired jobs: the conceptual ones are chosen by boys in both classes.

in published reports concerning the symptoms of psychiatric patients. Participants from the middle class tend to express themselves conceptually, those from the working class motorically. Because expressive styles are probably established in the first few years of a person's life, we now examine differences in parental reactions which might contribute to divergent styles. We shall focus on the activities and occupations that parents prefer for their sons, and such child-rearing practices as discipline, reward, and mothers' self-control.

### Mothers' preferences

*Interviews.* An introductory question called for a listing of activities that the mother would prefer her son to cultivate in his free time and the reasons for her preferences. The interviewer then asked her to choose the three most important reasons for an activity from a list of seven. Some were conceptual and some motoric. The list included: "It involves planning and organization," "It builds both a sound mind and a strong body," [15] and "It gives him plenty of exercise."

Next, the mother was questioned about the advice she would give her son about nonfinancial considerations in selecting a job. After this question she was asked to pick from a list of seven characteristics of any job, the three that she thought were most important.[16] We predicted that middle-class mothers would select activities permitting conceptual expression and that working-class mothers would select activities permitting motoric expression.

*Results.* Unlike their offspring, mothers from the two social classes differ significantly in their reasons for favoring a leisure activity for their sons. Table 15-1 reveals that the greatest contrast is in the choice of jobs. The differences between adults may reflect the long experience that they have had in their particular socioeconomic positions. They are probably better able than their off-

[15] Before we inserted this item we found that most parents mentioned it spontaneously and found it hard to choose from the remainder. By including it, we allowed them to make the spontaneous choice, which we did not count. Then, they had no difficulty in making the next selections, which we did count.

[16] Here again we had to insert an item that many parents mentioned spontaneously: "The child should be happy whatever he does." Almost all the women voted for the happy child. Then they expressed their next preferences with little hesitation.

spring to appreciate the satisfactions that are inherent in these class positions. As for the conceptual and motoric aspects of a job that the mothers consider most important, the differences between classes are significant and in the anticipated directions.

### Child-rearing practices

It would be difficult to understand the origins of motoric expression without considering the methods used by parents to train and restrict children in muscular expression and locomotion. When a baby first crawls and then walks, he requires considerable supervision, if only to protect his safety. He cannot be allowed to run into the street; he must be kept from the medicine cabinet; if he lives in the cramped quarters of a small city apartment, he must frequently restrict his movements.

The child also learns many incidental lessons in the course of his training. From his parents' methods of regulating his physical expression and locomotion, he may conclude that they require impossibly high standards of performance, that he can manipulate adults by the adequacy of his performance in front of strangers, or that uninhibited physical expression is dangerous. We were particularly impressed by the incidental learning which occurs when the child patterns himself after his mother. He may consciously copy her behavior or unconsciously identify with her. When he identifies, he internalizes her most potent child-rearing methods in their identical form in order to convince himself that he really wants to do what she urges.

Applying these premises to our research, we judged that the split by class in the sons' motoric and conceptual styles would be paralleled by a similar split by class in the techniques favored by parents. On the assumption that sons would pattern themselves after their mothers, we predicted that boys whose parents favored corporal punishment would be most motoric and that boys whose parents manipulated behavior psychologically would be most conceptual.[17] We also anticipated that parental use of concrete rewards would be associated with a motoric orientation in the sons, and that psychological rewards would be associated with a con-

[17] Chapter 3 describes our thinking about identification and contains descriptions of the specific techniques used to classify mothers with respect to each of the child-rearing methods.

ceptual orientation. If mothers retained emotional control while disciplining their children, we predicted that such children would be conceptually oriented.[18] Otherwise, we assumed, the children would be more motoric.

*Analysis.* We did not think it necessary to relate parental child-rearing practices to each index of conceptual and motoric orientation; we had no interest in the origins of any particular behavior. We consequently developed a single over-all index of expressive style. In constructing this index we arbitrarily decided to use the first tests, *statues* and *painting.* They seemed as representative of expressive style as any method we had developed. We classified subjects as most conceptual if they were most conceptual in their paintings and least motoric in the game of statues. We classified subjects as most motoric if they were most motoric in the game of statues and least conceptual in their paintings. A middle group consisted of children who were high in neither motoric nor conceptual scores.[19]

*Results.* As indicated in Table 15-2, expressive style is significantly related to each of the background variables. Mothers

TABLE 15-2

Child-Rearing Practices and Over-All Conceptual and Motoric Styles

| *Parental Practice* | *Trends: Boxes with Greatest Frequencies* | *N* | *Tau* | *Probability* |
|---|---|---|---|---|
| Discipline | Psychological & most conceptual; corporal and most motoric | 83 | .37 | $<.001$ (1t) |
| Type of reward | Symbolic & most conceptual; concrete and intermediate | 57 | .36 | $<.01$ (1t) |
| Mothers' affective control | Controlled & most conceptual; uncontrolled & intermediate | 83 | .25 | $<.01$ (1t) |

[18] The data were collected from the first sample of mothers. At the time they were seen we had not yet developed the questions on obedience, frequency of reward, weaning time, and harshness of toilet training, so we could not relate these conditions to expressive style.

[19] In this analysis we lost a number of subjects. A few were high on both conceptual and motoric tests, some were absent when one of the tests was being given, and a few could not be used because the mothers' descriptions of their child-rearing methods were too vague to be classified.

of motorically oriented boys are most likely to employ corporal discipline and concrete reward, to lose control of themselves, and to come from the working class. Mothers of the conceptually oriented are most likely to employ psychological discipline and symbolic reward, to retain self-control, and to come from the middle class.

These results are so consistent as to suggest a patterning of the parents' child-rearing practices. Possibly, a motoric orientation, membership in the working class, corporal discipline, and poor control are all characteristic of the same group of people. And, possibly, a conceptual orientation, psychological discipline, and good control are all characteristic of another group of people. If these conjectures are true, the association between expressive style and any parental method or socio-economic status should no longer be significant if we hold another background variable constant. We find the kinds of results we anticipate when we recompute a heretofore significant relation between expressive style and one background variable, such as social class, within the categories of another background variable, such as concrete and abstract reward. The significance vanishes for every association but one.

There is only one variable, affective control, which when held constant does not eliminate the significance of associations between child-rearing and expressive styles. In fact, they all remain significant. In retrospect, this finding seems reasonable when we remember that the parents were normal adults, most of whom were relatively controlled. Even those labeled as uncontrolled had only occasional lapses. Thus, while the difference between classes is significant, it is not very great.

From the findings just cited, we conclude that parents in the working class with motoric sons are generally the same people who use corporal discipline and concrete rewards. And parents in the middle class with conceptual sons are generally the same people who use psychological discipline and abstract rewards. However, most parents in the middle class who use psychological discipline do not necessarily retain control, nor are most parents in the working class who use corporal discipline necessarily prone to the occasional loss of control.

## Entrepreneurial and Bureaucratic Organization

In computing the previously reported association between expressive style and socio-economic status, we compared all members of the middle class with all members of the working class. In line with our interest in exploring entrepreneurial and bureaucratic settings,[20] we decided to compare expressive styles with respect to both social class and type of integration. We used not only the representative index of motoric and conceptual expression, but also the children's and mothers' attitudes, which were significantly related to expressive style.

No difference between the entire samples of middle- and working-class subjects is significantly contradicted by a difference within either the entrepreneurial or bureaucratic groups.[21] Of the four significant differences between the total samples of middle- and working-class subjects, two are repeated by the findings for the entrepreneurial group and two by the findings for the bureaucratic group. On the representative index of expressive style, the entrepreneurial groups show the same trend as the total sample, but the bureaucrats do not. Children in the bureaucratic working class are at least as conceptual as they are motoric. Possibly, this heralds the change that we anticipated in our discussion of bureaucracy. In their values about jobs both the entrepreneurial and bureaucratic subjects agree with the trend of the total distribution, but neither group produces a significant relation.

The entrepreneurial and bureaucratic mothers show the same trend in their values concerning leisure, but it is significant only within the bureaucratic group. While entrepreneurial mothers in the middle class give the opinions we anticipated, those in the working class surprise us by expressing many conceptual preferences. Apparently, they place a high enough value on the use of symbols to wish that their sons would learn to think conceptually. The bureaucratic mothers in the working class also show a trend

[20] We describe our method of classifying subjects in Chapter 2.
[21] The detailed results are included in Appendix D.

toward conceptual values, but it is not nearly so marked as that of the entrepreneurial mothers. However, when the chips are down —when the mothers have to think, not about their sons' leisure activities but about their occupations—the women become realistic and state preferences for values appropriate to the jobs which their sons will most probably have. The predicted divisions by class occur in both the entrepreneurial and bureaucratic settings.

## Testing Our Interpretations

It became necessary at one point to determine whether some source of error that allowed for alternative explanations of the results might have entered into our calculations. In Chapter 4 we noted the significant differences between the classes in intelligence. Our groups did not differ significantly in their spatial scores, but they did in their verbal and reasoning scores. Middle-class children were high on both tests. First, we checked to see whether boys with high scores differed significantly from those with low scores on any of the indices of expressive style. There are two such instances. Boys with high reasoning scores are inclined to choose conceptual hobbies and games, while boys with low scores choose motoric hobbies. When tested separately within the high and low distribution of reasoning scores, social class is no longer significantly related to choice of hobbies.

A second association, the significance of which changes only partially when computed separately for groups with high and low reasoning scores, is the one between social class and occupational preference. Among boys with high reasoning scores, class remains significantly associated with occupational preferences. The middle-class subjects select conceptual occupations, while those in the working class select motoric ones. But the significance disappears when scores are low. Apparently, middle-class boys, if they have low enough reasoning scores, do not pick conceptual occupations.

Three of the associations discussed in this chapter become insignificant when computed separately for groups with high and low verbal scores. One is the relation between social class and parents' preference for their children's occupations. We are not sure what this result means. Possibly, verbal ability is as good a measure of social class as parents' occupations and education. There is another possibility: Parents know how bright their children are—at least whether the intelligence is high or low—and adjust their preferences for occupations accordingly. When verbal ability is held constant, reward and mothers' effective control are no longer associated with expressive style. Again we can only speculate: We can postulate that boys with high verbal scores have the most intelligent parents, and that the more intelligent parents neither bribe their sons nor lose control while administering discipline. Boys with high intelligence may be more easily influenced by signs of respect than by bribes. Aside from the five associations just noted, none of the remaining twenty-seven are affected by separate computation within groups with high and low scores on any of the intellectual tests.

## Summary

Adolescent boys from the working class are predominantly motoric rather than conceptual when playing the game of statues, painting pictures, taking a block fitting test, or choosing hobbies and jobs. Boys from the middle class are more conceptual and less motoric in their reactions to the same activities. Apparently these expressive styles are quite general. The consistent differences between boys in the two social classes is more characteristic of subjects whose fathers work in entrepreneurial settings than subjects whose fathers work in bureaucratic organizations. Significant class differences in expressive style also emerge when the mothers express their attitudes to their boys' leisure activities and potential satisfaction from future jobs.

In addition to social status, child-rearing practices are significantly related to expressive styles. A conceptual orientation is typically associated with psychological discipline, symbolic reward, and maternal self-control. A motoric orientation is more characteristically associated with corporal discipline, concrete reward, and mothers' loss of control. Except for the latter, these parental behaviors overlap so much that the same middle-class parent who usually manipulates psychologically and rewards symbolically has a son with a conceptual style; the working-class parent usually employs corporal discipline and concrete rewards, and her son has a motoric style.

## References

1. Boisen, H. T. Economic distress and religious experience. *Psychiatry,* 1939, *2,* 185–95.
2. Carl, G. P. A new performance test for adults and older children: The Carl Hollow Square Scale. *J. Psychol.,* 1939, *7,* 79–199.
3. Davis, A., & Havighurst, R. J., *Father of the man.* Boston: Houghton-Mifflin, 1947.
4. ———. *Social class influence upon learning.* Cambridge: Harvard Univ. Press, 1948.
5. Efron, D., & Foley, J. P., Jr. Gestural behavior and social setting. In T. M. Newcomb and E. L. Hartley (Eds.), *Readings in social psychology.* New York: Holt, 1947.
6. McCarthy, Dorthea. Language development in the child. In L. Carmichael (Ed.), *Manual of child psychology.* New York: Wiley, 1946.
7. McNeil, E. B. Conceptual and motoric expressiveness in two social classes. Unpublished Ph.D. dissertation, Univ. of Michigan, 1952.

## PART FIVE

# POSTSCRIPT

# 16

## A FINAL REVIEW

We devote this concluding chapter to some random impressions of our methods and results. It is not necessary for us to engage in a systematic review. Too much of what we would say has already been covered in the chapters on theory and the reports of results. In any project that explores a new realm of problems there is much unfinished business. That is our concern here.

When we re-examine our methods, we try to convey a picture of their development. We have not usually done this in the reports of studies because we felt it would interfere with the clarity of the writing. Sometimes the final technique was very different from the one we had in mind when we first contemplated the problem. In the course of testing our methods we made many discoveries which affected both our procedures and our conceptions. Having completed the descriptions of the various investigations, we shall now review some of the problems that arose when we were constructing our instruments. We shall show how we arrived at solutions and discuss their effects on our conceptions and predictions. In addition, we shall highlight some of our unsolved methodological problems and raise some possible alternatives to our interpretations of results.

One of our goals in discussing results is to evaluate the significance for conflict of such background variables as a mother's characteristic type of discipline, or the time at which she weans her child. We shall re-evaluate some of our premises in the light of our findings. We shall review, for example, some of the deductions about the resolution of conflict that we derived from the epidemiological findings. We shall also re-examine some of the meanings and possible interrelations among moral standards, defenses, and expressive styles. Throughout the discussion we shall suggest some next steps in research. Finally, we shall speculate on some practical implications of our results for the work of the teacher, the psychotherapist, and the social worker.

## The General Methodological Approach

When we first conceived of the project, we knew we were interested in a general topic—the resolution of conflict. We intended to explore the relevance of moral standards and defense mechanisms to this topic. We also intended to investigate motoric and conceptual orientations, but we were not certain how they were associated with the resolution of conflict. Our previous research on one kind of conflict (5) and a study of Faris and Dunham's work prompted us to relate different social positions and child-rearing practices to moral standards, defense mechanisms, and motoric and conceptual styles. In general, we were raising problems that had been investigated most fruitfully by the psychoanalyst; we were planning to study them developmentally, and in a sociological context.

Our general topic seemed promising enough as a point of departure, but how were we to pursue it further? We were very conscious of the extent to which an investigator's questions and his methods of research determine the nature of his answers. In phrasing our questions we decided to depart from the traditional method of the clinician, who typically establishes his principles by making a thorough study of one or a few cases. Psychoanalysts have employed this method to create the building blocks of an impressive theoretical edifice. Yet, such an approach seems best suited to the initial exploration of an uncharted area. Once the general outlines of a system become visible, the study of individual cases sometimes reaches a point of diminishing returns. Then certain principles that are not readily tested by intensive case study may enter the province of faith. Certain extensions of the theory may not be explored because they require controlled investigations of adequate samples. A method that is thus very fruitful at one stage of development can, at a later time, hinder empirical work or the construction of a deductively related set of tested principles.

Whiting and Child have succinctly summarized some alternative methodological principles to which we subscribe. We quote here their discussion of the phrasing and testing of questions.

> A scientific hypothesis consists of a tentative statement of a relationship between two events. Most often, one of the events is considered as an antecedent and the other as a consequent. For evidence as to the validity of such a hypothesis, some means are needed for isolating this antecedent condition from other conditions and determining whether in fact this supposed consequent is observed with some consistency to follow or accompany it. In the study of the individual case no such means are available. If the antecedent and consequent specified in the hypothesis are both present, for example, so are an infinity of other conditions, and there is no way of knowing whether the supposed antecedent and consequent are genuinely related to each other, or whether on the contrary each may be the consequent of some quite separate set of antecedents among the infinity of other conditions which are present (8, pp. 8–11).

Whiting and Child go on to say that to study a hypothesis, the investigator should ideally fulfill three requirements pertaining to the sample, the manipulation of conditions, and the objectivity of methods. First, an adequate sample of cases is required to determine whether the association is an accidental or dependable one. Without a sufficient sample, an investigator may find it difficult to apply statistical techniques to his data. If he can apply them, he may still not be able to obtain results with sufficient statistical reliability. Second, to insure the fact that the antecedent is actually the antecedent, it should be produced by the experimenter. Finally, the evidence of the association between antecedent and consequent should be obtained, not by intuitive judgment but by objective procedures that can be repeated with the same outcome by other investigators.

Few studies in the social sciences can meet all of the three criteria. Like Whiting and Child, we had only partial success. Our numbers of subjects were usually sufficient to permit statistical analysis as well as the control of conditions which, had they been allowed to vary, would have complicated the interpretations of results. We also developed objective procedures for classifying our subjects on the different variables. Because of the nature of our problems, however, we could not hope to produce the antecedents, the background conditions, by our own actions: We could not direct parents to rear their children by specific methods. We could do the next best thing. We could, and did, select a sample with great care, so that we could specify many of the characteristics that might affect the results in ways we could anticipate. This helped us to isolate the antecedent variables from other conditions, thus permitting a partial fulfillment of Whiting and Child's second condition. Our controls increased the probability that the consequent was actually related to the postulated antecedent. We also felt that there were advantages in working with antecedent conditions defined by the structure of society rather than by the experimenter's manipulations. To begin with, social forces have created a much greater variety of child-rearing practices and resultant behaviors than we ever could by experimental manipulation. Second, in the artificial atmosphere of the laboratory it is difficult to elicit reactions that are representative of the subjects' everyday behavior. Their reports of reactions in the family are often more valid. Finally, compared to data obtained in the laboratory, subjects' reports of behavior are more fruitful in suggesting hypotheses and conclusions that might be helpful to the parent or educator.

## The Samples

In Chapter 2 we described the characteristics of our samples and our reasons for controlling certain conditions when we chose our subjects. The benefits provided by controls are gained only at a certain cost. The more conditions an investigator tries to hold constant, the smaller is the proportion of eligible subjects in the general population, and the longer it takes to locate them. These costs are illustrated by the difficulty we had in obtaining a sufficient number of subjects from a school of 1,400 pupils.

In restricting our sample to boys, we cut the potential number of subjects by half. When we further limited our group to white boys who were Protestants and born above the Mason-Dixon line, we narrowed the number to approximately 300. There were many other limiting conditions. We also eliminated children who were more than one year from the average grade of boys their age, were below average in intelligence, were emotionally unstable, came from broken or mobile families, or were not descended from families who came from northwest Europe. By the time we applied all of these controls to the original 1,400, we were lucky to find 15 children who were eligible subjects. There was still more attrition. One family had moved to another town, one family refused to permit their child to be a subject, and a few children were ill when we conducted some of the studies.

In short, we were mining a precious substance from an ore, most of which turned to dross. We hoped that, for purposes of research, the final precipitate would be superior to the original impure mixture. Our controls permitted us to rule out a number of alternative interpretations of our findings. We were confident that the results could not be attributed to differences between the sexes, between northerners and southerners, between the emotionally stable and unstable, and the like. To pay for this information, however, we had to work with relatively small numbers of cases. Usually, we had about a hundred subjects. In a typical analysis we divided the hundred into three types of discipline and each of them into the two categories of defense. If the cases were then randomly distributed, we had six categories, each with approximately seventeen boys. But not all subjects used every defense. The maximum of seventeen was sometimes reduced to five or less. In certain analyses this required the use of special techniques developed to analyze data obtained from small samples.

### Controls, representativeness, and the interpretation of class differences

Probably the most serious problem posed by the samples that we selected involves the interpretation of results. When social scientists refer to a particular social class they have in mind all the people in American society who have the characteristics included in a particular definition of that social status. To study such a group, an investigator should select a representative sample: a group of subjects who have all the characteristics of that segment of the society except its size. Almost no investigators achieve this goal in actual studies. Considering the size of our budget, we could not presume to try. We could have either controls or the approximation of a representative sample, but not both. We chose controls because they offered us greater advantages than a roughly representative sample. Yet, because of them, our working-class subjects were quite atypical. In the general population the working class exceeds the middle class in proportions of Negroes, descendants of immigrants from southeastern Europe, the educationally retarded, and broken families. By eliminating such cases, we chose nonrepresentative samples.

The lack of representativeness poses a difficult problem for the interpretation of some of our results. If the boys in our first two populations are not typical of their class, how do we interpret class differences in reactions to conflict? To what extent can we generalize significant differences to the population at large? Strictly speaking, we cannot; our group is a very special one. But let us consider its characteristics. By eliminating subjects from broken homes, we increased the similarity between boys in the two classes. This reduced the probability that differences between them would be significant. The same is true for most other conditions that we held constant, thus producing a nonrepresentative sample of working-class boys.

Had there been any interactions between the controlled variables and those under study, we would not have been able to approximate the kinds of results we might have gotten if our population had been truly representative. Since there was only one such type of interaction, the one involving verbal intelligence, we feel safe in saying that, in view of the nature of our controls, any significant results we did obtain are probably minimal. If our sample in each class had all the primary characteristics of the total population, it is likely that the number of significant associations would have been greater. We are therefore inclined to consider our findings as conservative estimates of the actual differences between boys in the two classes. Of course, these observations apply only to socio-economic comparisons and not to the interpretations of other results. It is difficult to see how their significance might have been affected by the representativeness of our sample.

It is also possible that we increased the number of significant results by holding some conditions constant. An instance of such a control is the selection of descendents of immigrants from northwestern Europe. Most of these people have been here for a minimum of two generations—usually more. When such families are still in the lower working class, they have often given up the attempt to improve their social status. Compared to the newer and more hopeful arrivals from southern or eastern Europe, the group from the northwest may thus be characterized by greater contrasts in the life styles of the working and middle classes.

### Small samples

A comparatively small number of cases poses special problems. In selecting our subjects, for example, we may have obtained most of our group from one end of the total distribution. If this were true, a second sample might have differed from the first in many respects. A serious bias in our sample would have curtailed the spread of certain variables and reduced the probability of obtaining significant results. The number we did obtain suggests that the sizes of our samples did not handicap us excessively. Of course, it is possible that some of our weak trends might have become significant with larger samples.

Another problem created by small samples pertains to the interpretation of chi squares. It is usually recommended that the smallest expected number in any box be at least five to ten cases. In a recent article Cochran (2) says that this number is arbitrary and that too little is known about the effect of a sample's size on chi square to permit the estimation of minimal amounts. He finds that if all expectancies in a chi square test are small, expectancies as low as two do not have an appreciable effect on accuracy. Such observations give us increased confidence in the possibility that the sizes of our samples did not seriously distort our analyses of data.

## The Story Completion Test

Because we were so concerned with the subjects' distortions of their conflicts, we inevitably thought of giving projective tests rather than interviews. When we considered various tests, we soon realized that we had to choose between two different types of techniques. Available to us were such methods as the Rorschach Test and the Thematic Apperception Test, both developed to measure a large number of variables and apparently adequate for certain clinical purposes. If these standard instruments did not suit us, we would have to construct special tests for the variables in which we were particularly interested.

### STANDARD OMNIBUS TESTS

In order to judge the possible value of standard clinical tests, we sought guidance from reports of studies in which these methods had been used. We illustrate such investigations by a hypothetical example. The investigator postulates an association between types of parental discipline and a variable, such as degree of narcissism. From questionnaires administered to parents, he selects two groups of boys in terms of the disciplines with which they have been reared. He administers the Thematic Apperception Test to the two groups. Then he rates or tabulates the frequency of references to narcissism in the stories the boys wrote about the pictures.

When an investigator estimates strength of narcissistic regression by counting references to it in stories about vague pictures, he is making a number of implicit assumptions. Since he is testing a postulated connection with events in childhood, the investigator is assuming that the pictures portray situations similar to those that aroused conflict in the subjects during the period of early rearing. He is also taking for granted that the picture cues stimulate forbidden needs that are strong enough to make the subject anxious. Most important, he is scoring the stories on the supposition that the subjects react to the conflict with narcissism rather than with other reactions that might have been learned in later years. In addition to such theoretical assumptions, some investigators also take for granted certain facts about their methods: that the relation between examiner and subjects has had a negligible effect on the results, and that the subjects approach the tests with similar understandings and motivations.

We think that more attempts to determine the validity of such assumptions would result in some marked changes in the methods of using projective tests. Possibly, the frequent invalidity of the assumptions accounts for one paradoxical phenomenon that we encountered in talking with some experienced investigators about the results of personality studies. If we asked whether we should modify our notions about the concept of oral passivity when we found a nonsignificant association between oral references on the Thematic Apperception Test and ratings of passive behavior, the social scientists' answers were usually negative. Most often, they attributed the lack of significance to the inadequacies of the projective test. When asked for interpretations of positive results, however, many investigators said, somewhat sheepishly, that they would interpret this as evidence in favor of the theory. If the purpose of doing research is to improve a body of theory, one may question the value of results that are accepted only if they confirm the original hypotheses. Empirical evidence is of little value unless it can provide negative as well as positive evidence for certain postulates. When we raised this point with some investigators, they gave us a surprising answer: They said that they would trust negative evidence if it arose in a psychotherapeutic interview instead of in a projective test.

It has become fashionable for critics to claim that projective tests, like vitamins and maternal love, have been oversold and to picture the clinician as an uncritical partisan. Yet we have not found the clinician willing to display a faith in his diagnostic instruments comparable to his faith in the therapeutic interview. The clinician faces a methodological problem common to every science, a problem that is most troublesome when a body of knowledge is first developing. Personality theory is still in its infancy. Most of its concepts have not been clearly defined. Many times, a variable is given an operational definition only with the greatest difficulty. Often, the instruments are poorly standardized. Since the theory is not always clear, and the validity of the techniques is not tested, it is not surprising that the researcher is inclined to retain a hypothesis even when he obtains negative results.

CAUSES OF INVALID LOW SCORES ON PROJECTIVE TESTS

Members of our project were reluctant to start research with so little faith in our methods. Why not, we reasoned, make a preliminary study of techniques? If we were fortunate enough to choose valid ones, we could then be relatively certain that the tests were not contributing a significant source of error to our results.

If we could have avoided the complicated task of designing our own instruments, we would have been happy to do so. To this end, we first examined the feasibility of using some of the popular projective tests. The literature was not encouraging. The reported validities are low in most carefully designed studies. Undeterred by the reports, we conducted a pilot study. We found, however, that we fared no better than others had. The tests rarely elicited the materials that we hoped to study. Yet, in some cases the responses gave very convincing pictures of the boys' reactions to conflict.

Why this inconsistency? In the hope of finding reasons for the variable results, we inspected the data from an earlier study of oral character (1) in which one of the writers had participated. In that investigation neither the Rorschach Test nor the Thematic Apperception Test was significantly associated with such behavioral criteria of orality as the quantity of ice cream consumed after lunch and the number of nonpurposive mouth movements. We had some confidence in the validity of the criteria because they were significantly related to a cluster of behaviors in accordance with predictions derived from psychoanalytic theory. Curiosity about the nonsignificant results prompted us to reread some of both tests. When we compared the subjects' responses with the criterion measures, we found that subjects with high test scores on orality were also high on the criteria: They ate a great deal of ice cream and they made many nonpurposive mouth movements. There was, however, a considerable group of subjects with low scores on the projective tests who were also high on the criteria. In other words, the high scores on this test tended to be valid, but not the low ones. When a subject got a low score, he was as likely to be very oral as he was very nonoral on the criteria.

Considerable speculation followed about these false negatives, whose occurrence we hoped to prevent in our research. We postulated two reasons for their existence. First, certain errors arise as a result of the relationship that the examiner establishes with the subject. Some of these were subsequently investigated in a series of experiments that have been reported elsewhere (6). It is the second source of false negatives that we wish to pursue here: the lack of structure in projective tests. An unstructured picture contains many stimuli, each of which has many attributes. When a subject makes up a story about a drawing of three people, all of whom are engaged in different actions with vaguely depicted utensils, he may respond to many different parts of the picture. He may concentrate on any or all of the people; he may highlight a function or a utensil; he may even focus on something in the background. In addition, a subject can talk about meanings that he derives from some of the shades of light and dark in the picture. Depending upon his needs, he selects from among these stimuli, and then weaves his choices into his story.

If an investigator were interested in determining all of the various needs or defenses of one individual, he could use all the material in the subject's stories. But the average investigator does not care to study all the information about one subject. He is usually concerned with one need or defense, which he hopes to use as a basis for comparing two or more types of people. In all the stories written by the subject, only those references are examined which are helpful in ranking him on the variable being investigated. Yet, since he has selected his own themes, there is no guarantee that all or any of the contents of his stories are pertinent to the problem under investigation. In short, the lack of structure in popular objective tests, which is sometimes their major asset to the clinician, can be a major drawback to the investigator.

As we view projective tests, they produce invalid low scores for three reasons. Let us assume that an investigator is studying a particular need. A subject whose need is strong may get a low score on the test because competing needs dominate his responses, because the need under investigation has previously been punished and he has learned to inhibit its direct expression, or because the test does not provide stimuli that are appropriate to the need. Unless we controlled such causes of false negatives, we could not hope to obtain valid results.

THE STRUCTURED STORY COMPLETION TEST

In the hope of eliminating false negatives, we chose the second methodological alternative, the construction of our own instruments. In most of our studies we decided to construct a story completion test, a method with obvious advantages over the omnibus type of instrument. We can best illustrate the advantages by describing some of the problems we encountered in constructing a test. Suppose we wish to identify the defense that a subject favors when he is torn between his anger and his moral standards. To make sure that there is a conflict, we insert it into the story beginning. We make up a theme about a boy who is going on a bicycle trip with some close friends.[1] In the theme he finds it hard to pedal when he starts out. A well-intentioned friend insists on straightening a part of the bicycle, despite the hero's doubts that it can be fixed without special tools. The part breaks, and the hero has to give up the trip. He sees his friend ride away with the others.

The hero should be frustrated and irritated at the helper, but also conscious of his good intentions. How do subjects complete the story? To find out whether the endings represent solutions of the conflict, we conducted a pretest. Suppose some boys write that the hero's brother comes home and offers his bicycle for the trip. This is a reasonable conclusion, but it evades the conflict. To prevent this ending, we change the story and state that the hero does not know exactly which route his friends took. It is consequently too late to find them even if another bicycle were available. Then we test the new version. We now find that in some stories the hero gets another bike and learns from an old traveler that the friends could have taken only one of two routes. When the boy tries one of the routes, he finds his friends. Again our subjects have ingeniously circumvented our goals. To preclude future use of this new evasion, we rewrite the incident. We say that the friends leave and there is no way of knowing where they have gone. We add that two hours pass, and that even if the boy knew their route, he would have no transportation. Finally, we state that he realizes he has missed the trip.

Now any story the subject makes up must take the frustration into account. At the same time, he is free to write anything he

[1] This story was developed by Douglas (3).

wishes. Hence, he can express his particular manner of resolving this kind of conflict. The lack of structured endings also makes it difficult for him to guess the purpose of the test.

In our initial studies we deliberately limited the beginnings of the stories to only one or two sentences on the assumption that some children would not be able to remember the details of longer themes. Later we included more details because we needed them to restrict the range of responses. Only with such a restriction could we interpret any ending as a resolution of a particular conflict.

When the stories became longer, we had to see whether the boys could remember all the details. We found they could take all the facts into account in organizing a plot. In fact, the increased length provided us with an unanticipated benefit. We got the impression that the additional details made the story beginnings lifelike and interesting to the boys.

Unlike an omnibus test, such as the Rorschach, the story completion test can be designed so that all endings are relevant to the study. Yet it retains many advantages of the omnibus type of projective test. It permits a range of responses rather than a dichotomous answer. It usually stimulates the subject to talk freely about himself because he thinks he is describing someone else. It also permits him to organize his response in any manner he chooses.

The story completion test has further assets. It can be administered to groups of subjects if the members are old enough to write. We consulted graded word lists when we constructed our stories, so that normal sixth-graders could—and did—take the test. It can be presented in a relatively short time; we were able to obtain endings to three stories in about twenty minutes.

### Overlap in scores from different tests

It was possible that scores from different tests of story completion were highly interrelated since they all required skill in verbal communication and an imaginative organization of details. Very high association between scores might mean that we were investigating the same variable, even though we were giving it different names in various studies. Even significant low associations among some variables would have contradicted some of our assumptions about the meaning of the variables. A significant relation between defenses in the first and second families, for example, would have contradicted the assumption that mechanisms in different families of defenses represent incompatible methods of resolving the same conflict. On analyzing the interrelations among scores from different tests, we find that none are significant. In other words, the various scores obtained from different stories are not measures of the same variable.

## Projective Tests, Arousal of Conflict, and Defenses

When we first decided to study defenses, we began by writing a number of stories about conflict. In each, a hero was inconvenienced by a strong person. Because that person was very attractive or very powerful, he could not be hurt directly. The story beginnings were presented at the same time that pictures of the events were projected on a screen. We assumed that the endings would contain many instances of defensive distortion. To our surprise, there were few endings from which we could infer specific defenses, although we had no difficulty in ranking the remoteness of the endings from the postulated original action tendencies.

In our first attempt we had developed a carefully structured instrument, but it did not measure what we thought it would. Rather than providing us with defenses, it gave us an unanticipated kind of information about a reaction, directness of displacement, which we were later to consider an expressive style.

### Intensity of Conflict and the Arousal of Defensive Distortions

We obviously needed to re-examine our blithe assumption that a story about conflict necessarily elicits defensive distortions. Like most investigators who use projective tests, we assumed that people readily distort conflicts in their problem areas, and that to elicit these reactions all we had to do was to present a story of conflict and a picture of the event. These are questionable assumptions. If a person is not under great stress, he can tolerate a certain amount of anxiety without resorting to a defensive distortion. Unless there is a serious external threat or a stimulus that intensifies a conflict about a forbidden action tendency, defenses are not necessarily employed.

Let us picture a subject who is taking the projective test. If there is no conflict, but only one unimpeded need, we can take for granted that the stronger this need is the more references he will make to it in the projective stories. The number of references to a need may still reflect its strength if it is much the stronger of two incompatible needs. When this occurs, the subject can tolerate the forbidden need. It must be the weaker of the forces in conflict and its strength must exceed a certain threshold before it arouses the anxiety that acts as a trigger for the defense. At that point, references to the direct expression of the need disappear from the story endings.

In our pretests we had done nothing to intensify forbidden hostile impulses other than to ask the boys to read a story about aggression. Psychologists commonly take for granted that a visual stimulus is sufficient for purposes of arousal. Yet we had no empirical reason to expect that if a forbidden need were called forth by the pictures or stories, it would be strong enough to create the minimal amount of anxiety required to activate any defenses. In fact, we had done everything within our power to diminish aggression. We took the boys from their classes, we fed them candy bars, and we were warm and respectful.

It was necessary that we provoke a sufficient amount of aggression to create anxiety to elicit defensive distortions. This suggested a new approach. Why not first request story endings under relatively neutral conditions? Then we could compare the endings with those written after we stimulated actual aggression. We would compare boys who increased their references to defenses from the first to the second set of stories with boys who did not.

Discrepancy scores were used in a number of our studies. The initial endings provided us with a baseline. They indicated how defensive the subjects were when they came to the testing situation, thus permitting some control of the differences in conflict that troubled the subjects when they first began the test. Without such a baseline, we might have misinterpreted the second set of stories. We can illustrate this point by the case of two boys who referred to many defenses after the actual arousal of anger.

The meaning of their scores depended on initial standings. One boy might have had a disagreement with his mother that morning and reacted with many defenses to the first set of stories. In that event, his performance on the second set of stories could have represented a decrease from the score on the initial set. Another boy who was not so angry when he wrote his first set of story endings might then have had a slightly lower terminal score than the first boy, but this score might have represented an increase compared to his original one. Only this second subject would have been counted as resorting to a defense, since only he increased his references to the mechanism after arousal of the forbidden action tendency. In short, we thought we could identify defenses more validly in terms of differential reactions to the actual arousal of a forbidden tendency than in terms of responses to a test given in a neutral situation.

Depending on the defenses that we hoped to elicit, we employed different arousal techniques in different investigations. When we obtained responses to conflicts about ambition, for example, we attempted to create real failures. When we studied reactions to conflicts about aggression, we tried to get the boys angry at their mothers. Once we used the technique of arousal, we obtained relations consistent with some of our theoretical expectations.

## Methodological Problems Involving Arousal

Arousal raises other questions. Do all subjects have to be aroused in order for them to produce defenses? Can instructions be changed so as to avoid the necessity of this procedure? Does one have to place the subjects under stress to obtain valid indicators of their moral standards or their expressive styles? The first two questions have become the objects of a study by Douglas (3). In essence, the results suggest very complex associations between the necessity for arousal and such characteristics as age and social class. After thinking about the second question, we decided that some kind of external stimulation was necessary when we wished to observe a reaction that the subject could not control and which he would ordinarily avoid. We could not see how defensive distortions would arise unless we created a minimal amount of anxiety.

CONDITIONS UNDER WHICH AROUSAL IS NECESSARY

Since completion of the studies reported in this book, we have experimented with the arousal of needs by specially designed instructions. In these we indicate that the events in the stories have actually occurred, and that the subjects are to describe the heroes' most probable behavior. Compared to our initial methods, we take much less pain to put the subjects at ease. Instead of being warm and eager to relieve any anxiety, the examiner is matter-of-fact and relatively expressionless. We get results with such an introduction that are significantly related to those obtained with the method of arousal.[2] We imagine that the newer method misclassifies some of the subjects whose forbidden impulses were aroused by events prior to the testing. Whatever the size of the resultant error, it is not great enough to preclude significant relations in our results. If arousing instructions are being contemplated, we recommend that whenever possible they be validated by comparison with the technique involving actual arousal.

We do not see that nondefensive reactions to conflict have to be aroused by special techniques. In the absence of conflict moral standards and expressive styles are usually not sources of anxiety in themselves; therefore, the average person is not reluctant to reveal them. In fact, the social approval that results from the expression of moral standards, or of appropriate expressive styles, probably motivates the subject to think about them when he is writing his story endings. It did not seem absolutely necessary, then, that we create real conflicts in our initial investigation of moral standards.

In the investigation described in the sixth chapter we had to obtain a number of different reactions to study the consistency of different moral standards. It would have been difficult to get enough information if we had engaged in the time-consuming process of arousing real guilt. As we might expect, the lack of arousal made it difficult to conduct an adequate investigation of defenses

[2] The results have been summarized in an unpublished paper by A. L. Kovacs entitled *Religion and the mechanism of denial.*

against guilt. While the records of our study show some externalization, it was not used frequently, and it was the only defense that occurred with sufficient frequency to permit a statistical analysis of the results. Strictly speaking, we cannot even be sure that we were analyzing a defense, and not some other reaction.

In the study of moral standards reported in Chapter 7 we tried to create actual guilt. The study contained fewer variables than the previous one, and the arousal was intended to maximize guilt and thus to improve the probability of obtaining significant relations. Although we cannot with certainty attribute our increased significance primarily to the stress, we are inclined to do so. Our doubt about this interpretation stems from the fact that we were no more successful in obtaining defenses against guilt than we were in the previous study.

### Degree and kinds of stress required for arousal

The design of arousal techniques provided us with some of our most vexing problems. We created conflicts with some qualms, but there seemed no way of avoiding this step. When we first planned an investigation of defense against aggression, we thought of making the subjects angry. We considered the possibility that the examiner might keep the boys waiting for an inexcusable time and then be unsympathetic in responding to their comments about his lateness. We discarded this plan very early. If the boys had legitimate reasons for being angry at the examiner, they would not feel guilty and they would have no reason to distort their action tendencies. It was necessary that we arouse incompatible impulses. That was why we tried to make the boys angry at their mothers for reasons that the boys could not accept, and why we tried to arouse the boys sexually in a situation that permitted no sexual expression. Pretests indicated that these methods elicited conflicting reactions: between guilt and the wish to hurt the mother in one study, and between the sexual impulses and strong inhibitory tendencies in another study. If we succeeded in creating these conflicts, the subjects waged internal battles instead of clashing with adults.

We feel that we have done little more than raise some of the most perplexing questions about the technique of arousal. The effects on conflict of various kinds and strengths of stimulation is a topic that deserves detailed study, as do the differences in the subjects' reactions. How much pressure did we apply to our subjects? With experience, the methods became increasingly drastic. In part, we adjusted the amount of stress to the type of conflict that we were investigating. Upon observing the boys in school, for example, we soon became convinced that no methods we might devise for creating threats of failure would be as unpleasant as the procedures in some classes. Although we did not begin to approach the threats used by some teachers, we felt that we successfully created in all the subjects a genuine concern with failure.

We were much more cautious in arousing anger. We did not want to make the boys excessively anxious about their anger at their mothers. Any concern that we developed about their anxiety was dispelled by the results. Because of our cautiousness, a much smaller proportion of subjects increased their defensive reactions than we anticipated. While a number of our relations were significant, we think we might have obtained more significant results had we created more stress. When, in subsequent studies, we devised methods of arousing sexual responses and fear of failure, we were much less cautious. Our results were correspondingly more clear-cut, and our methods still did not upset the men unduly.

### Determining the effects of arousal

How do we know that the subjects were aroused at all? We answered this question with only partial success because we did not consider it until we were actually collecting data from the second sample of boys, the ones in whom we tried to arouse anger and fear of failure. From the lack of complaints about our procedures, we gathered that we did not overwhelm the subjects. In the pretests, however, we found that most of the subjects displayed a great deal of affect. During the final interviews, when we explained that we had deliberately aroused guilt or fear, almost all the boys expressed some relief. Our subjective impressions gave us confidence that the methods had elicited rather strong emotional reactions in practically all subjects, but we cannot support these impressions in terms of an outside criterion. Unfortunately, we were not farsighted enough to devise such a criterion except in the study reported in Chapter 7. The research method was designed to stimulate at least a minimal amount of guilt. To determine the success of our attempt, we later interviewed all subjects and asked them to recall their reactions when they broke the machine. Our most direct question was: "What did you think and how did you feel when the machine broke down?" No subject thought that the incident was prearranged. Almost all the responses could be assigned to one of three categories. One consisted of such expressions of guilt as "I felt I had done something wrong," "It was my fault," "I felt guilty," and "I'll come back and make it up." A second type seemed to involve guilt, but with possible admixtures of shame. Examples were: "I must have gummed up the works," and "I felt embarrassed." A final category included responses which might be interpreted as fearful: "I was worried that your experiment would be spoiled," "I thought you would make me do it all over again," and "I felt that you thought I had broken it." Some of the descriptions that we coded as shame may have expressed guilt. Some which we coded as fear may also have expressed guilt—a guilt defended against by projection. Where we could not be sure of such interpretations, we separated the endings for further analysis.

Of our total sample of 107 subjects, 75 per cent described feelings of unquestionable guilt, 10 per cent expressed fear, 8 shame, and 7 expressed no unpleasant feelings. Did the 25 per cent who did not report guilt in the interview respond to the test differently from the 75 per cent who did? To answer this question, we compared the proportional shifts in guilt on the test among the three sex identities in the group who did not describe any feelings of guilt, with the proportional shifts among the three sex identities in the group who did report such feelings. We find that the relative frequencies of shifts are very similar for the same sex identities in both groups, indicating that the arousal technique must have affected all subjects in the same way, even those who did not report that they felt guilty. Of course, it is also possible to infer that it was some reaction other than guilt that accounted for our results. We cannot guess what other reaction it would be.

In the study of defenses described in Chapter 12 we tried to develop an independent criterion of the conflict created by the sexual arousal in the men with different types of sex identity. We conducted a pretest of a new technique of measuring palmar sweat, a commonly accepted index of anxiety. In the pretest, subjects held a bag of silica gel that soaked up sweat and was then weighed.[3] This standardized method, although valuable in other studies, distracted our subjects and interfered with their telling of projective stories. More damaging, the instrument was recognized by some of the more sophisticated college students as a method for determining fluctuations in anxiety. As a result, we temporarily gave up the idea of an independent instrumental criterion of arousal. An unobtrusive yet valid criterion remains to be developed.

A method of arousal must have the same meaning to all subjects if their responses are to be interpreted as comparable. Unless all subjects regard failure in a school task as a very unfortunate event, which is to be avoided if at all possible, the arousal of threats of failure may elicit noncomparable responses. Some may express reactions to boredom, and some may reflect defenses against failure. It might be claimed that boys in the two social classes attributed different meanings to the actual failures that they experienced. However, the possible difference in interpretation is not very pertinent to our results, since social status, by itself, is not significantly associated with denial of failure.

A final problem which bears on the significance of arousal was created by a few subjects who revealed no defenses in the story endings they wrote either before or after arousal. Possibly these boys did not become frightened of failing. It is also conceivable that their omission itself represented some kind of defense. Without data, we could not interpret the lack of productivity. Whenever subjects omitted references to a defense, we tried to find out whether they had any unique characteristics. In the study of sex identity, for example, we compared the sex identities of men who gave no defensive reactions with the identities of men who did. There are no significant differences.

In other studies subjects who produced no indications of defense were not distinguishable by the practices with which they had been reared, nor were they likely to come from particular socio-economic backgrounds. We also checked to see whether subjects who gave no manifestations of particular defenses tended to favor any other defenses more than the rest of the sample did. In the research on sex identity, for instance, we first located the

[3] The method was developed by R. A. McCleary and reported in the publication of the U.S. School of Medicine, Randolph Field, 1953.

FMs, FFs, and MMs who made no references in their story endings to mechanisms in the first family. Then we compared the distributions of these men on each of the other reactions to conflict with the distributions of the remaining men. If the disinclination of some MMs to make use of escape in the story endings had any special significance, for example, it might have been manifested by a tendency to favor some other defense like turning against the self. Such analysis yielded no significant results. In each distribution, the trends of men who had omitted certain mechanisms were the same as the trends of the other men. This type of comparison produced the same results in the three studies of defense. We found no evidence that the avoidance of a particular defense in story endings signifies a predilection for some other mechanism.

## Validity of Instruments

### Projective tests

The responses elicited by a projective test express impulse rather than action. We did not know how much the story endings depicted actual behavior. How could we tell, for example, whether the directness with which a boy expressed his aggression in story endings corresponded to the directness of his actual aggressive acts? When the behavior in the tests confirmed the predictions, we were willing to take the significant results as indirect evidence that the story endings probably corresponded to the subjects' typical actions. But how much faith could we have in such evidence? If the projective test was invalid, some of the results might have lacked significance, not because the predictions were incorrect but because the method was inadequate. It would have been desirable to obtain independent criteria for all the instruments. Because of the pressures of time, we were able to construct criteria for studying the validity of only two of our variables. One was the directness of aggression and the other was the parents' reports of toilet training. To resolve our doubts about the directness of aggression, we constructed an independent test of the boys' actual behavior toward teachers. We used students' ratings of each other rather than teachers reports to obtain the necessary information. In a pretest we found that teachers did not get to know all the students well because the classes were large. As a result, we did not get high enough reliabilities when we asked pairs of teachers to rate the same classes. Also contributing to the low reliability, we felt, was the intense emotionality with which some teachers reacted to their more aggressive pupils. A boy's classmates, we found, could produce consistent ratings if assured that the reports would be kept anonymous.

A subject was included in this part of the study only if there were four classmates who felt they knew him well. They answered two questions; in each it was necessary to choose one of two alternatives. The first question was: "When he gets scolded by the teacher or some other adult, does he (a) feel bad, or (b) get mad at the teacher?" The second one: "He would talk back to the teacher if he thought he were right: (a) yes, or (b) no." The answers of the four judges were pooled for each subject, and he was classified as being direct, intermediate, or indirect.

Data from the projective test agree significantly with the descriptions of actual behavior. Children who reveal indirect aggression in story endings are inclined to behave unaggressively toward their teachers, and children who reveal direct aggression in story endings are inclined to be overtly aggressive in their responses to teachers. Direction of aggression in reported behavior also parallels the story endings in its relation to social class and discipline. Direct expression of anger at the teacher, like direct expression in the story endings, is not significantly related to social class. It is significantly related to type of parental discipline. Psychologically manipulated subjects are generally judged by their peers to "feel bad" when scolded by an authority figure, and to be the sort of youngsters who do not "talk back" to the teacher, even when they feel they are right. Apparently, they express their anger in other ways. According to the peers, corporally disciplined children "get mad at" and "talk back" to the teachers. We were able to obtain ratings from classmates of only twenty-two of the thirty-three children in the group disciplined by intermediate methods. These ratings are divided almost equally among the different categories of aggressive behavior.[4]

[4] It would have been desirable to have obtained behavioral indices of the defenses, but there is a limit to the number of topics that members of a project can investigate. In a subsequent study Douglas (3) found a significant association between denial and sociometric ratings in some groups. Children who favor denial tend to be the isolates.

INTERVIEWS

The question of validity can also be raised with reference to the interviews with parents. There were many possible reasons for parents to distort the facts. Some were confused and anxious about their child-rearing procedures. Even the parents who were not troubled by anxiety may have forgotten some of the incidents—the timing of weaning, for example—that occurred many years earlier. Considerable evidence has been accumulated which calls the reliability and even the validity of such recollections into question. Interviews may be distorted for another reason. In order to hide their misdeeds, some parents may have deliberately falsified their answers. In view of all the possible pitfalls, the reader may well question our confidence in the material we collected from the mothers.

Because we had these pitfalls in mind, we took a number of precautions. In categorizing the mothers according to their methods of discipline and requests for obedience, we considered their responses not to one but to a number of questions. Then we took the pattern of responses into account in arriving at the code for a particular mother. We used patterns because we found in a pretest that we could not rely solely on the answers to specific responses. In her answer to one question a mother may have denied that she ever spanked her boy; in answering another the same woman may have described what he said when she spanked him for coming home late. Such contradictions were, of course, not the rule. Yet, we felt more confident about our final classifications because we took inconsistencies into account.

Only in the case of one child-rearing method, frequency of reward, did we make the mistake of relying on a single question. We have already indicated the paucity of significant relations between this measure and others. If a mother was inclined to deceive herself about her practices, or if she deliberately distorted the facts, we had no way of checking the validity of her report. We just had to accept it at face value. Possibly, a more fundamental weakness in any question about reward is the difficulty of identifying some of its forms. Most people can usually remember the last time they gave someone a gift, but they become very uncertain when they try to recall instances of responding to a gratifying act with a kind word, a pat on the head, or gesture of pride. It seems virtually impossible to obtain a valid measure of reward from interviews with mothers; one would do better to observe interactions between parents and their children.

Are current reports of ten-year-old incidents valid or reliable? While some parents could tell us the approximate time when they initiated a practice, they were often vague about the exact month. If they were certain about the time, it was usually because they could relate the practice to an event like a birthday. Many women could state with certainty, for example, that an event occurred before the child's first birthday or after his second.[5] We tried to capitalize on these observations; we divided the distributions of results into time periods of quarters or halves of the year. In the case of weaning practices, we felt fortunate that the median was almost at the end of the first year, a natural breaking point in the parents' memories. We were also fortunate in obtaining the wide variation of thirty months in the range of ages when weaning occurred. Assuming that most mothers did not deviate by more than a quarter year in their recollections of the actual age, the distinction between early and late weaning could have become blurred only in the cases of mothers who completed the weaning of their children when they were approximately one year old, the median age.

To what extent did the women distort the facts, either deliberately or unconsciously? We made one indirect attempt to check distortion in the accounts of bowel training. We assumed that if the mothers altered the facts, their reported practices would be consistent with methods recommended in the popular literature on child rearing. To determine the extent of their acquaintance with this literature, we asked the women whether they had read anything in magazines or books about bringing up children. Then we divided the mothers into those who had and those who had not read such material. Among those who had not read articles on bowel training, the number who were high in reported coerciveness is almost the same as the number who are low. Among the more

[5] This certainty can be viewed in two ways. We favored the interpretation that events close to the birthday are easy to remember. The alternative interpretation defines the birthday as a convenient but inaccurate peg. According to this viewpoint, an event like weaning may be shifted in retrospect in the direction of such landmarks as birthdays.

informed mothers, however, the number reporting coercive methods is twice the number reporting benign methods. Although these mothers read the articles that advocate delay in toilet training, they said they had started training early. Obviously, they did not distort their statements about toilet training to conform with methods recommended in popular journals.

TESTS OF SEX IDENTITY

We believe that the tests of sex identity represent our most effective methods. To begin with, we used standardized instruments for which adequate coefficients of validity and reliability had already been obtained. Discrepancies between the tests of unconscious and conscious sex identity signified defensiveness, not error. The objectivity of the instruments from which we derived our criteria probably contributed to the large number of significant associations in the two studies of sex identity.

## The Historical Definition of Problems

As we said in Chapter 5, we defined our problems in terms of developmental rather than contemporaneous relationships. We committed ourselves to a hazardous course in deciding on historical definitions. We can best highlight the difficulties of such an approach by referring to its alternative. In trying to explain differences in an expressive style, we might, instead of going back to earlier child-rearing methods or to socio-economic origins, have studied the connections between expressive styles and other contemporaneous dimensions of personality, such as extensiveness of relevant moral standards or the inclinations to favor certain defense mechanisms. Such hypotheses could not be viewed as either superior or inferior to the ones we investigated.

Contemporaneous problems involve relations between two or more current reactions, rather than between a current reaction and current indices of earlier events. It is often difficult to develop good criteria for identifying previous events. Social class is a good example of a very fallible historical criterion. Social class, it may be argued, is certainly not a clear concept; it is defined in many different ways. At best, its relation to child rearing or to expressive style must be very complex. Being in a particular social class can have many meanings for the origins of expressive styles. It may refer to current events or to events long past which are characteristically experienced by children of that social status; it may signify certain community pressures to which all members of any status are subjected; it may refer to particular sets of values shared by the members of a class; it may point to all or combinations of the meanings we have just listed. The possibility of so many meaningful links makes the interpretation of results very difficult.

Methodological criticisms can also be leveled against our study of child-rearing methods and their relations to the different aspects of conflict. Data about parental practices are usually obtained by the questionable method of interviewing anxious adults. Usually, the questions refer to a considerable range of years and can have very complex meanings.

These are cogent arguments. If they were our prime consideration, our selection of topics would have been determined more by expediency than by our theoretical interests. It is admittedly easier to collect data for a contemporaneous inquiry than a historical one, and the contemporaneous approach has the greater chance of producing significant results. But our interest in the developmental process committed us to the historical definitions of problems. We did not think that we had "explained" an event until we had related it to a necessary antecedent. Only by such an approach could we gain insight into the development of different defenses and expressive styles. Only such an approach could teach us enough about the origins of these manifestations of conflict to help the educators and clinicians who are trying to mold children according to socially acceptable ideals.

We chose the antecedent conditions of social class and various parental practices because they seemed most crucial to the process of socialization, and we intended to test some of the claims commonly made about these variables in the literature. We also hoped to evaluate the significance of epidemiological data for the socioeconomic distributions of the defenses which, according to psychoanalytic theory, are associated with the different disorders. We recognized that social class could be related to a particular defense for many reasons. At the same time, we were impressed by the significance of social class for some of the most crucial experiences and values in the society, and by the high correlations among the different definitions of social class. We had confidence, then, that we could reliably measure an important set of social forces which we believed would be related to the resolution of conflict. We anticipated that the nature of the resultant findings would, in turn, point to further problems of importance to our research interests.

## Social Class and the Resolution of Conflict

### THE MEANING OF SOCIAL CLASS

The finding of a significant association between social class and some reaction to conflict answers one question and raises another. Which of the many characteristics of social class accounts for the obtained association? The concept of social status is a collective one involving many component forces. The importance of these forces is suggested by the many significant findings involving social class. In our own project, for example, it is significantly associated with weaning, toilet training, discipline, and frequency of reward. In addition, it is connected with the inclination to use the second family of defenses, amount of denial among subjects with moderate intelligence, degree of repression, opinions about the necessity for corporal punishment, conceptual and motoric orientations, and tendencies to express aggression by fighting or fleeing. Social class is apparently a touchstone to many sources of reaction to conflict. But the significant results raise some difficult problems of interpretation.

In Chapter 15 we noted that social class is significantly related to expressive styles. When we hold any method of child rearing constant, the association between social class and expressive style disappears. In other words, parents in the middle class are the same people who use psychological discipline, retain self-control, and give frequent rewards. The total pattern of practices is related to expressive style. We cannot tell from the data whether any one of the practices is more important than others or whether all of them can be explained by a more basic variable, possibly one like power, which is connected with social status and which we did not measure.

The fact that different components of social class account for various significant findings becomes apparent when we compare the class differences in reactions to conflict. In our investigation of the second family of defenses, for example, we find that sons of white-collar workers are most likely to favor these mechanisms. Unlike the relations with expressive style, none of the parental practices are significantly associated with defenses in the second family. Whatever aspect of social class accounts for its association with expressive style overlaps with types of parental practices; whatever aspect accounts for the association with the second family does not overlap with types of parental practices. Different components of social class must account for the relations in the two studies.

These results suggest that the concept of social class refers to a group of variables; certain of these variables can and do account for relations with different personality traits. Such a conclusion is not necessarily discouraging. The kinds of association often indicate some of the directions that conceptions of socio-economic status may take. It is not difficult to make reasonable guesses about these conceptions. In the study of expressive style, for example, we imagined that it is to the economic advantage of white-collar workers to favor a conceptual orientation. In speculating about the frequency with which white-collar workers resort to the second family of defenses, we assumed that mechanisms like reversal and turning on the self are most efficient in resolving conflicts concerning certain types of aggression in a manner that is compatible with commonly accepted values in the middle class. When we considered the predilections for denial on the part of boys in the working class whose intelligence was average or less, we took for granted that they have to adjust to many hardships. Economic reward, values, degree of hardship—these are the kinds of variables which we think may evolve as the components of social class which are salient to personality.

## SOCIAL CLASS, CHILD TRAINING, AND PERSONALITY RESEARCH

Research on social class and reactions to conflict requires a sequence of steps. First, the investigator tests his initial hunches about the associations between social and personality variables. Then, depending on the data and the various impressions he gets from observing the subjects, he develops other hypotheses to account for the obtained results. A second step is then required to test the new hypotheses. Their investigation leads to the formulation of still further hypotheses. Only by such a continuous sequence of investigations will it be possible to isolate the specific variables which enter into the relations between social class and certain forms of behavior. The results of the present project suggest a number of leads which could become the hypotheses of a second stage of research. A typical instance is our assumption that hardship in the working class reinforces a tendency for boys of limited intelligence to deny their failures.

It would not be unreasonable for a skeptic to question the value of the first step. Why not, he might ask, go directly to the second step and test the association between amount of hardship and predilection for denial? Why bother with the concept of social class when it is so complex? We have three answers. First, social class suggests many such hypotheses, which might not occur to the investigator if he were studying other variables. Second, social class is one of the keys to the connection between social organization and individual behavior. When we inquire into the components of social class that are associated with expressive styles or defenses, we are taking a step in the direction of explaining individual differences in terms of the society in which the person is socialized. Third, social class defines a context which has to be considered in explaining the associations between some of the child-rearing practices and reactions to conflict.

The study of the second family of defenses provides a good illustration of the last point. Social class is significantly related to the inclination to favor these mechanisms. The nature of parental requests for obedience is not. When we combine them, their significant relation with shifts in defense indicates that requests for obedience have different meanings in the two classes. Arbitrary requests for obedience increase defensiveness in the middle class, but show an opposite trend in the working class.

Toilet training also differs in its relation to mechanisms of defense in the second family, depending on the social status of the subjects. Within the middle class, boys who are trained coercively are inclined to increase their references to the second family of defenses. Within the working class, boys who are trained early are least inclined to increase either. Apparently, coerciveness affects defenses primarily when it is used to implement the values, and the concomitant practices, of parents in a particular social class.

### Social class and morality

Sometimes, a significant result provides less food for thought than an unconfirmed hypothesis. One such group of relationships involves social class and the severity of various moral standards. Judging from the data, boys in the middle class do not differ significantly from boys in the working class in the severity of their guilt about disobedience, death wishes, or stealing. At first glance, this result seemed to contradict the reports that boys in the working class do not internalize standards as adequately as do boys in the middle class. Hence, the sons of manual laborers find it easy to disobey authorities, to express all kinds of hostile wishes, and to steal. Our data certainly indicate that they fight more than their counterparts in the middle class. Then why do we not find differences in the standards of the two classes? Behavior may vary with socioeconomic level, not because of contrasting standards but because of differences in the capacity to live up to them. It may be that social pressure to steal or lack of self-control make it difficult for the sons of some blue-collar workers to resist such behavior even when it is followed by guilt. These boys may feel compelled to steal or be disobedient to save face with their friends. Their antisocial behavior does not mean, however, that they suffer any less than middle-class boys from the pressures of internalized standards. To explain the behavior of boys in the two classes, then, we now postulate differences in the pressures to violate moral standards and in the abilities to implement them, rather than differences in moral standards themselves. If these assumptions are true, boys in the working class must suffer more often from guilt than do boys in the middle class. Of course, all these speculations apply only to boys who, like those in our studies, do not suffer from the pathologies of conscience.

## Social Integration

As we stated initially, the concept of integration was developed after we started our research on this project. Consequently, we could not completely satisfy all the criteria for identifying entrepreneurs and bureaucrats. We had to omit the criterion according to which men are classified as entrepreneurs when half of their income is earned from fees and commissions. The proportion of such cases in our population was probably small.

We tried to relate integration to reactions to conflict only when we first found that the social status was significant and that there were enough cases to permit a statistical analysis. Such analyses were possible in the investigations of the second family of defenses, repression, sex identity, and the conceptual and motoric expressive styles.

One impression conveyed by the different studies is that, of all the subjects, sons of entrepreneurs in the middle class are subjected to the most intense parental pressures. These boys must learn the defenses which turn aggression against oneself, reverse it, or diminish it. They must learn to avoid denial, to repress antisocial action tendencies, and develop a masculine identity. They must become accustomed to manipulating concepts as a means of solving personal problems. Most of our significant differences in integration involve comparisons between boys in the entrepreneurial middle class and boys with other patterns of stratification and integration. These findings parallel the ones reported for the associations between social positions and early child-rearing practices (7).

Among the bureaucratic subjects, the differences between the classes tend to be minimal compared with the differences among the entrepreneurs. The two classes of bureaucrats resemble each other in the uses of denial, the second family of defenses, and the conceptual and motoric styles. Within the bureaucratic group, the two classes differ significantly only in the rate of repression. Our speculations about this difference are contained in Chapter 10. The number of jobs in bureaucratic settings has been increasing and will probably continue to do so. Judging from the lack of socio-economic differences in reactions to conflict, it seems probable that status in a particular social class will become decreasingly important as time passes and bureaucratization progresses.

## Intelligence

Verbal intelligence is involved in some interactions that we had not anticipated. With high verbal scores, social class is not related to denial; with moderate scores, it is. The same holds true of the association with denial of requests for obedience and type of discipline. In addition, among boys whose parents have favored corporal methods of discipline, two-thirds of the group with moderate scores in intelligence advocate this method without qualification. Only about one-fourth of the boys with high intelligence are of this opinion.

How do we interpret the significance of intelligence for the resolution of conflict? We see three possibilities. According to the most obvious explanation, the duller boys are more affected by social pressures than are the brighter boys. If parents use very harsh methods, or their sons experience some of the frustrations which are the lot of people in the working class, boys who are not very bright may have little recourse but to deny the facts, especially when the pressures are very intense. But if the subjects are above average in intelligence, they may be relatively resourceful in adjusting to the vicissitudes of their existence. They may weather storms which cause boys with fewer intellectual resources to retreat into a world of fantasy.

Low intelligence is viewed as a result, rather than a cause, of denial in an alternative explanation of the findings. It assumes that practice in the avoidance of unpleasant facts handicaps a child in his learning of concepts and in the development of abstract thinking. The longer a boy practices denial, the lower his intellectual capacity becomes. In a group of early adolescents, therefore, we would expect to find a higher inverse relation between verbal intelligence and the inclination to increase denial than we would get in a younger group of children.

We must not overlook a third possibility, one that overlaps with the second. The test of verbal intelligence may reveal the extent to which a boy becomes socialized in accordance with the values of his social class. From this point of view, the boys with high verbal scores can be regarded as successfully trained in the skills most valued by the middle class. Such subjects can apply conceptual skills to the solution of personal problems. Compared to the sons of white-collar workers, sons of blue-collar workers receive less of the kind of training that helps one to do well on tests of one's intelligence, to question the values of one's social group, or to learn the more sophisticated defenses.

## Child Rearing

### Combinations of methods

It is the combinations of child-rearing practices that provide the most impressive relations with different reactions to conflict, particularly the mechanisms of defense. The data concerning child rearing and denial provide some typical examples of such relations. Shifts in denial vary significantly with the harshness of different combinations of reward and requests for obedience. The greatest increase in denial occurs when requests are arbitrary and reward is infrequent; the smallest increase occurs when requests are explained and reward is frequent. The combination of discipline and reward also interacts significantly with shifts in denial. Psychological discipline and occasional reward are associated with the greatest increase of the defense; mixed discipline and occasional reward are associated with the smallest increase.

### Internal consistency among child-rearing methods

The number of moral standards, defenses, and expressive styles to which the different child-rearing techniques are related is much greater than chance. It is possible, however, that we studied only one basic philosophy of child rearing and that its different variants created a spurious impression that we obtained many different kinds of significant relations. A concern with high achievement may, for example, be expressed by the tendency to push one's children prematurely into adulthood. Parents with such an orientation may wean their children early, initiate toilet training early, make strong appeals to guilt, and be forced, because their requests are initiated too early to be understood, to make arbitrary demands for obedience.

It is possible to conceive of a number of other general approaches to child rearing. Some parents may favor harsh methods because of hostility to their offspring. Some parents may favor benign methods because they believe in being permissive and letting their children work out their own problems. Some parents may be inconsistent because they are confused about the effects of different practices. Whatever the reasons, the different methods favored by particular mothers may all reflect common orientations.

If a general orientation underlies the parents' methods of weaning, bowel training, rewards, requests for obedience, and methods of discipline, we would expect them to be interrelated. This is not what we find. The various techniques are not significantly associated with each other.[6] There is one suggestive trend, but it is not significant. Parents who wean early are also likely to initiate bowel training early. Late weaning, however, is not connected with any particular method of bowel training. Possibly, some parents use harsh methods of weaning and training as the first of many opportunities to inculcate high standards of performance.

There are probably consistencies in some of the combinations of severe and benign practices. To motivate their children, for example, some adults may be initially nurturant and later show disinterest. The lack of specific relations among the child-rearing practices does not, therefore, rule out the possibility of a limited number of meaningful patterns. The lack of significance does suggest that the patterns are complex. Different parents probably apply the same practice with their own purposes and effects.

### Reconciling trends

Some knotty interpretive problems arise when we compare all the behaviors with which a particular method of child rearing is significantly associated. Weaning and toilet training, for example, are involved in most of the significant relations with the different moral standards. Two of three relations between weaning and severity of guilt are significant, and one is close to significance.

[6] Whiting and Child also find that weaning, bowel training, and discipline are not significantly related with each other.

Two of three relations between toilet training and severity are significant. Of three relations involving discipline, none is significant, and of the three involving obedience, none is significant. With one exception, however, the early child-rearing methods produce consistently nonsignificant results when related to the defenses. The exception is the association involving social class, toilet training, and repression.

Why the marked difference in the associations generated by the early and later child-rearing methods? We have some confidence in the reliabilities of the indices of obedience and discipline, since they are significantly associated with other reactions to conflict. In fact, we would not have been surprised if reports of oral and anal treatment had been relatively unreliable. Because the topics provided sources of considerable anxiety to some mothers, and years of time had elapsed since the events occurred, we initially had some doubts that the reported practices would be related to reactions in adolescence.

A clue to the different results for the two types of parental methods is provided by the fact that coercive toilet training and repression are associated within the middle class, but not the working class. Repression of failure requires a lengthy indoctrination. Before it can be effectively applied to anxiety, a boy must develop a sense of self and acquire the ideas of self-esteem and prestige. He must become proficient with the skills that are important in his social group. He must become acquainted with the values attached to different levels of achievement and the various indices of success and failure. It is extremely improbable that the timing of toilet training affects the inclination to favor repression. That harsh toilet training is associated with the mechanism in one social class but not the other suggests that the practice may be related to various values and practices which are characteristic of the social group and which are causally related to the use of repression. Harsh toilet training may be connected with the later goals of achievement, for example, and these may be more directly associated with the inclination to repress failure. In short, we assume that the differential relation to repression of toilet training within the two classes indicates that its meaning varies with the social context, and that the method is statistically related to later behaviors only because it is congruent with a cluster of later causal values and practices. In contrast, discipline and parental requests for obedience indicate types of coercion, but are probably not associated with specific groups of values. A mother may appeal to guilt or use physical punishment to enforce any requirement. She may use the same method to make her son fight for his rights or to punish him for fighting. Similarly, whether she makes arbitrary or reasonable demands is independent of their contents. Hence, maternal requests and methods of discipline shed less light on moral standards than do oral and anal methods.

### Type of discipline

Methods of discipline are significantly related to the two expressive styles, the indirectness with which subjects express aggression, and their conceptual and motoric orientations. The parental method is also associated with shifts in denial. By itself, however, discipline is not related to the second family of defenses, repression, severity of guilt, or defenses against it.

We imagine that it is the visibility of disciplinary methods which accounts for their associations with the expressive styles. If a woman uses her fists to punish her son, he cannot help but be painfully aware of her technique. If he identifies with her, he will unthinkingly employ the same technique in raising his children. He will express his anger directly just as she does, and he will become accustomed to seeking motoric outlets just as she does.

The association between discipline and denial requires another kind of reasoning. In speculating on the origins of the mechanism, we have stressed the importance of harsh child-rearing techniques. Both psychological and corporal methods seem to constitute stringent pressures, compared with the more flexible, mixed type of discipline. The pressures are even greater if the boys have only a moderate level of intelligence or reward has been minimal.

We have already suggested, in the discussion of weaning and toilet training, why we think discipline is not significantly related to the second family of defenses or to the different aspects of moral standards. Both kinds of reaction require indoctrination in particular values. By itself, the type of discipline does not create such an indoctrination.

## Some Practical Implications of Findings

In the reports of our investigations it was difficult to restrain our impulses to discuss some obvious implications of our results for the teacher, the psychotherapist, the parent, and others who work with children. We have avoided the topic up to now because we have not empirically tested any implications for educational or psychotherapeutic methods. Since this final chapter is devoted to speculations about findings, it seems an appropriate place for the consideration of practical implications.

Too often, the teacher comes from the middle class, or aspires to be in it. When she thinks of good students, she pictures boys with characteristics that are valued by white-collar workers. At best, she would like her pupils to be intelligent, to manipulate abstractions with some skill, and to set high goals of achievement. She also hopes that they will persevere when they are frustrated by a difficult task. At a minimum, she requires that they be clean, peaceful, and cooperative, and that they stop violating rules when she appeals to their guilt. She is likely to be disappointed by many sons of blue-collar workers in each of these respects. These boys often do poorly on intelligence tests. If they develop certain conceptual skills, they may hide this fact from their friends in order to save face. Boys in the working class dream about accomplishments, but their failures in real life create a fear of setting high goals.

Boys in the middle class persevere; they feel they must succeed in difficult tasks, and blame themselves when they fail. If they are in conflict about aggression, they are inclined to reverse it or to turn it inward. It is more difficult for working-class boys to persevere. If the task is difficult and their intelligence moderate, they may revert to denial. These children seem to have as many internalized prohibitions against direct aggression as the sons of white-collar workers, but social pressures and the internalized values of the group prompt them to fight. They are frequently plagued by problems of self-control and of guilt. When they express aggression, they tend not to blame themselves or to reverse their impulses. A recent study done on the project suggests that they probably externalize their guilt.

If a teacher is assigned to a working-class neighborhood, she will be sorely tried by her pupils unless she expects some of this behavior. Her greatest trials will be caused by her pupils' poor self-control, their difficulty in understanding concepts, and their lack of responsiveness to verbal appeals. These boys do, however, respond to another approach. If the teacher enables them to express themselves with the large muscles of the torso and limbs, her students may make surprising educational progress. If she appreciates their sensitivity to failure, and does not challenge them in a manner that might be very effective in a middle-class neighborhood, they may extend themselves to a surprising degree. If she does not appeal to their guilt because their behavior violates the norms of another social class, they may respond with warmth instead of their customary sullenness and resentment.

Like the teacher, the psychotherapist seldom questions the values of his social class. He thinks that a patient's prognosis is good if he is amenable to a verbal approach, if he favors such defenses as turning on the self and reversal rather than denial and projection, and if he persists in trying to solve his personal problems, even when he is anxious. These are traditional signs of promise for patients in individual psychotherapy. But the increasing number of blue-collar workers who are seeking help for their personal problems has made it obvious that traditional goals and methods must be modified. In clinics which serve patients in both social classes, a disproportionate number of blue-collar workers drop out of therapy very early because of dissatisfaction with the therapeutic procedure (4). It is important that psychotherapists learn more about the characteristics of manual laborers and about conditions under which these people mature. Their difficulty with verbal communication, their sensitivity to the threat of failure, and their inclination to deny severe problems are undoubtedly pertinent to the symptoms and behavior of many such patients.

It is difficult to devise methods to keep patients in therapy when they have been defeated by many failures, or are inclined to resort to denial of anxiety. But manual laborers react in these ways quite frequently, and effective methods are sorely needed to help people with such problems.

Our results indicate the desirability of exploring a variety of new psychotherapeutic techniques, particularly those in which words and concepts are subordinated to nonverbal and even motoric activities. Extensive investigation of group psychotherapy also seems indicated; some blue-collar workers respond well in a group in which they share their experiences with other people who have the same kinds of values, personal problems, and methods of communication.

Job counseling, a procedure related to psychotherapy, might benefit from the implications of some of our findings. Certain jobs typically held by members of the middle class seem to require a physical spontaneity which can only come from a motoric orientation. It is not enough to be able to "talk a good game" when a person aspires to be a dentist, an archeologist, or a surgeon. Some of the techniques of these professions require a type of physical skill and a capacity to manipulate objects which many people in the middle class can cultivate only with a considerable expenditure of time and effort.

Information about still other reactions to conflict might be helpful to the occupational counselor. An extended period of training is sometimes beyond the capacities of a very intelligent person who has a high fear of failure. Success on the job may require initiative, a capacity the expression of which may be hindered by unconscious femininity. If creativity is required on the job, a person may not be qualified if he occasionally becomes rigid or bereft of ideas because of his inclination to favor denial.

Our findings contain a number of implications concerning the desirability of certain methods of rearing children. Late weaning and toilet training, for example, are conducive to guilt about disobedience and stealing, but do not lead to guilt about hostile thoughts. Late training, particularly within the middle class, is also associated with minimal increases in denial. Thus benign methods seem to implement the values of the middle class, a fact which may explain their frequent recommendation by professionals who work with children's problems. If parents favor harsh methods, their children do not become very guilty about antisocial acts. Instead these boys become anxious about those impulses that they do not translate into action.

Judging from the variables with which discipline is associated, it is the mixed type that produces results which are socially most desirable. When mothers have been inclined toward mixed discipline, their sons are least likely to increase denial, are not excessively direct or indirect in their expression of aggression, and are usually intermediate in their conceptual and motoric orientations. In short, such boys are realistic, are neither uncontrolled nor overly constricted, and can express themselves flexibly by either motoric or conceptual means.

Unexplained requests do not necessarily produce undesirable behavior. We originally thought that children raised by means of unexplained requests would favor defenses in the first family, would find it difficult to control their impulses, and would unquestioningly follow parental rules once they were internalized. When analyzed by themselves, or in combination with other harsh methods, unexplained requests produce the anticipated results. But when combined with benign methods, unexplained requests are associated with defenses in the second family and with resistance to temptation.

We imagine that it is the context in which the requests are made which determines their effect. When the child is young, his parents must be arbitrary about certain rules: He must stay on the sidewalk whether or not he understands the reasons why he cannot run into the street. Some arbitrary requirements are still necessary later on. In fact, they constitute a source of security when a boy is testing limits and needs to be restricted.

## Some Unsolved Problems

### Social and individual concepts

A research project usually raises more issues than its members can ever hope to settle. One of the most fundamental issues, and one we share with many other projects in social science, involves the conception and phrasing of causal relations between societal and individual concepts. Up to this point we have reported connections between social class and expressive styles, to name one example, without discussing some of our doubts about the meaning of such findings. We have pointed out that social class, as a concept, encompasses so many different forces that its association with a particular individual trait is sometimes difficult to explain. We now come to a more serious problem. To date, no theorist has been able to successfully integrate concepts from the social and individual realms of discourse. The sociologist or anthropologist can often give a relatively clear account of the workings of a group, and even describe many operations of a social system. He is much more uncertain in his descriptions of personality. He may describe men in terms of the characteristics of the groups in which they participate. The investigator who is primarily concerned with groups may describe the behavior of individuals in terms of their roles. The concept of role has been defined in many ways. Role includes patterns of rights and responsibilities, patterns of values and of motives, and kinds of behavior, among others. Since individual differences can often be safely ignored in analysis of group phenomena, the concept of role is seldom handicapping in such research. The concept has not proved to be fruitful, however, in psychological research.

When the psychologist tries to integrate social and individual data, he is no more successful than the sociologist. Sometimes, he restricts himself to social questions. In that event, he usually ignores individual differences. When he does study individual differences, he often ignores the inescapable fact that people grow up in a society, and he is inclined to stress principles that originate in physiology and that link humans with lower forms of life.

The lack of theoretical systems to clarify the connections between social and individual concepts means that associations, even when they are significant, represent problems rather than solutions. Indeed, there are some scholars who think that the problems are insoluble. These men are of the opinion that social and individual phenomena represent two realms of discourse. Forces can interact within each realm, but not between them. From this viewpoint, an explanation of an individual variation in behavior cannot have much meaning unless the psychological results of membership in a social class are specified and measured. When they are, we may find many dimensions, the relations among which can vary considerably.

Although their meaning is still unclear, we still consider it important to investigate the connections between certain social and individual phenomena. Such empirical information can be helpful to the teacher and clinician. It can provide the theorist with leads which implement his basic problem of developing a system that integrates social and individual phenomena.

The need for an integrative theoretical system is indicated by such problems as developing a map of man's moral standards. It has not proved possible, thus far, to construct a system of classification that is purely intra-individual. While we have little doubt that the various moral standards are internally consistent in some way, the findings show that the consistency is a complex affair. Rarely are most of a person's standards either very flexible or very severe. Just how are they interrelated? We do not think that this question will be answered until a comprehensive theory of social organization is available. Moral standards originate as rules of groups. It is difficult to develop categories of standards without knowing how the rules implement a group's functions.

### Mechanisms of defense and expressive styles

Our findings have impressed us with the fruitfulness of attempting to solve problems connected with the learning of defenses. If defenses are acquired, they may vary with changing social conditions. The frequencies of such neurotic symptoms as hysteria, obsessions, and character disorders, each of which may be traced to certain clusters of defense mechanisms, seem to fluctuate in different times, places, and in different parts of the population. We imagine that the patterns of defense are constantly changing, to correspond with changes in the society.

Defenses are discussed in much of the clinical literature as though they are all socially handicapping. Many of our subjects used mechanisms which seemed to us to be socially adaptive. These are exemplified by story endings in which the hero accepts an irremediable situation graciously and says that his day will come, or in which he tries to understand the good intentions of the person who created the difficulty. There are many such defenses. Some seem very similar to rational solutions, and probably provide a much needed solace for the inevitable frustrations of everyday existence.

We have proposed two families of defenses, but we do not think that we have exhausted all the possible categories. The stories written by subjects contained too many kinds of substitution that were not covered by current systems of classification.

Even within the proposed categories, there are a number of unexplored mechanisms. These are suggested by the table for the second family of defenses, which also raises the possibility that there may be mechanisms in other societies which are seldom used in our own. Investigations need to be conducted of currently unlabeled mechanisms, of the conditions under which defenses are learned, modified, and used to facilitate socially adaptive behavior.

We believe that our methods of classifying reactions to conflict, and some of the empirical findings that we have reported, contain the seeds of many intriguing problems for research. Their variety is indicated by such topics as the associations between moral standards and different kinds of defense, the origins of such expressive styles as degree of self-control and adaptation to the limitations of time, the specific perceptual mechanisms involved in the operations of defenses, the social consequences of different reactions to conflict, the developmental sequences of the reactions, their variations in accordance with different parental values, familial constellations, and parent-child relationships, and their distributions among males and females and among members of different ethnic groups and religious faiths. We will have realized one of the major purposes of this volume if it has enabled the reader to appreciate the significance of such problems and to visualize methods of testing them more adequately.

## References

1. Blum, G. S., & Miller, D. R. Exploring the psychoanalytic theory of the "oral character." *J. Pers.*, 1952, *20,* 287–304.
2. Cochran, William G. The chi square test of goodness of fit. *Ann. Math. Stat.*, 1952, *23,* 315–45.
3. Douglas, Virginia D. The development of two families of defense. Unpubl. Ph.D. dissertation, Univ. of Michigan, 1958.
4. Hiler, E. W. An investigation of psychological factors associated with premature termination of psychotherapy. Unpubl. Ph.D. dissertation, Univ. of Michigan, 1953.
5. Miller, D. R. Responses of psychiatric patients to threat of failure. *J. abnorm. soc. Psychol.*, 1951, *46,* 378–87.

6. ———. Prediction of behavior by means of the Rorschach Test. *J. abnorm. soc. Psychol.*, 1953, *48*, 367–75.
7. ———, & Swanson, G. E. *The changing American parent.* New York: Wiley, 1958.
8. Whiting, J. W. M., & Child, I. L. *Child training and personality: a cross-cultural study*. New Haven: Yale Univ. Press, 1953.

# APPENDIXES

# APPENDIX A

# PROCEDURES USED TO OBTAIN THE FIRST TWO POPULATIONS

## SAMPLE ONE

It was first necessary that we select the schools from which we would recruit subjects. We were guided primarily by the average socio-economic position served by each school. We made our final choices after studying the United States Census and a 1951 sample of the metropolitan area made by *The Detroit News*. Using the census data as a guide, we selected a number of neighborhoods in the Detroit area. Within each, the majority of gainfully employed persons tended to be restricted to a particular socio-economic level. In 1951–52, the first year of our research, a slim budget limited us to parts of the Detroit area that were close to each other, so that little time was required for traveling from one school to another.

The city of Detroit provided a good sample of working-class boys who met our criteria, but not as many middle-class subjects as we needed. However, the relatively small city of Highland Park, functionally a part of Detroit and completely surrounded by it, promised to give us a group of families ranging from the working through the upper middle class. We chose five sampling areas in Highland Park and Detroit. We contacted the principal of a school within each area and gained his permission to examine the records of all children in the seventh, eighth, and ninth grades.

After combing the records of the five schools, we compiled a list of all boys who seemed to meet our qualifications. We planned to interview their mothers. On the basis of their reports on family backgrounds, we intended to eliminate those cases that did not fit our requirements. The interviews were also designed to give us information about child-training practices. A final purpose of the interviews with the mothers was to learn some facts that had been recorded vaguely, or not at all, in the school records. Such data included parental occupation, marital status, and religious preference.

INTERVIEWS WITH PARENTS

The interviewer introduced himself to each mother by saying:

> My name is ———. I'm from the University of Michigan. I am taking part in a public opinion study to find out some of the experiences of parents with growing children. I have some questions I'd like to ask you. Your answers will be entirely confidential. I am not trying to sell you anything. This is a scientific survey to find out what your experiences have been with children. We are very interested in your answers. But we are not taking your name. We want to find out, not about you in particular, but about the experiences of mothers in general.
>
> We got this address as being that of a family having a boy in the seventh, eighth, or ninth grade in school. Is that correct?

Actually, the interviewer did not recite this script exactly as it appears. He was instructed not to worry about the exact wording, but to cover all the points in a natural, conversational manner. Each interview was conducted like a public opinion poll, a procedure known to the vast majority of mothers. In no case was a mother told that we planned to study her child.

The interviews, which averaged an hour and ten minutes, ranged from problems of raising children to questions about the mother's philosophy of life, and, at the end, to information about the social position of the family. It is our impression that respondents enjoyed themselves. Frequently, members of our staff complained that the mothers talked too long and did not want to terminate the conversations.

Interviews were conducted by students at Wayne University in Detroit and the University of Michigan in Ann Arbor. The group from Wayne University did the work as part of a course requirement. We are indebted to Dr. Harold L. Sheppard of the Sociology Department of Wayne University for his help in training a number of his students for this phase of our study and for his expert advice about the structure of the metropolitan area. Interviewers from the University of Michigan worked as volunteers. We paid a few of the more skilled students from both universities to see parents who were not at home on the first or second calls.

To avoid biasing the trainees, none were informed about the purpose of the study. Their training began with lectures on such topics as the techniques of asking questions and following up answers, the possible reactions of working- and middle-class housewives to their middle-class visitors, and the reasons for recording every detail *verbatim*. Students then practiced the procedures with the instructors, who took the roles of different kinds of mothers. Next, the students interviewed some mothers who were not in the final sample. To insure a flavor of reality, the women were not informed that these were practice sessions. Finally, the interviewers were given the names and addresses of families to be visited. They were cautioned not to talk with mothers when their children were present. This meant that the work had to be done on weekdays and during school hours. If a mother could not be seen or was not at home on the first call, at least three other attempts were made to reach her.

SAMPLE TWO

In the initial study we did not get as many children from the upper middle and lower working class as we would have liked. Since a larger budget for the second year allowed us to do more traveling, we tried to select schools that would provide us with a population identical with the first one in social characteristics, but having more cases from the two extreme strata. To simplify our administrative problems, we decided to work entirely within the city of Detroit.

The same methods of selecting children from school files and seeing the mothers in their homes were carried over from the first year, but with one difference. In order to choose a group of boys with as narrow an age range as possible, we eliminated the ninth grade as a source of subjects.

The interviewers were mostly graduate students and a few undergraduate seniors from the University of Michigan, all of whom we were able to pay at professional rates. We repeated the training procedures of the previous year. Each trial interview was discussed in detail with a staff member. During the period of final interviewing, we observed each person's dress every day to make sure that it was conservative.

Two hundred and forty-five cases were selected for interviewing. First we mailed a letter to the parents, giving a brief description of the project and asking for cooperation. The purpose of the letter was to reassure any mothers who might resist being interviewed. It did not mention our plan to study the children; we feared that such information would make some mothers evasive.

Because we had found that some of the information in school records was unreliable, we checked it in our initial questions. This part of our questionnaire was a complete unit, so that an interviewer could gracefully end the matter if he discovered the family did not have the necessary characteristics. As in the first year, if the mother was not at home the interviewer returned at least three times.

A staff member read each record on the day it was obtained, and raised questions about unclear answers. In addition to maintaining our standards of interviewing, this intensive supervision helped to keep up the morale of the staff, who appreciated the careful attention to their work.

We were not able to reach 6 per cent of the mothers in the first sample and 7 per cent in the second. These proportions are characteristic of studies of the Detroit area. Compared to what we had been led to expect, we were gratified that only 10 per cent of the women in the first study and 8 per cent in the second refused to talk with us. Few mothers were uncooperative because of the subject matter. They usually explained that they could not interrupt other work. A poll did not seem an important enough reason for them to change their schedules.

As we anticipated, some people had been selected erroneously.

Because of mistakes or omissions in school records, we chose some subjects from Negro and non-Christian homes, some with parents who were separated or divorced, and a few with stepfathers or stepmothers. We lost 19 per cent of the first sample for such reasons, and 26 per cent of the second. Apart from the cases who violated our criteria, we had populations of 120 in the first sample and 145 in the second on whom we could test our hypotheses. Since we lacked the time and funds to study 145 cases available for the second sample, we eliminated another 21 families who were borderline in their class membership. This gave us a final population of 124 mothers.

We eliminated 14 cases who could have been labeled as either lower middle or upper working. To reduce the excess of boys in the upper working class, we excluded 7 of them at random. Unfortunately, we were forced by the limited number of working-class families descended from immigrants born in northwestern Europe to retain 11 boys, each of whom had a parent deriving from countries in eastern or southern Europe. These exceptions included one upper middle-class boy whose mother was born in French Canada; three lower middles, two with mothers of Polish descent, and one with a father of Slavic descent; six in the upper working class, two with Italian-born mothers, two whose mothers were born in Hungary, one whose mother was born in Poland, and one with a Lithuanian-born mother; and one in the lower working class whose father was born in Poland.

Following a new plan established by the Detroit Board of Public Education, we next sent a letter to the parents of each prospective subject describing the research we hoped to do and asking for the parents' written permission for their son to participate. Most of the letters were returned within a day. Ours was the first project to operate under the new regulations requiring parental approval before the schools would allow children to take part in research, and we were relieved when the final tally showed that 112 of the 124 parents to whom we had written returned the letters with their signatures. Nine failed to respond, and only 3 refused permission. These 12 parents were randomly distributed among the 4 social classes.

# APPENDIX B

## ADDITIONAL ITEMS USED TO CATEGORIZE DISCIPLINARY PRACTICES

1. Here are some ways parents have of punishing their children. Which of these do you do most, next, and next? (The interviewer handed the mother a card containing a typed list of practices.) Again it may be hard to pick your first three choices, but do the best you can to pick those that fit you best. (The interviewer then read them aloud.)

   a. Show him that you are disappointed in him, or that it makes you feel bad when he does wrong.
   b. Spank him or whip him for doing wrong.
   c. Scold him and warn him that you may have to spank or whip him if he ever does it again.
   d. Deprive him of something that he likes or expects.
   e. Tell him you can't love such a bad boy and others won't like him either.
   f. Don't show any feeling about it, but just ignore him until he is good again.
   g. If none of these fit, what *do* you do?

2. How important in general do you feel it is for a boy of your son's age to obey you when you tell him to do something? (If the respondent asked about obeying quickly, the interviewer said, "Just in general, how important do you feel it is for him to obey you?")

   a. Why do you feel this way?

b. What do you do if he doesn't obey?
c. How many times do you ask him to do something before you put your foot down?

3. Here is an experience one mother has. Let's call her Mrs. Smith. Mrs. Smith's son often gets very angry at her. He shouts at her, tries to kick and slap at her. What do you think Mrs. Smith should do?

a. What might be causing her boy to act this way?
b. If your own son did this, how do you think you would feel?

4. Many people feel there is such a thing as punishing a child too little. How do you feel about this? (If the respondent gave no reasons or a short answer, the interviewer asked, "Why? Can you tell me something about your reasons?")

5. Do you feel you are disciplining your child any differently from the way your parents handled you? (The interviewer recorded the woman's reaction to the question: whether she groped for an answer, for example, or whether she answered quickly. If she answered in the affirmative, he said, "In what ways?" and "Why?" if these had not been covered.)

# APPENDIX C

## STORY COMPLETION TESTS

STORIES IN CHAPTER 7

A1.

Bill never knew his parents, but he has always loved his Aunt Jane. Although she was ill with a weak heart, she raised him from infancy, and he has never had anyone but her. Bill appreciates her loving care, and has always confided in her because she is easy to talk to. One evening he brings Pat, a girl whom he likes very much, to meet his aunt. Pat and his aunt get along beautifully and Bill leaves the room for a minute. When he is taking Pat home, she smiles and tells him that while he was out of the room, his aunt told her that Bill has always worried about girls not liking him. For some reason Bill feels himself growing very angry. The next day, while he is speaking with his aunt, she begins to discuss Pat. Suddenly Bill tells her in a loud tense voice that he hates her for gossiping about his personal life. Aunt Jane gasps and starts to get up, but she falls to the floor, the victim of a fatal heart attack.

A2.

Jim loves to swim because he does it better than anything else. Jim's best friend, Bob, is also a terrific swimmer. Bob once saved Jim's life. Jim had been practicing alone at a small lake, and got a bad case of cramps in the middle of the lake. Bob heard Jim's cries for help, and pulled Jim to shore. Since then, Jim has become friends with Bob, and finds that they have many common interests. One summer day they are going swimming and they meet Sally on the way. They both like her a lot, so Jim asks her to come along. When they get to the lake, Sally wants to have them swim an underwater race. Jim and Bob agree to race thirty feet to the raft, turn around under water, and race back to shore. In front of Sally, Bob grins and asks Jim: "How much of a head start do you want?" Jim just says, "Let's start even," but he feels like slapping Bob. They begin the race. Underwater, Jim turns around before he gets to the raft. No one sees him, and he wins easily. Sally thinks he's terrific and sticks with him the rest of the time.

A3.

Whenever Joe wants advice or is in a jam, he can always get help or a couple of bucks from his Uncle Ted. Uncle Ted has been living with Joe's family for some time and he is responsible for putting Joe through college. One night Joe promises a friend he will walk over, but there is a heavy rain outside. His mother and Uncle Ted think he ought not to go because of the weather. Joe laughs and insists. And as Joe gets to the door, his Uncle says firmly: "Your mother and I think you ought not to go, and that's that." Joe is so mad he can hardly talk. He hates to be treated like a baby. He goes upstairs, but when the others have gone to bed, he sneaks downstairs and walks out. Feeling angry and defiant, he leaves the front door open. When he returns from his friend's house, he locks the door and goes to sleep. The next morning it is discovered that during the night a burglar has taken his uncle's wallet which had in it four hundred dollars and some very valuable papers.

B1.

Bruce feels pretty lucky to get Mrs. Miles as a teacher for his last semester of creative writing. She is an elderly woman who has a warm understanding of Bruce's writing, and her criticism of his work is always fair. She comments favorably on his themes, is really responsible for developing his talent, and finally gets him a job with a newspaper. Then Bruce begins a series of essays describing the character and personality of his girl friend, Nancy. Mrs. Miles points out that he is not writing as well as he can. One day Bruce is headed for home in his car, and spots Mrs. Miles on the corner. He offers her a ride and she accepts. On the way, Mrs. Miles remarks that she has marked his last essay and places it on the seat beside him. Bruce glances down at it and sees the comment: "You have written very poorly about an unworthy topic." Bruce is enraged and thinks: "I wish I never had to talk to you again." In his excitement, he misses a stop sign and smashes into another car. He is uninjured, but Mrs. Miles is killed instantly.

B2.

Tom likes to compete with Dick in most things. Tom is a little better in his studies, but doesn't take the initiative in making friends. Dick, his closest buddy since boyhood, introduces Tom to fellows and girls, makes him feel comfortable with people, and always helps him in tough spots. Because of Dick, Tom is happy in college and gets to have more confidence in himself. One day, just before the final exam in a very important course that they are taking, Tom finds in the library a terrific book that answers a lot of difficult points on the exam. That evening the other guys are kidding Tom about being a little shy around girls. Dick joins in, and starts to tell a friendly joke about Tom. Tom says nothing, but he feels like choking Dick. After the others leave, Dick asks: "Well, any new ideas on the exam?" Tom replies, "No. I guess I'll go study." And he walks off to his own room.

B3.

Don has always been crazy about basketball, and he was very proud when he made the team. The coach, an older man, likes Don a great deal. He teaches him everything he knows about basketball, and helps Don to plan his college career. The last game of the season is coming up, and it's a big one. The school is honoring the coach's retirement, and the team wants to win the game for him. During afternoon practice, Don makes a bad mistake in a play. The coach points to him and says to all the other boys: "That was an example of a stupid play." Don is embarrassed in front of the other boys. He thinks to himself: "To hell with you and the team too." During the big game, at first the team is red hot. The coach beams at everyone from the bench.

Then things begin going badly and the team is losing. Suddenly Don looks at the opponents' defense and sees a way that his team can score a lot of points. But he says nothing, and the team goes on to lose. The coach is heartbroken and the occasion is spoiled.

STORIES IN CHAPTER 9

1.

All his friends know that Billy is interested in music and wants to grow up to be a concert player. Some of them have laughed at him for his ambition, but he has continued his practicing, even though he has begun to find music is harder and harder for him as he goes on. One day a famous musician visits his teacher. It is arranged for Billy to play for him. He thinks he had played very well, but as he is leaving, he overhears the musician telling his teacher that Billy does not have enough talent to be a concert player and that it is a waste of money for him to be taking lessons. The teacher seems to agree with him. Billy doesn't know what to do.

2.

Pete's father has always wanted him to be good at sports and has encouraged him to go out for the school teams. Pete, though, is short and not very strong or fast. So in spite of practicing more than anyone else and trying very hard, he has been put off of every squad he has tried out for. He knows his father is very disappointed in him, and he is disappointed, too, because he likes sports. Finally, he tries lightweight wrestling. He is given a chance in a big match, but he is too anxious to do well, gets rattled, and is easily thrown. He is so angry and disappointed that he bursts into tears in front of the whole crowd. After the match, the coach tells him he should give up sports.

3.

Joe's family have just moved into town from their farm. Joe is very eager to make friends at school, but as time goes by, he finds that he is being left out of everything. Often he doesn't know what the other kids are talking about or laughing at because he just isn't one of the gang. Finally, though, he becomes better acquainted with a few of the boys. These boys all belong to a certain club. He's very happy because they don't ignore him or call him a "hick" the way all the others do. Now the time has come for the club to vote on new members. Joe has told the guys how very much he wants to be a member, and he knows that if he can't get into that club, no other one will take him. This is his only chance, particularly since there is a rule that a person can only be voted on once and can't be put up for nomination again. The day of the meeting, Joe goes home and waits by the telephone. Finally, that evening, there is a call for him. He rushes to the phone. It is Frank, the guy that Joe likes best of all the club members. But all Frank asks about is the homework assignment. Finally Joe asks him whether he was voted into the club. Frank says, "Oh, it's too bad, Joe but you just didn't make the grade." Joe hangs up.

4.

Jimmy is a freshman in high school. Nothing seems to have gone right for him from the very first day in high school. He's been having trouble with the work and knows that the teacher, whom he likes, thinks he's dumb. He can never think of the right answers when he's called on in class. He's also had trouble getting along with the other boys. The kids all seem to have it in for him. Now when anything goes wrong on the playground or in class, the kids or the teacher blame it on him. One day, he hears a couple of the guys talking about him in the locker room and saying that they aren't going to let him join any of their clubs because nobody likes him or thinks he's any good. Jimmy feels that he can't stand it any longer.

5.

John has just finished high school and now has to earn money to help his family. He has had several jobs but lost them all. Even his family have begun to wonder what is wrong with him that he couldn't keep the jobs. Now he has finally found another job, and he feels that he will never be able to face people if he gets fired again. But John's work is not good. He can't seem to keep the records straight. Every time he has to do some bookkeeping, the figures add up wrong. His boss keeps pointing out all the things he is doing wrong and either makes fun of his difficulties or gets mad at him and bawls him out. One day the boss calls him into the office. John knows that a customer has been complaining to him about one of John's mistakes.

6.

George has always felt he was no good. He has tried desperately to make a good impression on the other kids in the class and on his teachers, but usually they just laugh at him, or say "That's just George!" He always seems to be the one who makes stupid mistakes, who bumps into things, and who never seems to know what he is doing. He wishes he could be like the bright guys in the class, or like the guys who are so good at sports, and he has always dreamed that some day he will get a chance to show everyone that he isn't just someone to laugh at.

One day, his teacher brings the school's brand new movie projector into the room and announces that they will have a special treat—a movie! She asks if anyone in the class knows how to run a projector. George looks at the projector and thinks it is like one his father has, and he eagerly raises his hand. All the kids laugh, and the teacher looks dubious. But George assures her that he knows all about running the machine. As he gets to the projector, though, he realizes that it isn't like his father's. He is about to admit he's not sure about it after all, when he sees all the class watching him and the teacher looking at him with a surprised and pleased look on her face. Suddenly, he knows he can't fail this time, and sets about to put the film into the projector. Then he signals that all is ready. The teacher shuts out the lights. He starts the movie. There is a horrible sound of clashing metal, a smell of burning film, and the machine stops dead. The film and the projector are ruined. He knows what the teacher and the class are thinking of him. He turns to run out of the room.

STORIES IN CHAPTER 11

A1.

Harry's mother is away on a long trip. His aunt is staying with Harry. In the past, his aunt has often taken him to the movies, cooked his favorite meals, and let him stay up later than usual.

Harry likes his aunt and wants things to go well. But this time she seems irritable and blames him for things. While she is there, the biggest football game of the year comes along. Harry is more excited about this than anything else and has saved his money to buy a ticket. He is lucky enough to get the last ticket that was left. The day of the game, he comes home for lunch. While he was gone, his aunt, impatient with his not cleaning up his room, has cleaned it for him and even burned up some old useless papers that were lying around. She scolds him for having forgotten to pick up before he went out. After lunch, he goes up to his room to change his clothes for the game. The room is neat and spotless. He hurries because there is not much time before the kick-off. As he is about ready to leave, he goes to his desk to get his ticket. It isn't there. He searches frantically. He calls to his aunt, but she has gone to visit the neighbors. He looks and looks. The minutes go by. When the clock tells him that the second half is almost over, he gives up. He has missed the game! As he is sitting there, his aunt comes in saying, "Doesn't the room look better now?" Then she tells him about burning the papers, and he realizes that his football ticket was in the papers and she has burned it up.

A2.

Paul has always hero worshipped his father and loved his mother just as much. But his father died two years ago, and Paul's mother has just married a man Paul has always hated.

A3.

Dave's teacher takes a great interest in all the children and goes out of her way to help them whenever she can. She is very interested in encouraging Dave's artistic talent. There is going to be a school carnival, and she fixes it up so that Dave has the privilege of being excused from classes to help paint decorations. The day before the carnival a famous magician comes to the school to entertain the children. Dave has been hearing for weeks how this magician can take his own head off his shoulders, put it on a chair, and make it talk. Dave has always been interested in magic. Like everyone else, he wouldn't miss the show for anything, particularly since the magician is only stopping in town long enough to give the special show at the school before taking a plane on to his next engagement in New York City. Luckily, work on the painting is far enough ahead of schedule so that he is free to see the show. Or so the teacher has told him. But then, just before the magician's show, she comes to him looking worried. She has misjudged the amount of work to be done. It is a much harder job than she had expected. Since the teacher and Dave have been the only ones working on the project, there is absolutely no one else who can help them or do it for them. The teacher tells Dave they will have to give up everything else and work steadily on the job if they are to finish it before the carnival opens the next day.

B1.

Dan likes baseball, and the coach has spent a lot of time with him helping him to develop his ability. Dan feels that the coach is a real friend and with his encouragement has spent many hours practicing. Athletic practice has come to take a lot of his time away from other schoolwork. In Dan's senior year, his last at the school, the coach calls him in and says that he is very disappointed to learn that Dan is doing badly in his studies. Dan tells the coach that he does not like schoolwork and that he thinks he has become so good at baseball that he will make a career of professional ball, where it won't matter whether he has had good marks or not. But the coach says that he's been watching Dan very carefully and although the boy is quite good for a high school athlete, there is no chance that he could succeed in professional ball. The coach also says that he is surprised that Dan was foolish enough to forget that the main purpose of school is studies, not athletics. The coach says that he is going to drop Dan from the team for his own good. Dan knows that he is so far behind in his other work that he can just barely get caught up enough to graduate from school with his class.

B2.

Russ does not have a father, but he has always been close to his mother and loves her very much because of all she has done for him. But since she was ill five years ago, she has been somewhat nervous and has worried a lot about Russ. One day, Russ comes in very excited and happy. The first football tryouts of the year have just been held that afternoon, and Russ has played so well that the coach enthusiastically put him down for the squad. Russ tells his mother that everything is all set, and the only thing he needs now is her permission for him to play. He hands her the permission slip to sign. But his mother looks very upset. She says that she thought he knew how she felt about his playing football, that she is afraid he will get hurt. She doesn't like to stop him from doing something that he really wants to do so much, but ever since the boy down the street was badly hurt and almost killed the year before, she has felt that she can never let Russ play football. Russ tries to point out that football is really safe when it is played right. She looks down at the permission slip and thinks a long time. Then she shakes her head, says "I'm sorry, Russ," and tears up the slip. She goes to the phone, calls the coach and tells him her decision. The coach tries to get her to change her mind but it is no use.

B3.

Don always looks forward to his art class. He admires his teacher's ability to draw and is very grateful for the many hours of kind and encouraging help that she gives him. But sometimes he is uncomfortable because she tells him that he shows a lot of talent and he could become a really good artist if he weren't so sloppy. She drives him hard, trying to make him do better work. For a month he does his best. The morning of the art contest, he puts the finishing touches on his work and happily rushes to show it to his teacher. She spreads it out on a table to get a better look at it. "At last!" she says. "For once you have gotten over your sloppiness and can win a state prize." She starts to pick the picture up off the table. There is a loud rip. Without realizing it, she has put the painting down in some glue, and part of it has stuck. The whole center of the picture is torn in ragged strips. There is just no way it can be repaired, and there is no time to do another one.

STORIES IN CHAPTER 12

A1.

Same as B1 in Chapter 11.

A2.

Same as A1 in Chapter 11.

A3.

When Bill was very young his father died. His mother made many sacrifices for him and he loves her very much. Today he has wonderful news for her. At school he has been taking a driving course which he likes very much. The instructor told Bill that he can get him a good job for afternoons and Saturdays, because he is such a dependable driver. Because he is only sixteen years old, his mother needs to sign his license application. Bill tells the instructor he is sure he can get the permission; he feels that he can now start to repay his mother for all she has done for him. He tells his mother about his opportunity and asks her to sign the application. She hesitates and then refuses. She explains that she did not object to his taking the supervised school driving course, but she thought he knew she disapproved of young people driving without supervision. She thanks him for his fine intentions, but says she is worried by all the young drivers who get into accidents and that she cannot let him get his license. Bill tries to point out how careful a driver he is. He tells her the instructor picked him for the job. She listens patiently, and, after a long pause, says she is very sorry, and does not sign the slip. A few minutes later, the instructor calls to tell Bill that the job is all set and to ask if he can take the driving test that afternoon. Bill explains that his mother will not give her permission. The instructor speaks to her and tries to reassure her about Bill's driving ability and carefulness. She thanks him for helping her son but does not change her mind. Bill realizes that the possibility of any such job is gone.

B1.

Tom is the first violinist in the school orchestra. The music teacher has given him a great deal of encouragement with the violin and has taught him some conducting too. Tom feels that the teacher is a real friend. During his senior year Tom has spent so much time practicing for the annual concert that he is falling down in all his school studies. One day he gets a letter saying he will not graduate unless he improves his grades. Tom knows that if he does nothing but study for the rest of the semester he can graduate with his class, but he decides not to worry about it. He wants to go on with his music anyway. He doesn't really like nor does he need his other studies. He tells the music teacher the whole story that afternoon after rehearsal. The teacher says that Tom is a good violinist. He thinks Tom will always get pleasure from playing the violin but he is not good enough to become a professional performer. Besides, the teacher reminds him, if he wants to get further musical training at either the conservatory or the university, he has to graduate from high school and get good grades. How could Tom have been so blind as to forget that the first purpose of school is studies, not extracurricular activities? The teacher says that although he was counting on Tom for the concerts, he is going to drop him from the orchestra for his own good.

B2.

Same as B3 in Chapter 11.

B3.

Same as B2 in Chapter 11.

STORIES IN CHAPTER 14

1.

Jack has always admired the coach very much and wanted the coach to like him. He goes out for the baseball team, but the coach doesn't give him a fair chance.

2.

Bill looks up to and admires his sister, but when something goes wrong, she always tells his parents it's his fault. Bill doesn't know what to do.

3.

It is summer and Ed has a job working with a tough work-gang. One member of the work crew has been teasing and bullying Ed for weeks. Now the bully is asleep.

4.

Jim's mother is usually very patient and fair. But one day she sees Jim and his best pal, Bob, doing something she feels they shouldn't be doing. She immediately says she won't have such things going on in her house and tells Jim never to see Bob again.

5.

Paul loved his parents very much. But his father died two years ago, and his mother promised him then that she would not marry again without talking it over with him. But now she's telling him she's going to marry some man he's never met.

6.

John and his father are very close. But when something goes wrong, his father always blames John and not his brother. John doesn't know what to do.

# APPENDIX D

## Frequencies of Cells for Relations Cited in Summary Tables

RESULTS REPORTED IN CHAPTER 4

| | *Discipline* | | | |
|---|---|---|---|---|
| *Social Class* | *Psychological* | *Mixed* | *Corporal* | $N = 115$ |
| Middle | 29 | 5 | 4 | $\chi^2 = 49.45$ |
| Working | 9 | 28 | 40 | $P < .001$ (1t) |
| | | | | Sample 1 |

| | *Obedience Requests* | | |
|---|---|---|---|
| *Social Class* | *Arbitrary* | *Explained* | $N = 81$ |
| Middle | 16 | 27 | $\chi^2 = 9.40$ |
| Working | 28 | 10 | $P < .001$ (1t) |
| | | | Sample 2 |

| | *Maternal Control* | | |
|---|---|---|---|
| *Social Class* | *Present* | *Absent* | $N = 115$ |
| Middle | 24 | 14 | $\chi^2 = 5.05$ |
| Working | 30 | 47 | $P = .02$ (1t) |
| | | | Sample 1 |

| | *Reward* | | |
|---|---|---|---|
| *Social Class* | *Occasional* | *Frequent* | $N = 77$ |
| Middle | 13 | 19 | $\chi^2 = 2.69$ |
| Working | 28 | 17 | $P = .05$ (1t) |
| | | | Sample 2 |

| | *Type of Reward* | | | |
|---|---|---|---|---|
| *Social Class* | *Psychic* | *Neither* | *Concrete* | $N = 115$ |
| Middle | 25 | 6 | 7 | $\chi^2 = 29.52$ |
| Working | 12 | 37 | 28 | $P < .001$ |
| | | | | Sample 1 |

| | *Weaning* | | |
|---|---|---|---|
| *Social Class* | *Early* | *Late* | $N = 103$ |
| Middle | 33 | 22 | $\chi^2 = 5.26$ |
| Working | 17 | 31 | $P = .01$ (1t) |
| | | | Sample 2 |

RESULTS REPORTED IN CHAPTER 4 (Continued)

| Social Class | Discipline: Psychological | Mixed | Corporal | |
|---|---|---|---|---|
| Middle | 38 | 9 | 10 | $N = 105$, $\chi^2 = 6.08$, $P < .05$, Sample 2 |
| Working | 21 | 10 | 17 | |

| Social Class | Toilet Training: Not Severe | Severe | |
|---|---|---|---|
| Middle | 17 | 38 | $N = 104$, $\chi^2 = 2.83$, $P < .05$ (1t), Sample 2 |
| Working | 24 | 25 | |

RESULTS REPORTED IN CHAPTER 6

| Severity of Guilt about Death Wishes | Weaning: Early | Late | |
|---|---|---|---|
| High | 17 | 21 | $N = 101$, $\chi^2 = 10.88$, $P < .01$ |
| Medium | 24 | 9 | |
| Low | 10 | 20 | |

| Severity of Guilt about Death Wishes | Toilet Training: Not Severe | Severe | |
|---|---|---|---|
| High | 17 | 22 | $N = 100$, $\chi^2 = 8.41$, $P < .02$ |
| Medium | 6 | 25 | |
| Low | 16 | 14 | |

| Severity of Guilt about Death Wishes | Discipline: Psychol. | Mixed | Corporal | |
|---|---|---|---|---|
| High | 22 | 7 | 11 | $N = 108$, $\chi^2 = 5.86$, $P < .30$ |
| Medium | 22 | 6 | 5 | |
| Low | 14 | 8 | 13 | |

| Severity of Guilt about Death Wishes | Obedience Requests: Arbitrary | Explained | |
|---|---|---|---|
| High | 16 | 11 | $N = 78$, $\chi^2 = .77$, $P < .70$ |
| Medium | 11 | 12 | |
| Low | 14 | 14 | |

| Severity of Guilt about Death Wishes | Social Class: Working | Middle | |
|---|---|---|---|
| High | 18 | 22 | $N = 108$, $\chi^2 = 1.08$, $P < .60$ |
| Medium | 14 | 19 | |
| Low | 19 | 16 | |

RESULTS REPORTED IN CHAPTER 6 (*Continued*)

| *Severity of Guilt about Theft* | *Social Class* | | |
|---|---|---|---|
| | *Working* | *Middle* | |
| High | 20 | 13 | N = 104 |
| Medium | 29 | 32 | $\chi^2 = 5.46$ |
| Low | 2 | 8 | $P = .07$ |

| *Severity of Guilt about Theft* | *Weaning* | | |
|---|---|---|---|
| | *Early* | *Late* | |
| High | 15 | 14 | N = 97 |
| Medium | 25 | 33 | $\chi^2 = 8.49$ |
| Low | 9 | 1 | $P < .02$ |

| *Severity of Guilt about Theft* | *Toilet Training* | | |
|---|---|---|---|
| | *Not Severe* | *Severe* | |
| High | 13 | 17 | N = 97 |
| Medium | 22 | 35 | $\chi^2 = .18$ |
| Low | 4 | 6 | $P < 1.00$ |

| *Severity of Guilt about Theft* | *Discipline* | | | |
|---|---|---|---|---|
| | *Psychol.* | *Mixed* | *Corporal* | |
| High | 17 | 9 | 7 | N = 104 |
| Medium | 35 | 9 | 17 | $\chi^2 = 6.22$ |
| Low | 7 | 0 | 3 | $P = .19$ |

| *Severity of Guilt about Theft* | *Obedience Requests* | | |
|---|---|---|---|
| | *Arbitrary* | *Explained* | |
| High | 13 | 9 | N = 76 |
| Medium | 24 | 21 | $\chi^2 = .63$ |
| Low | 6 | 3 | $P < .80$ |

| *Severity of Guilt about Disobedience* | *Weaning* | | |
|---|---|---|---|
| | *Early* | *Late* | N = 88 |
| High | 19 | 29 | $\chi^2 = 3.71$ |
| Low | 25 | 15 | $P = .06$ |

| *Severity of Guilt about Disobedience* | *Toilet Training* | | |
|---|---|---|---|
| | *Not Severe* | *Severe* | N = 89 |
| High | 24 | 26 | $\chi^2 = 3.74$ |
| Low | 10 | 29 | $P = .05$ |

**RESULTS REPORTED IN CHAPTER 6 (Continued)**

| *Severity of Guilt about Disobedience* | *Discipline* | | | |
|---|---|---|---|---|
| | *Psychol.* | *Mixed* | *Corporal* | |
| High | 33 | 10 | 12 | $N = 95$ $\chi^2 = .79$ $P < .70$ |
| Low | 24 | 5 | 11 | |

| *Severity of Guilt about Disobedience* | *Obedience Requests* | | |
|---|---|---|---|
| | *Arbitrary* | *Explained* | |
| High | 19 | 19 | $N = 69$ $\chi^2 = .48$ $P < .50$ |
| Low | 19 | 12 | |

| *Severity of Guilt about Disobedience* | *Social Class* | | |
|---|---|---|---|
| | *Working* | *Middle* | |
| High | 26 | 29 | $N = 95$ $\chi^2 = .003$ $P < 1.00$ |
| Low | 20 | 20 | |

| *Resistance to Temptation Concerning Theft* | *Social Class* | | |
|---|---|---|---|
| | *Working* | *Middle* | |
| Yield | 29 | 32 | $N = 112$ $\chi^2 = .02$ $P < .90$ |
| Resist | 24 | 27 | |

| *Resistance to Temptation Concerning Theft* | *Weaning* | | |
|---|---|---|---|
| | *Early* | *Late* | |
| Yield | 30 | 28 | $N = 105$ $\chi^2 = .09$ $P < .80$ |
| Resist | 22 | 25 | |

| *Resistance to Temptation Concerning Theft* | *Toilet Training* | | |
|---|---|---|---|
| | *Not Severe* | *Severe* | |
| Yield | 25 | 32 | $N = 104$ $\chi^2 = .67$ $P < .50$ |
| Resist | 16 | 31 | |

| *Resistance to Temptation Concerning Theft* | *Discipline* | | | |
|---|---|---|---|---|
| | *Psychol.* | *Mixed* | *Corporal* | |
| Yield | 34 | 10 | 17 | $N = 112$ $\chi^2 = .60$ $P < .80$ |
| Resist | 28 | 11 | 12 | |

| *Resistance to Temptation Concerning Theft* | *Obedience Requests* | | |
|---|---|---|---|
| | *Arbitrary* | *Explained* | |
| Yield | 29 | 15 | $N = 81$ $\chi^2 = 4.24$ $P = .04$ |
| Resist | 15 | 22 | |

RESULTS REPORTED IN CHAPTER 6 (*Continued*)

| *Resistance to Temptation Concerning Disobedience* | *Weaning* | | |
|---|---|---|---|
| | *Early* | *Late* | |
| Yield | 35 | 44 | $N = 105$ |
| Resist | 17 | 9 | $\chi^2 = 2.69$, $P = .10$ |

| *Resistance to Temptation Concerning Disobedience* | *Toilet Training* | | |
|---|---|---|---|
| | *Not Severe* | *Severe* | |
| Yield | 33 | 48 | $N = 104$ |
| Resist | 8 | 15 | $\chi^2 = .08$, $P < .80$ |

| *Resistance to Temptation Concerning Disobedience* | *Discipline* | | | |
|---|---|---|---|---|
| | *Psychol.* | *Mixed* | *Corporal* | |
| Yield | 50 | 13 | 22 | $N = 112$ |
| Resist | 12 | 8 | 7 | $\chi^2 = 2.83$, $P < .30$ |

| *Resistance to Temptation Concerning Disobedience* | *Obedience Requests* | | |
|---|---|---|---|
| | *Arbitrary* | *Explained* | |
| Yield | 38 | 24 | $N = 81$ |
| Resist | 6 | 13 | $\chi^2 = 4.05$, $P < .05$ |

| *Resistance to Temptation Concerning Disobedience* | *Social Class* | | |
|---|---|---|---|
| | *Working* | *Middle* | |
| Yield | 42 | 43 | $N = 112$ |
| Resist | 11 | 16 | $\chi^2 = .32$, $P < .60$ |

| *Perceived Source of Standards* | *Social Class* | | |
|---|---|---|---|
| | *Working* | *Middle* | |
| Inner certainty | 27 | 45 | $N = 109$ |
| Thinks of others | 18 | 13 | $\chi^2 = 7.52$ |
| Hears voice | 5 | 1 | $P = .02$ |

| *Perceived Source of Standards* | *Weaning* | | |
|---|---|---|---|
| | *Early* | *Late* | |
| Inner certainty | 36 | 31 | $N = 102$ |
| Thinks of others | 13 | 17 | $\chi^2 = 2.80$ |
| Hears voice | 1 | 4 | $P < .30$ |

**RESULTS REPORTED IN CHAPTER 6 (Continued)**

| *Perceived Source of Standards* | *Toilet Training* | | |
|---|---|---|---|
| | *Not Severe* | *Severe* | |
| Inner certainty | 20 | 44 | $N = 101$ |
| Thinks of others | 16 | 15 | $\chi^2 = 5.53$ |
| Hears voice | 4 | 2 | $P = .07$ |

| *Perceived Source of Standards* | *Discipline* | | | |
|---|---|---|---|---|
| | *Psychol.* | *Mixed* | *Corporal* | |
| Inner certainty | 41 | 17 | 14 | $N = 109$ |
| Thinks of others | 15 | 4 | 12 | $\chi^2 = 7.89$ |
| Hears voice | 5 | 0 | 1 | $P < .10$ |

| *Perceived Source of Standards* | *Obedience Requests* | | |
|---|---|---|---|
| | *Arbitrary* | *Explained* | |
| Inner certainty | 26 | 28 | $N = 78$ |
| Thinks of others | 12 | 8 | $\chi^2 = 1.72$ |
| Hears voice | 3 | 1 | $P < .50$ |

| *Externalization after Theft* | *Weaning* | | |
|---|---|---|---|
| | *Early* | *Late* | $N = 105$ |
| Present | 22 | 17 | $\chi^2 = .78$ |
| Absent | 30 | 36 | $P < .40$ |

| *Externalization after Theft* | *Toilet Training* | | |
|---|---|---|---|
| | *Not Severe* | *Severe* | $N = 104$ |
| Present | 19 | 20 | $\chi^2 = 1.68$ |
| Absent | 22 | 43 | $P = .20$ |

| *Externalization after Theft* | *Discipline* | | | |
|---|---|---|---|---|
| | *Psychol.* | *Mixed* | *Corporal* | $N = 112$ |
| Present | 29 | 3 | 11 | $\chi^2 = 7.76$ |
| Absent | 33 | 18 | 18 | $P = .02$ |

| *Externalization after Theft* | *Obedience Requests* | | |
|---|---|---|---|
| | *Arbitrary* | *Explained* | $N = 81$ |
| Present | 21 | 15 | $\chi^2 = .18$ |
| Absent | 23 | 22 | $P < .70$ |

| *Externalization after Theft* | *Social Class* | | |
|---|---|---|---|
| | *Working* | *Middle* | $N = 112$ |
| Present | 20 | 23 | $\chi^2 = .003$ |
| Absent | 33 | 36 | $P < 1.00$ |

RESULTS REPORTED IN CHAPTER 6 (*Continued*)

| *Externalization after Disobedience* | *Social Class* | | |
|---|---|---|---|
| | *Working* | *Middle* | |
| Present | 29 | 29 | $N = 112$ |
| Absent | 24 | 30 | $\chi^2 = .16$<br>$P < .70$ |

| *Externalization after Disobedience* | *Weaning* | | |
|---|---|---|---|
| | *Early* | *Late* | |
| Present | 21 | 30 | $N = 105$ |
| Absent | 31 | 23 | $\chi^2 = 2.15$<br>$P = .14$ |

| *Externalization after Disobedience* | *Toilet Training* | | |
|---|---|---|---|
| | *Not Severe* | *Severe* | |
| Present | 26 | 28 | $N = 104$ |
| Absent | 15 | 35 | $\chi^2 = 2.86$<br>$P = .09$ |

| *Externalization after Disobedience* | *Discipline* | | | |
|---|---|---|---|---|
| | *Psychol.* | *Mixed* | *Corporal* | |
| Present | 38 | 7 | 13 | $N = 112$ |
| Absent | 24 | 14 | 16 | $\chi^2 = 5.73$<br>$P = .06$ |

| *Externalization after Disobedience* | *Obedience Requests* | | |
|---|---|---|---|
| | *Arbitrary* | *Explained* | |
| Present | 26 | 19 | $N = 81$ |
| Absent | 18 | 18 | $\chi^2 = .22$<br>$P < .70$ |

RESULTS REPORTED IN CHAPTER 9

| *Shift in Denial* | *Verbal Intelligence* | | |
|---|---|---|---|
| | *Low* | *High* | |
| Increase | 27 | 14 | $N = 96$ |
| No incr. | 23 | 32 | $\chi^2 = 4.52$<br>$P = .03$ |

| *Shift in Denial* | *Social Class* | | |
|---|---|---|---|
| | *Working* | *Middle* | |
| Increase | 19 | 22 | $N = 96$ |
| No incr. | 24 | 31 | $\chi^2 = .003$<br>$P < 1.00$ |

| *Shift in Denial* | *Obedience Requests* | | |
|---|---|---|---|
| | *Arbitrary* | *Explained* | |
| Increase | 21 | 15 | $N = 83$ |
| No incr. | 16 | 31 | $\chi^2 = 3.94$<br>$P = .05$ |

**RESULTS REPORTED IN CHAPTER 9 (*Continued*)**

| *Shift in Denial* | *Discipline* | | | |
|---|---|---|---|---|
| | *Psychol.* | *Mixed* | *Corp.* | |
| Increase | 24 | 3 | 14 | $N = 96$ |
| No incr. | 29 | 15 | 11 | $\chi^2 = 7.52$ <br> $P = .02$ |

| *Shift in Denial* | *Discipline* | | | | | | |
|---|---|---|---|---|---|---|---|
| | *Psychol.* | | *Mixed* | | *Corporal* | | |
| | *Low* | *High* | *Low* | *High* | *Low* | *High* | |
| | *Intel.* | | *Intel.* | | *Intel.* | | |
| Increase | 15 | 9 | 1 | 2 | 11 | 3 | $N = 96$ <br> $\chi^2 = 17.14$ |
| No incr. | 12 | 17 | 8 | 7 | 3 | 8 | $P < .01$ |

| *Shift in Denial* | *Reward* | | | | |
|---|---|---|---|---|---|
| | *Occasional* | | *Frequent* | | |
| | *Low* | *High* | *Low* | *High* | |
| | *Intel.* | | *Intel.* | | |
| Increase | 12 | 7 | 12 | 3 | $N = 78$ <br> $\chi^2 = 11.30$ |
| No incr. | 8 | 10 | 9 | 17 | $P = .01$ |

| *Shift in Denial* | *Obedience Requests* | | | | |
|---|---|---|---|---|---|
| | *Arbitrary* | | *Explained* | | |
| | *Occas.* | *Freq.* | *Occas.* | *Freq.* | |
| | *Reward* | | *Reward* | | |
| Increase | 12 | 7 | 4 | 6 | $N = 65$ <br> $\tau = .28$ |
| No incr. | 6 | 7 | 8 | 15 | $P < .01$ (1t) |
| Prop. incr. | .67 | .50 | .33 | .29 | |

| *Shift in Denial* | *Reward* | | |
|---|---|---|---|
| | *Occasional* | *Frequent* | |
| Increase | 19 | 15 | $N = 78$ <br> $\chi^2 = 1.18$ |
| No incr. | 18 | 26 | $P < .30$ |

| *Shift in Denial* | *Social Class* | | | | |
|---|---|---|---|---|---|
| | *Working* | | *Middle* | | |
| | *Low* | *High* | *Low* | *High* | |
| | *Intel.* | | *Intel.* | | |
| Increase | 18 | 1 | 9 | 13 | $N = 96$ <br> $\chi^2 = 11.83$ |
| No incr. | 12 | 12 | 11 | 20 | $P = .01$ |

| *Shift in Denial* | *Obedience Requests* | | | | |
|---|---|---|---|---|---|
| | *Arbitrary* | | *Explained* | | |
| | *Low* | *High* | *Low* | *High* | |
| | *Intel.* | | *Intel.* | | |
| Increase | 12 | 9 | 10 | 5 | $N = 83$ <br> $\chi^2 = 9.90$ |
| No incr. | 5 | 11 | 13 | 18 | $P = .02$ |

RESULTS REPORTED IN CHAPTER 9 (Continued)

| | Discipline | | | | | | |
|---|---|---|---|---|---|---|---|
| | Psychol. | | Mixed | | Corporal | | |
| *Shift in Denial* | Occas. Reward | Freq. | Occas. Reward | Freq. | Occas. Reward | Freq. | |
| Increase | 14 | 9 | 0 | 1 | 5 | 5 | $N = 78$, $\chi^2 = 18.05$, $P < .01$ |
| No incr. | 5 | 18 | 7 | 4 | 6 | 4 | |

| | Psychol. Discipline and Reward | | | | |
|---|---|---|---|---|---|
| | Occasional | | Frequent | | |
| *Shift in Denial* | Low Intel. | High | Low Intel. | High | |
| Increase | 7 | 7 | 8 | 1 | $N = 46$, $\chi^2 = 14.41$, $P < .01$ |
| No incr. | 3 | 2 | 7 | 11 | |

| | Obedience Requests | | | | | | |
|---|---|---|---|---|---|---|---|
| | Arbitrary | | | Explained | | | |
| *Shift in Denial* | Psy. | Mix. | Corp. | Psy. | Mix. | Corp. | |
| Increase | 13 | 1 | 7 | 10 | 2 | 3 | $N = 83$, $\chi^2 = 8.87$, $P = .12$ |
| No. incr. | 9 | 3 | 4 | 16 | 10 | 5 | |

RESULTS REPORTED IN CHAPTER 10

| | Social Class | | |
|---|---|---|---|
| *Recall* | Working | Middle | |
| Comp. | 30 | 15 | $N = 106$, $\chi^2 = 5.90$, $P = .05$ |
| Same | 13 | 13 | |
| Incomp. | 14 | 21 | |

| | Discipline | | | |
|---|---|---|---|---|
| *Recall* | Psychol. | Mixed | Corporal | |
| Comp. | 25 | 9 | 11 | $N = 106$, $\chi^2 = 5.60$, $P < .30$ |
| Same | 16 | 7 | 3 | |
| Incomp. | 19 | 4 | 12 | |

| | Obedience Requests | | |
|---|---|---|---|
| *Recall* | Arbitrary | Explained | |
| Comp. | 11 | 26 | $N = 92$, $\chi^2 = 6.72$, $P = .04$ |
| Same | 15 | 9 | |
| Incomp. | 15 | 16 | |

RESULTS REPORTED IN CHAPTER 10 (*Continued*)

| *Recall* | *Reward* | | |
|---|---|---|---|
| | *Occasional* | *Frequent* | $N = 84$ |
| Comp. | 15 | 19 | $\chi^2 = 1.59$ |
| Same | 13 | 9 | $P < .50$ |
| Incomp. | 12 | 16 | |

| *Recall* | *Social Class* | | | | | | |
|---|---|---|---|---|---|---|---|
| | *Working* | | | *Middle* | | | |
| | *Psy.* | *Mix.* | *Corp.* | *Psy.* | *Mix.* | *Corp.* | $N = 106$ |
| | *Discipline* | | | *Discipline* | | | $\chi^2 = 23.68$ |
| | | | | | | | $P = .01$ |
| Comp. | 6 | 3 | 6 | 19 | 6 | 5 | |
| Same | 9 | 4 | 0 | 7 | 3 | 3 | |
| Incomp. | 7 | 3 | 11 | 12 | 1 | 1 | |

| *Recall* | *Social Class* | | | | |
|---|---|---|---|---|---|
| | *Working* | | *Middle* | | |
| | *Early* | *Late* | *Early* | *Late* | $N = 99$ |
| | *Weaning* | | *Weaning* | | $\chi^2 = 9.02$ |
| | | | | | $P = .17$ |
| Comp. | 7 | 7 | 19 | 9 | |
| Same | 3 | 9 | 6 | 7 | |
| Incomp. | 6 | 13 | 7 | 6 | |

| *Recall* | *Social Class* | | | | |
|---|---|---|---|---|---|
| | *Working* | | *Middle* | | |
| | *Not Sev.* | *Severe* | *Not Sev.* | *Severe* | $N = 102$ |
| | *Toilet Training* | | *Toilet Training* | | $\chi^2 = 15.15$ |
| | | | | | $P = .02$ |
| Comp. | 9 | 6 | 7 | 21 | |
| Same | 4 | 9 | 2 | 10 | |
| Incomp. | 9 | 12 | 8 | 5 | |

| *Recall* | *Weaning* | | |
|---|---|---|---|
| | *Early* | *Late* | $N = 99$ |
| Comp. | 26 | 16 | $\chi^2 = 5.43$ |
| Same | 9 | 16 | $P = .07$ |
| Incomp. | 13 | 19 | |

| *Recall* | *Toilet Training* | | |
|---|---|---|---|
| | *Not Severe* | *Severe* | $N = 102$ |
| Comp. | 16 | 27 | $\chi^2 = 4.25$ |
| Same | 6 | 19 | $P = .12$ |
| Incomp. | 17 | 17 | |

RESULTS REPORTED IN CHAPTER 10 (*Continued*)

| | *Social Class* | | | | |
|---|---|---|---|---|---|
| | *Working* | | *Middle* | | |
| | *Occas.* | *Freq.* | *Occas.* | *Freq.* | $N = 84$ |
| *Recall* | *Reward* | | *Reward* | | $\chi^2 = 9.09$ |
| | | | | | $P = .17$ |
| Comp. | 6 | 5 | 9 | 14 | |
| Same | 7 | 4 | 6 | 5 | |
| Incomp. | 7 | 11 | 5 | 5 | |

| | *Social Class* | | | | |
|---|---|---|---|---|---|
| | *Working* | | *Middle* | | |
| *Recall* | *Arb.* | *Expl.* | *Arb.* | *Expl.* | $N = 92$ |
| | | | | | $\chi^2 = 12.18$ |
| | | | | | $P = .06$ |
| Comp. | 6 | 5 | 5 | 21 | |
| Same | 9 | 3 | 6 | 6 | |
| Incomp. | 11 | 8 | 4 | 8 | |

| | *Obedience Requests* | | | | | | |
|---|---|---|---|---|---|---|---|
| | *Arbitrary* | | | *Explained* | | | |
| | *Psy.* | *Mix.* | *Corp.* | *Psy.* | *Mix.* | *Corp.* | $N = 93$ |
| *Recall* | *Discipline* | | | *Discipline* | | | $\chi^2 = 17.54$ |
| | | | | | | | $P = .07$ |
| Comp. | 8 | 1 | 2 | 15 | 7 | 4 | |
| Same | 12 | 2 | 2 | 4 | 4 | 1 | |
| Incomp. | 7 | 2 | 6 | 10 | 1 | 5 | |

| | *Reward* | | | | | | |
|---|---|---|---|---|---|---|---|
| | *Occasional* | | | *Frequent* | | | |
| | *Psy.* | *Mix.* | *Corp.* | *Psy.* | *Mix.* | *Corp.* | $N = 85$ |
| *Recall* | *Discipline* | | | *Discipline* | | | $\chi^2 = 15.17$ |
| | | | | | | | $P = .13$ |
| Comp. | 6 | 4 | 5 | 14 | 2 | 3 | |
| Same | 10 | 3 | 1 | 6 | 2 | 1 | |
| Incomp. | 6 | 0 | 6 | 11 | 1 | 4 | |

| | *Obedience Requests* | | | | |
|---|---|---|---|---|---|
| | *Arbitrary* | | *Explained* | | |
| | *Occas.* | *Freq.* | *Occas.* | *Freq.* | $N = 74$ |
| *Recall* | *Reward* | | *Reward* | | $\chi^2 = 13.32$ |
| | | | | | $P = .04$ |
| Comp. | 6 | 3 | 4 | 14 | |
| Same | 9 | 5 | 5 | 3 | |
| Incomp. | 5 | 9 | 6 | 5 | |

RESULTS REPORTED IN CHAPTER 11

| *Shift in Defense* | *Social Class* | | |
|---|---|---|---|
| | *Working* | *Middle* | |
| Increase | 12 | 26 | $N = 88$ |
| No incr. | 29 | 21 | $\chi^2 = 5.04$, $P = .03$ |

| *Shift in Defense* | *Obedience Requests* | | |
|---|---|---|---|
| | *Arbitrary* | *Explained* | |
| Increase | 15 | 17 | $N = 77$ |
| No incr. | 17 | 28 | $\chi^2 = .32$, $P < .60$ |

| *Shift in Defense* | *Discipline* | | | |
|---|---|---|---|---|
| | *Psychol.* | *Mixed* | *Corp.* | |
| Increase | 21 | 8 | 9 | $N = 88$ |
| No incr. | 28 | 10 | 12 | $\chi^2 = .02$, $P < 1.00$ |

| *Shift in Defense* | *Reward* | | |
|---|---|---|---|
| | *Occasional* | *Frequent* | |
| Increase | 13 | 17 | $N = 68$ |
| No incr. | 18 | 20 | $\chi^2 = .01$, $P < 1.00$ |

| | *Social Class* | | | | | | |
|---|---|---|---|---|---|---|---|
| | *Working* | | | *Middle* | | | |
| *Shift in Defense* | *Psy.* | *Mix.* | *Corp.* | *Psy.* | *Mix.* | *Corp.* | |
| | *Discipline* | | | *Discipline* | | | |
| Increase | 5 | 2 | 5 | 16 | 6 | 4 | $N = 88$ |
| No incr. | 12 | 7 | 10 | 16 | 3 | 2 | $\chi^2 = 7.67$, $P = .18$ |

| | *Obedience Requests* | | | | | | |
|---|---|---|---|---|---|---|---|
| | *Arbitrary* | | | *Explained* | | | |
| *Shift in Defense* | *Psy.* | *Mix.* | *Corp.* | *Psy.* | *Mix.* | *Corp.* | |
| | *Discipline* | | | *Discipline* | | | |
| Increase | 8 | 1 | 6 | 11 | 4 | 2 | $N = 77$ |
| No incr. | 11 | 2 | 4 | 15 | 8 | 5 | $\chi^2 = 2.32$, $P < .90$ |

| | *Obedience Requests* | | | | |
|---|---|---|---|---|---|
| | *Arbitrary* | | *Explained* | | |
| *Shift in Defense* | *Occas.* | *Freq.* | *Occas.* | *Freq.* | |
| | *Reward* | | *Reward* | | |
| Increase | 8 | 5 | 3 | 10 | $N = 60$ |
| No incr. | 4 | 10 | 12 | 8 | $\chi^2 = 7.99$, $P = .05$ |

RESULTS REPORTED IN CHAPTER 11 (*Continued*)

| Shift in Defense | *Social Class* Working: Expl. Requests | Working: Arb. Requests | Middle: Expl. Requests | Middle: Arb. Requests | |
|---|---|---|---|---|---|
| Increase | 3 | 7 | 14 | 8 | $N = 77$ |
| No incr. | 14 | 12 | 14 | 5 | $\tau = .28$ |
| Prop. incr. | .18 | .36 | .50 | .60 | $P = < .01$ (1t) |

| Shift in Defense | *Social Class* Working: Occas. Reward | Working: Freq. Reward | Middle: Occas. Reward | Middle: Freq. Reward | |
|---|---|---|---|---|---|
| Increase | 5 | 5 | 8 | 12 | $N = 68$ |
| No incr. | 10 | 12 | 8 | 8 | $\chi^2 = 4.53$ |
| | | | | | $P < .30$ |

| Shift in Defense | *Reward* Occasional: Psy. Discipline | Occasional: Mix. Discipline | Occasional: Corp. Discipline | Frequent: Psy. Discipline | Frequent: Mix. Discipline | Frequent: Corp. Discipline | |
|---|---|---|---|---|---|---|---|
| Increase | 6 | 3 | 4 | 13 | 0 | 4 | $N = 68$ |
| No incr. | 10 | 3 | 5 | 12 | 4 | 4 | $\chi^2 = 5.76$ |
| | | | | | | | $P < .40$ |

RESULTS REPORTED IN CHAPTER 14

| Aggression | *Social Class* Working | Middle | Prop. Middle | |
|---|---|---|---|---|
| Very indirect | 15 | 10 | .40 | $N = 115$ |
| Somewhat ind. | 23 | 11 | .32 | $\tau = .07$ |
| Somewhat dir. | 23 | 11 | .32 | $P < .30$ (1t) |
| Very direct | 16 | 6 | .27 | |

| Aggression | *Discipline* Psychol. | Mixed | Corporal | |
|---|---|---|---|---|
| Very indirect | 13 | 7 | 5 | $N = 115$ |
| Somewhat ind. | 14 | 11 | 9 | $\tau = .30$ |
| Somewhat dir. | 6 | 12 | 16 | $P < .001$ (1t) |
| Very direct | 5 | 3 | 14 | |

| Aggression | *Type of Reward* Psychol. | Neither | Concrete | |
|---|---|---|---|---|
| Predominantly indirect | 21 | 23 | 15 | $N = 115$ |
| Predominantly direct | 16 | 20 | 20 | $\chi^2 = 1.44$ |
| | | | | $P = < .50$ |

RESULTS REPORTED IN CHAPTER 14 (Continued)

| *Aggression* | *Attitudes About Control*: For Expression of Feelings | For Some Control | |
|---|---|---|---|
| Predominantly indirect | 21 | 38 | $N = 115$ |
| Predominantly direct | 17 | 39 | $\chi^2 = .16$<br>$P < .70$ |

| *Aggression* | *Mothers' Control*: Absent | Present | Prop. Pres. | |
|---|---|---|---|---|
| Very indirect | 6 | 16 | .73 | $N = 115$ |
| Somewhat ind. | 13 | 21 | .62 | $\tau = .26$ |
| Somewhat dir. | 18 | 16 | .47 | $P < .001$ (1t) |
| Very direct | 17 | 8 | .32 | |

| *Direct Attack* | *Social Class*: Working | Middle | |
|---|---|---|---|
| Present | 42 | 14 | $N = 115$<br>$\chi^2 = 2.52$ |
| Absent | 35 | 24 | $P = .06$ (1t) |

| *Direct Attack* | *Discipline*: Psychol. | Mixed | Corporal | |
|---|---|---|---|---|
| Present | 11 | 18 | 27 | $N = 115$ |
| Absent | 27 | 15 | 17 | $\tau = .25$ |
| Prop. pres. | .29 | .55 | .61 | $P < .001$ (1t) |

| *Flight* | *Social Class*: Working | Middle | |
|---|---|---|---|
| Present | 23 | 3 | $N = 115$<br>$\chi^2 = 5.82$ |
| Absent | 54 | 35 | $P < .01$ (1t) |

| *Flight* | *Discipline*: Psychol. | Mixed | Corporal | |
|---|---|---|---|---|
| Present | 3 | 5 | 18 | $N = 115$ |
| Absent | 35 | 28 | 26 | $\tau = .32$ |
| Prop. pres. | .08 | .15 | .41 | $P < .001$ (1t) |

| *Boys' Opinions Corp. Discipline* | *Social Class*: Working | Middle | Prop. Middle | |
|---|---|---|---|---|
| Necessary | 33 | 2 | .06 | $N = 107$ |
| Qualified | 23 | 20 | .47 | $\tau = .37$ |
| Unnecessary | 14 | 15 | .52 | $P < .001$ (1t) |

RESULTS REPORTED IN CHAPTER 14 (*Continued*)

| *Boys' Opinions Corp. Discipline* | *Discipline* | | | |
|---|---|---|---|---|
| | *Psychol.* | *Mixed* | *Corporal* | |
| Necessary | 5 | 8 | 22 | N = 107 |
| Qualified | 19 | 13 | 11 | $\tau = .25$ |
| Unnecessary | 13 | 6 | 10 | P < .001 (1t) |

| *Boys' Opinions Corp. Discipline* | *Verbal Intel. in Working Class* | | *Prop.* | |
|---|---|---|---|---|
| | *Low* | *High* | *High* | |
| Necessary | 21 | 7 | .25 | N = 57 |
| Qualified | 8 | 10 | .56 | $\tau = .32$ |
| Unnecessary | 4 | 7 | .64 | P < .01 (1t) |

| *Boys' Opinions Corp. Discipline* | *Verbal Intel. in Corp. Disciplined* | | *Prop.* | |
|---|---|---|---|---|
| | *Low* | *High* | *High* | |
| Necessary | 14 | 4 | .22 | N = 36 |
| Qualified | 3 | 6 | .67 | $\tau = .33$ |
| Unnecessary | 4 | 5 | .56 | P = .03 (1t) |

| *Peer Ratings* | *Aggression in Stories* | | *Prop.* | |
|---|---|---|---|---|
| | *Indirect* | *Direct* | *Dir.* | |
| Aggressive | 13 | 23 | .64 | N = 95 |
| Moderate | 17 | 16 | .49 | $\tau = .28$ |
| Unaggressive | 19 | 7 | .27 | P < .01 (1t) |

| *Peer Ratings* | *Discipline* | | | |
|---|---|---|---|---|
| | *Psychol.* | *Mixed* | *Corporal* | |
| Aggressive | 9 | 6 | 21 | N = 95 |
| Moderate | 13 | 7 | 13 | $\tau = .25$ |
| Unaggressive | 12 | 9 | 5 | P < .01 (1t) |

| *Peer Ratings* | *Social Class* | | *Prop.* | |
|---|---|---|---|---|
| | *Working* | *Middle* | *Middle* | |
| Aggressive | 28 | 8 | .22 | N = 96 |
| Moderate | 20 | 14 | .41 | $\tau = .17$ |
| Unaggressive | 15 | 11 | .42 | P < .05 |

RESULTS REPORTED IN CHAPTER 15

| *Signs of Motoric Dilation in Playing Game of Statues* | *Working Class* | *Middle Class* | N | $\chi^2$ | *Probability* |
|---|---|---|---|---|---|
| Either hand waist high | 54 | 22 | 99 | 13.13 | <.001 (1t) |
| Other | 6 | 17 | | | |
| Both hands waist high | 40 | 16 | 99 | 5.32 | .01 (1t) |
| Other | 20 | 23 | | | |
| Either hand shoulder high | 39 | 16 | 99 | 4.57 | .02 (1t) |
| Other | 21 | 23 | | | |
| Legs spread apart | 40 | 18 | 99 | 3.30 | .04 (1t) |
| Other | 20 | 21 | | | |
| Body not vertical | 37 | 17 | 99 | 2.43 | .06 (1t) |
| Other | 23 | 22 | | | |
| Body not facing camera directly | 42 | 12 | 99 | 13.13 | <.001 (1t) |
| Other | 18 | 27 | | | |
| Most motoric | 23 | 5 | | | |
| Intermediate | 22 | 15 | 99 | $\tau = .29$ | <.01 (1t) |
| Least motoric | 15 | 19 | | | |

| *Signs of Dilation and Constriction in paintings* | *Working Class* | *Middle Class* | N | $\chi^2$ | *Probability* |
|---|---|---|---|---|---|
| No recognizable objects | 6 | 12 | 99 | 5.53 | .01 (1t) |
| Recognizable objects | 54 | 27 | | | |
| Four or more colors | 25 | 23 | 99 | 2.18 | .07 (1t) |
| Less than four colors | 35 | 16 | | | |
| Large painting | 40 | 34 | 100 | 4.70 | .02 (1t) |
| Other | 21 | 5 | | | |
| Paint only | 19 | 4 | 99 | 4.93 | .05 (ns) |
| Pencil and crayon | 41 | 35 | | | |
| Structural use of black paint | 43 | 23 | 99 | 1.19 | .13 (1t) |
| Other | 17 | 16 | | | |
| Small painting | 12 | 4 | 99 | 1.02 | .15 (1t) |
| Other | 48 | 35 | | | |
| Most conceptual | 18 | 22 | | | |
| Intermediate | 27 | 13 | 99 | $\tau = .26$ | <.01 (1t) |
| Least conceptual | 15 | 4 | | | |

RESULTS REPORTED IN CHAPTER 15 (*Continued*)

| *Instructions for Spatial Problem* | *Working Class* | *Middle Class* | N | $\chi^2$ | *Probability* |
|---|---|---|---|---|---|
| Goal oriented | | | | | |
| Above median | 13 | 29 | 85 | 8.61 | <.001 (1t) |
| Below median | 28 | 15 | | | |
| Motoric directions | | | | | |
| Above median | 15 | 11 | 48 | .04 | <.50 (1t) |
| Below median | 13 | 9 | | | |
| Conceptual directions | | | | | |
| Above median | 5 | 13 | 37 | .32 | <.30 (1t) |
| Below median | 8 | 11 | | | |

| *Boys' Preferences for Leisure and Occupational Activities* | *Working Class* | *Middle Class* | *Proportion Middle Class* | *N* | $\tau$ | *Probability* |
|---|---|---|---|---|---|---|
| Reasons for leisure activities | | | | | | |
| Conceptual | 13 | 8 | .38 | 114 | .07 | .26 (1t) |
| Intermediate | 8 | 7 | .47 | | | |
| Motoric | 52 | 26 | .33 | | | |
| Hobbies and games | | | | | | |
| Conceptual | 10 | 11 | .52 | 113 | .18 | <.05 (1t) |
| Intermediate | 11 | 8 | .42 | | | |
| Motoric | 51 | 22 | .30 | | | |
| Satisfactions of job | | | | | | |
| Conceptual | 22 | 19 | .46 | 113 | .24 | <.01 (1t) |
| Intermediate | 9 | 10 | .53 | | | |
| Motoric | 42 | 11 | .21 | | | |
| Jobs expected | | | | | | |
| Conceptual | 15 | 16 | .52 | 111 | .19 | <.05 (1t) |
| Intermediate | 17 | 8 | .32 | | | |
| Motoric | 40 | 15 | .27 | | | |
| Jobs liked | | | | | | |
| Conceptual | 35 | 24 | .41 | 113 | .09 | <.20 (1t) |
| Intermediate | 15 | 5 | .25 | | | |
| Motoric | 23 | 11 | .32 | | | |

| *Mothers' Preferences* | *Working Class* | *Middle Class* | *Proportion Middle Class* | *N* | $\tau$ | *Probability* |
|---|---|---|---|---|---|---|
| Reasons for leisure activities | | | | | | |
| Conceptual | 26 | 19 | .42 | 117 | .19 | .02 (1t) |
| Intermediate | 36 | 18 | .33 | | | |
| Motoric | 16 | 2 | .11 | | | |

RESULTS REPORTED IN CHAPTER 15 (*Continued*)

| *Mothers' Preferences* | *Working Class* | *Middle Class* | *Proportion Middle Class* | N | $\tau$ | *Probability* |
|---|---|---|---|---|---|---|
| Satisfactions of job | | | | | | |
| Conceptual | 8 | 14 | .64 | 102 | .37 | $<.001$ (1t) |
| Intermediate | 29 | 13 | .31 | | | |
| Motoric | 33 | 5 | .13 | | | |

| *Background Conditions* | *Significances of Interrelations among Background Conditions:* *Type of Discipline* | *Type of Reward* | *Affective Control* | *Expressive Style* |
|---|---|---|---|---|
| Social class | $<.01$ | $<.01$ | $<.05$ | $<.001$ |
| Type of discipline | | $<.01$ | $<.01$ | $<.001$ |
| Type of reward | | | $<.20$ | $<.01$ |
| Affective control | | | | $<.01$ |

| *Expressive Style* | *Discipline:* *Psychol.* | *Mixed* | *Corporal* | |
|---|---|---|---|---|
| Intermediate | 11 | 13 | 11 | $N = 83$ |
| Most motoric | 3 | 3 | 13 | $\tau = .37$ |
| Most conceptual | 17 | 7 | 5 | $P < .001$ (1t) |

| *Expressive Style* | *Type of Reward:* *Symbolic* | *Concrete* | *Prop. Sym.* | |
|---|---|---|---|---|
| Most conceptual | 14 | 5 | .74 | $N = 57$ |
| Intermediate | 12 | 13 | .48 | $\tau = .36$ |
| Most motoric | 3 | 10 | .23 | $P < .01$ (1t) |

| *Expressive Style* | *Affective Control:* *Present* | *Absent* | *Prop. Pres.* | |
|---|---|---|---|---|
| Most conceptual | 20 | 9 | .69 | $N = 83$ |
| Intermediate | 15 | 20 | .43 | $\tau = .25$ |
| Most motoric | 7 | 12 | .37 | $P < .01$ (1t) |

| *Expressive Style* | *Working Class* | *Middle Class* | *Prop. Middle* | |
|---|---|---|---|---|
| Most conceptual | 12 | 17 | .59 | $N = 83$ |
| Intermediate | 21 | 14 | .40 | $\tau = .37$ |
| Most motoric | 18 | 1 | .05 | $P < .001$ (1t) |

**RESULTS**

| Condition | *Entrepreneurial Subjects* Social Class: Working | Social Class: Middle | Proportion Middle | | *Bureaucratic Subjects* Social Class: Working | Social Class: Middle | Proportion Middle | |
|---|---|---|---|---|---|---|---|---|
| Representative index: | | | | | | | | |
| Most conceptual | 1 | 10 | .91 | $N = 35$ $\tau = .63$ | 10 | 7 | .41 | $N = 48$ |
| Intermediate | 8 | 4 | .33 | | 13 | 11 | .46 | $\tau = .20$ |
| Most motoric | 11 | 1 | .08 | $P < .001$ | 7 | 0 | .00 | $P = .15$ (1t) |
| Child interview: satisfactions of job | | | | | | | | |
| Conceptual | 11 | 9 | .45 | $N = 45$ | 11 | 8 | .42 | $N = 63$ |
| Intermediate | 2 | 5 | .71 | $\tau = .28$ | 6 | 5 | .45 | $\tau = .21$ |
| Motoric | 15 | 3 | .17 | $P = .06$ | 25 | 8 | .24 | $P = .10$ (1t) |
| Maternal interview: reasons for leisure activities | | | | | | | | |
| Conceptual | 11 | 7 | .39 | $N = 45$ | 13 | 10 | .43 | $N = 65$ |
| Intermediate | 15 | 8 | .35 | $\tau = .07$ | 18 | 10 | .36 | $\tau = .25$ |
| Motoric | 3 | 1 | .25 | $P < .40$ | 13 | 1 | .07 | $P < .01$ (1t) |
| Maternal interview: satisfactions of job | | | | | | | | |
| Conceptual | 2 | 7 | .78 | $N = 39$ | 6 | 7 | .54 | $N = 56$ |
| Intermediate | 14 | 5 | .26 | $\tau = .48$ | 12 | 8 | .40 | $\tau = .38$ |
| Motoric | 10 | 1 | .09 | $P < .01$ | 21 | 2 | .09 | $P < .05$ (1t) |

# INDEX


Aberle, D. F., 335
achievement, 11
act, 128-129
action tendencies, 123-126, 138
  components of, 126-131, 138-139
affect, 130
"afraid-sleep," 199
agent, 130-131
aggression, 11-12, 20, 50, 57, 59, 66, 155, 295, 438-439
  conflicts involving, tests of, 257-262, 270
  directness of, 24, 28-29, 295, 319-321, 323-327, 329-333
  directness of, method of study of, 317-321
  early expressions of, 273-275
  expression of, to teachers, 333-334
  modified by identification, 73-75
  against self, 283-284
  and self-modifying defenses, 262-265, 270-271
alcoholism, 13
Allinsmith, B. B., 78, 315, 335
Allinsmith W., 86, 132*n.*, 136*n.*, 139, 141*n.*, 149*n.*, 157*n.*, 176
Allport, G., 296, 303, 312
Alper, T., 250, 251, 252, 254
altruistic surrender, 209*n.*
ambition, 11
anger, expression of, 315-317
Anrep, G. V., 312
anxiety, 17
Aronfreed, J., 92, 143*n.*, 177*n.*, 182*n.*, 186*n.*, 193
arousal, methodological problems involving, 374-380
  of anger, 257-259
  of feelings of failure, 217-218
  of guilt, 180-181
  of sexual conflict, 277-279
authoritarianism, of mothers, 81
  *see also* discipline

Baldwin, A. L., 38
Barber, B., 67
Barker, R. G., 67, 115
Bateson, G., 199, 211
Beaglehole, E., 67
Beardslee, B. J., 80, 83, 213*n.*, 230, 256*n.*, 271
Beardsley, R., 51
behavior, modification of, 73-76
Beier, E. G., 38
Bendix, R., 67
Benedict, P. K., 67
Benedict, R., 67, 212, 288
Bennett, E. L., 313
*berdache,* 275
Beres, D., 335
Bettelheim, B., 95, 212, 335
Bexton, W. H., 67
Binet, A., 312
Blackwell, H. R., 312
Block, J., 312
Block, Jeanne, 312

Blum, G. S., 402
Boisen, T. H., 356
Breese, F. H., 38
Breuer, J., 139
Broom, L., 67
Bruner, J. S., 312
bureaucratic setting, 264-265, 271, 390-391, 444
  class differences in, 63-65
  expressive style in, 340, 353-354
  incidence of repression in, 242-243
  membership in, 65-66, 67
  and sex identity, 182-183
  *see also* social class

Calden, G., 230
Carl, G. P. A., 356
Carmichael, L., 356
Carothers, J. C., 67
caste, 52
Centers, R., 67, 115
Champney, H., 38
Chandler, K., 314
character, in conflicts, 31-34
cheating, 77, 164*n.*
chi square test, 36
Child, I. L., 39, 76, 95, 96, 361, 362, 393*n.*, 403
child, socialization of, 12, 13
child-rearing practices, 385
  combinations of, and defenses, 226-229, 392-395
  and denial, 222-226
  and incidence of repression, 243-244, 245-249
  influence of social class on, 6-8, 70-72, 111-112
  in relation to guilt, 163-164
  standards of, 30
  and type of expressive style, 350-352, 355-356
Clark, R. A., 288
Clark, R. E., 67
class, *see* bureaucratic setting, entrepreneurial setting, middle class, social class, working class, *and* upper class
Cochran, W. G., 365, 402
Cohen, Y., 95
Colby, K. M., 139
conceptual orientation, by social class, 342-347, 354, 355
  *see also* expressive style
conflict
  arousal of, in projective tests, 277-279, 372-380
  characteristic responses to, 3-4
  frequency of, and sex identity, 191
  related to social class, 56-57, 58-59, 66
  resolution of, 14, 386-389
  and sex identity, research concerning, 276-280, 287
  significance of, 29-34
  stabilized, 9-11, 15, 17
  *see also* defense mechanisms *and* moral standards
conformity, 64
conscience, 164
  *see also* guilt *and* moral standards
control, 309
  degree of, 24
  loss of, 328-329
conversion neurosis, 32-34
Cooper, M., 68
corporations, 63-65
  *see also* bureaucratic class
Cowen, E. L., 38
culture, and personality disorders, 44-45

Dakota Indians, 275
Davis, A., 67, 115, 335, 356
death instinct, 317*n.*
death wishes, 145-146, 163, 427
  guilt about, 156-160
defense mechanisms, 11, 15-17, 19, 21, 22
  by class, 48-50, 386, 387
  and combinations of child-rearing practices, 392-395
  definitions of, 194-197, 210-211
  differences among, 196-199
  of first family, 201-205, 211
  of second family, 205-210, 211
  shift in, table of, 437-438
  during story-completion tests, 280-288, 373, 374
  study of, 401-402
  typology of, 199-200
delinquents, 77
Demerath, N. J., 67

denial, 20, 27, 59, 65, 198, 282, 381 *n.*, 387, 388, 392, 432-434
child-rearing practices, 222-223, 229-230
compared to repression, 232-233
related to combinations of child-rearing practices, 226-229
in working class, 241, 242
denial in fantasy, 20-21, 213-214
importance of verbal intelligence for, 220-222, 224
projective test of, 214-220
dependency, 84
depression, 44, 47, 48, 50-51
Detroit, 407
Deutsche, J. M., 312
directness, in expression of aggression, 24, 28-29
continuum of, 319-321
and discipline, 323-327, 334
and social class, 329-333
*see also* aggression
dirt, and aggression, 295
discipline, 154-155, 225, 227-229, 391, 394, 395, 398-399, 412-413, 426-435, 438, 439-440, 443
classification of, 77-79, 267, 271
corporal, 76-77, 332-333
and directness of aggression, 323-327, 331, 334
psychological, 75-76
related to aggression, 7
and repression, 243, 245
severity of, 27
disobedience, 146, 161-162, 163, 164, 165
externalization after, 168-170
related to temptation, 172-173
*see also* obedience
displacement, 20, 22, 188, 206, 207-209
substitutions in, 23-25, 291-296
Dobu, 45
Dollard, J., 319, 335
Doob, L. W., 319, 335
Douglas, V., 279*n.*, 374, 381*n.*, 402
Dreyer, A., 176
Dunham, H. W., 39, 45-47, 68

Eaton, J. W., 67
education, 54-55
Eells, K., 68, 115
Efron, D., 356
Eisenberg, P., 312
Eissler, R. S., 140, 335
Ellis, W. D., 255
emotional dilation, 284-285, 287
emotional dilation-constriction, 24
energy, nature of, 122
entrepreneurial setting, 63, 65-66, 67, 264-265, 271, 390-391, 444
and expressive style, 340, 353-354
incidence of repression in, 242-243
and sex identity, 182
*see also* social class
Erickson, M. H., 22, 39
Ericson, M. C., 67
Eriksen, C. W., 39
Erikson, E. H., 95, 139, 335
expression, substitute, 8-9
expressive style, 11, 23-25, 26, 93, 137, 284-287, 289-290, 297-298, 386, 387, 443
by class and parental reaction, 348-352
classification of, 304-305
conceptual orientation of, 24, 26, 342-347
definitions of, 296-297
examples of, 337-338
and motoric orientation, 24, 26, 341-342
perceptual dimensions of, 299-303
sources of difference in, 305-308
extensity, 132
of moral standards, 134-135
externalization, 173-174
definition of, 138
rating of, in projective tests, 150-151, 168-170
after theft, 168
after disobedience, 168-170

failure, 215
fear of, 11
repression of, 240
fantasy, 198, 201-202
denial in, 20-21, 213-222, 224
Faris, R. E. L., 45-47, 67
father, influence of, in child-rearing, 71-72
fear, and guilt, 166-167
Fell, Jesse W., 238

femininity, *see* sex identity
Fenichel, O., 139, 150, 176, 312
Fenton, John, 191
Ferenczi, S., 154, 176, 202*n.*, 212
Feshbach, S., 288
Firth, R., 68
Flügel, J. C., 136*n.*, 139, 150*n.*
Foley, J. P., Jr., 356
Fonda, C. P., 39
Franck Kate, 95
Franck's Drawing Completion test, 14, 92-94, 287, 288
Freedman, R., 68
Frenkel-Brunswik, E., 300, 303, 307, 312
Friedman, C. R., 139
Freud, Anna, 20, 39, 95, 140, 195, 212, 230, 254, 290, 312, 335
Freud, S., 22, 36, 39, 49, 122, 139, 195, 212, 234, 254, 317, 335
Freudian error, 22
frustration, 319*n.*
Fuller, R. C., 68

Gardner, B. B., 67
Gardner, M. R., 67
Glueck, E., 95
Glueck, S., 95
Goldstein, K., 312
Gough, H. G., 94, 95, 114, 287, 288
Gowland, F., 288
Green, A., 293, 313
Greenacre, P., 39
Greening, T. C., 157*n.*, 176, 186*n.*
Grosser, D., 176
guilt, 7, 14, 64, 91, 132, 135-136, 142, 389, 393, 427-429
  associated with psychological discipline, 75-76
  criteria for identifying, 147-149
  defenses against, 150, 188-190
  and fear, 166-167
  interpretation of findings concerning, 162-168
  related to sex identity, 187-190
  severity of, 137-138, 139, 153-156
  severity of, test results on, 156-168
  *see also* externalization *and* moral responses

Hartley, E. L., 67, 335, 356
Hartmann, H., 140, 335
Hartshorne, H., 164*n.*, 176
Hathaway, S. R., 95
Havighurst, R. J., 115, 335, 356
Hebb, D. O., 140
Herman, H. M., 345*n.*
Heron, W., 67
Highland Park, 407
Hiler, E. W., 402
Hilgard, E. R., 95, 291, 312
Hoffman, M., 176
Hollingshead, A. B., 60, 61, 68
Holzman, P. S., 301, 302, 312
homeostasis, 122*n.*
homosexuality, 90
  *see also* sex identity
Horney, K., 212
hostility, 45
Hunt, J. McV., 39, 140
Huschka, M., 95
Hutt, M. L., 74, 95
Hutterites, 44, 48, 50
hypothesis, definition of, 361-362
hysteria, 32-34, 45, 59, 310, 311

identification
  definition of, 73
  in discipline situations, 75-76
  in sex identity, 89-90
Ifaluk, 45, 137
imagery, in defense, 203-205
income, 54*n.*
influence techniques, 174
Inkeles, A., 95
integration, social, 52, 390-391
  *see also* bureaucratic setting *and* entrepreneurial setting
intelligence, verbal, of subjects, 103, 391-392, 432, 440
interviewers, 409, 410
interviews
  of mothers, 408-409
  validity of, 382-384
isolation, of affect, 57, 208

Jacks, I., 67
Jaensch, W., 312
Janke, L. L., 115
Janowitz, M., 61

Kalhorn, J., 38
Kardiner, A., 212
Keller, J. E., 333*n.*
Klaus, E. J., 181*n.*, 193

Klein, G. S., 297, 301, 302, 312
Kluckhohn, C., 212, 335
Knight, R. P., 95, 139
Koffka, K., 212
Kounin, I. S., 67, 115
Kovacs, A. L., 375
Krech, D., 299, 306, 312, 313
Kretchmer, E., 313
Kris, E., 335
Kruechel, B., 140, 313
Kubie, L. S., 140

Lacey, J. I., 293, 313
Landis, C., 68
Lansky, L. M., 92*n.*, 160, 165, 182*n.*, 272*n.*, 288
Latscha, R., 39, 288
Lazarus, R. S., 39
learning, and rewards, 82
Lemkau, P., 68
Lenski, G. E., 61
Levin, M., 39, 116
Levinson, D. J., 95
Lewin, K., 140, 212
Lin, T. Y., 68
Lippitt, R., 176
Lipset, S. M., 67
Long, L., 313
Lorand, S., 335
Lowenfeld, V., 299, 313
Lowenstein, R. M., 140, 335
lower class, *see* working class
Lunt, P. S., 68

McCarthy, D., 339, 356
McCleary, R. A., 379
McClelland, D. C., 140
Maccoby, E., 39, 116
McDougall, W., 122, 140
McKinley, J. C., 95
MacKinnon, D. W., 95, 176
McNeil, E. B., 337, 356
McNemar, Q., 39
Maller, J. B., 176
Malzberg, B., 68
manic-depressives, 4, 44, 46, 47, 49
Marquis, D. G., 291, 312
masculinity, 7
  degree of, 88-92
  tests of, 113-114
  *see also* sex identity
Mason, G., 251, 252, 255
May, M. A., 176
Mead, M., 199, 211, 306, 313
Meeker, M., 68
mental illness, 13
  *see also* personality disorders
middle class, 4, 28, 66
  and aggression, 262-263
  and child-rearing, 7
  conflicts found in, 56-57
  criteria of, 53-54
  and directness of aggression, 321-322, 327
  self-attack in, 50
  values of, 55-56
  *see also* bureaucratic setting, entrepreneurial setting, *and* social class
Miles, C. C., 96
Miller, D. R., 52, 62, 65, 68, 74, 95, 116, 193, 263, 271, 403
Miller, N., 39, 140, 335
mobility, of subjects, 104-105
Mood, A. M., 39
moral responses, 141-144
  projective test of, 144-147
    interpretation of, 147-152
    sample and controls used in, 152-153
moral standards, 11, 26, 37, 50-51, 131-133, 401
  contents of, 50*n.*
  definition of, 132-133
  extensity of, 134-135, 139
  internalization of, 12-13
  lack of, 77
  perceived source of, 173-175, 430-431
  projective test involving sex identity and, 177-181
  related to sex identity, 185-192
  and resolution of conflict, 136-138
  results of violation of, 135-136
  *see also* values
morality, and social class, 389
mothers
  identification with, in discipline process, 75-76
  interviews of, 408-409, 410-411
motoric dilation, 441
motoric orientation, by social class, 341-342, 355
  *see also* expressive style
Mowrer, O. H., 150*n.*, 176, 335
Mullahy, P., 313

Murchison, C., 140
Murray, H. A., 95, 140, 176, 255, 335
Myers, J., 61

Naegele, K. D., 335
needs
  classification of, 123-126
  definition of, 120-123, 138
  sexual, 13
neurosis, 8, 45, 150*n.*, 310
  origins of, 18
  and social class, 4
Newcomb, T. M., 68, 335, 356
normality, concept of, 122*n.*
Nowlis, J. W. M., 96

obedience, 224-225, 226-227
  and defenses, 265-267, 271
  parental requests for, 79-81, 155, 426-432, 434, 436, 437
  and repression, 243-244, 245-247
object, 129*n.*
obsession-compulsion, 45
obsessives, 48-49, 50
Ordan, H., 313
orientations
  conceptual, 24, 26, 341-342
  motoric, 24, 26, 341-342
Osborn, R. C., 116

Page, J., 68
paranoia, 34
parents
  identification with, 26-27
  preferences of, concerning expressive style, 349-353
  social class of, and child-rearing, 71-72
  *see also* interviews, mothers, sex identity, *and* social class
Parsons, T., 140
passivity, 24, 190, 285-287, 295, 308
perception
  alteration of, as denial, 233-234
  experiments concerning, 298-303
personality, in conflict situations, 31-34
personality disorders
  cross-cultural studies of, 44-45
  by social class, 45-50, 339
Platsky, E., 331*n.*
Polansky, N., 176
Pollack, H. M., 68
population, selection of, 100-105
power, 52-53
projection, 20, 59, 77, 138, 150-151, 188, 198, 206, 235
projective tests, 366-367
  and arousal of conflict, 372-380
  invalid low scores on, 368-370
  of moral responses, 144-147
    methods and interpretation of, 147-153
  validity of, 380-381
psychoses, 49-50
  and social class, 4
psychotherapy, and social class, 397-398
punishment, corporal, 76-77, 332-333
  *see also* discipline

Queen, S. A., 68

rage, 163*n.*-164*n.*
Rapaport, D., 140
recall, 434-436
  *see also* repression
Redlich, F. C., 68
Reich, W., 32, 39, 296, 298, 307, 313
repression, 20, 21, 209, 234, 394
  class as factor in, 240-242, 253
  compared to denial, 232-233
  as defense, 235
  and discipline, 243, 245
  and obedience, 243-244, 245-247
  personal traits and, 251-254
  tests of, 236-240
  *see also* recall
research
  characteristics of samples in, 105-112, 362-365
  implications of findings of, 396-399
  methodology of, 360-362
  plan of, 36-38
  problems involving arousal in, 374-380
  selection of subjects for, 100-105
  sex identity in third sample of, 112-115
  stages in, 99-100
  statistical methods of, 34-36

unsolved problems for, 399-402
*see also* interviews *and* story-completion tests
responses, moral, *see* moral responses
reversal, 20, 57, 65, 66, 199, 235, 387
rewards, frequency of, 82-83, 155, 225-226, 226-228, 327-328, 426, 428, 433, 434, 435-438, 443
and defenses, 268-269, 271
validity of reports of, 382-383
Rhodes, D. A., 145*n.*
Roe, A., 299, 306, 313
Rorschach, H., 313
Rokeach, M., 300-301, 313
role, concept of, 400
Rose, A. M., 67
Rosen, E. A., 95, 288
Rosenzweig, S., 250, 251, 252, 255, 313

St. Augustine, 30, 39
Saloman, A., 312
sample, research, 362-365
selection of, 407-408, 409-411
small, 365
Sanford, R. N., 88*n.*, 96
scapegoats, 14
Schachtel, E., 306, 313
Scheerer, M., 312
schizophrenia, 4, 34, 59, 310, 311
class incidence of, 44-45, 46, 47
Schlaegel, T. F., 306, 313
Schlesinger, H., 301, 312, 313
Schlosberg, H., 312
Scholl, R., 313
Schroeder, C. W., 68
Scott, T. H., 67
Sears, P. S., 96
Sears, R. R., 39, 96, 116, 335, 336
self-punishment, 44, 49
Selznick, P., 67
severity, of standards, 132
Sewell, W. H., 96
sex, of subjects, 102
sex identity, 87-88, 272-273, 281
and conflict, research concerning, 276-280, 287
developmental stages in, 90-92, 273-274, 275
differences in, 275-276
Franck's test for, 92-94
and loss of control, 190-192
origins of, 88-90
and severity of moral standards, 185-190
and social position, 182-185
in third sample, 112-115
validity of tests of, 384
shame, 135-136
Sheppard, H. L., 409
Shils, E. A., 140
Shire, P., 79, 321*n.*
Shuttleworth, F. K., 176
Sigel, I. E., 176
Smith, J. E. K., 39
Smith, M. B., 209*n.*
Smith, R. L., 293, 313
social change, 47
social class, 5-6, 8, 52, 155-156, 441-444
and child-rearing practices, 111-112
and conceptual orientation of expressive style, 342-347, 353, 354, 355
and conflict, 66
criteria for determining, 53-55, 60-62
definition of, 52-53
and denial, 223, 241, 242
and differential personality disorders, 4, 45-48
and directness of aggression, 321-327, 334
and expressive style, 309-310, 339-346, 348-352
as factor in guilt, 161*n.*, 426-430, 431-443
as factor in repression, 240-243, 245-247, 253
interests and activities by, 347-348
and morality, 389
and motoric orientation of expressive style, 341-342
predictions involving, 28-29
related to perceived source of standards, 173-175
and requests for obedience, 266-267, 271
and resolution of conflict, 386-389
and self-modifying defenses, 262-265, 270-271

social class—(*cont'd*)
significance of, 384-385
of subjects in sample, 106-108
*see also* bureaucratic class, entrepreneurial class, middle class, upper class *and* working class
socialization, 12, 69-70, 385
early, 83-87
*see also* child-rearing practices
socio-economic class, *see* social class
Solomon, R. L., 174
Spiro, M. E., 68, 140
Spock, B., 96
standards, moral, *see* moral standards
statistical tables, explanation of, 34-36
status, social, 13, 28, 386
Sterba, R., 96, 140, 313
story-completion tests, 144-145, 366-367, 414-425
structured, 370-371
stratification, social, 52
*see also* social class
Strauss, A., 140
Strong, E. K., 96
subjects
mobility of, 104-105
selection of, 100-105, 112-115
in sex-identity study, 276, 279-280
substitutions, 23-25, 132
learned dimensions for, 292-296
unlearned dimensions for, 291-292
*see also* displacement
suicide, 44
Swanson, G. E., 52, 61, 62, 65, 68, 116, 160, 193, 263, 271, 403
Symonds, P. M., 212, 336

Taba, H., 335
Taylor Manifest Anxiety Scale, 294
temptation, 429-430
resistance to, 174
test results concerning, 170-173
Terman, C. M., 96
theft, 146, 160-161
Thematic Apperception Test, 367, 368
Thurstone, L. L., 116, 193, 230, 271, 288, 300, 313, 336
Thurstone, T. G., 116, 193, 230, 271, 288, 336
Tietze, C., 68
toilet-training, 7, 27, 85-86, 229, 269, 270, 388-389, 394, 427, 429, 430, 431, 435
coerciveness of, 86-87
early, and guilt, 154
mild, 166
Tomkins, S., 39
Tooth, G., 68
Torgoff, I., 176
tragedy, 31

upper class, included in survey, 53*n*.
*see also* social class

values
of middle class, 55-56, 64
of working class, 57-58, 64
*see also* moral standards
Vernon, P. E., 296, 303, 312
visions, 49

Walker, E. L., 157, 163
Wapner, S., 298, 314
Warner, W. L., 68
weaning, 7, 21-28, 70-71, 163-164, 229, 269-270, 393, 426-432, 435
early, and guilt, 154, 161
harshness of, 86
importance of, 84-85
late, 166
*see also* child-rearing practices
Weil, R. J., 67
Welch, L., 313
Werner, H., 298, 314
Whiting, J. W. M., 39, 76, 96, 174, 361, 362, 393*n*., 403
Williams, A. H., 68
Wilson, D. C., 68
Winter, William D., 145*n*., 149*n*.
withdrawal, 137, 198, 282
Witkin, H. A., 302, 306, 314
Wittenborn, J. R., 96
Wolfenstein, M., 30, 39, 313
working class, 7, 28-29, 54, 66
and aggression, 263-264, 322-323, 327
and conflict, 58-59
incidence of denial in, 241, 242
and schizophrenia, 4
values of, 57-58, 64
*see also* social class
Wright, H., 67, 115

Zeigarnik, B., 236, 255